TREASURY MANAGEMENT IN INDIA

Dr. V.A. Avadhani

M.A., Ph.D. (Neb.), LL.B., C.A.I.I.B.

- Retired Adviser in the Reserve Bank of India
- Former Director of Research and Training in Bombay Stock Exchange
- Former Adviser in Hyderabad Stock Exchange
- Visiting Faculty in Finance

Himalaya Publishing House

ISO 9001:2015 CERTIFIED

Edition : 2010
Reprint : 2014, 2017, 2018
Reprint : 2023

Published by : Mrs. Meena Pandey
for **HIMALAYA PUBLISHING HOUSE PVT. LTD.,**
"Ramdoot", Dr. Bhalerao Marg, Girgaon, Mumbai - 400 004.
Phone: 022-23860170, 23863863; **Fax:** 022-23877178
E-mail: himpub@bharatmail.co.in; **Website:** www.himpub.com

Branch Offices :

New Delhi : "Pooja Apartments", 4-B, Murari Lal Street, Ansari Road, Darya Ganj, New Delhi - 110 002. Phone: 011-23270392, 23278631; Fax: 011-23256286

Nagpur : Kundanlal Chandak Industrial Estate, Ghat Road, Nagpur - 440 018. Phone: 0712-2721215, 2721216

Bengaluru : Plot No. 91-33, 2nd Main Road, Seshadripuram, Behind Nataraja Theatre, Bengaluru - 560 020. Phone: 080-41138821; Mobile: 09379847017, 09379847005

Hyderabad : No. 3-4-184, Lingampally, Besides Raghavendra Swamy Matham, Kachiguda, Hyderabad - 500 027. Phone: 040-27560041, 27550139

Chennai : No. 34/44, Motilal Street, T. Nagar, Chennai - 600 017. Mobile: 09380460419

Pune : "Laksha" Apartment, First Floor, No. 527, Mehunpura, Shaniwarpeth (Near Prabhat Theatre), Pune - 411 030. Phone: 020-24496323, 24496333; Mobile: 09370579333

Cuttack : Plot No. 5F-755/4, Sector-9, CDA Markat Nagar, Cuttack - 753 014, Odisha. Mobile: 09338746007

Kolkata : 3, S.M. Bose Road, Near Gate No. 5, Agarpara Railway Station, North 24 Parganas, West Bengal - 700 109. Mobile: 09674536325

Printed at : Geetanjali Press Pvt. Ltd., Nagpur. On behalf of HPH.

PREFACE TO THE THIRD REVISED EDITION

Since the last revision of this book, many changes took place in the banking and financial fields, to which the Treasury Management is more relevant. The present revision took advantage of incorporating these changes in this book to the extent possible. These operations of Treasury are not only relevant to banking and financial field, but to all corporate units which have financing, trading and investment operations.

Treasury management is a specialized subject in the finance area. It encompasses the funds management and investment management along with the trading operations in the financial markets. The functions of Treasury involve all the above items *inter alia*. To the extent that the companies have problems of liquidity and solvency — short term and long term — they have the need for Treasury management. This book makes a comprehensive treatment of all related aspects of the Treasury operations. Planning and budgeting and forecasting the funds flows and shortages and surpluses to be taken care of by the Treasury have become a part of this book.

All the operations of the Treasury in the markets and investment management of their portfolios are discussed in this book along with the risk management techniques adopted by them. The various contextual and environment problems to the Treasury have found a place in this book. This is thus a comprehensive treatment of a narrow and highly specialized subject of Treasury management.

All the financial markets are well regulated by RBI and SEBI with good infrastructure, institutional framework, with depth and width in the markets, which makes it a challenge to the Treasury to make efficient operations. The latest policy changes of all the relevant policies affecting the money & capital markets, gilt edged and forex markets etc. have found a place in this book. In the present context of the Indian economy, moving towards globalization, deregulation and privatization, the markets have become more competitive which makes more challenging the task of Treasury manager.

In all the areas that this book is concerned, the material has been updated and many changes have been incorporated to make it more comprehensive and useful to all the readers and students of this subject.

The author acknowledges gratefully all the comments of the teaching faculty and the co-operation and help of the Himalaya Publishing House.

- AUTHOR

CONTENTS

PART – I

SCOPE AND COVERAGE

1 INTRODUCTION TO TREASURY FUNCTION

The definition of Treasury is the treasure or valuables of the government, centre and states and extended to semi-government bodies, corporates and non-corporate bodies, financial institutions including banks who operate this treasury. Treasury management therefore refers to all activities involving the management of revenues, inflow and outflow of government, banks and corporates, etc.

Treasury function as defined above is a general concept applicable to all funds managements and in its wider form it encompasses cash, currency and funds, including credits, inflow and outflows as part of the general financial management. If it is the same as financial management, there would be no need for a seperate treatment of treasury in this book, but treasury is a special term within the compass of the broader term "finance."

To be more specific, it is that part of the financial management which deals with the treasury as a profit centre, utilising the treasure that any unit acquires in best possible manner, with the least-cost-profit maximisation motive. The inflows of cash currency and funds and outflows of the same are to be matched, and a delicate balancing of the assets with liabilities is aimed at with a view to optimise the market value of its shares and its net assets. It is thus, an independent function.

Treasury has both macro and micro aspects. Government as the sovereign power is the source of all treasure of the land. Its creation of money as a vehicle of facilitating trade, industry and business is the starting point for the function for treasury operations for micro units. The Reserve Bank of India as a banker to the Government creates the currency on behalf of the government and manages the government debt. It is also a banker to banks in that it controls the credit creation of banks. The same issued by the government, currency created by the RBI and credit instruments of banks are all the subjects of management of the treasurer.

Evolution of Fund Management Function

Fund manager is a general term, applicable to the private sector, while treasury management relates to the special term of management of cash, currency, credit of the sovereign power of the country. Foreign exchange and government debt are the two aspects or sources for currency. The markets involved are money market for cash, currency and credit and foreign exchange market for foreign currency deals and gilt edged market for government securities and the debt markets. The treasury management has wider implications of management of all government and semi-government instruments as also the currency, credit and corporate debt instruments. So, although in effect the funds management is the same thing as treasury management and also commonly understood as synonymous in usage, the differences are subtle and imply the sourcing of funds, either from money market, government securities market or the forex market.

Thus, the above concepts of fund manager and treasury manager are used in this book in a common sense and refer to the same meaning and objective of the efficient use of funds and disposition in various avenues for the maximum returns and minimum risks. The needed expertise is the same at the conceptual sense, although operational efficiency needed in each of them, namely, Money Market, Treasury Funds [cash and credit] and Forex operations in the financial system, are substantially different from each other.

Macro Sense of Treasury

As against the textbook definition, referred to above, the common man's understanding of Treasury refers to the Government funds, as the Government is the sovereign authority which has created the currency system of the country and manages the circulation of cash and credit through the banker to the government and banks, namely, the Central Bank of the country. In India it is central government, which has a unified control on coins, currency and credit system in the country. The Reserve Bank of India is the Central bank of the country, which has been given the monopoly powers of creation of currency, and its management in the interests of public, trade, industry and business. The Central Government, with the Parliament as the sovereign authority, delegated to it by the public through the democrate process of elections has all the powers of creation, of coins, currency and credit, their management and destruction or amendments and modifications, etc. The stability of the value of money or currency in the internal and external dealings, namely, its internal purchasing power and external value of the rupee has to be maintained in the public interests and for promoting trade, business and industry. This responsibility is given to the Reserve Bank of India.

Treasury Concept — Historical Evolution

Historically the Treasure was gold, silver and precious metals mined from inside the soil of the land of a Kingdom and belongs to the King, who or his family used to exercise their rights on the treasures of the land. That was the source of wealth for the Kingdom and with that they used to acquire other physical goods such as weapons, horses, goats and consumer goods. Down from the centuries, upto even 19th century, gold coins or silver or copper coins etc. used to serve as money and that was the treasure of both the King and his subjects.

When British East India Company came to trade with India, these treasures were used to exchange goods and for trade both by the Indian traders and foreigners. Thus, treasure was the means of executing trade, business and commercial transactions in those days and even today, gold was stored as an asset or wealth and used as and when necessary for precautionary purposes and contingencies, depending on the needs. Based on the ideology of sovereign power (namely, the emperor or King) holding or owning the treasures of the country, the present day usage of the term Treasury or Treasury chests belonged to the Government and the power to create money (in the place of gold) rested with the sovereign power of the country.

Linkage of Domestic Currency with Foreign Currency

From the very beginning of East India Company, and their trading with India, the major concern of British Government was to repatriate funds back to England. Originally, gold and silver coins constituted the mode of such transmission of funds. Later, the system of council drafts (Bills and telegraphic transfers) was used for supplying rupees in India for acquisition of Sterling for payment of Home charges by British India Government to Britain and as these bills were sold by Secretary of State of Council, they used to be called the Council Bills for supply of rupees for Sterling and reverse councils for the opposite deals of supply of Sterling against Rupee. When India had to pay abroad, the Rupee was exchanged for Sterling at 1s.4d. per rupee for a long time. It was only in 1927, the rate was fixed at 1s.6d., under the Act with the Sterling on a gold basis and maintainance of the value of the rupee at 1s.6d. for a fairly long time, the system which emerged in due course operated as Gold Exchange Standard for Indian Currency. During the early years of 19th century, Silver constituted the support for the currency, later replaced by gold standard and subsequently by Gold Exchange Standard to be completely replaced by Sterling Standard or Foreign Exchange Standard by immobilising the role of gold and silver in the sixties. After September 1931, with the departure of Sterling from gold, the Rupee Sterling link also lost gold link and it became Rupee-Sterling link. The exchange rate between Rupee-Sterling continued at 1s.6d. upto 1966, when the rupee had to be devalued.

Legal Basis of Treasury Instruments

The Fund Manager operates in the Financial Markets, in a manner that the efficient deposition of funds leads to the maximisation of income and minimisation of risk. He deals in coins and currency, which are issued by the Government under the Indian Coinage Act as amended to date, and under the RBI Act (Section 22). These are made legal tender by Section 26 of the RBI Act and the monopoly of Note Issue and Coinage is shared by the RBI with the Government. This is evident from the insignia or symbol of the Government and the name of the Reserve Bank of India inserted on the face of the notes. Whenever the Government issues currency notes, as in the case of one rupee notes, they are in replacement of coins, which the Government mints under the India Coinage Act. Similarly, when the coins of higher denominations of Rs. 2, 5, 10 etc. are given, they are given under the provisions of the Indian Currency Act in replacement of currency notes. Thus, the Indian Coinage Act and Indian Currency Act provide the legal basis of coins and currency.

Similarly, the legal basis of bank instruments is under the Banking Regulation Act and Negotiable Instrument Act. The issue of cheque, DD, MT, TT etc. are all governed by the relevant provisions of Negotiable Instruments Act for which knowledge of law and practice of banking is necessary for the Treasury Manager.

The development of the Money Market is based on the negotiable instruments such as commercial bills, CDs and CPs etc. which are all bills of exchange coming under the Negotiable Instruments Act and the relevent provisions of Indian Stamp Act will also apply to such bills unless the Government has exempted any category of such documents from payments of stamp duty.

The issue of Government Securities is for raising funds for the Government by borrowing under the Indian Public Debt Act. The Management of Government Debt, the regulation relating to the issue of such securities are all provided in the Public Debt Act. Now the bearer bonds or securities are no-longer issued by the Government and all registered securities are dealt with by the RBI as the banker to the Government and as the Government's agency for Debt management. Thus, the emergence of Government Securities market is therefore based on the Public Debt Legislation.

The foreign currency dealings and the forex market are governed by the FERA and the provisions and guidelines made thereunder, including the exchange control manual of the RBI. Law and practice of Foreign Exchange is therefore a prerequisite knowledge for forex fund operations.

The other financial markets have the legislative backing of Companies Act, Securities Contract Regulation Act and Securities and Exchange Board of India Act and a host of other enactments which are all relevent to the dealings in these markets.

The control and regulation of the capital market, new issues etc. is as per the powers given to the SEBI, under SEBI Act. Although new issues and mechanism of new issues — rights, prospectus, allotment of shares are all set out in the Companies Act, their mode of issue, contents of prospectus etc. as also the operations of companies in relation to new issues and stock market are controlled by the SEBI. The trading of securities on the stock market is under the Securities Contracts (Regulation) Act and the rules made thereunder, namely, S.C.(R) Rules. But these activities are also regulated by the SEBI. The stock exchanges, stock brokers and sub-brokers etc. are all the intermediaries in the capital market who are regulated by the guidelines and directions of the SEBI. So all powers of the SEBI Act, and the powers under the Companies Act have been delegated to SEBI by the government, in respect of investment activities in the stock and capital markets.

In addition to the above Acts, sometimes dealings of Forex operations involve the knowledge of Customs Act, import export policy under the Trade Control Act and knowledge of the law and practices in the foreign exchange dealings or trade and payments.

In respect of domestic markets the fund managements require a thorough background of the law and practice of banking, legal and regulatory provisions under RBI Act, Banking Regulation Act, Indian Contract Act, Transfer of Property Act, particularly for leasing, hire purchase and related transactions.

TREASURY AS MONEY MANAGEMENT

The basis of treasury operations is money and near money assets like money market instruments, government securities, new and existing securities of corporate units, etc. The money in terms of foreign currencies is traded in the forex market. All the above markets are inter-related and are based on money, cash and credit instruments in rupees or in foreign currencies. These are the areas where the treasury manager operates.

The chart-1 depicts the various phases of money and monetary assets involved in treasury management, and are explained in terms of markets: cash created by the RBI including coins minted by the Government of India is the basis of credit creation and is called high powered money. On the basis of high powered money, credit instruments like Demand Drafts, Mail Transfers, Cheques, Pay Orders, Telegraphic Transfers etc. are all created by the banks to augment the money supply and increase the quantity as well velocity of circulation of money, for helping the trade and industry.

Among these markets, the major segment is call-money markets for borrowings and lending of overnight money to money up to 14 days. Treasury bills of the Government of India, Commercial bills of trade or finance, Participation Certificates, Commercial Paper, Certificates of Deposits and Factorisation Bills are discounted and traded in the money market. This market is supervised and regulated by the Discount and Finance House of India on behalf of the Reserve Bank of India for smooth functioning of the market.

MONEY MANAGEMENT

Domestic Money | Foreign Money

	Credit	Inter-bank Money	Govt. Securities (Gilt-Edged) Market		Foreign Currencies and Credit Instruments
Cash	DDs MTs Cheques	TBs	Equity Preference Shares Debentures		Foreign Currency Notes
Created by RBI	TTs Bankers Drafts & Pay Orders Etc.	Commercial Bills PCs CPs CDs FBs	P.S.Bonds UTI Bonds Other Bonds		Foreign Currency Bonds Forward Currencies
		D.F.H.I.			Net Balances
	Created by Banks	Money Market	Stock Market	New Issues Market	Forex Market

Chart 1.1

In the capital market, long-term funds are dealt with and borrowings and investments mainly in the following categories take place in this market. The money claims in this market are for more than one year and has two segments, namely, primary market for new issues and secondary market for trading of existing securities.

1. Government funds or securities, semi-government bonds, PSU bonds etc. in the gilt-edged market, which is a part of the long-term wing of the trading.
2. Equity shares, preference shares, debentures of various types like FCD, PCD and NCDs, etc. of corporates.
3. UTI units, schemes etc., mutual fund schemes and similar long-term institutions and their issues.

In the forex market, foreign exchange dealings are effected involving the conversion of rupee into foreign currencies, and *vice versa*. The foreign exchange dealings are based on the need for rupee, against foreign currencies for export receipts and other non-trade receipts or for conversion of rupees into foreign currencies, for import payment or other payments abroad. Inflows and outflows of funds take the form of rupee and foreign currencies, which is reflected in the forex market.

In addition to currencies and short-term credit instruments, the other instruments traded in this market are short-term notes, long and medium term bonds, forward currencies, etc. The deployment of foreign funds take place in this market in a mix of such instruments, referred to above.

Conclusions

The Treasury function refers to trading and operations on the Treasury funds, namely the cash, credit, domestic and foreign money. Treasury management is a special aspect of financial management, dealing with only trading, investment, cash and credit markets as opposed to manufacturing and marketing aspects of corporates. The domestic markets are money debt, and government securities markets, while foreign markets include both foreign exchange and foreign currency markets. All these operations in markets involve risks and hence risk management and hedging in derivative markets are all part of Treasury management, including the environmental aspects of these markets and institutional and structural factors in these markets.

❑ ❑ ❑

2 MACRO TREASURY OPERATIONS

Historical Evolution

The era of uniform currency began in India in 1835, when the silver rupee of 180 grains of 11/12, fineness was declared legal tender throughout British India; that was in fact the coin that had been in circulation in some parts of the country at that time. The mints were open to the public for free coinage of the metal. The Act of 1835 permitted the minting of gold coins of the same weight and fairness and that was the gold mohur, equivalent to the value of Rs. 15 per £ at that time, and of the minting of five, ten and twenty rupee pieces. In terms of notifications issued by the government, public treasuries were to accept silver coins as legal tender, but also gold mohur in payment of taxes and other dues. Besides, currency notes issued by Presidency Banks of Bengal, Mumbai and Chennai which started issuing them during 1809 to 1843 were in circulation.

As per the Paper Currency Act 1861, the sole right of note issue rested with the government. The paper currency reserve was to consist of silver coin and bullion, of gold coin bullion in the reserve upto 25% and the government securities upto a maximum of Rs. 4 crores initially. Arrangements were made for issue of notes in exchange for gold coin and bullion in terms of Section IX of Paper Currency Act, 1864. Sovereign equivalent to Rs. 10 and half sovereigns of Rs. 5 were accordingly issued at that time for public use and operations of Treasury. Currency controller used to manage these operations, on behalf of the Government of India.

British India Government maintained some gold reserves, against which they gave the Indian rupees and British sovereigns were also made legal tender at Rs. 15 per pound. These gold and gold coins were later called gold standard reserves. For payments to be made in Britain, the mechanism of telegraphic transfers was used. The evolution of coinage and currency system in India was guided more by the Government's obligations for payments to home country, Britain and at the same time provide coins at stable value.

There was the Coinage Act 1870 and Paper Currency Act 1882 which controlled the issue of gold coins and currency. These acts were emended in 1893 to allow conversion of gold into gold coin, issued at a rate of 1s.4d. per rupee, use of sovereign and half sovereigns at Rs. 15 per sovereign and currency to be issued to Controller General in exchange for gold. ('s' stands for Shilling and 'd' stands for Pence, belonging to British currency).

Paper Currency Act

In terms of India Paper Currency Act 1927, the exchange value of the rupee was fixed at 1s, 6d, the gold equivalent of the rupee being 8.47512 grains fine; sovereign and half sovereign were discontinued. The currency authority was given powers to buy and sell gold at fixed parity.

Under Coinage Act, 1870, amended in 1893 there was closure of Indian Mints for free coinage of gold and silver to public. Rupee coin was defined in RBI Act as silver rupee, which were legal tender under the Indian Coinage Act 1906.

During 1874 to 94, there was a steady fall in the value of silver in relation to gold and the fate of Bimatelism (of gold and silver) was sealed then. Mints were closed to the free coinage of silver. But gold was accepted for minting or for exchange into rupees at a rate of 7.5344 grains of fine gold equivalent to an exchange rate of 1s. 4d. to rupee.

Foreign Currency Dealings

From the very beginning of the history of currency, the government was concerned with the payments to British Home Government by the British India Government, being the legacy of East India Company to meet Home charges. For meeting these payments the secretary of state in council sold council drafts by tender for delivery of sterling in England by payment of rupees in India from Government funds. These council drafts were used originally to acquire sterling to meet Home charges in England. Later, it was extended to meet all requirements for Indian currency. Shipments of silver or gold were made unnecessary by this mechanism. Since 1904, there was a standing offer by government to sell council bills in rupees for sale of sterling for use in England, and the government provided for reverse council bills for sale of sterling for rupees also. Later on, these council bills and reverse council bills became the mechanism used to finance trade and payments between India and Britain.

Gold Exchange Standard

The gold standard could not be adopted in India as Indian public did not prefer the use of gold coins and bullion except as wealth for storing and not for circulation. With Sterling on a gold basis, and maintenence of rupee at 1s.4d. for a fairly long period, the system which emerged in due course is the gold exchange standard. In this, gold was exchanged into rupees, but reverse is not true. Under the Indian Coinage Act as amended in 1940, standard silver coins were not issued to public. New rupee coins of metals other than gold and silver (such as copper, nickel with or without some silver content) and zinc etc., were issued since 1940.

New one rupee currency notes, printed in England were started for issue in the place of rupee coins, in July 1940 and the subsequent issue of one rupee notes was in substitution of one rupee coins. All small denomination coins were also issued under the Indian Coinage Act, by the government.

Currency Chests

The Government accounts used to be maintained by Treasury and it has kept balances with Imperial Bank of India or earliest Presidency banks of Mumbai, Chennai and Kolkata. They used to maintain currency chests as receptacles of stock of new and reissuable notes, rupee coins, and small coins. The Treasury or agency of the Bank provided with the currency chest, can withdraw funds, according to requirements when its payments exceed its receipts on any day and if there are excess receipts, such funds are deposited back in currency chests. The provision of currency chests at as many places as possible helped the physical transactions without the need for physical transfer from one place to another at frequent intervals.

Supply of Cash Country-wide

The provision of adequate supply of currency and coin was the responsibility of the government which it discharged by providing currency chests at the branches of Issues Department of RBI, at branches of Imperial Bank of India (later SBI) which carried on the business of Government treasury and maintained these chests at all district headquarters where the Government has offices, where the Tehsil or District centres are located; adequate supply of rupee coins and currency denominations are provided there for the benefit of public.

The currency chests are listed by revenue officers to provide exchange facilities for higher denominations to lower denominations of coins and currency notes, and *vice-versa,* depending on the requirements of trade and industry. This will also provide for exchange of soiled or old notes for new ones. The currency chests also provide the mechanism for provision of remittance facilities to the banks and public in the areas served by them. These currency chests at different centres with Government departments are part of the Treasury and the responsibility of maintaining them has been given to the RBI when it was setup from the controller of currency which had since ceased to exist.

Post RBI Period — Foreign Currency

The system of council bills and reverse council bills, referred to earlier, was replaced by TTs and MTs by the Imperial Bank of India, set up in 1921, by the amalgamation of three Presidency banks. Exchange banks operating in India even before the 19th century continued to facilitate trade and payments between India and Britain and other foreign countries while the Imperial bank thus helped to Government transactions at home as well as abroad, the Exchange banks specialised in foreign deals of trade and Industry.

After the RBI was set up in 1934, the control of both currency, domestic as well as foreign, and banking was brought under one fold and accordingly RBI was having issue department as well as banking department. To facilitate foreign transactions, RBI was given the responsibility of gold and Sterling reserves and the maintenance of external value of the rupee at 1s.6d. per rupee. The RBI continued to use the medium of Imperial Bank of India and later the State Bank of India since 1956 for distribution and regulation of currency chests, maintained by them and through the Government Departments, maintaining currency chests at District Headquarters. Meanwhile, many Indian Joint Stock Banks started their foreign Departments and the Exchange Banks along with these Indian Banks began to operate the foreign dealings involving foreign funds management and credit transactions for foreign trade receipts and payments.

Treasury and Supporting Legal Powers

I. Government of India

Sovereign power of the people and Indian coinage Act and Indian Public Debt Act replaced by Government Securities Act

Reserve Bank of India Indian Coinage Act and RBI Act — Indian Currency Act gave unlimited legal tender for RBI Guaranteed by Govt. smaller coins are of limited legal tender.

II. Reserve Bank of India has power for currency distribution, as it is fully owned by the Government since 1948 and manages the currency of the country in India guaranteed by the government of the country and the currency is full legal tender.
Domestic Currency is rupee and it is full legal tender of the country and is backed by the Gold, Foreign Assets, and Government of India Securities and their Guarantee;

III. Forex Instruments/Foreign currencies
Indian Rupee was for long linked to Sterling upto early seventies. For foreign payments and receipts foreign currencies are exchanged for the Rupee: such foreign currencies are Sterling, Dollar and other Convertible Currencies.

IV. Credit instruments on the basis of the rupee :
Bills of exchange, Trade bills, Finance Bills, MTs, TT, DD, etc.

V. Credit Instruments on the basis of Foreign Currencies
MTs, TTs, DDs, Sight Bills and usance bills, documentary bills, clean bills, trade bills etc. are bills in foreign currencies, bills for collection, bills for negotiation, confirmations, guarantees, etc.

RBI's Treasury Function

The Macro-treasury manager is the RBI. At the district level, the Tehsildars or Revenue officers keep the custody of the currency chest which are the replicas of the Government treasury. Money due to the government is credited into this chest and money is taken out of the chest for expenditure of the government. Court fees, revenue cess on land, their fees, penalties, and other charges due from the public to the government are credited to these chests. If there are excess funds received than spent on any day, they are credited to the currency chests. If there is shortfall in revenue over expenditure, it is replenished by the Issue Department of the RBI. One of the three functions of the issue department of the RBI is the maintenance of the currency chests of SBI offices at district and state headquarters and where the SBI does not have an office, the district tehsildars or district collectors keep the currency chests. Traditionally the Imperial Bank and later the State Bank of India (after 1956) does the government business of effecting the receipts and payments where the RBI has no office. Where the SBI has no office, the Tehsildars keep the currency chests. To keep new notes in exchange of soiled and torn out notes and to replenish the currency and coins in the currency chests and to keep the accounts of these inflows and outflows is the responsibility of the RBI. The currency chests are the extended arms of the Issue Department of the RBI.

RBI's Functions : The three functions of the RBI referred to above are (i) issue of currency notes (ii) distribution of smaller coins and one rupee coins and rupee notes on behalf of the Government (iii) maintenance of currency chests and facilitate the seasonal adjustment of the currency in circulation by replenishing the currency chest and by taking away the excess funds from the chest. Wherever there are treasuries, there are currency chests. The currency chests are the miniature treasuries of the Government. Under the Section 38 of the RBI Act, the sole agency for distribution of currency and coins is given to the RBI which shares this responsibility with SBI and more recently with all nationalised banks also. One rupee coins and notes and smaller denomination coins are issued by the Government under the Indian Coinage Act, but distributes through the RBI. Under Section 22 of the RBI Act, RBI is given the monopoly power of note issue in India. All rupee notes above rupee one are issued by the RBI. Both currency and coins are distributed by the RBI through SBI, other banks and the currency chests of the Government of India, as per the requirements of the public, trade and industry in India.

Currency Notes

As referred to earlier, currency chests are receptacles of currency and coins kept at various places in the country as extensions of the issue department of the RBI. The currency chests are maintained at various offices of the issue department of the RBI at the SBI offices, and the subsidiaries and sub-treasuries at district and taluka or mandal headquarters. In addition to SBI many public sector banks have been entrusted with the treasury function of keeping their chest making payment and receipts on behalf of the Government.

Objectives and Currency Chest Operation

The basic objective of keeping the currency chests at various places in India is to facilitate quick dispersal of currency and coin to distant places, in India to facilitate remittances to banks and the public economising the available cash by banks and government so that they can do business on a minimum cash basis and to enable the public, to exchange currency for coins and *vice versa*, soiled and torn notes for good ones and higher denomination notes for smaller denominations and *vice versa*. The SBI and its subsidiaries take the responsibility for safeguarding the currency chest, maintained in their premises and the state governments ensure the safeguarding of the currency chest with the treasuries and subtreasuries maintained at district and taluka headquarters. Police "Bandobast" for safe custody of these treasuries and chests is the responsibility of the state government.

Implications of Currency Chest Operations

Currency chests being the extended arms of the issue department of RBI, any deposit of money notes into these chests would tantamount to curtailment of currency and coins with the public. The disbursal of currency and coins from these chests would enlarge the currency and hence money supply with the public. The coins are the assets of the issue department, which along with gold, foreign securities and rupee securities of government are the assets to back the issue of fresh currency by the issue department of RBI. If therefore coins are returned back into currency chests, they will increase the assets of issue department against which, the Issue Department can create additional currency. Thus, expansion of currency and its contraction are taking place on the continuous basis, due to the operation on currency chest. As the currency and coins are the constituents of money supply, the expansion of them leads to the expansion of the latter and *vice versa*. The created currency is exchanged with the rupee securities of the Banking Department for backing the currency creation by the Issue Department and the Banking Department takes the created currency for its payments or cash balances. Thus, the currency created by the issue departments goes to the public through the treasuries or through the banks from the banking department of the RBI. The mechanics of operations of the issue and banking Departments of the RBI enlarge and contract the money supply in the economy in the form of coins and currency.

Money supply with the public (M1 concept of RBI) includes, currency and coins outside the treasuries and banks and current deposits of banks and (their created credit) and other deposits of RBI on which cheques can be drawn by the public.

Sectoral Picture of Macro Treasury

Government is the Sovereign power which has control on cash and currency circulated in the country. The issue of coins and currency is based on the treasures of the government in the form of gold and silver stocks which are supposed to back such issue. More recently, government securities and their promissory notes became the basis of such issue. In fact, the coins of gold and silver were first replaced by the paper currency on the one hand and coins of base metals like copper, nickel, bronze, zinc etc., on the other. To supplement the available currency and to facilitate trade and business, credit instruments came into vogue in the form of promissory notes to pay at a future date by the trade and industry. Thus, on the one hand the government promissory notes became the basis for coins and currency, rather than precious metals like gold and silver and on the other hand, the promissory notes of trade and industry (Business Sector) became the source of credit instruments.

Government and Business are the main sectors which borrow and spend or invest more than their revenues or incomes. These borrowings and promissory notes become the origin of treasury bills, commercial bills, etc., traded in the money market. Their medium and long-term borrowings, investments etc. become the basis of government bond market and corporate bond market (securities or debentures in the legal parlance). The intermediation of these instruments is the responsibility of the finance sector consisting of the banks, commercial and cooperatives, Regional Rural banks, financial institutions, non-bank finance companies, etc.

The chart below depicts this specific relationship leading to the emergence of Treasury markets. Government is the source first of cash and currency and then their borrowings lead to the credit markets.

Industry	Govt. Sector	Households
I > S Borrowings > Lending Net Deficits	I > S Cash & Currency Treasury Bills Govt. Bonds & Securities Net Deficits	S > I Expenditure < Income Lending > Borrowings Net Surplus
	Intermediation — Finance Market	

I = Investment
S = Savings

Chart 2.1

The operations of finance sector are designed to help the real sectors, namely, the Government and Semi-government bodies, business trade and industry and household sector. The larger their role of intermediation and development the larger is the growth of the economy and the improvement in the standard of living of the people. The funds management or the treasury management arises out of the needs of various micro units of business, trade and industry to manage their inflows and outflows as also their balances, efficiently in a way that they maximise the productivity of finance operations, optimise the returns and minimise the risk in such operations.

Foreign Sector: In the above chart, the economy is a closed economy and no consideration is given to the foreign operations and their impact. If the economy is an open economy there will be imports, exports, invisible receipts and payments through travel, transport, investment, insurance etc. There can also be capital inflows and outflows for investment, borrowing and lending etc. as between India and foreign countries.

The foreign transactions lead to the foreign sector and involve exchange of rupees to foreign currencies and *vice versa,* trading in foreign credit instruments etc., which lead to the forex market. The chart below depicts the interrelations of the domestic markets and foreign markets.

Domestic Markets	Foreign Sector
I > S	Lending > Borrowing
Net Govt. Borrowings	Inflows > Outflow
Net Industry Borrowings	S > I
Borrowings > Lending	Foreign Currency
Net Deficits	Borrowings, Bank Credit, Euro Bonds
Domestic Funds	Foreign Funds
Intermediation — Forex Market	

Chart 2.2

The above forex market is linked to domestic markets through currencies and credit transactions, inter-market flow of funds, inter-sector deals and are open to the fund manager to operate in any of these markets or all of them.

Linkage of Macro Treasury Operations with Micro Fund Management

We have seen the emergence of markets from the domestic operations and foreign operations of micro level productive units say, a company or a business unit etc. It explains how physical operations result in financial operations, which in turn lead to inflows and outflows of funds, net balances, in domestic and foreign currencies. Such operations may also be due to government departments, corporate public sector undertakings and individuals in the household. These flows of funds and net balances are managed by the fund manager through appropriate strategies of investment, disinvestment, borrowings and lendings, loans and advances, intercorporate deposits, etc.

The physical operations and financial aspects of them are shown in both domestic and foreign sectors. The government sector, business sector and household sectors operate in both domestic financial markets and also the Foreign finance markets. The domestic markets are the money market, government securities market, new issues market, stock market and bullion market. These are in turn related and linked to the forex market through the operations of the domestic sectors, units and organisations in the business of exports, imports, travel, insurance transportation, investments etc. and through interchange of rupees to foreign currencies and *vice-versa*. It can then be concluded that treasury management involves operations in cash, currency and credit instruments, in any of the above markets.

Conclusions

This chapter traced out the historical evolution of currency and credit system in India which is the basis for Treasury operations. The macro level pyramedical system of currency chests, Treasury with SBI, the erstwhile Imperial Bank of India, and Issue Dept of the RBI at the top, replacing the functions of controller of currency are the pillars on which the Currency System in India is built. The Credit System is built up on the promissory notes issued by banks and the RBI, leading to the Banking Dept of the RBI which makes the RBI Controller of Currency and Credit and thus act as the macro treasurer of the nation. The micro level of operations treasurer are linked to the macro level and the sectoral interlinkages have been shown in Treasury operations in the various markets, both domestic and foreign.

❑ ❑ ❑

3 SCOPE AND FUNCTIONS OF TREASURY MANAGEMENT

Inter Linkages with other Functions

This chapter attempts to set out the needed background information and prerequisites for treasury function. This function is part of the total managerial function of any economic unit, be it a company, non-corporate body, partnership firm etc. The managerial function has three major heads like the Hindu Trimurty gods.

(i) **Production function :** Output and capacity building and capacity utilisation, product mix, input-output matrix, etc.

(ii) **Marketing function :** Sales and distribution network for marketing of the output, logistics, inventory management, etc.

(iii) **Finance function :** This function has three further minor heads, namely, input financing, output financing and funds management. Treasury function falls within the framework of funds management.

All these are depicted in the chart below :

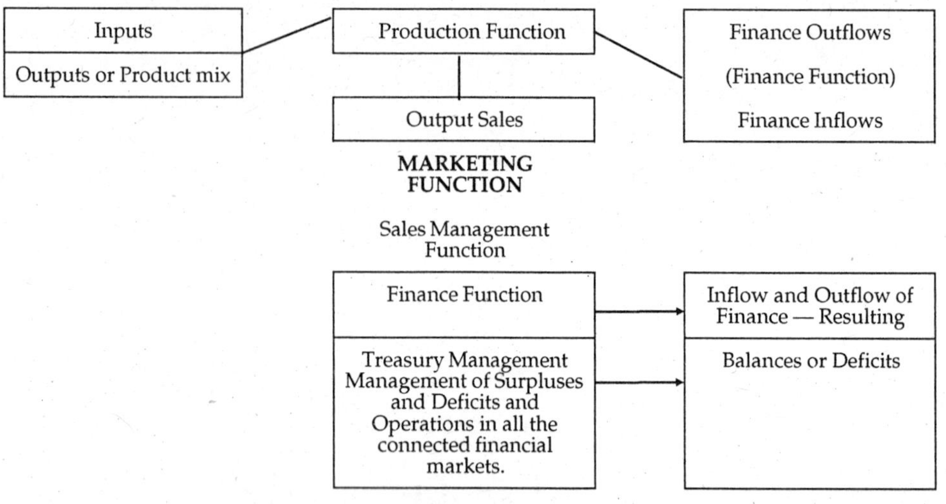

Chart - 3.1

The macro operations of the economy by the government, business and foreign sectors require the availability of cash currency and credit. In broader terms all financial resources including forex reserves are to be made available to the micro economic units, say companies. Similarly, the operations at the national level involve return flow of funds, repayment of loans, taxes, fees etc. to government, business and foreign sector. Such ebb and flow of funds are part of the financial functioning and follows from interrelations between real economy and money economy.

Project Finance and Investment

Any business enterprise requires finance to start business operations. The first requirement is in terms of capital for setting up the project. The project finance needs long-term funds. The specific sources of long-term funds, used for investment in land, factory, building, plant, machinery, equipment, etc. are the following:

(1) Issue of ownership securities : Equity and preference shares. These funds are contributed by promoters public financial institutions, mutual funds, banks etc. Preference shares can be issued as ownership funds, if the company is already existing and needs additional funds.

(2) Loans and advances from financial institutions and banks : While FIs provide long-term loans, banks provide term loans of 5 to 7 years or working capital term loans. These loans can be both secured and unsecured and are of long-term in nature.

(3) Debentures or debt capital : These are issued by an existing company in need of funds for project completion, expansion and diversification, etc. They are funds contributed by public financial institutions and banks. They can be both secured and unsecured.

(4) Public deposits : Existing companies with an equity base or networth and if they have potential to increase debt in relation to equity can raise

funds of three to five years (starting with one year) in the form of deposits from public, firms and companies.

(5) Internal accruals in the form of reserves and surpluses, past profits and provisions, if any, in the case of an existing company can also be used in the financing of investment.

Working Capital Finance

Once the company starts operations of production and manufacture they need working capital funds also. These are required to meet the payments for inputs, labour, raw materials, spare parts, electricity, etc. used in the daily production operations during the process of utilisation of plant and machinery and pending the receipts from sales and services, the payments are to be made in advance. In such cases, all companies provide some buffer resources from the loans/advances or working capital term finance taken from the banks or financial institutions. If those are not provided for and if provided, not adequate, they resort to the short-term finance from the following sources :

(1) Cash credit/Overdraft limits from banks.

(2) Loans for working capital from banks.

(3) Trade credits or suppliers credits which are normal for manufacturing company.

(4) Dealers / Stockists deposits with the company for supplies, if the product sales depend on them.

(5) Instalment credit from other companies such as lease / Hire purchase companies which are paid in instalments.

(6) Customer advances for supply of goods if the goods are specific to the customer needs.

The requirement of working capital funds depends on the nature of company's activities. For finance companies or service companies, non-manufacturing trading companies, the need for such funds is small or negligible. For manufacturing companies, such need is large and inevitable. The needed funds and sources supplying the funds will depend on the nature of the product and the company. For example, for companies manufacturing machinery and capital equipments specific to the customer needs, capital required is large and customer advances will also be large.

Overall Finance Function

At the micro level, the finance function starts with the capital structuring, scouting for the least cost combinations of capital for financing of the project and forecasting the sources and uses of funds. In this function one has to co-ordinate with the production and operations manager, sales or marketing manager and all of them constitute the management team.

The inflows and outflows and their co-ordination and synchronisation and making arrangements for meeting any gap between them is one side of the coin. The other side of the coin is the funds management of the surpluses and maximisation of returns from these funds. These two sides of the coin generally go together due to functional inter-dependence; but while the former is referred to as the finance function for managing the inflows and outflows, the latter is the treasury function, namely, management of the surplus funds for profit. These two together have to be viewed and analysed for overall assessment of the financial efficiency. So a finance manager need not have a treasury function or *vice versa* although they are two sides of the same activity. The term "funds manager" is also used to refer to the latter function of the management of cash balances and credit facilities. As cash and credit go together, again there is need to have a co-ordinated funds management for each micro unit, which put together cash and credit components of funds management. So treasury function is a special aspect of funds management dealing with cash and credit.

Micro and Macro Operations

The Treasury Management has both macro and micro aspects as referred to earlier. At the macro level, the pumping in and out of cash, credit and other financial instruments are the functions of the government and business sectors, which borrow from the public. These two sectors spend more than their means and have to borrow to finance their ever growing operations. They accordingly issue securities or promissory notes which are part of the financial system. These borrowings for financial needs are met by the surplus funds and savings of the Household Sector and the Foreign Sector, who have incomes more than their expenditure in total. The micro units utilise these flows and build up their capacities for production of output and this leads to the productive system and this in turn results in the consumption and distribution of goods and services resulting in financial inflows and outflows for the micro units. These relations are depicted in the chart below :

Macro Transactions	Micro Transactions	Leads to
Govt. Borrowings— →	Expenditure > Income	Gilt-edged Market
Industry & Business Borrowings— →	Investment > Savings	New Issues and Stock Markets
Foreign Sector →	Exports/Imports, Inflows and Outflows	Forex Market
Financial Sector — Money Market, and Related Markets.		

Chart - 3.2

Environment of Finance

No company can operate in a vacuum. Its assets are both financial and physical. As such, there are both quantifiable and non-quantifiable factors involved in financial performance, forecasting and the achievement of targets.

The company's finance manager is the kingpin around which the operations of company revolve. His operations and performance have an impact on the company itself and the financial system and the economy in the broader sense. The finance function is therefore an eyesore of all operations of the company at micro level and macro level.

All these above agencies will be examining the micro unit from the macro angle and compare the company's performance with other companies in the same industry and the industry in total. Physical targets, operations and performance will boil down to how efficiently the financial goals are achieved, the inflows and outflows and total balances and how productively and profitably they are deployed and managed in the best interests of the company.

Finance Functions and Treasury Operations

The objective of the finance function of a manager may be set out in different ways. He may aim at optimising the value of his assets or wealth or minimising the worth of his liabilities. Put in differently, he may maximise his gross profits or net profits or aim at optimising the market value of his company shares. Looked at from any angle, the management basically aims at economy, efficiency and productivity leading to greater profitability. For this purpose, he concentrates on the efficient management of cash and credit so far as the financial aspect is concerned. But more importantly, he has to consider the production function of which cash and credit are inputs. The manager has to take into account the national and international forces in the preparation of plans and budgets for resource inflows and outflows and in input and output markets. In the raising of funds and use of such funds, the costs of alternative uses and sources have to be considered both at home and abroad.

In terms of the real sector or the financial sector, he has to observe the criteria of efficiency and productivity etc., in the input market and output market and in allocation of physical resources or financial resources. In the input and output markets as well as in financial markets, both domestic and foreign forces have to be reckoned with.

Input Market

In the input market, physical and financial inputs are fed into the productive system. Physical inputs relate to physical capital equipment, plant and machinery, raw materials, spare parts and intermediate products, etc. Financial inputs relate to money spent on wages for labour, payments for raw-material, electricity etc. or cash kept for current liabilities or contingencies. Such inputs can be secured both from domestic markets and foreign markets. As such, a cost calculus has to be made for the right mix of inputs and the right sources of supply of such inputs so as to minimise the costs for a given product mix. It is possible that some raw materials or spares are more cheaply available abroad than at home and assuming a free access to such market with or without licences or subject to government regulations if any, the manager may plan for a mix of inputs at the least cost, subject to the technical feasibilities in the production process. The markets, both domestic and foreign, have to be accessed for these inputs in terms of costs and prices and alternative sources of supply explored. In the supply of financial inputs for production purposes one has to take into account the need for cash and credit and the relative proportions of each both from home and abroad and to assess their relative costs. Marginal costing of cash and credit is part of the wider subject of cash management. The cash component as an input in the production function is part of the subject of production management, while the overall management of all funds — sources and uses of cash, credit and other financial assets — is in the domain of financial management.

In a subsidiary or branch of a foreign company, foreign sources play a more important role even in financial inputs. Such exercises relating to financial inputs have to be made after an assessment of cash inflows and outflows, both on current and capital accounts. On the capital account, sources and uses of funds for investment also become an important pre-requisite for planning and budgeting. These will be discussed below under sources and uses of funds.

Output Market

In the output market, the sale of final and intermediate products can be made both in domestic and foreign market. International marketing and international finance are closely interlinked and flows of finance follow the flows of trade. Marketing is an important pre-requisite for trade. International trade and international finance are close complements to domestic trade and finance. The costs of production and selling costs and the available margins both on domestic sales and foreign sales have to be considered. Here again, it is assumed that there is a free market abroad or trading is possible, subject to an export licence or after satisfying all the requirements of the government policy in this regard. A cost calculus has to be made for planning for the right mix of sales at home and abroad. For an assessment of the demand prospects abroad, we need to know the alternative sources of supply in such markets, costs and prices of such alternative sources, transport and selling costs etc. which are the subject of international economics and finance. As sales has two components of cash sales and credit sales, trade and finance go together, which the finance manager has to bear in mind.

Sources and Uses

At the micro level of a company an analysis of the sources of funds reveals that broadly there are three categories of sources : (i) Savings of the company which are its retained earnings, (ii) External sources (domestic) from the capital and money markets such as banks, all-India or state-level financial institutions, government or the public, and (iii) foreign sources, namely, institutions and persons abroad. The last category can in turn be specified as follows: (a) credit from private parties, *viz.*, trade credit, buyers credit, etc. (b) foreign government credit, *viz.*, government to government line of credit, foreign aid or grants or loans, (c) resources from international or interregional bodies such as IFC, IBRD, foreign banks or Euro-currency markets etc., and (d) Non-resident individuals and institutions.

The same analysis holds good at the sectoral and national level. In fact, the emergence of international financial markets can be traced to this sectoral interdependence, including the foreign sector and intra-national dependence. Basically, as no country is self-sufficient but it is dependent on other countries for something or the other, international economic and commercial relations emerge.

In a similar fashion, it would be appropriate to set out the pattern of use of funds of any company into various sectors of the economy, including the foreign sector. Dispensation of funds for current or capital expenditures in domestic markets and international markets can be separately set out. Such an analysis is particularly more relevant to multinational corporations and branches or subsidiaries of foreign companies in whose case foreign markets and foreign sources of supply play an important part. The head office or the holding company may spend a part of its funds in investment in the host country, make inward remittances for working capital or investment purposes and outward remittances for royalty and dividend payments or technical fees, etc.

Sectoral Interdependence and Sweep of Treasury Operations

International financial markets emerged out of the felt need to facilitate operations of nations arising out of the commercial and financial transactions with the rest of the world. This emergence can be attributed logically to the inter-relations of the economic unit with the corporate sector and of latter with other sectors of the economy, including the foreign sector. It would be apt to set out here the inter-relations between the micro-level operations of a finance manager with the macro-level working of the corporate sector and foreign sector. A finance manager is a micro unit in the corporate sector. The environment he faces is competition from other similar units in the corporate sector and as suppliers of inputs or as consumers of output. Besides, this corporate sector in turn, is interlinked with all other sectors of the economy. The micro-level manager is thus faced with a total environment of the economy which includes foreign sector, and it is thus necessary for him to be familiar with the international financial system, as much as to the domestic financial system. It is in these domestic and foreign markets that the treasurer operates at the micro level of a corporate unit. The sweep of treasury operations encompasses all financial markets and connects all sectors of the economy.

The corporate sector is a part of the total business sector having trading and manufacturing activities. The corporate sector is also connected with all sectors of the economy, namely, government sector, household sector and foreign sector either as suppliers of inputs or as consumers of output. Besides, all these domestic and foreign sectors are inter-connected through the flow of funds and savings from one sector to the other. In each sector, there are both savers and investors. Only the household sector is a net saver in India. Besides, the household sector is also a supplier of factors of production such as labour, management, enterprise etc. Foreign sector may be a net saver, if there was a net balance on current account of our balance of payments leading to the accretion to our foreign exchange reserves. India is running huge deficits in merchandise trade account for some time which would offset any positive balance on the invisible trade account. This would mean a negative savings in the foreign sector leading to a loss of our foreign exchange reserves. If there is a net inflow of funds from abroad either as foreign credits, grants etc. or borrowings from foreign governments., international bodies etc., there may be a positive balance in the balance of payments and foreign savings would accrue. The surplus savings in some sectors would flow into other sectors with deficit. In the corporate sector where investment is invariably more than their available savings, the units have to depend on other sectors to finance them. These savings may flow directly from the government sector or household sector or indirectly through financial institutions, banks and other agencies. It would thus be clear that the corporate sector is intricately connected with all other sectors of the economy either as suppliers of inputs of production or suppliers of factors of production, including land, labour, capital or enterprise or consumers of their products or services. They are also connected with other sectors of the economy through inflow or outflow of funds or savings or financial assets — moneys or near money assets or financial flows.

Another aspect of inter-dependence of the various sectors of the economy is government and foreign private investment in the domestic economy or Indian investment abroad. This investment may take the form of (i) equity participation in Indian enterprises (ii) investment in bonds or debentures, (iii) granting of loans or credits to the private sector, (iv) joint ventures in third countries and (v) technical consultancy or know-how participation etc. Transfer of technology is also one of the aspects of the international commercial and financial relations which is necessary for a sustained rate of growth at the lowest possible costs and the highest level of productivity.

All the inputs of the corporate sector come either from the household sector as labour, capital or enterprise or from Government sector as infrastructure, land, electricity, water etc., or from agriculture or industry (business sector) as raw materials, intermediate products, spares, parts etc.

Particularly more relevant for our discussion is the contribution of finance sector towards inputs of the corporate sector in the form of loans or equity for working capital or physical capital, plant, machinery, spares, raw materials, etc. or financial inputs in the form of short-term credits or investment in financial assets, etc.

Such inter-dependence between the corporate sector and other sectors is also noticed in the field of outputs. The main consumers of some products may in fact be the business or government and not always households only. Either in respect of consumer goods or capital goods, there is a good element of foreign demand, particularly from the less developed countries. In view of the vastness of our domestic markets, the executives of the corporate sector rarely explore the foreign markets, unless the products are export-oriented. With the projected expansion of the industry and limitations in the domestic markets and the recent trends towards globalisation, the present executives may have to think more in terms of foreign markets than of domestic markets. More recently, export oriented industries and 100 percent export units are being encouraged by the government in the light of the prevailing balance of payments difficulties of the country and increasing export shortfalls. Besides, the philosophy of the government is also veering round the view of making our economy more competitive with globalisation and a greater role allocated to the private sector and export sector. The cost consciousness and competitiveness has increased when facing the foreign sector which can be hardly overemphasised when the chill winds of competition and cost consciousness make the executives of the corporate enterprise more alert and informed on both the domestic and external sectors. The foreign environment would be equally important and more challenging than the domestic markets due to the ever changing scene of demand and supply forces, competition and cost price factors operating from all sides of the world. These may hopefully improve the efficiency of factors and lower the costs of production.

There is another reason why the foreign sector is more important to India, namely, the limits are already reached in the domestic markets and the scope for further expansion of markets lie abroad. Besides, there is the debt service burden which we carry due to our reliance on foreign credits during the last few decades of our planning. This burden can be discharged by a continuous flow of goods and services outside the country leading to an export surplus or a current account surplus for the nation.

In the output market, the domestic household sector has been the main consumer in India, followed by the government sector which needs the output of the corporate sector both for capital formation and current consumption. Besides, the government with its expanding role in the economy has a greater say in the affairs of the corporate sector despite their avowed policy of a greater role for the private sector in the years to come. The business sector comprising industry and agriculture continue to consume the products of the corporate sector as intermediates or raw materials for manufacture or further processing. These provide inter-linkages of corporate sector to other sectors and to the financial sector in particular.

Conclusions

The treasury function involves a complex set of operations in cash and credit markets and is interlinked to all the other functions of the corporate unit or bank, starting with its close links with Financial function for funds management, it is connected with production and marketing functions at the micro level and with the other sectors of the economy and with the foreign sector at macro level. Arranging for cash and credit to the corporate unit, the treasurer has to interact with all the domestic and foreign sectors and the related markets. In particular it is related to socio-economic environment through money, stock and securities markets govt. debt market and foreign money market and foreign exchange and currency markets. Thus, the scope of treasury function is very wide and encompasses a variety of operations in the finance area.

❑ ❑ ❑

4 ACCOUNTING AND LEGAL BACKDROP

Accounting Backdrop for Treasury Operations

The need for analysis and forecasting for the purpose of treasury operations was referred to earlier. The data, necessary for the purpose emanate from the accounts — income and expenditure statements, balance sheet statements and other related statements. The analysis of these statements is the basis for assessing the financial performance of any company or organisation.

Banks are providing credit on the need based assessment and not on security alone. For this purpose, the viability of the project, financial soundness of the company and the prospects for its operations are examined by banks. The assessment of credit needs of any unit is based on the purpose, project and performance (three ps). For such assessment by bankers, financial analysis and tools of analysis are required, which necessitate expertise in accounting concepts and their interpretation and statistical tools for analysis and forecasting. Thus, a banker, a manager or an investor would look into the accounts of company their financial data and financial statements for analysis and interpretation. It is in this background that source of knowledge of the accounting concepts and conventions should be familiar to the treasury manager and funds manager.

The Top management has itself a deep involvement in such analysis and their interpretation. They have to plan for the financing of current operations capital needs for expansion and diversification and for raising of such resources from the least cost sources and least cost combinations of capital. They are interested in the efficient use of capital and to keep cost of capital and labour as low as possible to maximise the profits and to improve the net worth of the company, so as to keep share price rising and investors happy. Managements are interested in proper accounts and their analysis for planning and control while the treasury manager in particular is interested in cash flows, funds flow, surpluses and deficits on various accounts, the costs of alternative sources and the returns on alternative avenues of investments of funds etc. The Treasurer has to arrange for borrowing and examine the alternative sources and the least cost combination.

Major Accounting Statements

The accounts of a company or any economic unit are recorded on a daily, monthly and annual basis. The physical operations of the company involve financial commitments, *viz.*, inflows and outflows. The most important statement for the accounts are the income and expenditure statements giving out the financial results of the operations over any period of time, monthly, quarterly, half yearly or yearly profit or loss position seen from statements as also the disposition of profits through profit allocation statement. There are a number of other statements all presented in the form of schedules to the balance sheet. Balance sheet is a standing position of the company in terms of assets and liabilities at any point of time presented in India every six months and yearly. The net results of the company in the form of profit or loss are carried to the balance sheet. The assets and the liabilities of any unit should be equal and balance themselves and hence called balance sheet. Thus, next to income expenditure statement, balance sheet is the most important accounting data for the financial analyst. Not only the above published data, but the unpublished internal records of stocks receivables payables etc. are necessary for assessing the company's financial position.

In these and other financial statements there are a number of concepts which are subject to ambiguity and misinterpretation. Some such concepts are discussed in the subsequent paras. In fact, each item in the balance sheet and income expenditure and other related financial statements should be clearly understood by the analyst although only a few of the ambiguous and complicated concepts are discussed in this chapter.

Accounting Principles

The norms of the Institute of Chartered Accountants and provisions of Company Act, along with the guidelines under the Act govern the accounting principles and practices, followed in India.

The knowledge of the more important principles involved is an asset for the financial analyst.

The majority of the companies follow these right principles of accounting, which are prudent and conservative. Some of these accounting principles are set out below.

1. Conservatism: This principle embodies prudence whereby all losses, whether likely or realised are recognised while profits are recognised when they are actually earned. As per the RBI guidelines to NBFCs, the prudential norms for income recognition are : Income part due but not received within 6 months of due date is not to be booked, until actually received. Similarly, non-performing assets (NPA) are to be separated. The definition for the NPA is a credit instrument in respect of which, interest and principal instalments have become due for a period of more than six months. Such assets are required to be provided at the rate of 10 to 50% of the amount (depending upon period of overdue from 6 months to 3 years). An asset considered uncollectable has to be provided for at a rate of 100% of the amount, as per the RBI guidelines to finance companies.

In respect of valuation of inventory or any asset, the market price or cost price whichever is lower is to be taken. There should not be undue overvaluation or undervaluation of assets and valuation should be realistic. Prudence also dictates the need for making provision in anticipation of doubtful debts or bad debts, adoption of written down values for charging the depreciation and amortisation of intangible assets. Similarly, liabilities should not be undervalued as assets should not be overvalued.

2. Consistency: Whatever method is adopted for valuation of assets or for charging depreciation the same should be adopted throughout the years for comparison and consistency. Some companies change the accounting practice with a small footnote at the end. Thus, excise duty paid in some assets deducted from sales income are sometimes shown separately as expenditure. Similarly, cash discount received on purchase is treated in one year as revenue and in another year a reduction in purchase price. If any change is needed for window dressing, the change should be explained with adequate reasons giving the implications of the same to the company's financial position. The same practice should be followed uniformly every year instead of changing year after year.

3. Sound Practices in Reporting: Every expense item is to be supported by a voucher and if that is not possible with petty cash entry that has to be maintained separately and debit and credit vouchers should be passed, supported by proper receipts, wherever possible. This is called objective evidence approach. Besides, accounts should be kept on the basis of either accruals or realisation. The interest accrued is generally taken as credit, while payments made on a cash basis. This leads to overestimation of revenue, relative to expenditure. There should be a uniform policy of reporting either on accrual basis or on cash basis and not a mixture depending on the circumstances.

4. Materiality: As there may be minor expense or credit items, all major items are to be recorded individually and minor events to be clubbed together. Reporting of minor stationery items and minor petty cash items can be clubbed into a major reporting item by putting an indent for use of a section or a division. In respect of such events, the section and division will record the minor details and the major items of expense or revenue will go to the accounting books. What is major or minor or what is material or not has to be decided by the accountant and is a matter of judgement. Only consistency in treatment is to be maintained.

5. Disclosure: This principle of disclosure refers to full and fair disclosures of all material facts in company finances. Through proper accounting methods, certain disclosures are made compulsory by law and formats are laid down by the Companies Act for income expenditure statements and balance sheet statement, with a view to force full disclosures by the company. Even by practice, good companies have always followed this principle, in giving detailed notes and footnotes on any changes in practices and in the case of intangible assets or contingent liabilities, etc. The various schedules to the income expenditure statement and balance sheet, as per the Companies Act, provide the necessary disclosures by the companies.

As per the Government guidelines, under the Companies Act, all companies have to have a uniform accounting year of April to March and departure from this rules should be an exception. Similarly, listed companies have to show quarterly unaudited results to the public and disclose in the balance sheets the sources and uses of funds and achievements *vis-a-vis* the targets or projections, given at the time of new issues. The companies have to finalise all their financial statements and annual report within six months from the date of the closure of accounts, namely, by September for the accounts closed in March. The quarterly results are to be ready within a month of the close of the quarter.

Other Disclosures

Disclosure requirements are laid down in the Companies Act, government guidelines and the listing agreement with the Stock Exchanges, which all listed companies have to observe. The Financial Analysts and Treasury Managers have to be familiar with these requirements, under the Law.

As per the latest government guidelines, the companies have to keep accounts on cash basis or mercantile basis. All the companies have to follow the prevailing guidelines from April 1996 onwards. The following details are to be provided in the Director's Report, as per the companies (Disclosure of Particulars in the Report of Board of Directors) Rules 1988 :

1. Measures taken for pollution control and abatement under Water Pollution and Control of Pollution Act.
2. Conservation of energy and measures taken in the direction of economising the use of electricity.
3. Technology absorption and measures adopted for saving scarce water and energy resources.
4. Research and development efforts to absorb the foreign technology and development of import substitutes.
5. Insurance of all insurable interests of the company.
6. Foreign exchange earnings and outgo during each of the years.

As per the Section 217 (2A) of Companies Act each company has to reveal the names of employees drawing above Rs.25,000 P.M. in the Balance Sheet, or any other amount as may be laid down by the government.

All accounts are kept in nominal rupees and although rupees of last year or a few years back are not comparable with the present rupee no attempts are made to present inflation adjusted figures in the balance sheets, which are more scientific.

Under Section 212 of the Companies Act, the subsidiaries of companies and their details are to be given separately specifying their holdings in these subsidiaries. It is now made necessary for companies to present a consolidated position including those of W.O.S. (Wholly Owned Subsidiaries). Investments in non-traded assets and those of non-marketable nature are to be presented separately. Uniformity and consistency in practices is also required to be adhered. Any changes have to be explained and their implications for the accounts and their comparison are to be set out in the Auditor's Report or footnotes.

Some Accounting Misconceptions

1. There is need to distinguish the cash from funds flows as there is difference between them.
2. Premium on issues made, although received in cash do not form part of profits of the company but are to be shown as free reserves in Balance Sheet.

3. Profits are a liability and losses are assets and reduce the capital available.
4. Work in progress and miscellaneous expenditure not written off form part of the assets.
5. Depreciation is another accounting concept, much abused by the companies and financial analyst has to note the method of depreciation adopted, and examine consistency and comparability of their figures. In fact, cash profits should include depreciation figures with net profits.
6. Ability of current assets and the non-performing nature of these assets are to be noted. Not all current assets are of the same quality as some may be sub-standard and some may be bad debts.
7. Inventories of yester years may not be valued as the inventories of current years as the costs per unit may differ for each year.
8. The RBI guidelines for income recognition and provisioning for bad and sub-standard debts are to be observed by all companies.
9. Some companies show huge cash and bank balances and they are not necessarily creditworthy or efficient as they may be having arrears of P.F. contributions, tax payments, etc. They may be inefficient in the use of cash balances.
10. Sales income is sometimes presented with and is also clubbed with other income, which is in the nature of trading, or speculation and it is not a correct method.
11. Financial analyst has to take care of the accounting malpractices, changes in accounting systems and practices of companies.
12. Revalued assets may be put along with other assets not revalued and no indication may be given about why revaluation is done.
13. Profit figures can be manipulated by showing changing provisions for taxation, depreciation, DRR, CRRF etc.
14. The company's treatment of depreciation, secret reserves, contingent liabilities and intangible assets are the items where the financial analysts have to be careful in their analysis and interpretation.

Contingent Assets

Another item in the Balance Sheet, which is subject to liquidity and different interpretations is Contingent Assets. It is a category of assets, which need not be shown in the balance sheet proper. But the usefulness of these assets is a matter of discretion to the analyst and the company claims need not be taken as totally true and realisable.

Some examples of contingent assets which are shown in notes to balance sheet and not balance sheet proper are given below :

1. An option to apply for shares — rights, warrants, coupons, etc.
2. A legal action on infringement of copyright, patent, etc.
3. Possible refund of taxes paid.
4. Possible recovery of written off debt on legal action.

Financial analysts may have to take each item separately and assess the extent of bonafides and usefulness of item for overall credit rating of the company or for proper evaluation of assets *vis-a-vis* liabilities.

Some miscellaneous assets are reported in balance sheets, the details of which should be looked into carefully by the analysts. These are the non-current assets of a duration of life of more than one year. They may be unquoted investments, loans and advances to employees, directors, deferred charges, prepaid expenses etc. and advances made to subsidiaries or investments for housing for employees etc. These non-current expenses are treated as assets and many of them may not be realisable in cash, within a short period of less than one year.

Intangible Assets

Another grey for financial analysts is the intangible assets. All types of malpractices, window dressing and cover up operations are possible due to intangible assets as in the case of contingent liabilities. They are no doubt useful in the business, but the extent of the usefulness is a matter of discretion, unlike in the case of physical assets.

Under this category, the following are a few examples, which are found in the balance sheets of many companies :

Goodwill, patents and trademarks, designs and copyrights, preliminary and unwritten off-expenses, deferred revenue expenditure, bad and doubtful debts, carry forward losses, development expenses etc.

Normally, appearance of these items is an indication of doubtful nature of the healthy financial position of the company, as sound and growing companies or blue chip companies do not carry such items, as they would write them off from their profits and surpluses. To the extent that they appear, they deem to wipe out the capital of the company and in ascertaining the true networth of the company, the analyst has to reduce them from the owner's funds.

Contingent Liabilities

Schedule VI of the Companies Act mentions some items as examples of contingent liabilities. As these are not shown in the Balance Sheet, but in a footnote, many analysts ignore such data, although they are very relevant for a correct analysis of the financial position. If the contingent liabilities of a current nature along with the reported current liabilities in the Balance Sheet exceed the amount of current assets, the company becomes highly risky. Sometimes guarantees given by a company result in a liability much more than originally estimated. Contingent liabilities are a potential risk for the company, which if not prudently assessed will lead to wrong conclusions about the company. The liabilities which are mentioned as contingent liabilities in the footnotes are given below as a few examples :

1. Guarantees given by the company.
2. Claims of the government on the company, not acknowledged as due by the company.
3. Uncalled liability on partly paid shares.
4. Arrears of fixed cumulative dividends.
5. Bills discounted but not matured.
6. Estimated amounts of contracts, remaining to be executed on capital account and not provided in the balance sheet.
7. Contested amounts of excise claims.
8. Dues contested in a court, but pending before the final court order.

There can be many more such contingent claims on the company, which might have been underestimated by the accountants, but have to be assessed by the financial analysts, carefully.

Depreciation: Confusion also arises out of the use of the concept of depreciation. It was already referred to as a non-cash expense item and funds are retained in the company. Depreciation refers to write off of the values of fixed assets. The Companies Act 1956, in Schedule VI, enumerates the following items as fixed assets.

Goodwill, land, buildings, leaseholds, railway sidings, plant and machinery, furniture and fittings, property development, patents, trade marks and designs, the stock and vehicles. Of the above some like good will, patents, trade marks and designs are intangible assets, but writing off of their values is permitted, revaluation of assets again lead to fictitious assets, which financial analysts should not take into account, for valuation of shares as they are not free reserves as per the definition of the government.

Obsolescence is also partly similar to depreciation since technologies may change leading to obsolescence of plant and machineries. All physical assets except land depreciate with time, but some physical assets also lose their value due to obsolescence, which means loss of usefulness of an asset, caused by supersession of one type of machinery by another and more advanced. Changes in tastes, styles, and fashions bring in new products, which make the old products obsolete and with that machinery producing them also lose their value. New inventions and innovations have produced new machinery, which make the old machinery obsolete. The financial analysts have to take due care of such possibilities in valuation and analysis of financial statements for arriving at the net asset value of the company.

Methods of Depreciation

The following are the factors which are considered for providing depreciation on fixed assets.

1. Projected life period of the assets based on expert opinion and prevailing practice.
2. Estimated salvage and resale value of the asset *vis-a-vis* the cost of acquisition.
3. Method adopted for depreciation.

The methods, usually prevailing for depreciation are the following :-

1. Straight line method: Under this, a constant proportion of the original cost of the assets less the scrap value is provided every year, as a fixed amount.

2. Written down value method or diminishing value method: Here a fixed percentage say 20%, is written off every year on the diminished book value of the asset, till the asset is reduced to the scrap. This method is approved by the Income Tax Department. This will lead to reduced amounts of write off year after year, as the book value diminishes from the original cost.

3. Sum of the years digits method: The depreciation provided under this method also gets reduced year after year. To give an example, if the life of the asset is 5 years, the sum of the digits is 1+2+3+4+5 = 15, and the first year deduction will be 5/15, followed in later years by 4/15, 3/15, 2/15 and 1/15, leading to total write off in 5 years.

4. Depreciation fund method or redemption fund method: Under this, an equal amount is written off every year, by debiting it to the profit and loss account and crediting it to the depreciation fund account. The yearly instalment is calculated in such a manner that, if the amount is invested at compound interest, it will accumulate to an amount equivalent to the cost of the asset minus scrap value over the period. The provisions are not retained in the business but invested in some securities, with reinvestment facility, so as to get back full value of the original cost of the asset.

5. Annuity method : When the funds are to be retained in the business, and book value is written down every year, by provision for depreciation, the instalment to be provided periodically is calculated as per the Annuity Table as a fixed amount. Here the presumption is that money invested in an asset earns interest at a fixed rate, which is debited to the asset account at reduced value of principal, each year. This method, generally prevalent in respect of long leases of large capital goods involves a provision at a fixed rate, but the amount provided declines year after year, as the interest charge keeps on decreasing although the principal amount repaid is the same every year.

There are a number of other methods, for providing depreciation, which are less frequently used. These are based on the concept of the endowment for a fixed period, or revaluation of the asset, or based on the value of output each year or machine hour product etc. Sometimes all the assets are grouped together and a flat rate of depreciation is charged every year for the total value. This clubs all the assets together and a fixed life period say 5 to 8 years is decided and depreciation accordingly provided. This method, called global method is not permitted under the Companies Act, in India.

Each method has is own advantages and disadvantages. Most commonly used methods are the straight line method on the original cost, and the written down value method on the book value of the asset. Whatever is the method, accounting standards dictate, that the same method should be continued throughout the life of the asset, while in fact a number of companies change these methods of providing depreciation depending on their profits and management policy.

Legal Backdrop*

Treasury Manager need not be a legal expert but his company or the bank being governed by some laws, some legal knowledge is also necessary. Treasury Managers in banks are to be familiar with the Law and Practice of Banking, FERA, Exchange Control Manual and RBI guidelines. Whether dealing with companies or firms, or with other banks, they have to manage, financial assets and investments, credit instruments, like Bills Receivables, Payables Cheques, DDs, etc. They should have a background of the Banking Regulation Act and Negotiable Instruments Act. Besides, as Finance Managers or Treasury Operators, they enter into a number of contracts in the form of purchase, sale or transfer, the knowledge of Indian Contract Act, Transfer of Property Act, Stamp Act and similar legislation should be familiar to them. A Treasury Manager in Leasing and Hire-purchase finance company has to be thorough with the Transfer of

---

* See the Author's Book on "Investment and Securities Markets in India" for detailed treatment.

Property Act and such provisions of the Contracts Act, I.T. Act etc. as are necessary for his work.

As this book is not intended to be a legal brief for Treasury Manager, it is not proposed to deal with all these laws here. In particular a Treasury Manager in a Joint Stock Company has to be thorough with the Companies Act, as the later deals with all the operations of companies from inception to winding up. Indian Companies Act and provisions of Negotiable Instruments Act are commonly useful for all operations in financial services and instruments. The Treasury Manager in a Bank has to be more thorough with the law and practice banking, B.R. Act, RBI Act, N.I. Act, F.E.M.A., Govt. Securities Act, Indian Contract Act, etc.

Lastly, Indian Stamp Act and State Stamp Acts are all relevant to dealing in negotiable instruments, other than cheques, which have to be stamped. All promissory notes, bills payable or receivable are subject to stamp duties, as in the case of transfer deeds, share and debenture certificates and rights. All these are to be executed on approved formats and stamped. Some stamped on ad valorem basis, some to be on fixed amounts and some with revenue stamps, some with judicial stamps, broker's stamps, adhesive stamps, share stamps, and imprest stamps etc. These are to be clearly known to all finance managers.

The company solicitors, or the legal department of the company will generally take care of all the formalities required under the law. There are many statutory obligations under the Law imposed on the company secretary also. But to the extent that these provisions of Companies Act, relate to offer of public issues through prospectus, letter of offer, rights issue or warrants and debentures, they are governed by the respective provisions of the Act. Even raising deposits from the public is governed by Section 58 A & B of the said Act in addition to the existing guidelines in this regard by the RBI and the Department of Company Affairs of the Central Government. There are special provisions relating to the issue of debentures under Sections 117 to 120 of the said Act. In financial planning and raising of resources, the financial manager should be familiar with these legal formalities as much as the company secretary.

The Treasury Managers operate in money market, controlled by the RBI, gilted securities and semi-government securities, managed by the RBI and the forex market, which is again regulated by the RBI. This makes it incumbent for all treasury managers to be familiar with the working and policies of the RBI as published in their monthly and annual reports and their press briefings on a daily or regular basis. RBI's policy statements and their weekly statement of affairs showing the changes in the balance sheet of the RBI, and the fortnightly data on the balance sheet of scheduled commercial banks, published by the RBI contain a wealth of information affecting these markets, which the Treasury Manager should know how to analyse.

The commercial bills, and other trade bills, discounted by treasury managers and all the instruments in money market which they deal in, including the inter-corporate investments are negotiable instruments, controlled by the Negotiable Instruments Act. Bills of exchange, transfer deeds, share certificates are examples with which they deal frequently and require endorsements and the rules regarding their validity, endorsement, negotiation, presentation and blank transfers etc. are all governed by the Negotiable Instruments Act.

As all their deals are contracts entered into for purchase, sale repos, swaps, switches etc., by the treasury manager which are regulated by the Indian Contracts Act, or Securities Contracts (Regulation) Act, the time and place of execution of deeds and their validity are to be ensured by the treasury manager in all his transactions and these operations are aided by his knowledge of Indian Contract Act, Securities Contracts (Regulation) Act and Negotiable Instruments Act.

Particularly relevant are the actionable claims on money dealt with under Sections 18 to 30 of the Sale of Goods Act and Transfer of Property Act which deal with actionable claims, or monetary claims and their transfer. They come under the Transfer of Property Act (Chapter VII) relevant to hire-purchase and leasing. All such transfers of property rights have to be executed by writing and signing by the persons competent to contract on behalf of the company or bank. Mortgages, leases, charges involving transfer of some rights in property, movable or immovable, are effected by executing deeds and depositing the title deeds to goods and such deeds are duly executed and registered as per law. The property transferred can also be actionable claims, debt or monetary claim or securities, which are governed by the same provisions under the law. Section 54 of Transfer of Property Act lays down the mode of such transfer of claims, through execution and registration. The payments or receipts of money depend on these monetary claims which determine the inflows and outflows of funds, for which the treasury manager is concerned with the knowledge of the Sale of Goods Act, Transfer of Property Act and the commercial terms used in practice are relevant to the Treasury Managers as receipts and payments due to transfer of such money claims depend on the terms of credit, grants, terms of payment allowed and also the prevailing practices in this regard. It is thus, clearly seen that the efficient operations of treasury management involve adequate knowledge of the relevant Acts and the policies of the government and the RBI. The information system which should be built for efficient treasury operations are dealt with in another chapter.

Conclusions

Treasury Manager needs to be a good Financial Analysis with knowledge of Basics of Accountancy Principles and Practices — Costing, managerial accounts, Law and practice of banking and commerce. In practice as Treasury management involves operations in various financial markets, he should have a thorough grasp of the practices, legal aspects and accounting principles involved in these operations. Some basic knowledge of secretarial practices and Chartered Accountancy will be an added advantage. This chapter prepares the ground for the material in Part II on Analysis and Planning, Forecasting and Budgeting which are all necessary part of the kit of the Treasury Manager.

❑ ❑ ❑

PART – II

ANALYSIS AND PLANNING IN TREASURY FUNCTION

5 FINANCIAL STATEMENT ANALYSIS

Analysis and Planning

In treasury function, or the management function, planning and budgeting are very essential to achieve the targets and to keep effective control on costs. Analysis of the data and information is necessary for performance budgeting or for planning and budgeting. Performance budgeting is referred to as setting physical targets for each line of activity and the basis of management objectives and delineate the basis of activity to achieve the targets. The Financial outlay or expenditure needed for each is earmarked to choose the least cost mode of activity to achieve the targets. Productivity and efficiency improves by decentralisation of responsibility and that is achieved by performance budgeting, where each department or section is made a profit centre and is accountable for its targets, financial involvement and profits in financial terms, relative to the targets in physical terms.

This type of planning involving performance budgeting is best suited for services industry say finance company or bank where each department can function in a decentralised manner and achieve the targets planned for. The cost of production concept is not suitable for the service sector, as in the financial services and banking. The treasury function is also amenable to performance budgeting, as targets can be set in the forms of services to be rendered, payments and receipts and net profits generated by each operational department or centre.

Zero Base Budgeting (ZBB)

Another tool of analysis and performance is ZBB which involves, both planning and budgeting, department wise or activity wise. The ZBB is defined as follows :

It is planning and budgeting process requiring each manager to —

(i) Establish objectives for his function and gain agreement on them with top management.

(ii) Define alternative ways of achieving these objectives.

(iii) Select the most practical way of achieving each of the objectives or the objective.

(iv) Break that alternative into incremental levels of effort, required to achieve the objective.

(v) Assess the costs and benefits of each incremental level of activity in terms of human and financial resources and their inputs and outputs.

(vi) Describe the consequences of approval of that alternative in the best and worst scenarios.

Why ZBB

It is called Zero Base, as we assume that the job on hand is scrapped and if we start afresh what are the alternatives to it. ZBB is a search for better alternatives to the existing one. The question that finance manager should ask is "Why does this section costs so much to us and what alternatives have we considered." What is the operation, that the section is doing and what are the alternatives to it.

An effective way to reduce costs and improve efficiency and productivity is the ZBB. To achieve the strategic goals and to ensure that they are achieved within the available resource constraint (amount allotted to the section), we need the ZBB method of planning, particularly in the service sectors and finance area.

Where can it be used: Although ZBB can be used in all activities of manufacture, trading etc. specific mention of the following areas may be made in particular as highly suitable :

"Finance and accounting, personnel, marketing sales, research, engineering and product development, capital budgeting etc."

Objectives of ZBB

The objectives of ZBB may be set out as :

(i) To allocate better the scarce financial resources.

(ii) To improve decision-making process.

(iii) To facilitate, planning and achievement of targets at least cost combination.

(iv) To reduce costs in general and of costs of personnel in particular.

How to use ZBB

The planner has to integrate planning with budgeting. He has to set out the alternatives in the form of decision-making tree and alternatives are the branches. The best branch is the one with least cost combination. Thus, decision-making is simplified. The budgetary process eliminates the need for juggling with numbers as in normal budgetary exercises and in physical budgets. The analysis and decision making are integrated without the need for too many calculations.

The planner has to prepare a set of decision packages and rank them in the order of priority. Those above a predetermined level of affordability will give the decision point. That one which is just above the break-even point within the resource constraint will be chosen and the alternatives deferred.

The chart for preparing the decision packages will develop the alternatives for decision-making. The components of the chart will be as shown below :

(1) Division/Decision-making unit (packaging unit)

(2) Desired result and the present expenditure (X)
Packing 1 lakh units per month — present results (y)

(3) Description of Activity.
10 clerks plus one supervisor will work for 6 to 8 hours to pack one lakh units physically in boxes purchased from outside.

(4) How and when accomplished
No. of working days.
No. of hours.
Daily turnover of packing etc.

(5) Alternative ways.
   (a) Giving contract to an outside agency.
   (b) Purchasing a machine for keeping the products in boxes.
   (c) Reduce the box size or adopt a new box which will reduce time.

(6) Benefits of each of these alternatives and costs involved in each are shown.

(7) Consequences of eliminating the activity, *viz.*, no packaging and goods are sold unpacked only.

(8) Benefits — costs are placed in order for each of the alternatives to the present set-up of activity.

(9) Alternatives are marked in the order of benefits and costs — highest benefit and lowest cost in the order — quality and quantity both being considered.

(10) Prepare the decision packages for the final selection of the top management. The finance manager can keep watch on the decisions made in each of the departments and their total effect on the company's finances.

Financial Statement Analysis

Introduction: Financial analysis of a company is necessary to help the manager to decide whether to buy or not the bonds/instruments of that Company. The soundness and intrinsic worth of a company is known only by such analysis. The market price of a share depends, among others on the sound fundamentals of the company, the financial and operational efficiency and the profitability of that company. These factors can be examined by a study of the financial management of the company. All investors need to know the performance of the company, its intrinsic worth as indicated by some parameters like book value, P/E multiple etc., and come to a conclusion whether the share is rightly priced for purchase.

This, in short is the importance of financial analysis of a company to the funds manager. In this chapter Finance Manager and Funds Manager are the terms used as synonymous with Treasury Manager, with the proviso that their specialisations are different. Treasury Manager is part of the Finance Team and has to be familiar with all these functions, and has to participate in their decision making.

What is Financial Management

The financial management of a company is concerned with management of its funds which reflects how efficiently the company is managing its funds. The overall objective of all business is to secure funds at low cost and their effective utilisation in the business for a profit. The funds so utilised must generate an income higher than the cost of procuring them. Here it is to be noted that all companies need both long-term and short-term capital. The finance manager must therefore keep in view the needs of both long-term debt and working capital and ensure that the business enjoys an optimum level of working capital and that it does not keep too many funds blocked in inventories, book-debts, cash, etc.

Financial analysis is analysis of financial statements of a company to assess its financial health and soundness of its management. "Financial Statement Analysis" involves a study of the financial statements of a company to ascertain its prevailing state of affairs and the reasons therefor. Such a study would enable the public and investors to ascertain whether one company is more profitable than the other in the same industry or business and also to state the causes and factors that are probably responsible for this.

Components of Financial Statements

The term financial statements as used in modern business refers to (i) the balance sheet, or the statement of financial position of the company at a point of time and (ii) income and expenditure statement, or the profit and loss statement over a period. To this is added, the profit allocation statement, which reconciles the balance in this account at the end of the period with that at the beginning. Thus, the financial statements provide a summary of the accounts of a company over a period of one year, and the balance sheet reflecting the assets, liabilities and capital as at a point of time say at the end of the year.

Analysis and Interpretation

With a view to interpret the financial statements, it is necessary to analyse them with the object of formation of an opinion with respect to the financial condition of that company.

This analysis involves the following steps:

(a) Comparison of the financial statements, over two or three years.

(b) Ratio analysis.

(c) Funds flow analysis.

(d) Trend analysis.

The salient features of each of the above steps are discussed briefly in this chapter.

Comparison of the Financial Statements

Comparison is the precondition for a meaningful interpretation. It may be :

(a) figures of one year with that of another year.

(b) inter-firm comparison of figures, within the same industry.

(c) comparison of one product figures with that of another product; and

(d) comparison of budgeted figures with the actual figures.

For the purpose of analysis, the figures in the balance sheet and the income statement are to be arranged properly which will facilitate the work. The statements are prepared on single (vertical) column form as shown below for this purpose.

Balance Sheet as at	
Fixed Assets	
Investments	
Working Capital:	
Current Assets	
Less:	
Current Liabilities	....
Net Current Assets	
Total Capital Employed	
Less:	
Funded Debts/Borrowed Funds.	
(Debentures and Long-term liabilities)	....
	....
Shareholder's own funds	....
Represented by:	
Preference Share Capital	
Equity Share Capital	
Reserves and Surplus	....
Less:	
Preliminary Expenses	....
	....
Profit and Loss Account for the year ended	
Sales (Net)	
Less:	
Cost of goods sold	....
Gross operating profit:	
Less operating Expenses (Office, selling and distribution expenses)	....
Net Operating Profit:	
Income credits (other income)	....
Earning Before Interest and Tax (EBIT)	
Profit After Tax (PAT)	....
	....

Meaningful analysis can be achieved by comparing the financial data and ratios of one firm with that of another. This process is called inter-firm comparison. When the performance in various departments of a single firm is compared, the term used is intra-firm comparison.

For inter-firm comparisons the financial statements must be made as far as practicable, comparable so as to derive reliable conclusions on analysing. The stated amounts of the two enterprises must be on the same price levels, and the accounting methods used by them must be similar.

Ratio Analysis

The ratio is a statistical yardstick that provides a measure of relationship between any two variables. It can be effectively used as a tool of management along with Fund Flow Statements and Trend Analysis for interpretation of the financial statements. As ratios are simple to calculate and easy to understand, there is a tendency to employ them profusely.

The ratios are conveniently classified as follows :

(i) Balance Sheet Ratios which deal with the relationships between two items or groups of items which are both in the balance sheet, e.g., the ratio of current assets to current liabilities (Current Ratio).

(ii) Revenue Statement Ratios which deal with the relationships between two items or groups of items which are both in the revenue statement, e.g., ratio of gross profit to sales, or gross profit margin.

(iii) Balance Sheet and Revenue Statement Ratios which deal with relationships between items from the revenue statement and items from the balance sheet, e.g., ratio of net profit to owned funds (Composite Ratios).

(a) Revenue Statement Ratios	**(b) Balance Sheet Ratios**
(i) Gross Profit Ratio	(i) Current Ratio or Working Capital Ratio
(ii) Operating Ratio	(ii) Liquid Ratio or Quick Asset Ratio or Acid Test Ratio.
(iii) Interest Coverage Ratio	(iii) Debt to Equity Ratio
(iv) Expense Ratio	(iv) Asset to Equity Ratio
(v) Net Profit Ratio	(v) Equity to Networth
(vi) Stock Turnover Ratio	(vi) Equity to gross block

(c) Composite Ratios

(i) Return on total Resources
(ii) Return on Own Funds
(iii) Turnover of Fixed Assets
(iv) Turnover of Debtors

Usefulness of Ratio Analysis

Ratio analysis should be based on some common standards such as comparison between two companies in the same industry and within the same assets group. Since the performance of companies varies from industry to industry and from location to location, the ratios are not comparable exactly.

What is proper for hotel industry which is seasonal in nature may not be true for cement and steel industry which belong to infrastructure sector.

The use of ratio analysis depends on the object in mind. The question to be put to oneself is what do I want to know of the company? Let us say its capital efficiency is to be examined. Then ratio such as gross block to equity or fixed assets to share capital or net profit to capital employed etc., are to be used. Thus, there are different ratios for different purposes.

Ratio analysis will be meaningful to establish relationships regarding financial performance, operational efficiency and profit margins with respect to companies within the same industry group.

In addition to the Ratio Analysis, Financial Analysis involves Fund Flow Analysis and Trend Analysis. Fund Flow Analysis involves the examination of sources and uses of funds. Thus, inflow of funds is due to sales, and other income, whereas uses are increase in investment or purchase of assets or for regular wage and other payments etc. Cash accruals and how they are utilised will be studied in this process.

Fund Flow Analysis

The balance sheet of a company reveals its financial status at a point of time. The financial executive must know the flow of funds underlying the balance sheet changes. The operation of business involves the conversion of cash into non-cash assets which are recovered back into cash form. The statement showing sources and uses of funds is properly known as "Fund Flow Statements." It shows the ebb and flow of funds into and out of the business. It covers all movements that includes an actual exchange of assets and only transactions representing book-keeping adjustments are not reported. Thus, funds flow statement is a useful tool in the kit of financial management and is a report of the financial operations of the company. The term funds should not be interpreted as literal cash, but it extends the concept to include assets or financial resources which do not effect cash or working capital. Cash flow is different from funds flow. The latter is a wider term and includes cash and non-cash items. Examples are the purchase of property in exchange for issue of shares and bonds. The broader approach provides a more complete and informative presentation.

The changes representing the "sources of funds" in the business may be due to :

(a) Sale of assets,

(b) Increase in liabilities, addition to current liabilities, increase in long-term debts and issue of debentures,

(c) Increase in net worth, addition to owned funds, reserves and surplus, retention of earnings.

changes showing the "uses of funds" include:

(a) Additions to assets — fixed and current,

(b) addition to investments,

(c) decrease in liabilities by paying off,

(d) Decrease in net worth by incurring of losses, withdrawal of funds from business and payment of dividends.

If the net profit for a particular accounting year is a source of funds, a net loss as shown by an income statement is an application of funds. This is so because where a loss has been incurred, funds have gone out of the business.

The changes in net working capital take place either by the decrease in current assets and increase in the liabilities as sources of funds and the reduction in current liabilities as uses. These changes in net working capital are available from the comparative balance sheet. An increase in net working capital in this manner presents a net application of funds. A statement of source and application of funds can be prepared from the two comparative balance sheets with an accompanying increase-decrease column. From the standpoint of the balance sheet funds may come from three sources; increase in liabilities, a decrease in assets and an increase in net worth. The increase in net worth is used to represent two sources of funds, namely, net profits and contribution of own funds. Likewise, applications represent three uses of funds; decrease in liabilities, increase in assets and decrease in net worth. Here again, the decrease in net worth represents the uses, namely, net losses and decrease in capital funds.

The fund flow statement helps in guiding the destiny of a business by enabling the executive to visualise the movement of funds that constantly take place. A failure to detect pattern of change can perpetuate undesirable trends and lead to financial difficulties. An extended reliance on external sources can create a top heavy capital structure. This statement helps in detecting the sources for financing the heavy accumulation of inventory and book-debts. It is also helpful in forecasting the flow of funds. It is used for projecting working capital requirements. It also highlights future need for funds and plays an important role in the evaluation of trade credit.

Trend Analysis

Trend analysis refers to comparison of some important ratios and rates of growth over a time period of a few years. These trends in the case of GPM or sales turnover are useful to indicate the extent of improvement or deterioration over a period of time, in the aspects considered. The trends in dividends, E.P.S., assets growth or sales growth are some examples of the trends used to study the operational performance of the companies. Any temporary deviations due to insolvency of the company can be known from the trends in current ratio or quick ratio. So also a temporary rise in inventories to sales would indicate sluggish demand for the products of the company, leading to liquidity problems.

Thus, the trends of the results, rather than the actual ratios and percentages, are important. Structural relationship taken from the financial statement of one year only are of limited value and the trends of these structural relationships established from statements over a number of years may be more significant than absolute ratios. Financial analysis helps to know-how well the business is operating in comparison with planned performance and if actual results are not good enough, what should the future indicate for the company. The financial results of all business are affected by general economic conditions by competition, and local factors relating to company.

It should be particularly emphasised that one particular ratio used without reference to other ratios may be very misleading. In other words, the combined effect of the various ratios must be considered in arriving at a correct diagnosis which will be of assistance in interpreting the financial condition and earning performance of the business. Each ratio plays its part in this interpretation.

Finally, it should be realised that ratios are only a preliminary step in interpretation and must be supplemented by rigorous investigation into all aspects of operations of company before safe conclusions can be drawn from them. Trend analysis should supplement the ratio analysis to assess the good and bad aspects of working of a company.

More importantly not only the objective factual data should be analysed from balance sheet and income-expenditure statements of the company, but a scrutiny of subjective factors indicated in the directors and auditors reports should also be made, with particular reference to any mention in footnotes to contingent liabilities, unpaid taxes, doubtful debts etc. Besides research into practical day-to-day operations of the company can be done only by a plant visit and study on the spot the prospects of the company in the coming year or two.

Industry Study – Example

Given below is an exercise in actual company anlysis within the pharmaceutical industry. The two companies chosen are the best in the industry with different profiles. Their Annual Reports present the trend data for about five to ten years. To be brief, some selected variables on the financial performance of each of these companies are given below. The Treasury function involves the financing and investment decisions together and hence on exercise on the choice of the company within an industry is attempted here. After the choice of the company the intrinsic worth, past performance and present trends and forecasting of the future price have to be done, before a final investment decision is taken. For this purpose, the trend analysis and ratio analysis etc. may have to be undertaken, with the help of Balance sheet data, Financial funds flow data, etc.

In the Table below, the data on Ranbaxy and Dr. Reddys are juxta posed, for the year ended Dec. 2004 and March 2005 respectively, which are proximate enough for comparability. The market price of Dr. Reddys is almost double that of Ranbaxy. The equity base of Dr. Reddys is one fifth but the Reserves is almost near to that of Ranbaxy. The book value of Dr. Reddys share is four times that of Ranbaxy. This explains why its market price in double that of Ranbaxy. Its P/E ratio is also twice that of Ranbaxy. But Ranbaxy has a law Debt-equity ratio, better profitability, higher EPs and a stronger equity base. Dividend distribution is only 60% for Ranabaxy, as against 100% for Dr. Reddys. Both are having strong fundamentals and good prospects for the future earnings flow. The decision of the choice is left to the reader. *Prima facie,* the choice may fall on Ranbaxy due to its lower M.P., better equity base, lower P/E multiple, but more in depth analysis of the product range, their demand etc. have to be looked into and such research is left to the reader.

Pharma Industry
Financial Ratio Analysis (in Rs. Crores)

Variables	Ranbaxy (at and Dec. 2004)	Dr. Reddys (at end March 2005)
Equity	185	38
Reserves	2322	2036
Networth	2507	2069
Debt Capital	926	273
Current Assets	3546	1828
Current Liabilities	1917	441
Debt Equity Ratio	5.1	7.2
Current Ratio	1:1.8	1:4.1
Book value per share	64	272
Gross Block	2313	1004
Inventories	1435	418
Sales	5532	1694
Ratio of Sales to Inventories	3.8	3.9
Ratio of Sales to Gross Block	2.3	1.7
Ratio of Gross block to Equity	12.5	26.4
EBDIT/Gross Profits	1081	166

Net Profits	699	65
EPS Earnings pershare	Rs. 29	Rs. 22
Face value of share	Rs. 5	Rs. 5
Average market price	Rs. 450	Rs. 827
P/E multiple	Rs. 15.5	Rs. 37.6
Dividend %	60%	100%

Source: Annual Reports of the Companies.

CASE STUDY ON MANAGEMENT OF BANK FUNDS
The Karnataka Bank, Mangalore

The Karnataka Bank is a private sector Bank listed on the BSE and NSE. Its market price is now ruling around Rs. 90 and its EPS was Rs. 14.5 at end March 2006. Its P/E ratio is 6.2

It has an equity base of Rs. 121 crores and Reserves of Rs. 989 crores, resulting a net worth of Rs. 1110 crores and the book value of share of Rs. 10 at Rs. 92.0. It has deposits of Rs. 13,243 crores and borrowing of Rs. 182 crores a total of debt of Rs. 13,425 crores, enjoying a leverage of 110 times (which is normal for banking operations).

As on 31-3-2006

Its current assets are as follows :

	Rs. Crores
Cash and Balances with RBI	535
Balances with Banks and Money at cell	679
Current Assets total –	1214

Current Liabilities are as follows :

Contingent liabilities	Rs. 2,412
Bills for collection	463
Other liabilities and provisions	416
Total Current Liabilities	3271

For banks, current ratio and debit equity ratio are not relevant. Their liquidity and solvency are taken care by the RBI through risk weighted capital adequacy norms, credit and investment ratios, (CRR and SLR etc.). From the above data, it is apparent that its current liabilities are not only covered by current assets, but are 2½ times more than current assets.

As per bank norms, the cash reserve ratio (CRR) at 9.2% of deposit liabilities (NDTL) is much higher than the stipulated ratio (5%) the SLR was also higher at 30%, as against the stipulated 25%, taking only the government and approved securities.

Balance Sheet of Karnataka Bank
As on March 31, 2006

(in Rs. Crores)

Capital and Liabilities	Rs. (in crores)	Assets	Rs. (in crores)
Capital :	121	Cash and Balances with RBI	535
Reserves and Surplus	990	Balances with banks & Money at call, etc.	679
Net worth	1,111	Investments	5,548
Deposits total	13,243	Advances	7,791
Borrowings	183	Fixed Assets	104
Other liabilities & Provisions	416	Other Assets	294
	14,953		14,953
		Contingent Liabilities	2,412
		Bills for collection	463

Profit and Loss Account

Income:	
Interest income	1,018
Other income	167
	1,185
Expenditure:	
Interest expended	652
Operating expenses	204
Provisions and contingencies	152
	1,008
Profit:	
Net profit for the year	176
Proposed dividend	5

No. of Shares outstanding	Rs. 1,212 (Nos)
Face value of shares	Rs. 10
Market Price	Rs. 86
Earning per share	Rs. 14.5
Capital adequacy ratio	14.16

The above CRAR is as at end March, 2005 (RBI data)

Karnataka Bank has good profitability as return of 1.17% of total assets is good and it has been consistently rising from 0.7 1% in 1999-2000. (net profits as age of total assets). Operating profit as percentage of working funds was also high at 3.16%. Non-interest income which represents the Treasury income, among others, is also good at 2.05% as against interest income of 7.79%. (RBI data).

The segmental results as published by the Karnataka Bank itself, are as follows : These show the Treasury operations, as compared to the Banking operations proper of the Bank.

Table – Segmental Results of Karnataka Bank for the year ended March (Rs. in crores)

Particulars	Treasury		Other Banking Operations		Total	
	2006	2005	2006	2005	2006	2005
Revenue	220	295	965	766	1185	1061
Results	12	82	284	183	295	265
Assets	2616	2215	12194	10196	14810	12412
Liabilities	2546	2117	12102	10135	14648	12252

The rest of the particulars come under the category of unallocated items, under either segment. A look at the above table shows that the Treasury operations were at a low ebb in 2006 as compared to 2005. Besides the Treasury operations account for only one fifth of the total operations of the Bank, which shows the smaller importance of the Treasury to the Bank operations. The result as a percentage of Revenue was 28% in 2005 but fell to 5% in 2006. As a general trend, the Treasury operations in 2005-06 were at a lower level than in 2004-05. The bank has excess investments over the level required under SLR, on which it can do trading but the level of Treasury operations are not significant, reflecting the lack of expertise and opportunities.

❑ ❑ ❑

6 CORPORATE BALANCE SHEET ANALYSIS

Financial Analysis and Investment decision making depends on the Balance Sheet Analysis, which is necessary for Treasury Management also. Balance Sheet Analysis in financial studies involves the use of the Financial data available in balance sheet and income and expenditure statements of a company. The objective of this analysis is to know the overvaluation or undervaluation of a share as judged by its intrinsic worth and compare it with its market price and that of the similar companies within the same industry. The company's performance in terms of its physical operations is reflected in its balance sheet and income and expenditure statements. The financial worth of a company can be assessed from such studies.

Annual Reports

The main components of the Annual Reports of Companies containing Balance Sheet and Income and Expenditure data are as follows :

1. Chairman's Speech to its Investors: This would bring out the management's views of the company's performance in the backdrop of the economy and industry, its plans for expansion or diversification if any, difficulties or problems faced by the company, and their plan of action to meet these challenges and the immediate future prospects of the company etc.

2. Director's Report: This is a factual account of the operations of the Company during the past year and the financial results of these operations, profits or losses, the allocation of profits for depreciation, interest, taxes, dividends etc. After allocating these sums, the residual profits are ploughed back to the reserves or losses are written off. The input availability, market for the outputs, labour problems, Government policy changes with regard to them, if any, exports or imports made by the company etc., are all presented in this report for the benefit of its shareholders.

3. Balance Sheet and Income and Expenditure Accounts: These accounts are accompanied by the profit allocation statements and the detailed schedules for each of the items in the accounts. The method of presenting these data varies from company to company although the contents are almost the same. These data would reflect the *prima facie* position of the company's operations and the financial results of these operations.

4. Auditors' Report: This is a statutory report testifying the correctness of the accounts and giving their own comments on the practices and procedures of the company. The real position of the company's operations is known from the footnotes to the accounts and the comments of the auditors. They indicate the contingent liabilities, bad debts, changes in accounting practices adopted to camaflouge the poor financial performance, method of providing for depreciation, provisions for D R R fund and other statutory obligations, revaluation of assets if any, dividends not paid, advance calls etc. In fact, the most vital information to be provided to investors as per the Companies Act is contained in the footnotes. As such the financial analysts should examine carefully these notes and auditors' report to make any correct assessment of the valuation of company's intrinsic worth.

Market Price and Corporate Performance

The market price is a function of demand and supply for its share which in turn depends on the corporate performance.

The market price of a share thus depends on the company's performance, reflected in the earnings per share or cash earnings, dividend record or bonus payments by the company. Besides, the share price also depends on the goodwill factors which are subjective in nature such as management reputation, expansion plans, tax planning, technological set-up, reputation of collaborators and locational advantages. The management rating is subjective and is a factor contributing to the goodwill of the company. This goodwill also depends on the Government attitude to the management, Government policy with regards to the imports etc.

Honesty, integrity and consistency of management gives good rating for the company. The price of a share also depends on subjective factors like sentiment of the market, phase of the market such as gloom, fear, indecision, optimism and euphoria etc.

Briefly the market price of a share depends on some fundamental factors like intrinsic value of the share, subjective and goodwill factors and sentimental factors depending on the phase of the market. The intrinsic worth of the company is judged by the net present value derived by discounting future returns on share, book value of the share, earnings per share etc.

Types of Companies

At any stage in the economy, there are different types of industries, some start up companies, some mature and grown, some expanding into growth industries and some showing decline in their prosperity and popularity.

Similarly, in each industry there are different types of companies, some growing, some stagnant and some declining. There are thus, different types of industries within the economy. An astute analyst should try to identify the potentialities of each of these groups and concentrate on the growth oriented industries and emerging blue chips and established blue chips. Within each industry, there are some companies which are turn–around companies showing signs of emerging into blue chip companies.

Blue chip companies are in simple language, growth oriented companies showing signs of expansion, diversification, modernisation of technology and reputation for consistent profitability and profit margins to sustain the consistent dividend distribution, growing profits and expanding net worth.

The managements of these companies have got a dynamic and growth oriented policy and have a reputation for a vision for future growth and expansion and maintain a sustained growth in assets, sales turn-over and profits. Emerging blue chip companies are those which are turn-around companies and exhibited potentiality to growth and expand in gross block, sales and net profit. The actual Blue Chip Companies like Colgate, TELCO, Hindustan Lever, SPIC, L&T etc., have a consistent record of dividend pay outs, growth in dividends, expansion and bonus from time to time. The main characteristics of the blue chip companies may be set out as follows:

1. These companies belong to the industry groups which are in general expanding and growing.
2. They are market leaders as in the case of Indian hotels in the hotel industry, ACC in cement industry, Bajaj Auto in scooter industry and Colgate in toothpaste industry.
3. These companies show capacity to diversify and grow and generate larger gross block, higher sales turnover and growing profit margins. They continuously expand the capital base in terms of debt or equity or rights etc.
4. They have purposeful tax planning and consistent modernisation and expansion plans. They have the capacity to meet the emerging challenges like input or labour problems.
5. The management out-look is dynamic and their vision is ambitious expansionism. They are highly aggressive leaders in the industry.
6. They have also commitments to research and development and are quick to adopt new technologies and lower costs and increase profits.

Growth Companies

These companies are very attractive to the long-term investors as the return to the equity shareholders in such companies is continuously expanding due to dividends, growth in dividends, networth, bonus and rights etc. Besides in view of the consistent good performance, detailed monitoring by investors of such companies may not be necessary. They are a good hedge against inflation and rising costs. The investor is also benefitted by capital appreciation or capital gains and through multiplying their original investment in a short period of time. The investor has only to identify such scrips and make long-term investments in them which will ensure steady return on their investments, safety, marketability and continued capital appreciation, regular dividends, rights, bonus shares etc.

The examples of such growth shares which should be included in the portfolio of every investor are Bajaj Auto and Telco in the automobiles, Tisco in steel industry, East India Hotels in hotel industry, CEAT Tyres and Apollo Tyres in tyre industry, Brooke Bond and Tata in tea industry, Britannia in food industry etc.

Cyclical Companies

Some categories of industries are cyclical in nature whose fortunes may depend upon the business cycle and trading like shipping, tea, fertilizers and coffee etc. They make sometimes huge profits and sometimes poor profits depending on the cycles. ACC, Nagarjuna, Tata Tea etc. are examples in this category.

Defensive Shares (Stable Companies)

Another category of companies has defensive shares whose prices are stable and do not fluctuate widely. Normally, they pay regular dividends within a narrow range and have standard practices of ploughing back profits and declaration of modest dividends. These are defensive shares whose dividends are stable and profits and profitability are expanding but at a consistent and slow rate. Asian Hotels and Videocon etc. are examples.

Discount Shares

Besides, there is a category of discount shares whose prices are depressed due to low profits but with a hope of higher profitability in the immediate future due to the change in the management or in Government policies or due to new technological changes. Among the companies in this group, there may be many undervalued shares whose potentialities for growth are high and therefore they are called turn-around companies or emerging blue chips. The category of blue chips emerges out of corporate performance and can be attributed to rich parentage arising from the foreign collaborators or foreign technicians ambitious and driving promoters, unique products, special technologies, marketing strategies, management reputation, etc.

How to Locate Emerging Blue Chips

Research on the companies' operations and their financial results is necessary for locating emerging blue chips. This can be done through fundamental analysis which helps us to decide on what to buy and what to sell. This research has to be both on the desk and on the field. On the desk, the financial results and balance sheets have to be examined to locate the potentiality of companies to emerge as turn-around companies. *Prima facie,* such companies have been in losses for a year or two but due to some expected management changes or policy changes of Government or demand changes leading to higher capacity utilisation or due to new projects in the last phase of completion, these companies show the potentiality for turning into profitable projects in the coming year or two. Research on the field and to interview the officers of the companies, visit to the plant and secure the opinions of the experts, suppliers, stockists is necessary. This fundamental analysis is to be supplemented by technical analysis to decide on when to buy and when to sell.

Some companies may be building up gross block due to expansion and diversification but sales are not rising fast enough due to low capacity utilisation. Then the company may not be making adequate profits to service investors temporarily. Some companies may have both gross block and sales rising but gross profit margin is low due to high costs of manufacture and poor sales due to inefficiency, but improvements in technology may be expected to increase the profits and the company may be in the process of growth as a blue chip company. One can easily locate an example of turn-around company or an emerging blue chip company. Amar Raja Batteries, Western India Industries etc., are some examples of turn-around companies which have come out of the red.

The expertise of the analyst lies in locating the emerging blue chips. The blue chips of yesteryears are no longer the blue chips of today. Similarly, there is no guarantee that the blue chips of today will be the blue chips of tomorrow. Thus, for long in the eighties, scrips like Reliance, Orkay, Century etc., were the blue chips. In the nineties, the Essar Gujarat, Videocon, or Reddys etc., took over the lead. Many service industries like ICICI, SBI, and HDFC have also emerged as blue chips.

Established Blue Chips

For a conservative investor established growth stock with assured return are attractive. These companies are leaders in the industry like Reliance and Raymonds in the textiles and Tisco in steel etc. They have a strong capital base and networth, well established financial position, organised and professionalised management. They reward the investor with uninterrupted dividends, steady rise in capital values and bonus from time to time or rights or other privileges. Such companies are worth holding for long and are recommended in all the portfolios of investors. The risk of holding such scrips is low and their Betas[@] are generally around the market Betas and their rewards are also around average performance of the market. Investors in such blue chips as ACC, Colgate, Hindustan Lever etc., have benefitted by regular dividends and bonus shares.

The characteristics of the established Blue Chips are as follows :

1. Management rating: Highly professionalised and efficient management, reputed for honesty and integrity. Financial practices and accounting are consistent and dependable.

2. Gross profit margin and sales turnover are high and the company captured a substantial chunk of market demand. The quality and after sales service are the strong points of the company and they are one of the leaders in the industry.

3. Dividend record: The company has been making continuous profits of which a reasonable dividend is declared. A prudent policy of ploughing back profits for expansion and diversification is also pursued.

4. The company's net worth is high relative to equity and is expanding year after year. The leverage enjoyed by equity through long-term borrowings (debt) is also high. Their long-term solvency is rated high.

5. The current liquidity position is also strong. Their current assets cover their current liabilities including contingent liabilities by more than twice and their sales management is such that inventory holding is always optimal. Their sales and distribution strategies are sound and cash efficient.

6. The company has expansion and diversification plans for future growth as reflected in the rise in net worth and gross block. Such expansion plans are ac-

---

@ Beta is a mesaure of the risk of retun of an individual scrip relative to total market risk of return. It is in practice calculated by the average percentage change in the price of a scrip to the average percentage change of the market prices represented by the Index.

companied by tax planning so as to conserve resources for growth. Alternatively, the company is already diversified and has still expansion plans.

7. The management has a vision for the future of the company and their policy is ambitious expansion and growth. The policies adopted are result oriented and efficiently executed.

8. The company's networth is growing due to ploughed back profits and funds are available for bonus payments to satisfy the investors from time to time.

9. The market price of such shares is rising consistently and steadily and any possible fall in price in bear phase is small and temporary. The price fluctuations are narrow and the long-term trend of its price is upwards.

10. The company has earned a reputation for fair practices and their servicing of investors through dividends, bonus allotments, share transfers etc., is generally rated good.

Having discussed above the major characteristics of a blue chip company and an emerging blue chip company, it will be appropriate to set out here an example in the form of a case study of what is not either of them.

CASE STUDY OF A COMPANY* (MONOZYME INDIA LTD.)

History

"Monozyme" was set up and registered in 1989, with an authorised capital of Rs. 40 lakhs and paid up capital of Rs. 3 lakhs. Its objectives include production of diagnostic enzymatic kits and of bulk drugs.

From the beginning, it had collaboration with the Technology Development and Information Company of India Ltd., (TDIC). The original project was for manufacture of enzymatic kits with a capital investment of Rs. 69 lakhs, of which the TDIC had financed Rs. 56 lakhs. The products being import substitutes, TDIC took the interest in the company. It had initial problem of lack of working capital, which it had secured only in 1992 from Allahabad Bank. It had started manufacturing protein, Calcium, Phosphorus, HDL Cholesterol, Glucose etc., in 1991-92. Since May 1991, commercial production of a few items of clinical chemistry kits was started.

In 1993 it had entered into a tie up with Euro Genetics, N.V. Belgium for the manufacture and marketing of ELISA range of kits. The new project, which was undertaken in 1993, was expected to be financed by a public issue of Rs. 2.5 crores. In Nov. 1993, the company made a public issue for a total capital of Rs. 2.40 crores.

During the initial years it had continued to import bulk drugs and sell them in India after repacking, which involved trading activity even after five years, trading activity surpassed the production and manufacturing of the kits and drugs.

To Examine : Objectives of the Case Study

1. The management of solvency;
2. The management of liquidity;

---

* As the discussion is only for academic purposes, the year to which the data relates does not make much difference.

3. Accounting methods; and
4. Sales and profitability.

Brief Description: 1994-95 is its 6th Annual year, their accounts are closed for June 1995 and June 1994. The accounts presented for 1994 are for 15 months and for 1995 for 12 months.

It is registered at Hyderabad for the preparation and manufacture industrial enzymes and diagnostics kits, such as for thyroid and fertility panels. Although bulk drugs project was planned, it is kept in abeyance, as according to the company, the demand for the latter is less in the coming years.

(1) Management of Solvency

	Rs. crores		Rs. crores
Funds (Equity)	3.10	Total Borrowed funds	0.93
Reserves	.45	of which from banks for working capital	0.32
Net worth	3.55	long-term funds	0.61

The company has mixed up the long-term and short-term funds, which is irregular. Taking only long-term funds, the solvency is excellent with equity debt ratio at 1:0.17, with high potential borrowing capacity and future for leverage. But why is it not using the leverage now? Inefficiency and wrong planning are the reasons, as the project planned is postponed, and sales and trading are mixed.

Interest burden accounts for 18% of sales income and 1/3rd of gross profit (EBIDT)

(2) Management of Liquidity

	Rs. crores		Rs. crores
Current Assets including Inventory	2.85	Current Liabilities	0.90
		Bank Borrowing	1.95
Current Assets excluding Inventory	2.24		
Current Ratio : 1:2.32	2.85	Quick Ratio : 1 : 1.83	2.85

Note: Bank borrowings is for net working capital needs.

Under both the ratios, the liquidity position of the company is good. But how did it bring about? It is holding Rs. 3.8 lakhs in cash and in bank current account Rs. 1.98 lakhs – a total of Rs. 5.8 lakhs is wasted without any return and a loss of potential return in intercorporate funds of 16% to 18% in those years. Besides current assets include bad debts of Rs. 50,000 and accrued interest of Rs. 9.28 lakhs. If one is asked whether their management of liquidity is apparently good, it is definitely not good despite a high current ratio, due to the fact that they are keeping idle balances of Rs. 5.8 lakhs and their trading income is more than their sale income. If only the sale income proper of its own products is taken, their inventories are 48% which is definitely a symptom of inefficiency.

There are many miscellaneous items of expenditure equal to Rs. 1.31 crore, which is not written off by revenue-income, but shown in the capital side, as an asset. Nearly rupees one crore is deferred revenue expenditure.

(3) Accounting Practices : From the data in the Balance sheet, the true picture does not evolve. In the Auditor's Report, Liabilities due are stated as follows :

For P.F. Insurance etc. :	Rs. 1.68 lakhs
For sales tax dues etc. :	Rs. 3.24 lakhs
Total outstanding for more than six months due but not paid.	Rs. 4.92 lakhs

It closed its accounts in June and for the year 1994, it was accounted for 15 months. In the accounting policies of the company there are other points to be noted also. All accounts are kept on historical cost basis and not cash basis (as is required under the Budget 1995-96). Depreciation is on a straight line method. Sales are inclusive of excise duty and net of discounts. Its sales include sale from diagnostic goods and sale from trading goods. As the company is trading sales tax is due. The value of traded goods purchased is Rs. 2.42 crores while the sale price is Rs. 2.55 crores. Why is the company doing these accounting practices? It is to camouflage the real position of the company by an accounting jugglery to show a very good picture of the company with good liquidity and profitability. The fact that it has accrued interest income of Rs. 9.3 lakhs while it pays interest charges of Rs. 2.2 lakhs shows that it is revealing a cash rich position at the expense of dues to be paid, postponed to the extent of Rs. 4.9 lakhs as shown earlier.

(4) Sales and Profitability: Its total sales income is Rs. 3.82 crores of which Rs. 2.55 crores (nearly 66%) is due to trading activities; although the objectives of the company permit trading, the prospects of company for growth are stunted because of trading activity. Its losses are covered up by accounting malpractices. Its losses in 1994 were Rs. 14.66 lakhs and profits for 1995 were Rs. 31.23 lakhs. This amount as a proportion of sales is only 8%, while, as percentage of equity, it is 10%. The R.O.I. is therefore 8 to 10% and that is grossly inefficient way of using the capital (equity or networth, as the case may be).

The irregularities in accounting are many in this case, which any expert financial controller should be able to decipher. Some examples are given below :

1. Working capital borrowing from banks is shown under long-term funds, along with other term loans.
2. Current inventories are taken as given by the management and are high, relative to its own products.
3. Deferred revenue expenditure is shown as an asset (of Rs. 1 crores) and share issue expenses of Rs. 34 lakhs.
4. Pre-operative expenditure of Rs. 35 lakhs are not written off. (All the above details and the discussion is based on their Annual Report, 1994-95).

If we take the Director's Report alone, it has a gross operating profit of Rs. 36 lakhs and cash profits of Rs. 41 lakhs. But if we analyse the data after adjusting all the irregularities and the notes in the Auditor's Report, (dues of Rs. 5 lakhs), there will be a loss of about Rs. 1 crore, wiping out the net worth to Rs. 2.56 crores from Rs. 3.56 crores. At this level of net worth, the share price can rule only at less than face value. But due to camouflage of figures, it was sometimes quoted very high at Rs. 45. It had a 52 week low of Rs. 7 also as the investors analyse the company, as shown above deleting all the window dressing and malpractices in accounting, through equity research.

Profitability: To enable the reader to assess himself, the summary of Balance Sheet and Profit & Loss Account is given in the next two pages.

Monozyme India Ltd.
Balance Sheet
(As on June 30, 1995)

	Source of funds		Rs. crores
1.	Shareholders capital		3.10
	Reserves		0.45
	Owned Funds		3.55
2.	Loan Funds :		
	Secured loans		0.55
	Unsecured loans		0.38
			0.93
	Total Funds or sources	Rs.	4.48
	Application of funds :		
I.	Long-term (Fixed Assets)		
	1. Net Block		0.87
	2. Pre-operations expenses		0.35
			1.22
II.	Current Assets :		
	1. Inventories		0.61
	2. Accrued Interest		0.09
	3. Sundry Debtors		1.36
	4. Cash and Bank balance		0.06
	5. Loans and Advances		0.73
			2.85
	Less :		
III.	Current Liabilities (Sundry Creditors)		0.90
IV.	Net Current Assets (II – III)		1.95
V.	Miscellaneous expenditure not written off		
	Preliminary and share issue expenses		0.34
	Deferred revenue expenses		0.97
			1.31
	Total uses (I + IV + V)	Rs.	4.48

Profit & Loss Account for the year ended 30th June 1995

			Rs. crores
I.	**Income**		
	(a)	Sales of Diagnostic Products	1.26
		of Traded goods	2.55
			3.81
	(b)	Other income	0.17
	I.	(a+b) total Income (adjusted for Stocks)	3.98
II.	**Expenditure**		
	(a)	Stock and materials	2.79

	(b) Wages and salaries	0.15
	(c) Other general expenses (Administration and Selling)	0.51
		3.45
	Interest 0.17	
	Depreciation 0.05	
	Taxes Nil	
	(d) Total of I, D, T.	0.22
		3.67
	Net Profit	0.31

Notes : 1. Its gross block (or net block) is low relative to its equity. It is using the extra funds for trading.

2. It has carried Rs. 31 lakhs to the balance sheet as profits and has not declared any dividend. It has been in existence for the last six years.

3. As it is for illustration, the date of the data and the company are not relevant.

Remarks

Funds manager may get familiarised with accounting jugglery, malpractices and inefficient management in production, marketing and finance costs. In 1993-94 it had sales of Rs. 218 lakhs and gross profits of Rs. 40 lakhs. After payments of interest (no taxes) and providing for depreciation, it had net profits of Rs. 29 lakhs. Of the total sales an amount of Rs. 75 lakhs were from diagnostic kits (1/3rd of the total) and Rs. 143 lakhs from sale of trading goods (of bulk drugs imported). During 1993-94 the previous year's losses of Rs. 15 lakhs were wiped off and balance of profit of Rs. 14 lakhs was carried to reserves.

During 1994-95 it had a net profit (after depreciation and interest) of Rs. 31 lakhs which together with the previous year's reserves totalled up to Rs. 45 lakhs and carried to the balance sheet.

Equity shares issued to public during 1993-94 were for Rs. 2.40 crores of which Rs. 52 lakhs were allotment money not received. The paid up equity stood as at end June 1994 at Rs. 2.67 crores. As at end June 1995, paid up equity capital rose to Rs. 3.10 crores and reserves stood at Rs. 45 crore.

Inefficient Capital Use: Sales increased from Rs. 2.18 crores in 1993-94 to Rs. 3.81 crores in 1994-95. As the previous year was for 15 months, comparison is not possible. But net profits as percentage of sales was 13% in 1993-94 and 8% in 1994-95 which is poor reflection of efficiency in the use of capital. Another measure is sales to net worth, which showed a ratio of 0.77 in 1993-94 and a ratio of 1.07 in 1994-95. Profits as a percentage of networth was 11% in 1993-94 and 10% in 1994-95 which did not show any improvement. Poor utilisation of owned funds and borrowed funds is seen in the rates of gross block to owned funds and to total funds which stood at 28% and 22% respectively.

It is a lesson on window dressing of accounts. This is an ideal case study of what financial mismanagement is. It has raised an amount of about Rs. 2.4 crores of rupees from the public for the project of bulk drugs for which this money was meant but was used for trading and working capital purposes. The gross block built up was only for Rs. 1.0 crore. The project could not be completed due to delays, rise in costs and change in market conditions and most important due to managerial inefficiency. This is also an example of diversion of funds.

Secondly, it has insufficient net inflows to build up reserves but the reserves shown in the balance sheet of Rs. 45 lakhs is a make believe show. It has continuously shown a large gap between the expenditure and receipts and cash earnings or the difference between inflows and outflows is poor. So this will not help the build up of reserves, complete the projects on hand and to have the plant and machinery installation for bulk drugs as originally planned. In the management of working capital, its inventories are high relative to sales of its own products and trading margins are low on traded goods. Low bank borrowings and high level cash and balances reflect poor funds management. All these factors reflect poor funds management accompanied by inefficient management policies.

At the other end, we should present a case study of a company, whose financial management is excellent and which is an established blue Chip Company. This is the case of Reliance Industries Limited, which is briefly set out below:

CASE STUDY – EXAMPLES OF RIL

The best example of an established Bluechip Company is Reliance Industries Ltd., which has a good Corporate Ranking in the fortune global 500 list of world's largest corporations and found a place in the elite world's top 25 climbers.

The company's financial highlights are as shown below for the latest year 2005-2006

Indicators	2004-05	2005-06
Debt to equity ratio	0.46:1	0.44:1
Current ratio	1:1.7	1:1.5
Book value (Rs.)	289	357
EPS (Rs.)	54.2	65.1
EBDIT (Rs.)	14,261	14,982
EBDIT as % of Gross Turnover	19.5%	16.8%
RONW	21.9%	22.7%
Market Price (March Average data) (Rs.)	544	755
Book value to M.P.	1.9	2.1
P/E ratio	10.1	11.6

Source: Balance Sheet of Reliance, 2005-06.

It will be soon from the table that liquidity and long term solvency are good. Profitability as judged by EPS, RONW, profit to sales ratio is also good. What is more important is that these ratios are consistently rising. Dividend pay out is 100% which rose consistently from 35% in 1997-98. EPs also rose from 14.4 in 1996-97 to 65.1 in 2005-06.

❑ ❑ ❑

7 FINANCE AND INVESTMENT DECISIONS

Finance Function and Accounting Function

The finance function is different from Accounting function. The latter involves only recording of transactions, verification of the authorisation for expenditure, keeping evidence in the form of vouchers, custodial services for cash credit instruments and securities and record all inflows and outflows in cash and credit vouchers, bills etc. One keeps accounts as per the nature of the benefits and trading and commercial transactions, taking place. The finance function on the other hand is different in that it goes beyond the mechanistic accounting of income, expenditures, assets, liabilities etc. It is concerned with how to plan for raising of resources for the capital expenditure and current expenditure, inflows and outflows of cash and credit and in brief to attend to all activities in relation to quality and quantity of funds required and sub-serve the goal of management, namely, minimise the costs and maximise the profits. The objective of all economic activity is to maximise the returns with the constraint of given costs or minimise the costs with the constraint of given return.

Responsibility for Sound Financial Position

Finance function, as elaborated above is a vital element in the corporate activity and is the life blood of all economic activity. Its main aim is to keep the company in sound financial health. The health of any economic unit depends on its financial position. The finance function is entrusted with this crucial job of keeping the unit sound and healthy and secure strong financial state of the unit.

To secure the sound financial health, the Treasury manager or finance manager has to perform the following functions:

1. Investment function and decisions.
2. Financing function and decisions.

1. Investment Function: This relates to the efficient use of funds in alternative activities open to the economic unit. This takes care of the utilisation of finances as per the capital budgetting decisions and current operating budget. The aim is to secure optimum return from each line of activity and thereby maximise the share price of the company. It has to plan for proper investment strategy both in the short-run and long-run with the above objectives. The utilisation of funds, as and when they accrue should take care of the two conflicting trends in corporate finance — one there should not be any idle funds, as that will reduce the total returns for the firm and will lead to uneconomic use of funds and second, there should not be risk of loss of liquidity for the firm from the anticipated and unanticipated expenditures cropping up from day-to-day. Liquidity and returns are the conflicting objectives to be pursued by the Treasury manager in a judicious manner. Illiquidity leads to risk but the larger the illiquidity the larger is the return. So a delicate balance between these two conflicting goals of high returns and high liquidity has to be aimed at in the finance function which is comparable to walking on a razor's edge. It is in this context that the finance function becomes crucial to the company's survival and growth. So far as the investment decision making is concerned, it is referred to in the subsequent pages in this chapter. Investment decision process helps the finance function to make right decision with the above objectives in mind, to make proper use of funds through various investments, advances, etc.

2. Finance Decision: This refers to the securing of the right sources of finance which are cheap or economical and which provide sufficient quantum at the right time as and when needed. The finance function involves decisions on the least cost combination of funds for long-term capital use and short-term working capital purposes. The analysis of sources and uses of funds is relevant in this context. The uses are the investment decisions while the sources are the financing decisions.

What should be the leverage for the company? How much debt and in what forms is it to be raised and when? What is the least cost combination for capital structure — methods of financing fixed assets of the company, which is a major study in corporate finance? How to ensure that the company has sufficient working capital and as and when needed, the funds are available to the company. He has to ensure the proper quality and quantity of finance for the firm in its activities throughout the year. For this purpose he has to plan and budget for the financial inflows and outflows. This requires also coordination with other managerial functions, namely, production, sales and human resources, (production, marketing and HRD functions). It is in this sense that finance function is the most critical function for any firm whether it is manufacturing or trading company or whether it is finance or investment function. The relative importance of the finance decision and investment decision will vary depending on the nature of the firm's activities.

3. Mergers and Acquisitions: Both as a finance decision and investment decision, an example is to acquire an existing non-profit making company, as a source of funds as also an investment decision which with proper tax advantages, taken into account, will make the merged unit more healthy, both operationally and financially. Mergers and acquisitions are governed by SEBI guidelines, but, if they are voluntary and friendly mergers or acquisitions, the guidelines are less rigorous and sometimes bail out takeovers are encouraged by the government.

Mergers are combining the two companies by takeover of assets and liabilities at the rates at the current juncture of merger, as per the market prices. Takeover or acquisitions are purchase of the shares of the company at the market prices or at the negotiated prices. As per the SEBI guidelines these negotiated prices, should be related to the historical market prices and they should keep the interests of minority shareholders and the public in mind.

Treasury manager should be in a position to judge and assess how the financial inflows and outflows will be affected by the mergers and plan a revised budget in the event of the merger or takeover is effected. He should be competent to assess the fairness of share prices for acquisition or the asset revaluation for mergers. Either a source of finance or as an investment decision, the merger or takeover has to be justified as in the best interests of financial health of the company and for the maximisation of share price of the company.

Stock splits, Bonus issues etc. are also examples of both finance and investment decisions in a sense with which Treasury Manager has to be thoroughly conversant.

Responsibility of Finance Manager

Finance Manager is a wider term which includes also the functions of Treasury Manager. The finance manager has two duties of taking decisions both in the areas of financial resources and investment of resources. He has to take responsibility for finance decision and investment decisions which are part of the overall finance function. He has to integrate the finance function with production and marketing functions. As finance has tentacles with all other activities of the firm, the finance manager has broad spectrum of responsibility in (i) planning of physical and financial aspects of the operations; (ii) budgeting of financial resources — sources and uses of funds — (iii) integrate finance decision with investment decision and (iv) co-ordinate the various functions of the management with the finance function.

Routine Duties of Finance Manager

The routine duties of finance manager include the following, among others:

(1) Keeping a track, month-wise, of all cash inflows and outflows and their variance with budgetary projections.

(2) Maintain a record of all receivables and payables, credit instruments, credit sales, deposits, loans and advances etc.,

(3) Study regularly the quality and quantity of current assets and liabilities and position of current liquidity.

(4) Assess from time to time the long-term and short-term solvency of the company and its overall solvency position.

(5) Keep liaison with stock exchanges, where the company's shares are listed for a study of share price movements and analyse the relation of the financial position of the company with share prices.

(6) Keep liaison with banks and FIs for any changes in limits or to inform them of any imminent changes in company's financial position or policies. Payments of interest and instalments of principal are to be ensured at the right times, for which the finance manager has to arrange funds out of his budget.

(7) Keep liaison with Registrar of Companies and Government Departments connected with investment and financing decisions for any information regarding the imminent changes in policy or from operational angle.

(8) Keep abreast with all legal and procedural requirements for raising funds and making investment decisions. Knowledge of law under Companies Act, SEBI Act and other relevant enactments as listed in an earlier chapter is essential for all finance managers.

(9) Keep the top management or the board informed of any likely changes in the financial position of the company either due to external reasons or internal factors such as production and sales etc., provide contingency plans with a view to meet the emerging situations.

(10) Help the top management with all requirements of new issues prospectus, letter of offer statement in lieu of prospectus, negotiations with merchant bankers, underwriters etc. and with bank borrowings or dealings with financial institutions.

Finance Function and Investors

In the finance functions, one has to keep the investors' satisfaction as one of the goals. In the best interests of the company, which is also the interests of the investors, who are owners of the company, the finance function should aim at regular dividend payments and through tax planning and expansion programmes, promote the growth of the company and increase its networth. This networth and book value along with net profit or earnings per share would reflect the true fundamentals of the company, which is the basis for share price formation to a large extent. Among the internal factors, influencing the company's share price, the main factors are its fundamentals, reflected in book value and earnings per share, along with the solvency and liquidity of the company. All these variables are influenced by the financial operations of the company for which the finance manager is responsible.

Banks and FIs

Similarly, the finance manager has to keep bankers and FIs, connected with the company satisfied so that the future requirements of the company are met by them without any difficulty for which regular payment of instalments of interest and principal is necessary. Besides, the operations in cash credit account should be regular and the banker should be informed regularly of all important developments in the company. The relations with these institutions should be friendly and co-ordial which is again a responsibility of finance manager.

Finance Function — Characteristics

If should be flexible, easily adjustable to changing conditions. Alternatives and standby policies are to be kept ready in the plan for both finance decision and investment decision. Short-term liquidity and long-term solvency and profitability to increase net worth on a continuing and consistent basis are the basic objectives which should be kept in mind for alternatives to be pursued.

Investors should be kept happy by a policy of regular dividends and increasing book value (or net worth); this will increase the share price. Only if the public and investors are satisfied with the financial image of the company, will the company succeed in raising fresh resources from the public, if necessary in the form of deposits from the public, rights to the existing shareholders or public issue through prospectus or private placement, etc.

Besides, the finance function should aim at keeping the management free from interference from banks and FIs and even debenture trustees by keeping them happy through regular servicing of all debtors. The staff and workers of the company have to be reimbursed with salaries and perquisites and bonus consistent with profitability and productivity of the labour. The company has to satisfy the statutory requirements of P.F. contributions from employers and pollution control, water treatment plant, etc. The finance function should keep the government and semi-government authorities satisfied, so as to allow free operations of management without much interference from them.

Decisions Tree Approach to the Finance Function

It has been noted already that finance function has two major aspects, namely, investments decision and finance decision. In either case, the decision has to be based on analysis and alternatives, available or opportunities, open. For each alternative, there are costs and benefits and costs are the outflows and benefits are the inflows of cash or funds in each of the investment proposals or financing alternatives. To study the cost/benefit for analysis for each alternative, the decision tree approach or opportunities can be placed in the order of net benefits or in terms of their profitability. There are various methods or principles on the basis of which projects can be marked in the order, namely :

(1) Pay back period : The number of years in which original investment can be recouped.

(2) Return on investment method – which will take into account average return or return on average investment (R.O.I.)

(3) Present value return which discounts to the present day all the future cash flows from an investment during its life time.

(4) Minimum total cost or lowest unit cost of each project but this cannot be the criteria in respect of those for statutory obligation (like pollution control or water treatment plant) or for welfare of the staff (like staff housing project), in which case project has to be implemented, irrespective of the cost benefit flows. Some projects like diesel generating sets for emergency needs of electricity are not subject to the same 'criteria' as referred to above. The above criteria are applicable to normal projects with risks and returns and costs and benefits.

Decision Tree Analysis with Certainty – Example (in Rs.)

			1st year	2nd year	3rd year
Project-A	Investment Rs. 12,000 spread over 3 years.	Cash inflow	4,000	5,000	6,000
		Cash outflow	4,000	4,000	4,000
Project-B	Investment Rs. 12,000 spread over 2 year.	Cash inflow	7,000	10,000	—
		Cash outflow	4,000	6,000	—

Given the risk free rate for discounting as 10%

and present value factor for one year 0.909
for 2nd year 0.826
and for 3rd year 0.751

(for 10% discount factor)

	Project - A	Project - B
Present value of Cash inflows: in Rupees		
1st Year	3636	6363
2nd Year	4130	8260
3rd Year	4506	-
Inflows Total:	1,2272	1,4623
Present value of Cash outflows: in Rupees		
1st Year	3636	5454
2nd Year	3304	4956
3rd Year	3004	-
Outflows Total:	9944	10,410

I. Project — A = $\frac{12,272}{9944} \left(\frac{\text{Inflow}}{\text{Outflow}}\right) = 1.23$

II. Project — B = $\frac{14,623}{10,410} = 1.40$

Both are positive net returns. But Project-B is preferred, as it has higher positive return.

Advantages: Net present value takes the time factor into account. Both cash inflows and outflows are spread over the life of the asset and present values for both inflows and outflows are taken into account.

Take another example :

Original investment in a machine = Rs. 30,000; cash flows generated by the machines are as follows:

	Machine — A (in Rs.)	Machine — B (in Rs.)
1st Year	16,000	12,500
2nd Year	16,000	12,500
3rd Year	—	12,500
Total Returns	32,000	37,500

Based on simple average returns Machine-B is preferred as it gives additional 7,500 over 3 years (average per year of about Rs. 2,500) while Machine-A gives additional Rs. 2,000 (average per year of about Rs. 1,000).

Based on N P V at 10% discount factor.

NPV (MACHINE-A)		NPV (MACHINE-B)	
1st year (0.909×16000)	= 14,544	(0.909 × 12500)	= 11,362
2nd year (0.826 × 16000)	= 13,216	(0.826 × 12500)	= 10,325
3rd year NIL		(0.751 × 12500)	= 9,388
NPV of Total Flows	27,760		31,075

Machine A is to be rejected as it gives

negative NPV (Less than 1) = $\frac{27,760}{30,000} = 0.925$

Machine B has given positive NPV return and has to be preferred

$$= \frac{31{,}075}{30{,}000} = 1.036$$

In case of decision tree analysis with uncertainty of flows, probable return or inflow has to be weighted with total of weights as (1). All the alternative flows with weights will be considered for decision of finance/investment on the same lines as shown above.

FINANCE AND CONTROL

Finance function encompasses the monitoring of the budget, control on the progress of budget and financial operations and review. Sometimes the chief finance officer is made the controller with a separate finance manager to look after function of funds management. In such an event, controller's function has to be clearly distinguished from that of the finance executive. In practice now-a-days, the finance function has come to include treasury function also. To distinguish these two functions, following official statement of the Board of Directors of the Financial Executive Institute of USA is reproduced below :

CONTROLLERSHIP	TREASURERSHIP FUNCTION
(1) Planning for Control	**(1) Provision of Capital**
To establish, co-ordinate and administer as an integral part of management, an adequate plan for control of operations. Such a plan would provide to the extent required in the business profit planning programmes, for capital investing and for financing sales forecast, expenses budgets and cost standards together with the necessary procedures to effectuate the plan.	To establish and execute programme for the provision of capital required by the business including negotiating the procurement of capital and maintaining the required financial arrangements.
(2) Reporting and Interpreting	**(2) Investor Relations**
To compare performance with operating plans and standards and to report and interpret the results of operations to levels of management and to the owners of Business. This function includes the formation of accounting policy, the coordination of systems and procedures, the preparation of operating data and of special reports as required.	To establish and maintain adequate market for the company's securities and in connection therewith to maintain adequate liaison with investment bankers, financial analysts and shareholders.
(3) Evaluation and Consulting	**(3) Short-term Financing**
To consult with all segments of management responsible for policy or action, concerning any phase of the operation of the business as it relates to the attainment of objectives and the effectiveness of policies, organisational structure and procedure.	To maintain adequate sources for the company's current borrowings from commercial banks and other leading institutions.

(4) Tax Administration To establish and administer tax policies and procedures.	**(4) Banking and Custody of Securities** To maintain banking arrangements to receive and have custody of and to disburse the company's resources and securities and to be responsible for the financial aspects of real estate transactions.
(5) Government Reporting To supervise and coordinate the preparation of reports to government agencies R.O.C., SEBI etc.	**(5) Credits and collections** To the granting of credit and collection of accounts due to the company including the supervision of required special arrangements for financing sales such as time of payment and leasing plans.
(6) Protection of Assets To assure protection to the assets of the business through internal control, internal auditing and assuring proper insurance coverage.	**(6) Investments** To invest the company's funds as required and to establish and coordinate policies for investment in pension and other similar trusts.
(7) Economic Appraisal To continuously appraise economic and social forces and Government influences and to interpret their effect upon the business.	**(7) Insurance** To provide insurance coverage as required.

Investment Decision

Treasury work involves investment decision-making as already referred to. This decision-making process, *inter alia* depends on the (i) Availability of surplus cash/funds or as part of the business of the company or bank or financial institution and on (ii) Analysis of the data and information about the market forces, whether it is money market, gilt-edged market or forex market.

All operations, in any of the financial markets involve investment decisions. Actual investment operations and market forces are discussed later. Here, the analytical framework for decision is set out.

Decisions are of three types:

(i) to buy (ii) to sell (iii) to hold

Decisions may be relating to shift from (i) one market to another market (ii) from one segment or instrument of the market to another of the same market and (iii) from one maturity to another maturity in respect of the same instrument or from spot to forward market and vice versa and from one yield to a higher yield etc.

Factors influencing decisions are:

(1) Fundamentals of the company, credit rating of the instrument.

(2) Risk return characteristics of the instrument or asset.

(3) Expectations of the price rise or fall.

(4) Current mood of the market or the segment of the market concerned.

(5) Investor's perception of whether the price is undervalued or overvalued.

(6) Investor's preference and the company's needs for liquidity, income etc.

(7) Statutory obligations to invest any properties in a particular asset as in the case of the regulations of RBI for investment of finance companies in government bonds/securities upto a minimum.

(8) SEBI guidelines for investment as in the case of mutual funds and venture capital funds etc.

Normally, manufacturing companies which are profit making ones have some investments in short-term assets like treasury bills or commerciai paper or bill discounts, in money market for quick conversion into cash, as and when need arises. If there are still extra funds, they are invested in medium and long-term instruments including new issues of companies and under writing, if it is a mutual fund or merchant banker or broker firm.

Planning in Investment

(a) Buy low and sell high is the principle for all investments which will appreciate in market prices, as in equity.

(b) Current yield should be high with instruments of the same maturity.

(c) Maturity has to be planned in a manner that some investments mature every year for meeting any contingencies or for any event like purchase of a capital equipment or repayment of debt due or for any instalments due to banks.

If the company or firm is a trading company, it has to keep the speculative element to a manageable proportion. Either in stock market or forex market sometimes open positions are kept uncovered for speculative gains. It is possible that there may be losses also sometimes. So a limit of such open position is to keep at 10 to 15% of the total fund invested — a stop loss order at 10% of total funds.

Prudence pays and greed should be avoided by all fund managers. If the temptation is there and gains have come, by keeping open positions, the manager is apt to fall a prey for increasing the stakes. Hearsay and rumours should not be the basis for any investment decisions. If by any chance despite the limits set for speculation there are continued losses due to slide of the currency held open in the forex market or shares traded/overbuying or oversold, there should not be panic and profits and losses have to be taken as part of the game.

Maturity of Investments

Short-term investments are to be undertaken (i) for excess inflow for a short period, as per the budget or (ii) for payments after 3 to 12 months ahead and funds are kept earning until the date due for repayment or payments. In the process he has to attempt the proper asset liability mix for the company and undertake asset liability matching. Long-term investments are permitted, if the operations of the company involve such investment activity or there is need for expansion into subsidiary or to improve the profitability through high returns in some other activity.

Some investments are also needed for spread of risk or for tax planning purposes. Besides, the statutory and healthy guidelines require some funds to be set apart for staff welfare schemes or payment of compensation or pension etc.

These funds can be invested by the company for a future date with a maturity falling due, when funds are necessary and every year some amount has to fall due in maturity. Adjustments of maturities in investments as per the future requirements of the company and for satisfying the requirements of risk return features, as needed by management are the responsibility of the Treasurer of the company.

Investments can also be planned and budgeted in the Annual Plans and amounts be set apart for short-term and long-term investments separately. The actual investment decision is to be made at the time of need depending on the state of the market, risk-return features of the instrument and the requirements of the company and maturity pattern, needed for efficient funds management. The responsibility for all such activities and decisions with regard to investment is that of the Treasurer of the company.

Conclusions

In this chapter, the functions of the Treasuer are distinguished from those of the Finance Manager, Funds Manager, and Controller. Planning and Budgetting go together for taking any Financing decision and Investment decision. The Treasurer of a company is concerned with all these functions and has to operate in coordination with the Finance Manager and Financial Controller. Their functions overlap and the functions of controller and distinguished from those of treasurer. But Finance Management involves and encompasses all the functions of Financing and Investment decisions, with which the Treasurer is also concerned.

❑ ❑ ❑

8 FINANCIAL FORECASTING

Financial planning and Budgeting are necessary for Financing and Investment decisions, with which the treasurer is concerned, as seen in the last chapter. This chapter deals with the related subject of Financial forecasting, which is necessary for Financial planning and funds flow analysis.

What is Forecasting?

Financial forecasting is a part of financial planning necessary for efficient funds management. The funds manager should not only know the past and present trends by analysis for planning, he should also have estimated forecasts of future flows of funds. Forecasting involves estimates of future conditions of the business on a systematic and dependable basis. As the future is uncertain, management decisions will have to be made in the darkness of events to come, relating to sales production, pricing and costs, profit margins and inflow and outflow of funds. Forecasting is a part of the Management Information System (MIS) and helps to clear the uncertainty of the future and provides a guiding light for decisions on future actions and making for dependable planning. Forecasting is the basis for planning of both finance function and Investment function of Treasury Manager.

Why Forecasting?

Forecasting is necessary, due to the uncertainty of the future on which financial decisions are to be made. It involves a reasonable estimate of the likely events or probable alternative scenarios likely to emerge. It involves the analysis of available data or information and prepares the best basis possible for the formation of business estimates. On the basis of these analysed data, the alternatives possible may be set out and the best possible likely events are forecast. The more realistic the forecasts are, the more efficient are the business decisions and treasury manager's operations.

In business activity starting with the project preparation, some estimate, of the inputs and outputs and capacity, creditor and possible production levels at different capacity utilisation levels, the sales and profit margins on the basis of costs of production are to be forecasted. Thus, forecasting for financial planning is applied in :

(i) capital investment decisions (ii) budgetary control of financial operations (iii) estimates of working capital requirements (iv) profit projections, cash inflows, outflows and net cash flows (v) making investment decision through projection of present value of future returns.

Apart from the above financial projections the business decisions which also effect the financial planning are the need of forecasts of business indicator and trends. Such forecasts are needed for performance budgeting, strategic planning, production mix and output planning marketing strategy, planning and stock controls, distribution strategies, credit sales, and collection procedures, profit margins, etc.

Starting with the forecast of inputs needed for a given level of output, the likely flow of output, labour to be employed, sales cost of production, profit margins and other business activities are all planned on the basis of forecasts only. The results of business and the operations of business at various stages require financial planning and thus, financial forecasts of the needs for capital, sources and cost of funds, working capital requirements and estimates of inflows and outflows of funds.

Functions — Forecasting

The following major functions are performed by financial forecasting :

(1) To pursue a course of action plan in physical operations of production, sales etc., which will result in some financial inputs and outputs.

(2) To impose budgetary control based on the action plan, monitor the progress of the operations and resulting financial inflows and outflows and take corrective actions through financial discipline and making changes in financial allocations.

(3) To provide warning signals for impending troubles from physical operations or from external factors, leading to financial crisis and to take measures to prevent such crisis before hand and to ensure safe current liquidity for the company.

Basis of Forecasting

(1) Study of the past data and information and understanding why changes in the past took place in production, sales, stock, costs etc. The past trends, ratios, rates of changes, acceleration or deceleration in rates etc., would help to constitute the basis for future projection. If no past is there for a new company, the trends in the industry are studied.

(2) Study of business environment, macro-economic and financial parameters which change the trends in the company's output, sales, profit margins, like business cycle within the industry or economic trends, credit and banking trends and market changes.

(3) Selection and availability of data on factors influencing the business variables like GNP, industrial production, inflation, money supply, export, trade

etc. at macro level, and the market demand for its products, its own labour, raw-materials and other input supplies, necessary for production, at the micro-level have to be selected and data collected and analysed for trends and possible changes.

(4) Analysis of data for forecasting is done on the basis of reasonable relationship established between the selected data and company's own performance indicators but the rationale for such relationship has to be established, by the study of the past data. Such relationship is used for drawing some dependable conclusions about the future trends/events which is called forecasting.

Techniques of Forecasting

In general, the methods of forecasting are of many varieties, namely, simple statistical tools like charts, graphs on trend, and more complicated techniques like regression and correlation, programming and econometric models.

The following are some of the commonly used methods of forecasting.

(1) Historical Analogy Method: This is based on the projection of the future trends on the basis of similar conditions prevailing in the past in India or outside and the consequent changes that took place at that time in India and abroad. Demand for a product is estimated on the basis of business cycles and the historical analogy method of the demand in a past period with similar conditions of recession or boom, in business activity.

(2) Field Surveys and Opinion Polls: This is based on the information gathered by the questionnaires, field surveys conducted and opinion polls taken. The data may be collected on random sample method, simple expert opinions on a selected sample of the market distributors, consumers etc.

This method is used to quantify the demand changes, likely response to price changes, taste and habit changes among consumers, margins required by traders and distributors and those offered by other competitors in the market. A consensus view can be obtained by averaging the views (use of Delphi Method).

(3) Index of Business Conditions: Important business indicators may be used to project company's market demand, sales and project margins. These are mainly macro indicators like GNP, WPI, Industrial Production (I.P.), Stock prices, Bond prices, etc. There are many other indicators like the credit trends of banks, interest rates, money supply and budget deficits etc. Many of these indicators and all of them reflect different activities in macro production, trade, business, finance etc. These macro factors will influence the micro level position of the company and forecasting is done on the basis of above barometers and some established relations.

(4) Extrapolation: This method assumes that the past trend continues and there is a consistency in its travel. Thus, the past trend is extrapolated and elongated to derive the coming trends. Therefore the appropriate trend curve and the values of parameters are determined. There are many alternative trend curves and suitable ones may be selected.

(a) *Arithmetic Trend:* This is a straight line of arithmetic average and the growth will be at a constant absolute amount.

(b) *Semilog Trend:* This is based on the constant percentage change each year or half year. Since the periodic changes are constant in logarithms the line will have the advantage of a straight line when drawn as a graph with a logarithmic vertical scale and years on the horizontal scale. The same can be projected for the next year.

(c) ***Modified Exponential Trend:*** This curve assumes that each increment of growth will be a constant percent of the previous one. This will result in a line, which tends to approach but never reaches a constant asymptote, which may be thought of as an upper limit.

(d) ***Logistic Curve:*** This has both an upper asymptote and a lower one. It assumes a law of growth involving increasing increment from an initial low level and then gradual slowing down of growth as maturity is approached. The GOMPERTZ curve has similar properties, referred to above and is used to describe the growth of industrial output. To choose one of the above curves, the actual data and their nature have to be examined and the best suitable curve is to be chosen depending on the nature of the data. For example, demand for a consumption good may become asymptotic after a stage, say in the case of jute and tea products. The curve may have arithemetic or geometric trend, in case of growing and sunrise industries like telecommunications, satellite networking, computer software etc. The product and its nature and the company's share in the market generally influence the nature of the curve.

(5) Regression Analysis: The dependent variable to be projected is rationally expected to depend on some independent variables. If sales are to be projected and they are expected to depend on the disposable income of the people, sales can be regressed on the disposable incomes. If sales depend on the advertisement expenses, then sales can be projected for every level of advertisement expenses. If any dependent variable is dependent on one independent variable as in the examples above, it is called simple regression. The equation for it is :

$x = a + by + e$

x is sales a dependent variable

y is advertisement expenses

'a' and 'b' are constants and 'e' is error term to capture all other variables not considered.

In the graph alongside, these relations are shown.

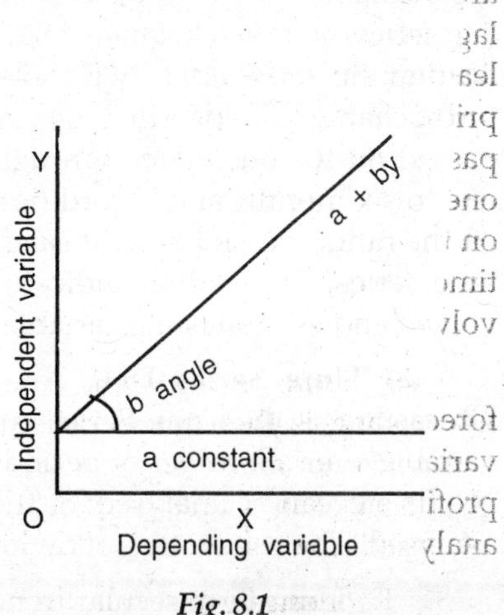

Fig. 8.1

Values of x and y in the time series data of the past are used to calculate "a" and "b" values which can be used to calculate X for given value of Y.

If there are one, two or more than two independent variables like Y_1, Y_2 etc., then it is called multiple regression equation which requires, calculation with calculators or with computer programming. In the case of linear relationship, multiple regressions can be worked out more easily and in the case of non-linear relationship only computer programming can help in this process. Examples of linear and non-linear relationship are given below.

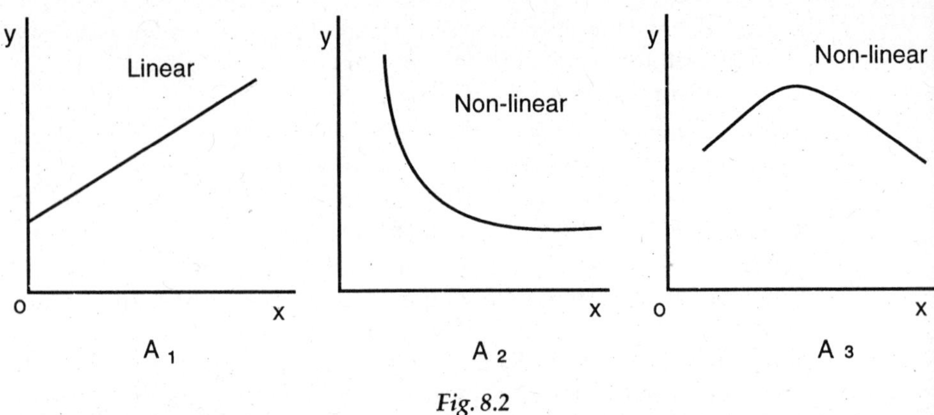

Fig. 8.2

(6) Econometric Models: Leaving mathematical formulas, there will be an explicit mathematical model and a large number of equations will be there setting out the relations between different variables, in linear or non-linear fashion. Thus, there may be as many equations, as there are relations. Thus, sales depend on output, advertisement expenditure, number of dealers, number of stocking centres, etc. Thus, it becomes one equation, where sales are dependent on a number of variables. There can be another equation of output depending on plant capacity, electricity supplied, shifts worked etc. This determines output and sales may also depend on output among others. Thus, there can be any number of equations in an econometric model, which help to determine output, sales, profits, costs etc. All these equations are solved through computer programming with a number of observations over years. The variables used and the relations established should be chosen after a lot of research, and the relations should have an economic rationale.

(7) Lead — lag Analysis: If there are two variables and their time series data are available, the lead-lag approach establishes a relationship of lead series and lag series and the average lead or lag is determined. Thus, if cost series are leading the price series by the extent of six months on an average, one can predict price changes, depending on the cost changes. Thus, excise duty increase is passed on to consumers, through a higher price and normal time lag for this is one to six months and accordingly price realizations can be estimated depending on the ratio of cash to credit sales. Thus, the corporate analyst has to identify in a time series, the leading indicators and lagging indicators and the time lag involved and estimates the variables depending on the other.

(8) Time Series Data Analysis: The most popular method for business forecasting is the Time Series Analysis. This requires collection of data on any variable over a number of periods — months or years. Thus, sales or GPM or net profits etc. can be analysed; or the data of sales over months can be collected and analysed. They show the following components, in the series :

1. Long-term secular trend — based on general tendency.
2. Seasonal variations over some months due to climate etc.
3. Cyclical variations due to cycles of trade, recession or boom over quarters or years.
4. Irregular or erratic variations due to factors such as war, earthquakes etc which are irregular and unpredictable.

The analyst should separate all these parts of the time series data.

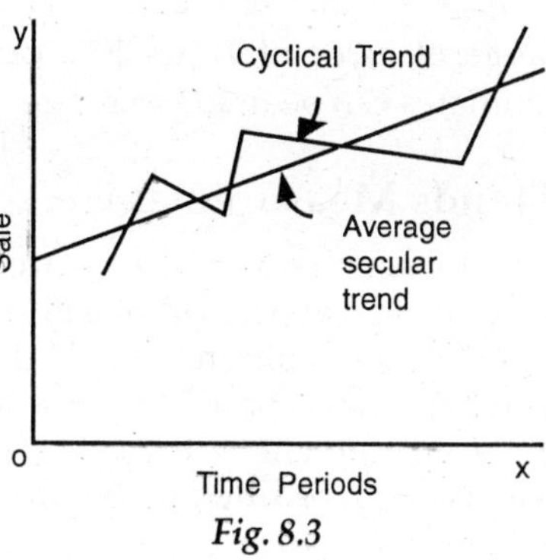

Fig. 8.3

Thus, Y = T x S x C x I, where Y is the sum total of 4 elements of Time Series or total features of the data T = Trend, S = Seasonal Variation C = Cyclical changes, I = Irregular variations. Despite its theoretical nicety it is difficult to identify these elements in reality. These can be grouped at least under major heads in practical business field, namely, secular trend (T) and cyclical seasonal variations (C). These are reflected in the alongside graph.

(9) Use of Moving Averages: In the use of time series to smoothen the undue fluctuations we can derive moving averages of 3, 6 or 9 months and arrive at a more smooth curve to enable us to know the true secular trend on the basis of which the trend forthcoming can be forecasted by simple graphical method, or extrapolation. Moving average method, ratio to trend method or link relatives method can be used to measure seasonal variations.

Example of Moving Average Calculation (M.A.)

Calculation of say 5 year M.As

Year	No. of autos sold	5 yearly totals	5 year M.A.
1985	23	---	
1986	26		
1987	28	129	26
1988	32	118	24
1989	20	104	21
1990	12	86	17
1991	12	63	13
1992	10	56	11
1993	9	55	11
1994	13	56	11
1995	11	59	12

First total the first five initial observations and divide by 5, then omit the first and take 2 to 6 observations and divide by 5 and so on. Calculation of a larger number yearly M.A.s makes the curve much smoother. The larger the number of periods, the better is the curve. Let us see trend curve fitting with M.A. method. All the figures of M.A.s in above data are used for the curve.

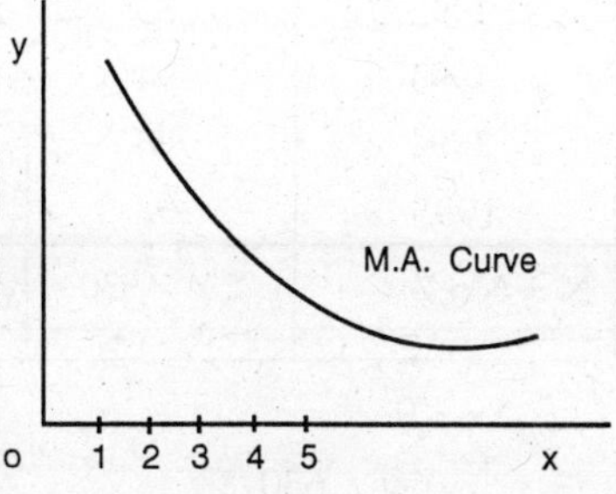

Fig. 8.4

If the years chosen or periods chosen for the calculation are coinciding with the cycle, better results can be got. If the above M.A. curve is extrapolated, then we get the next M.A. and from that the actual can be derived for the next year. These estimates are rough and crude and extreme care has to be taken in their use. A range of error of 10 to 20% can be easily expected if properly calculated, and estimates can be made to range within some limits.

Trends Measurement

Linear trends are measured by fitting a straight line trend (Y = a + bx). The curve can be expressed by simple graphic method drawn by hand or by equation given above, with time series, data of x and y. For non-linear relations, we can use graphic method or moving average method or second degree parabolic reflected in the measurement by logarithms by taking the curve becoming a straight line and equation can be fitted in log form as shown below :

$\log Y = \log a + x \log b + x^2 \log c$

Where the variably x, y 'a and b' and c are explained above

Without logs the equation is

$Y = a + bx + cx^2$

In the real world the curves are parabolic in the sense that the demand for a product will continue to grow for some years after which the growth decelerates and even becomes negative. Then the curve after reaching a point tends to go down.

TREND EXTRAPOLATION

Trend analysis is often used to forecast the future levels of the variable concerned. As referred to earlier the trend equation for a straight line is given as Y = a + bx. – 'a' and 'b' can be worked out by solving two normal equations.

$Y = a + b\Sigma x$

$\Sigma Y = a\Sigma x + b\Sigma x^2$

a = constant, thus Y = a, when $\Sigma X = 0$

b is the rate of change or gradient of the fitted trend line.

To give an example of the use of trend equation, consider the following data.

Table 8.1

Year	Production Y (000 tons)	Deviation from middle year (x)	XY	X^2	Trend values (ye)
1989	80	–3	–240	9	84
1990	90	–2	–180	4	86
1991	92	–1	–92	1	88
1992	83	0	0	0	90
1993	94	+1	+94	1	92
1994	99	+2	+198	4	94
1995	92	+3	+276	9	96
N = No.7	$\Sigma Y = 630$	$\Sigma x = 0$	$\Sigma xy = 56$	$\Sigma x^2 = 28$	$\Sigma y = 630$

$\Sigma x = 0$

$$a = \frac{\Sigma y}{N} = \frac{630}{7} = 90; \qquad B = \frac{\Sigma XY}{\Sigma X^2} \quad \frac{56}{28} = 2$$

The trend values (ye) are calculated as follows :

For	x = -3	ye = 90 + 2x -3	= 90 - 6	= 84
	x = -2	ye = 90 + 2x -2	= 90 - 4	= 86
	x = -1	ye = 90 + 2x -1	= 90 - 2	= 88
	x = 0	ye = 90 + 0	= 90	= 90
	x = +1	ye = 90 + 2 × 1	= 90 + 2	= 92
	x = +2	ye = 90 + 2 × 2	= 90 + 4	= 94
	x = +3	ye = 90 + 2 × 3	= 90 + 6	= 96

For graphic presentation, the chart below shows the actual data and trend line for the data in the above example.

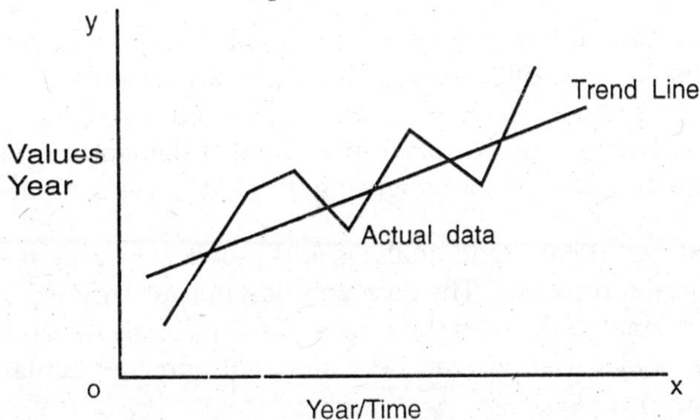

For 1996 the trend line can be elongated to arrive at say 100. Thus, the graphic method can also be used for estimation.

The same linear form of data and curve are drawn and we can use logarithms and convert them into straight line and use the calculation in the same fashion.

Financial Forecasting Techniques

Of the techniques referred to above, financial forecasting has to be applied normally to output sales, cash flows, receivables, payables, etc. For the above variables, the techniques which are more useful are the following:

(1) Field Surveys for estimation of demand for a brand product changes in taxes etc. which affect consumer goods, sample studies region-wise, state-wise and area-wise, or income group-wise will help to forecast likely changes in demand and sales.

(2) Economic and Business Indicators: These will influence needed capacities to be built, capital investment to be made, diversification and expansion etc. depending on the changes in the business parameters like fall in GNP, reducing the demand for the product, or new technology. Reducing costs for a product which is a substitute for the company's product will lead to fall in demand for the present product of the company. This will necessitate a change in product mix. Depression or recession in automobiles reduced the demand for cars during 1992-94 and thereafter the boom conditions prevailed leading to a rise in their production and sales in 1995 and 1996.

(3) Extrapolation of the data can be done by the trend in growth rates of sales, receivables, cash inflows etc. It can be done graphically or algebraically or in a tabular form. If there is no visible trend despite the smoothening of curve by

M.A. method, smoothening by the simple exponential method may be adopted. This means that the forecasted value of the series at time period 't', namely, yt includes a fraction of the forecasted error of the previous period. Thus, to predict the value of the time series at time t + 1, we have the equation as :

$$yt + 1 = a\,(yt - Yt) + Yt$$

In this equation, the difference between the actual value yt and the forecasted value Yt for the same period is more than in the previous period (t-1) by a fraction say "a". This fraction "a" of this difference is derived from the past period difference (Yt)

Exponential smoothening is a special kind of weighted moving average and is found to be useful in applications to financial variables like sales, inventories, receivables etc. This should be used when long period time series data are available. When sales actually made differ from estimated demand then the past actual and their estimate can be used for weighting the next year's estimate.

(4) Time Series Data: Trend analysis and moving average method can also be used in financial forecasting. The data on sales, output, inflows through receivable etc. can be estimated through the time series data analysis. In these series, the cyclical and seasonal variations can be eliminated and the secular trend can be identified for such analysis.

(5) Regression Method can also be found to be useful for forecasting the financial data with somewhat good mathematical background and knowledge. Simple linear regression model of the type of (Y = a +bx) is very easy to use with a good number of observations of Y and x, (say sales and cash inflows or output and sales).

Forecasting of Cash Flows

Receivables and payables can be estimated on the basis of sales or projected sales. This will indicate the inflows and outflows. Products item/category-wise or department-wise estimates can be made and added together. Cash sales and credit sales and their proportion can be used to project month-wise inflows depending upon the maturity of bills. Thus, cash sales are 30% and credit sales 70%. Assuming a total sales of Rs. 100, the credit sales with one month bill, of 20% two month bill of 20% and three month bills of 30%. Month-wise inflow forecasts for the coming months is as follows:

First Month		2nd Month	3rd Month	4th Month	
Cash Sales	30	+30 cash	30+	30+	etc.
Credit Sales		20 Bills	20+	30+	etc.
			20+	20+	etc.
				10+	
Total inflows	30	50	70	90	etc.

Annual, half yearly or quarterly earnings data can thus be derived from such estimates. Similarly, outflows can also be estimated.

Growth Models

If the past earnings were growing at an arithmetic average growth rate, then we can have the models as follows: where g is the growth rate, and average growth rate ($\bar{g}$).

$\bar{g} = 1/n \, \Sigma \, gt$

From the above next quarter or half year earnings can be estimated.

If the past earnings were growing at an average compound rate, then g is the average compound growth rate.

$$g = \left(\frac{vt}{vo}\right)^{\frac{1}{t}} - 1$$

where $vt = vo\,(1+g)^t$

If once g is known as the compound growth rate, then based on the value of this rate, next quarter or half yearly sales or earnings can be estimated.

Quarterly or half yearly earnings model can also be built on regression basis. If it is auto regression model then the quarter 't' earnings will depend on the last quarter t-1, plus an error term. The equation for this model is :

Earnings in period t = Et.

Earnings in period t - 1 = Et - 1

e is the error term.

Thus, Et = Et - 1 + e.

If it is a general regression model of the type of equation y = a + bx

y is the dependent variable, sales, and x is the independent variable say output or price per unit or industrial production or any other variable.

Other Methods of Estimation

Net market share approach can be used to estimate sales of a company. If for example the share of Birla Cement is 10% of total sales of cement in a year (the total for the country) and if the total demand for cement is estimated at x units, the demand for Birla Cement would be $\frac{1}{10}x$.

The sales estimate or output estimates can also be based on the proportion of capacity of the company to the total capacity of the industry in the country. This assumes uniform capacity utilisation in all units or that the capacity utilisation of the company is about the same as the average capacity utilisation for the whole industry.

Earnings and expenses items can be estimated independently and net cash inflow can be derived by deducting the estimated expenses from estimated earnings. If a company is a finance company and not a manufacturing company, there will be no scope for estimating sales on the basis of the methods, discussed earlier. For finance companies auto regression methods or trend growth rate methods are to be adopted. Earnings have to be estimated on the basis of activities say leasing, hire purchases etc. on a service unit or department basis.

For such companies involving no manufacturing, trend method and extrapolation methods can also be used. Besides, regression models can be used on the basis of following relationship. The variables are as follows: Earnings after tax (EAT) is a function of tax rate (T), R = Before tax return on assets, L/E leverage provided by debt (L) to equity (E), Equity and effective interest rate (I) are the variables generally considered.

The equation is as follows:

$$EAT = (1 - T)\left[R + \frac{R - I \times L}{E}\right]E$$

$$R = \text{Before Tax Return on Assets} = \frac{\text{EBITD}}{\text{Total Assets}}$$

$$I = \frac{\text{Interest paid}}{\text{Total liabilities}} \text{ or } \frac{\text{Finance expense}}{\text{Borrowings}}$$

Earnings are a function, in the long-run of a number of variables such as :

(1) Utilisation of asset base (TA/E) = Total assets/Equity

(2) Profitability of sales (GPM) = GP/Sales

(3) Effective cost of Borrowed funds; Finance costs/Total Borrowings

(4) Leverage enjoyed = Borrowed funds/ equity

(5) Effective Tax rate.

Depending upon the funds manager's expertise, research can be conducted on the factors influencing sales, inventories and earnings, under any of the methods discussed above.

Cash Flow Forecasting

Cash outflow and cash inflows are due to payables and receivables in addition to cash receipts for sales and other income and cash payment. Separate estimates can be made of cash receipts and receivable as also for cash payments and other payables. The circular relations between cash, sales etc. can be set out as follows:

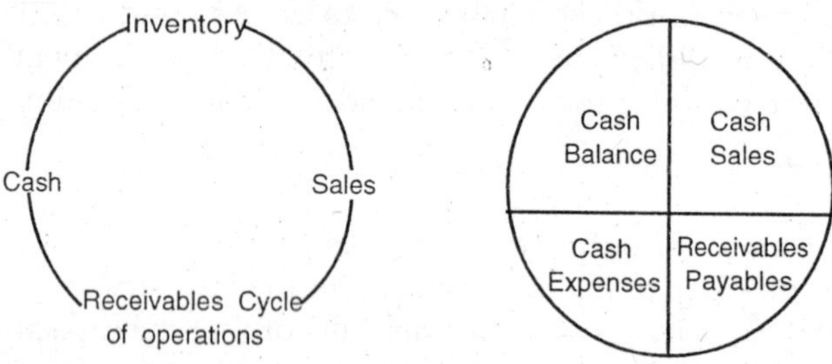

Fig. 8.5

Using these relations, item-wise receivables and payables can be estimated to prepare the budget and make up an action plan for the next year, or quarter.

Budgeting and Financial Planning

Budget is an estimate of receipts and expenditure. It can be both on capital account and current account. The finance manager has to prepare an annual budget and split it into quarter-wise details. On the capital side any investment for repairs and maintenance of plant, equipment and machinery are included. Capital receipts may be from internal accruals, borrowings from public (deposits), banks or financial institutions (loans and advances) or from foreign equity or loans.

A Proforma Budget on Capital Account

	Receipts		Expenditure
(1)	Internal Accruals	(1)	Work in progress
(2)	Reserve Funds	(2)	New equipment and parts needed
(3)	Bank Term Loans	(3)	New plant and machinery ordered
(4)	F.I. Term Loans	(4)	Miscellaneous capital assets

A Proforma Budget on Revenue Account

(1)	Sales income (net of excise)	(1)	Cost of manufacture (wages/salaries, stores, other inputs)
(2)	Other income	(2)	Non-factory expenses (Administration, sales expenses etc.)
		(3)	Miscellaneous expenditure

Total Income - Total Expenditure = EBIDT

Net Profits = EBIDT – Interest, Depreciation & Taxes

In budgeting, the first step is to fix physical targets for sales, income and expenditure and profits are estimated as residuals. The financial side is the statement of profit-loss account. Targets are set for output month-wise and division-wise. The corresponding costs are worked out on the basis of past data on cost per unit, division-wise or product-wise. The price multiplied by estimated sales will give sale income. The other incomes are from trading, investments and real estate. The cost of production is similarly estimated on the basis of units produced and cost per unit. Here the output is assumed to be equal to sales; if not, the stocks will change accordingly.

As a next step, other administrative and selling expenses, statutory dues, P.F. and other contributions, taxes, dues etc. are provided for. Finally, net earnings are arrived at of which interest and taxes are paid and the left over funds are their cash accruals which form part of the sources of funds.

As part of financial planning quarter-wise estimates are made for inflows and outflows and the gap has to be met by arrangements with bank credit (on cash credit/over draft basis). The inflows and outflows are the result of physical operations of output, sales and accruals of other incomes and materials, parts and spares, electricity and stores etc.; expenses are to be estimated on the basis of item-wise details given above.

For financial planning it is also necessary, and also for working capital finance from banks, to prepare the fund flow statements. Based on the various items of assets and liabilities and their variations, the sources and uses of funds are estimated on a quarterly basis. The proforma generally used by banks for their assessment is as follows:

	Sources		Uses
1.	Profits before tax	1.	Increase in gross block.
2.	Depreciation	2.	Decrease in liabilities or repayments of debt or public deposits.
3.	Net earnings	3.	Increase in inter-corporate investments.
4.	Increase in capital (Equity/preference, if any)	4.	Decrease in short-term bank borrowings. (including bills discount)
5.	Increase in debt (Debentures, deposits)	5.	Decrease in other current liabilities.
6.	Decrease in inter-corporate investments	6.	Increase in other assets.
7.	Increase in short-term bank borrowings (including bill discounts)	7.	Increase in inventory.
8.	Increases in other liabilities	8.	Payment of taxes.
9.	Decrease in other assets	9.	Payment of dividends.
10.	Decrease in inventory	10.	Payment of arrears of P.F. and other dues etc.

As the sources and uses have to be balanced the final adjustment is made by a financial plan of low-cost borrowing or bank funds. The cost of capital, availability, easy access etc. are the criteria, adopted by funds manager, for funds flow statement. Normal principles like, efficient use of funds, minimising the average cost of capital and maximising the profit margins are adopted by the funds manager. The annual plan and quarterly breakdown plans are set well before the year starts. Afterwards monitoring revision and policy changes for balances, outflows and inflows are initiated during the year.

Conclusions

This chapter has highlighted techniques of forecasting – statistical and econometric to be used by Treasury Manager. Financial forecasting goes with the budgeting and planning exercises which together help the Treasury manager perform his functions for short term and long term financial needs of the company.

❑ ❑ ❑

9 SHORT-TERM FINANCIAL PLANNING

Management Function and Planning

Financial Planning, either for short-term funds or long-term finance cover the following important steps to be adopted by the top management, which in this case is the Treasury Manager. The plan should set out the quantity and quality of funds required during a time frame determining or forecasting the need for funds and their timing of the need. Secondly, it should set out the least cost sourcing for the needed funds. Thirdly, it should be the function of Treasury manager to arrange for sourcing of funds, cash management and management of receivables, payables and working capital finance. Financial planning also involves laying the policies for administration and control of the budget which incorporates the plan. According to Walker and Baughn, "Financial planning pertains only to the function of finance and includes the determination of firm's financial objectives, financial policies and financial procedures."

Thus, the three components of financial plan are :

(1) Objectives: To increase productivity and reduce costs so as improve the profitability.

(2) Financial Policies: To lay down total quantity of capital and cost of capital, least cost combination leading to efficient capital structure; capital budgeting decisions and policies for maximisation of wealth through gearing of equity; proper sourcing of funds, preparation of budgets both for capital and current accounts; control on book debts, proper collection policies etc.

(3) Financial Procedures: To follow some guidelines for project implementation or for controlling current and capital expenditure and setting out procedures for raising funds, taking investment decisions, arranging for bank finance and collection procedures for bills due, book creditors and receivables etc.

Financial plans are based on forecasts and they should be as scientific as possible, there should be forecasts of both inflows and outflows and a plan to match both in quantity and timing. The co-ordination of various departments is to be secured by treasury manager say from materials purchase department, inventory control department, production department, sales department etc. The financial plan should also be flexible and provide for alternatives in case of any failure or deviations from projections.

Objectives of financial plan are the Beacon Light of the direction for the plan to proceed. For this, annual or quarterly budgets are prepared and implemented. The implementation is strictly as per the guidelines and policies of Top Management (Board of Directors). The financial guidelines should be spelt out, clearly in a manual to be followed by the treasury managers; a few examples of which are set out below:

(1) Finance for permanent needs should come from permanent sources and not from short-term funds, normally.

(2) The core part of inventory and a portion of short-term assets should be financed by long-term funds only.

(3) Plan well ahead for any contingent needs of financial crisis or liquidity crunch.

(4) Maintain personal contact with concerned government departments, bankers, financial institutions concerned and keep track of capital market and the company's share price behaviour in the light of the stock market behaviour.

(5) Plough back profits as much as possible and increase the net worth so as to maximise share price of the company, for its investors.

What is Short-Term Finance ?

Short-term finance includes all types of finance for a duration of one day to a few months upto say one year. The instruments or forms in which the finance is required are cash, credits for varying periods, bills, cheques, DDs, TTs, MTs etc. These are moneys or claims on money in different forms like credit cards, overdraft facilities, IOUs, etc. Short-term finance is thus money or near money assets easily convertible into cash at short notice or in a few days. The purposes for which cash is needed are transactions of daily nature such as for daily wages, raw materials, travel, incidental expenses, etc. Cash is also needed for emergencies like sudden payments of bills due or to meet accidents or for servicing for meeting a breakdown in plant, machinery, fire in building etc. Economy in cash is involved through use of cheques, bill finance or postponement of payments by use of credit cards for some purchases and payments.

Role of Cash

Economy in cash is needed because cash is scarce and has alternative opportunities. Cash is no doubt absolutely necessary to meet the above payments or requirements, but it is barren, as it does not by itself generate any further income. Besides, to hold money in cash is a waste due to opportunity incomes lost

Secondly, as money loses its value due to inflation or rise in prices, cash earns a negative income in real terms. Thirdly, cash held in hand is subject to the fear of theft, or loss due to fire, accident or wear and tear. Thus, cash is absolutely necessary, but to an optimum extent. If minimum cash is not there, problems of illiquidity, risk of loss of credibility so essential in business will arise. If excess cash is there, there is a problem of loss of income and reduced profitability or even waste of scarce resources.

Cash Ratio

Cash ratio is the ratio of cash held in hand to total current liabilities, which cash helps to meet, for a growing concern. This ratio varies from concern to concern and case to case and period to period and cash needs determine cash ratio. Technical solvency of a concern is measured by cash ratio or the gap between inflows and outflows, which cash helps to meet. Another ratio which also measures the solvency and liquidity of the company is the current ratio or quick ratio.

$$\text{Thus, Current Ratio} = \frac{\text{Current Assets}}{\text{Current Liabilities}}$$

$$\text{Quick Ratio} = \frac{\text{Current Assets} - \text{Inventories}}{\text{Current Liabilities}}$$

Optimum cash ratio is known by experience of business, and factors influencing the cash needs.

Factors Influencing Cash Needs

Current operating cycle determines the needs of cash. If sales to inventory ratio or turnover is high, then inventory will be low and sales will be made as inventories are built up. Secondly, the larger the sales in cash, the lower is the need for holding cash for transactions and emergencies. Thirdly, if debtors delay the payment or credit sales are high, there is delay in return flow of funds and of cash inflow. If cash sales are high and if credit sales, resulting in book debts or in receivables, are realised well in time then again cash is generated. This cash inflow as against cash outflow determines the cash ratio. The cash is utilised for purchase of inventories, which again get converted into sales and cash again. This operating cycle can be set out as follows :

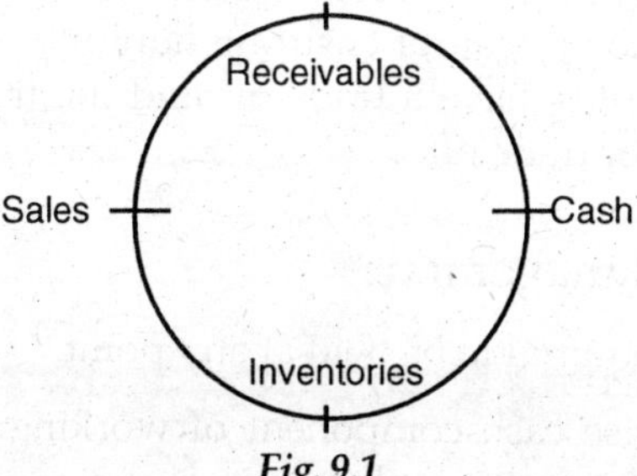

Fig. 9.1

Sales to receivables to cash to inventories and sales again is the operating cycle.

Efficient cash management involves the following steps :

(1) To reduce the operating cycle — the shorter the period — a reduction from 2 months to one month — the more is the saving in credit costs and increase of efficiency.

(2) To improve the quality of current assets like book debts, bills receivables, short-term credits, sundry debtors, investments, etc. would improve the cash realisations in time and promptly.

(3) To make proper planning of cash inflows and outflows through budgetary exercises. Month-wise inflows and outflows are planned and the gaps are arranged to be filled in by bank demand drafts and short-term trade credits etc. and provision to be made to invest profitably if there is excess of inflows.

A and B are excess cash outflows, in Figure 9.2. Gaps are to be anticipated and provision is made.

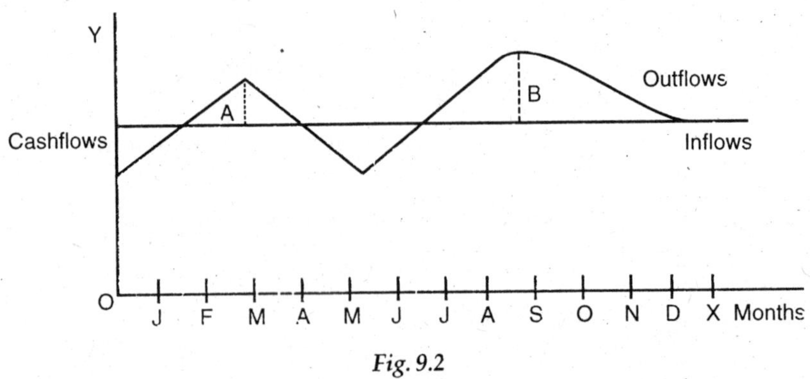

Fig. 9.2

(4) Where operating income falls short, the budget has to provide for income generation through other sources like investments in those periods of shortfall — operating income and non-operating income are to be compensating and offset-ting.

(5) To avoid excess liquidity situations and also shortfalls of cash in the business concern.

(6) To provide for seasonality in sales, and inflows through study of past trends and for possible bad debts or delay in receivables — a contingent provision of 10% on either side of the budget for ensuring liquidity of the firm is necessary. The liquidity and profitability have a trade off and the treasury manager has to strike an optimum point for trade off.

Principles of Cash Management

(1) Minimum cash required to be held at any point.

(2) Cash sales increase cash component of working capital and should be used to make cash payments as they fall due.

(3) Credit sales may lead to book debts or bills. While book debts have to be tactically realised without becoming bad debts, bills will be realised when due and care in respect of both is necessary. When these are realised, cash is also increased.

(4) While the above funds should be credited to bank's cash credit account, if they are by cheques, they are to be ploughed into cash pool if received in cash and used for payments due on a daily or weekly basis.

(5) The tendency to keep excess balances on the one hand and possible shortfall in cash on the other should be avoided by proper planning. Here comes the importance of collection procedures.

(6) The minimum cash required is known by past experience of a study of past few year's net cash payments and net cash balances maintained each month on a monthly basis in the past.

(7) If the cash shortage is expected, as per the budget estimates then cheque payments may be encouraged and even insisted. While receiving, they may insist on cash, but while paying, they may pay by cheque only. Cheque will give breathing time of a few days, while bills will give more time of one to three months.

(8) Improvement in cash receipts can be planned, when the budget indicates a likely shortfall, through better inventory management and more efficient portfolio management. Here comes the importance of quality of assets.

(9) The watch words of CRASH Management of cash in working capital are the minimum holding of cash, increased cash sales, and aggressive collection of receivables.

The above principles of efficient cash management should be scrupulously adhered to by Treasury Management.

Planning for Short-Term Funds
Cash Flow Statement

Sources of Cash	Uses of Cash
Net profits before taxes	Increase in Book debts
Borrowings from Directors	Increase in Inventories
Deferred payments	Repayment of deposits or
Public Deposits	loans, borrowing, etc.
Depreciation provisions	Increase in Receivables
Development rebate reserves	Tax payments
Sales on cash	Dividend payments
Bills maturing	Interest on loans
Receivables paid	Repayment of deferred
Sale of fixed Assets	payments due, etc.
Sale of Investments	

Bank Overdrafts and borrowings in the form of public deposits will fill the gap between the above two.

Cash Forecast and Budget

When we prepare statement of inflows and outflows on the basis of our past experience and present trends we have to forecast the cash flows. The treasury manager has to forecast both cash flows and funds flows. The difference between them is that the former includes only the cash accruals or outflows, while the latter includes cash and all funds in the form of credits, economic values, claims on money or investments, etc.

Cash Budget includes the (i) Cash receipts from sales and debts, (ii) receipts from non-cash operations, like sale of investments and capital gains, (iii) sale of fixed assets and (iv) any dues from investors, employees, etc. On the payment side it includes, (v) payments on account of operations, (vi) Adhoc payments due for royalties, dividends, income tax etc. (vii) unavoidable capital expenditure, (viii) any payments due to employees, investors, etc.

Cash Budget Proforma

		Monthwise		
		Jan.	**Feb.**	**March**
(1)	Opening Balances of cash.			
(2)	Cash Sales.			
(3)	Cash from Credit sales made earlier.			
I.	**Total Cash Receipts**			
	Payments for operations (A)			
	Purchases :			
	Purchases on Credit earlier but paid in cash			
	Purchase in cash			
	Selling and administrative expenses			
	Other payments (Non-operational) (B)			
	Bank instalments			
	Hire purchase instalments			
	Others, if any			
II.	**Total Cash Payments (A + B)**			
	Closing Cash Balances (I – II)			
	Expectation for Forecast of			
	(1) Sales			
	(2) Purchases.			

Objective of Cash Management

As referred to earlier cash has actual and potential uses; it is useful for transactions and payments for contingencies. It satisfies the psychological feeling of wealthiness and comfort to be able to meet any contingencies. The companies and firms keep generally sufficiently large cash reserves for contingencies. Even banks and financial institutions lack in planning and efficiency and waste a large proportion of resources in the form of cash. This is because of undue weight to that physical and psychological feeling of comfort, which is generated out of actual possession of cash. Besides, cash being most liquid it is preferred to other financial assets. But it has no income generation and hence unprofitable to hold cash. Cash has alternative uses and has potential income generating power. So there are two opposing forces — one to keep as much cash as possible and the other to keep as little cash as permissible. There is a clash of two opposing forces — one with high liquidity and zero profits and the other with low liquidity and high profits. The efficient manager has to weigh the alternatives, plan the forthcoming cash uses and generate as much surplus of cash as possible which has to be channelled into income generating assets. It is this movement of Cash into Credit Instruments from M1 to M2, M3 and M4 etc., and Money Market Instruments and short-term instruments which generates money market operations.

Thus, cash is money and liquidity and it has value and is scarce. Its proper use is to generate cash surpluses and activate idle balances by conversion of cash into near money assets which are income earning and to increase the returns in an every growing fashion. All this needs the expertise of a treasury manager.

Target of Micro Cash Management

Of the above concepts of M1 to M4 most individual spending units use M1 as it is the most comprehensive definition encompassing important functions of money, namely, medium of exchange and measure of value. How can we economise in the use of M1? Its components are coins, cash and chequing deposits with banks (both savings and current accounts). Coins and currency is one category, which can be economised by conversion of it into deposits with banks. The second category can be economised by conversion of bank money into near money in the form of fixed deposits with banks and instruments in the money market and other financial markets. By conversion of cash into bank money, some interest is earned where no positive return is possible on cash. By conversion of bank money into money market instruments of short-term maturity, a higher return and larger income are possible, but liquidity is sacrificed.

By a process of generating cash surpluses through economising in the use of cash, cash management can reduce costs and increase revenue. Cash surpluses can be generated through (a) synchronising the timing of income with expenditures and (b) matching the quantum of income with expenditure on a regular basis. Economy in the use of cash is possible through planning of inflows and outflows in terms of quantum of such flows over a period and secondly by synchronising the timing of such outflows in accordance with inflows.

Generating cash surpluses is not the end in itself. These surpluses should be used for investment in near money assets of short duration and by lending to other spending units who are in deficit. Thereby these surpluses which would have earned no return or a negative return would now not only earn a positive return but with a possibility of maximising returns as investments extend into money market assets of increasing maturity.

Micro cash management involves economising the use of cash, which is scarce and channelling the cash surpluses, so generated into income earning assets of varying maturities in the money market, thereby earning positive net returns on such cash and yet ensure liquidity as and when necessary. Management should aim at minimising the cash use and maximising the income earnings, out of such cash. This is the quintessence of the theory and practice of cash management. Here the trade offs involved are : the more the liquidity, the less is the profitability — the larger the cash holding, the less is the income earning assets. The less the liquidity, the greater is the chance of becoming insolvent.

Managing Liquidity

Liquidity means cash or nearness to cash. Management of receivables matching of inflows and outflows of cash, referred to earlier is the objective of treasury manager. The liquidity of the firm is safeguarded by such matching and also by keeping some funds in cash always, which should be minimum to meet any exigencies. This matching has two aspects : (1) one in terms of quantum of flows and (2) another in terms of the time period of flows. Receipts and payments being a daily affair, assets and investments, including capital and current account should be of such maturities that some always mature every month. In between months, the current sale income or non-operational income will meet the outflows. Management expertise involves matching of these inflows and outflows in terms of timing as also in quantum.

The mismatches are to be met by arranging for trade credits, bank borrowing and bill finance. If there are excess inflows, they are deployed profitably by investing in money market or in short term lending in I.C.D. segment or any other near money assets.

It is important that any corporate unit has to maintain its liquidity and solvency. For this purpose, sufficient cash holding along with a proper matching of inflows and outflows is necessary. Besides, the current assets should be nearly two times or more than current liabilities, so that any liabilities as they fall due can be met by conversion of current assets into cash and maintain the liquidity of the company.

Mismatch of Assets and Liabilities

It is in this context that matching of assets and liabilities is necessary and expedient. By matching, one means that the maturity mix in (current account current assets and liabilities) and in capital account (fixed assets and long-term borrowings) should be such that maturity of liabilities mix should be similar to that of asset mix.

The mismatch is possible, if short-term funds are diverted to long-term investments and long-term funds are used for working capital purposes. In the case of corporate units, equity is too small and borrowed long-term funds are too large which will result in a mismatch of owned funds to borrowed funds leading to a high risk scenario. Such mismatches in the current asset-liability mix are not advisable.

Mismatches in the current account also create a greater risk of illiquidity for the firm. These result from long credits for buyers while suppliers give short credits. Mismatch may also occur due to differences in maturities in the items of current assets and current liabilities.

Inflows and outflows of cash and funds should match.

(Receipts – Payments = Lending – Borrowing)

The above formula states that the excess receipts are invested for an income or lent outside, while deficit in receipts is met by borrowing — through private credits and bank finance. In all those cases of mismatch, the time element and quantum flow involved should be kept in mind by the treasury manager.

Asset-Liability Mix

The treasury manager has to operate with a view to balance inflows with outflows on the one hand and on the other, keep the asset-liability mix balanced. Thus, a company which has assets of long duration can have liabilities of short duration. There can be a mismatch leading to problems of illiquidity, operational inflexibility and difficulty of borrowing from banks or FIs. Assets can be short-term and medium when liabilities should be of long-term. The rate of interest or yields on short-term and long-term will play a part in the development of the asset-liability mix.

Examples of Mismatch

Thus, the treasury manager is operating in Money Market with most of his funds tied for 90 days to 180 days, when his liabilities are maturing in 30 days. A treasury operator in government securities has some investments in 90 day treasury bills and 10 year government bonds. In between if any liability is maturing, the company will face financial crisis. The investments should be spread in a uniform pattern of maturities, say 6 months, 9 months, one year and so up the line. The same principles of the spread of the assets will apply whether the treasury manager is operating in government securities, money market or forex market. But, more scientific planning can be adopted for making corresponding maturities of assets for all maturing liabilities or expected maturities of liabilities. Strict adherence to proper maturity mix may sometimes conflict with the objective of risk minimisation or maximisation of returns. A proper trade off and a judicious planning are necessary for achieving a workable mix, if not an ideal mix.

Treasury Manager and ALM

ALM means Asset-Liability Management which in essence means the management of entire balance sheet. In the latest liberalised economic scenario with freedom to operate in any market by the treasury manager there is abundant scope for him to increase profitability by managing properly the asset liability mix. For this purpose, continuous monitoring of both current and fixed assets and identifying the mismatch in the assets and liabilities, in terms of quantum and maturities is necessary. The assets composition and liabilities composition can be changed to (1) match the maturities (2) meet the gap or deficit in any maturity period and (3) utilise the surpluses profitably in the money market. He should identify the interest sensitive assets or liabilities — say too much of cash or low yielding bonds; when interest rates are rising and operate on them in a manner, that he can take advantage of interest rate changes and emerging new financial instruments and new opportunities.

Gap Analysis

The Treasury Manager has to classify the asset into Rate Sensitive Assets (RSA) and Rate Insensitive Assets (RISA) and corresponding liabilities. The gap between rate sensitive assets and liabilities (RSA – RSL) has to be identified and the gap to be filled in by high interest yielding assets or low interest liabilities. He should also aim at filling the gap between RSA and RSL, so that the fixed interest assets are financed by fixed interest liabilities so that the interest rate risk is lowered. Similarly floating rate assets should be matched by floating rate liabilities. Gap analysis and ALM should go hand in hand for the manager to take full advantage of changes in demand and supply conditions on markets and interest rate changes.

Managing Receivables

Receivables arise out of credit sales of any economic unit. If sales are made on short-term, credits and dues are settled in time, the payables can also be settled by the company in time and there will be no problem of illiquidity. But if the debtors take longer time, then the level of book debts will go on rising, working capital funds are blocked up causing scarcity of funds for current operations.

There are many methods by which the average period of receivables can be brought down by the finance manager. The receivables as a ratio of sales will indicate the extent of credit, period and the sales strategy. The average period of receivables can be brought down by (1) more cash sales (2) less credit sales (3) efficient and quick collection system (4) improve the quality of credit sales in the sense of making credit sales only to highly creditworthy buyers and (5) reduce the period of credit. Here credit risk assessment is necessary.

Without allowing sales to fall, if the above methods are adopted, quality of output or products is maintained and improved and after sales service is efficient and prompt, then the average period of receivables can be brought down, without impairing the profits of the company. The date on receivables and sales should be over a period to design a strategy to improve the sales and at the same time reduce the period of receivables.

Average Period of Receivables

Receivables period is important for knowing the bank credit and trade credits required by the company. It also reflects the efficiency of sales strategy and collection strategy and the overall competency of the management. The period of credit allowed is ascertained first by dividing the credit sales by 12, which will give average monthly credit sales. If the average monthly credit sales is used to divide the receivables figure, we get average collection period.

Example

ABC company has sales of total Rs. 4.5 crores of which credit sales is Rs. 2.4 crores.

Average monthly credit sales is $\frac{2.4}{12}$ = Rs. 20 lakhs.

The total receivable are Rs. 50 lakhs.

Period of receivables is 50/20 = 2.5 months ($2\frac{1}{2}$ months).

This figure can be brought down by quicker collection process or reducing the total credit sales etc., which was referred to earlier.

At this stage, it is necessary to set out the terms by which receivable data are set out by various corporates, namely, credit bills/advance payments/sundry dues/receivables/sundry debtors/account receivables.

Credit collection period is defined as : No. of days = 360/credit sales during the year ÷ Account Receivables.

The smaller the number of days, the higher will be the efficiency of credit collection of the firm. This ratio helps in planning for matching the credit inflows with outflows.

"Banks do not advance against receivables beyond 180 days maturity or outstanding for more than 6 months. Receivables in the form advances given to sales men, employees or for suppliers are not counted as receivables by the bankers but as advances or loans. If receivables or acceptances or bills have extended credit periods, they are not acceptable to the banks again for bank finance.

Liquidity Crunch

Book debts are good as they are self-liquidating, so long as they are of creditworthy clients. Book debts outstanding for longer periods of 3 to 6 months and those given to unknown parties or doubtful of realisations are not generally acceptable to banks for lending to the corporates. If a large component of book debts of a unit is of those categories and they fail to pay, the problem of liquidity crunch will arise. The companies have to be extremely cautious in the credit sales and given to known and creditworthy parties only so that liquidity of the company is not impaired. Liquidity is also not impaired, if there are no party-wise or drawee-wise limits of such credit. If credit rating of the parties or debtors is not considered and extensions are granted for making payments, liquidity crunch may crop up again.

Bank advances against hypothecation of book debts, which are good, are granted after keeping a margin on them. Overdrafts are also granted on the security of trade bills. The documentary bills, cheques, clean bills of good parties are discounted by banks, as the bills are paid by drawees on due dates and cheques by drawers and are thus self liquidated except when they are not dependable parties. But as banks keep margins and examine the nature of the parties they take their own precautions and exclude the over due bills and supply bills. They extend need based credit on the basis of receivables and bills, which are acceptable and creditworthy. The supply bills drawn for supplies by first rate companies, Government and Semi-Government bodies are accepted by the banks, for finance. Generally, banks try to avoid these supply bills, as some of them may be accommodation bills. In the case of deferred receivables, involving sales on long-term repayment basis, if they are for indigenous machineries, the banks finance them and get refinance from IDBI.

The credit policy as laid down by RBI has directed banks to reduce cash credit component and increase loan component, so as to enforce financial discipline on borrowers and reduce their dependance on banks. Now the bank policy is to encourage the credit worthy companies to secure finance through commercial paper (C.P.) issued in the market. At the same time security is less important and needs are more important for bank finance as the banks are asked to provide need based finance, but at the same time, this is to be given to the parties which are creditworthy. Creditworthiness of the project is more important than the creditworthiness of the party.

Thus, the corporate units have to take care to see that they are creditworthy and that their book credits are good and provision is made for bad and doubtful debts. The banks have to see to all these factors, before giving an overdraft or cash credit limit. Sometimes they take second mortgage of fixed assets for granting such limits. Banks consider the financial position of the company in a broader perspective through a study of their annual and monthly sales, average period of credit enjoyed from suppliers and agents, peak level and seasonality in sales, proportion of book debts in Balance Sheet, credit rating of debtors, collection procedures and management efficiency and a host of other financial factors.

Managing Payables

Sundry Creditors arise out of supply of stock in trade and are a source of short-term funds to the company. They include bills payable, trade acceptances, trade creditors, advance payments received, which all come under the category of payables, which are short-term credits and categorised as sundry creditors in the Balance Sheet on the liabilities side.

To be eligible to receive such credits from other than banks, the economic unit has to prove its credibility, integrity and financial soundness. As the bank finance is scarce and more expensive units depend more on sundry creditors. But it is unhealthy practice to have sundry creditors higher than sundry debtors. The company may get into debt trap if the creditors are more and powerful while debtors are shy and do not pay in time. To keep up its commitments on creditors it has to keep quality of book debts high and arrange for bank finance to meet the emerging gap between them. The gap between the sundry creditors and sundry debtors is the amount, expected to be taken care by the banks or from the market through CPs, or public deposits..

By following a Judicious Credit Policy one can reduce the length of credit period extended by the creditors, which is taken into account by the banks in granting credit. Funds can be got from banks for unpaid stocks and diverted into other activities without making payment for stocks supplied.

Transaction Period

When the company sells through the distributors there is a time gap between the sale and receipt by them and their payment to the company. This time gap is called transaction period. If paid in cheque it takes a few days of say two or three days. If paid in cash it is one or two days. But if payment is by credit/bills, then the sight bill gives time of 10 to 15 days grace period. If sold by usance bills, the time period may vary from 30 days to 90 days. The finance manager has to calculate the weighted average time period by taking the time period for each category and weighting it by the amount of sales under that category.

To give an example

			Weights
Cash sales	:	30%	0.3
Cheque sales	:	30%	0.3
Credit sales	:	40%	0.4
Total Weights			1.0

Calculation of weighted transaction period :

Category	Weights	Average Time Period	Weighted Average
Cash	0.3	1 day	0.3
Cheque	0.3	3 days	0.9
Credits	0.4	30 days	12.0
			13.2

Roughly 13 to 15 days is weighted period for transaction (about 2 weeks)

The transaction period is useful to estimate the working capital finance required by the company. The finance manager has to arrange the financing of it for 15 days through trade credits, private credits and bank credit, with the proportion of each of them depending on the cost and availability of them, so that the company can have least cost combination of financing them.

This concept is also useful to determine the efficiency of operation. To reduce this period is efficiency and if the period exceeds 180 days, as in the case of some state governments and semi-government undertakings and departmental undertaking it is inefficiency. Secondly, the need for external sources (banks for example) is reduced if exact matching of average period of receivables to that of payables is secured. The ideal situation is cash and carry when there will be no creditors and debtors which is not possible in real life. But when there are both creditors and debtors, then the company has to manage the transaction periods of both in a manner that they synchronise as far as possible. If that is not possible, the next best alternative is to plan for a gap which is manageable and as low as possible, and plan accordingly to finance the gap by bank credit — bill finance or cash credit or by overdraft from banks. If exact synchronising is achieved, inflows tally with the outflows both in quantum and time, then bank finance for receivables is not needed as they are met by payables.

Managing Inventory Periods

Inventory is the stock of goods, either raw-materials, semi-finished goods or finished goods. Every business need some inventories and these are part of current assets of the company. The components of inventory are — indigenous and imported raw-materials, stores, spares and supplies of stationery, office supplies, goods in process, semi-finished goods and finished products. As production requires continuous supplies of raw-materials, spares and inputs, inventory is essential for production. Inventory is also necessary for sales, as some stocks of goods are to be supplied at various centres as and when required because the demand may be recurrent or seasonal or irregular and if supplies of output have to meet this demand, it has to be stocked in anticipation of demand, otherwise sales will suffer.

Period of Inventory Holding

The objective of any firm is to reduce the cost of holding inventory and maximise profits. The best alternative is to have stocks which are just adequate for sales in any period and that will lead to least cost situation. But as that is not possible, firms stock the output in anticipation of sales.

$$\text{Ratio of turnover of Inventory} = \frac{\text{Cost of Sales}}{\text{Inventory Cost}}$$

$$\text{Or} = \frac{\text{Net Sales} - \text{Operating Profit}}{\text{Value of Inventory}} \text{ (Which is the cost of sales only)}$$

Note: Both should be valued in the same rupees.

This ratio indicates how funds invested in inventory are turned over. The higher the turnover, the better is the inventory management and less is the cost due to the smaller amount of money blocked in inventory. This ratio of the inventory turnover can also be used to find the period of inventory holding.

$$\text{Average holding period} = \frac{\text{Days in a year}}{\text{Inventory Turnover}}$$

Example :

Assume sales are for Rs. 50 lakhs in a year (cost of sales)

Inventory in the beginning Rs. 30 lakhs

Inventory at the end Rs. 20 lakhs

Turnover of Inventory

$$\text{Average inventory in the year} = \frac{(50) \text{ sales}}{(30\text{–}20)} = \frac{50}{10}$$

$$\text{Ratio of Turnover} = 5 \text{ times}$$

$$\text{Average stocking period} = \frac{360}{5} = 72 \text{ days}$$

(72 days or 2 months and 12 days)

The lower this average stocking period, the more efficient is the financial management and larger will be the profitability, *caeteris paribus.*

Similarly, the turnover of raw materials work in progress and of finished stocks can be worked out as :

$$\text{Turnover of raw materials} = \frac{\text{Annual Consumption}}{\text{Average stock of raw materials}}$$

$$\text{Turnover of work in progress} = \frac{\text{Annual production}}{\text{Average work in progress–stock}}$$

$$\text{Turnover of finished goods stock} = \frac{\text{Cost of goods sold}}{\text{Average stock of finished goods}}$$

The holding periods of stock are seen from these data and these periods, vary from the nature of the goods, technology used, state of market demand and sales strategy and a host of other factors.

Inventory Management

Management of inventory has two principles to be observed : (1) These should be adequate for continuing sales without any break, (2) These should be low enough to save the cost of holding them. The objective is to maximise profits out of minimum working capital, sunk in the inventory. The techniques of inventory management should be known to the Management. Overstocking and under stocking are to be avoided by a study of the past trends and industry norms.

Inventory – Cash – Sales Cycle

Operating cycle is 2 months (60 days)

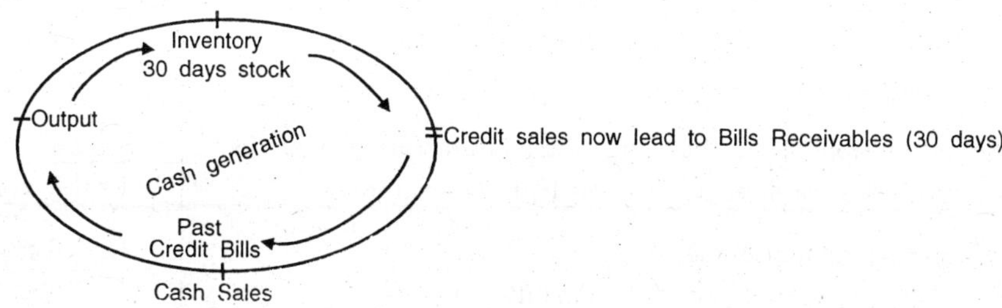

Fig. 9.3

Normally, banks are reluctant to finance inventory stock. The larger the credit stock, the larger is the need for bank finance. Cash sale on Commission or discounts if practiced will reduce the profits. If the stock are undervalued, it may be because the company wants to build secret reserves and show less profits.

One symptom of inefficiency is over stocking of goods, as the value of stock involves cost and over stocking leads to higher costs. Over stocking of scarce raw materials or parts is common, but speculative over stocking is risky. Sound financing and healthy practices do not allow such malpractices and banks inventory valuation is on cost price basis or market price basis.

Stocking requires efficient handling for efficient distribution, after sales service and for reputation and credibility. Losses may arise due to falling prices and costs, or from obsolescence, improper storage etc. Proper internal control and reporting mechanism has to be developed in each company for storing just minimum adequate stocks. The treasury manager has to keep himself informed of the costs in maintaining a given level of stock, wastages, etc. involved for his planning of short-term finance.

Bank Finance for Inventory

To a limit, banks finance inventory on the basis of cost price or market price, whichever is lower. The stocks being tangible assets, hypothecation or pledge is taken for lending against stocks. Banks give guarantee or letter of credit to suppliers for and on behalf of money from their clients varying from 20% to 50%, depending on the client's credit rating and the nature of the commodity. Pledge involves that the goods are in the custody of the banks which is not favoured, if there is a quick turnover of sales. In the latter case hypothecation is preferred as the custody of stock is with the customer. Sometimes clean advances are given to the customer if he is highly creditworthy and a well-known party.

Calculation of Working Capital Requirements

The preparation of the working capital estimate is shown below, for illustration as this will facilitate the Finance Manager or Treasury Manager to plan accordingly. Suppose the average credit period is 2 months then the calculation is as follows :

Example :	**Rs. lakhs**
2 months raw-material requirements	40
2 months consumable stores	20
2 months value of stock in process	20
2 months stock of finished goods	60
$2\frac{1}{2}$ months value of receivable	30
(average period of receivables is $2\frac{1}{2}$ months calculated before)	
One month provision for administrative and manufacturing expenses	10
The above periods are assumed for simplicity in the example	Rs. 1.8 crore
Total working capital requirement is	Rs. 1.8 crore
Deduct 2 months trade credit available and bills payables	Rs. 0.4
Deduct liquid surplus (current assets minus current liabilities)	Rs. 0.4
Net working capital requirements	Rs. 1.0 crore

The above time periods are arrived from the average storing period of raw-materials or consumables, namely, average stock of raw-materials / consumables divided by average daily consumption of them during the year. The average processing period is average stock in process divided by the daily cost of finished goods during the year. The average storage period of finished goods is the average stock of them divided by the cost of daily finished goods sold during the year.

Double Finance

Some companies get credit from suppliers and also draw bank credit to finance the inventory. This type of finance is avoided by banks. For this the Chore Committee (1979) recommendation was the use of drawee bills by suppliers who will be paid by the banks directly, namely, to suppliers. Daheja Committee (1969) and Tandon Committee (1975) have drawn attention to provision of double finance and divertion of funds by borrowers/clients of banks. To avoid this the concept of working capital gap (WCG) has been developed by Tandon Committee. The WCG is arrived at after taking into account creditors for purchases and other current liabilities, other than bank borrowings. At present, these items are deducted from the total working capital requirements and as such double finance is not possible. Banks are not allowed to provide bridge loans now to finance and investment companies. They are expected to monitor the end use of all loans beyond a limit. The cash credit component of total credit to the borrower is now reduced to 40% in 1996 for advances above Rs. 20 crores and this was later replaced by discretionary finance by banks. As part of discipline on borrowers, the total loan component is now given as advance.

The bank will first assess the average length of credit extended by non-bank creditors. The following formula is used for calculation of the length of this credit.

$$\text{Length of credit} = \frac{\text{Average creditors and bills payable}}{\text{Average daily credit purchases in the year}}$$

This will help the banks to making projections about the amount of credit that may be made available from these sources in future. Banks deduct the quantum of sundry creditors and advance payments to the company in making bank finance available to them. The net bank finance for working capital is arrived therefrom.

Estimation of Working Capital Requirement

Items for which working capital is needed are (1) Materials, (2) Wages (3) Overheads. In respect of materials, required quantity and their cost are to be estimated for (i) raw-materials (ii) work in progress (iii) finished goods (iv) credit to debtors minus credit from creditors.

In respect of wages, the amounts paid in various departments for work in progress and for finished goods, has to be added together for all categories of workmen.

In respect of overheads as also incidentally for maintenance, repairs, etc. additional expenses are to be added together.

All the above components are to be estimated month-wise and quarter-wise for forecasting and planning the working capital requirements.

Illustration – Case Study :

The company named "SMART" has to estimate the working capital requirements, with given data as shown below :

Budgeted Sales = Rs. 2.6 lakhs (26,000 Units)		
Cost per unit of Raw Materials	-	Rs. 3/-
Cost per unit of Labour	-	Rs. 4/-
Cost per unit of Overhead	-	Rs. 2/-
Cost per unit of profit	-	Rs. 1/-
Total Cost per unit	-	Rs. 10/-

From the past experience, raw materials are held for three weeks and finished goods for two weeks. Factory processing will take 3 weeks, suppliers will give 5 week credit while the customers will take 8 week credit.

Solution for the above case :

Calculation is by weeks with 52 weeks in a year.

Inventories :

Stock of raw materials	$= 26000 \text{ units} \times 3/52 \times 3$	
(Processing period is 3 weeks and stocks for 3 weeks)		= Rs. 4,500
Raw materials	$= 26000 \times 3/52 \times 3$	= Rs. 4,500
Labour	$= 26000 \times 3/52 \times 4$	= Rs. 6,000
Overheads	$= 26000 \times 3/52 \times 2$	= Rs. 3,500

Stock of Finished goods :		
Raw materials	$= 26000 \times 2/52 \times 3$	= Rs. 3,000
Labour	$= 26000 \times 2/52 \times 4$	= Rs. 4,000
Overheads	$= 26000 \times 2/52 \times 2$	= Rs. 2,000
Sundry debtors	$= 26{,}000 \times 8/52 \times 9$	= Rs. 36,000
(8 week credit is given and cost per unit is Rs. 9)		
	Total so far	Rs. 63,000
Minus Sundry creditors $26000 \times 5/52 \times 3$		= Rs. 7,500
(5 week credit is taken and cost per unit of raw material is Rs. 3)		Rs. 55,500
Net working capital required is Rs. 55,500/-		

Excess Liquidity

If these funds are secured from bank finance or other private credit, there can be full finance for working capital purposes and as per the budget planned. But sometimes, deficits might arise due to cost overruns, which has to be planned by the treasury manager to finance from contingency overdrafts from banks or public deposits or some loans from directors. There can also be surpluses on the planned amount, due to various causes. Surpluses might also arise due to new issues floated recently, extra-operating and non-operating income such as through investments or capital gains, sale of capital assets, or the savings of employees in pension and gratuity funds. The treasury manager should have contingency plans to utilise such surpluses profitably by investments in money market or other short-term investments.

Bank Finance Norms

Inventory and receivables comprise the bulk of the current assets. Norms were laid down by the Tandon Committee for holding periods of inventory and receivables, industry-wise. As per this Committee recommendations, banks started financing only that part of the inventory and receivables, which are not financed by private credit, and the non-core part of inventory not financed by long-term loans. The core part of the inventory is to be financed by term loans. The banks calculate the requirements of working capital finance as per the above norms for holding inventory and receivables and decide the non-core part of inventory for calculating the working capital limit to the units. The actual valuation of inventory is on a cost price or market price basis, whichever is lower and the inventory holding of the company will not be the basis of fixing Net Bank Finance Limit for the unit.

As per the latest RBI policy, banks have been given discretion in lending but they would observe the lending discipline of asking the units to follow the industry-wise norms for inventory and receivables, submission of quarterly data on their sales, bills receivables, and other current liabilities. The banks are free now to use their discretion on the inventory portion, and the receivables portion which they should finance under working capital limits. The finance manager would have to find alternative methods of finance, if they need more funds than what has been granted by the bank. Here the finance manager has to estimate the total funds needed and the bank finance granted and plan for least cost combination of other sources for total funds required. More recently, there is a well developed market for Commercial paper, Bill discounting, Term money, Certificates of deposits, etc. either as sources or uses of funds for the creditworthy companies, with which Treasury Manager has to be familiar.

Methods of Financing Working Capital

The financing of current requirements should not normally be by long-term sources but some business enterprises and industry units resort to this practice. In the case of many institutions in the capital market, the bills due to be paid and moneys due to the company may not synchronise. There is a gap thus arising out of differences in timing of receipts and payments and their quantities.

To reduce this gap is one problem of the treasury manager; second and more important problem is the least cost method of financing it. To reduce the gap itself involves a cost. This cost is to be compared to the cost of financing the gap, say through bank credits, public deposits, etc. The management expertise lies in planning well, maturity wise amounts involved in receivables and payables, so as to minimise the reliance on the bank credit and reduce costs and increase efficiency.

After making provisions in the form of cash and current account balances with banks for liquidity, the problem of filling up the gap in working capital has to be attended and that requires the expertise of working capital management in any company.

Sources of Finance

For any company, the normal sources of working capital finance are as follows :

(a) Bank credits,

(b) Trade credits,

(c) Intercorporate funds, bills discounting or rediscounting, etc.,

(d) Medium-term funds through deposits, term-loans from banks etc., diverted for short-term purposes,

(e) External commercial borrowing (ECBs).

In the case of finance companies, trade credits are moneys in the pipeline to be paid to companies, specialists, brokers, service agencies and other intermediaries in the capital market. Many finance companies including the mutual funds and merchant bankers depend on money market instruments and short-term investments for easy liquidity and conversion into cash. Their holding of cash is generally less than one percent of their current assets. In some companies, cash goes up to 5% of the current assets.

As referred to earlier, the major source of short-term funds for working capital purposes is bank credit. The banks provide cash credit loans or advances, overdraft facility, or bills discounting facility; most of them are of short-term nature.

The finance companies specialising in lease, hire-purchase and housing finance depend more on long-term funds, in view of the nature of their activities. Mutual funds, merchant bankers and investment companies depend more on short-term funds from public and banks. Having a large component of their current assets in money market instruments, their short-term requirements are generally met by discounting bills, commercial paper or treasury bills, etc. The details of money market instruments are discussed in a separate chapter.

MEASURES OF EFFICIENCY

Bills receivable is the first indicator of efficiency in Credit Management. This depends upon the management's credit and collection policies. The larger the proportion of credit sales the larger will be the bills receivables. Of the total sales, what is the proportion in the form of loans, advances, bills receivables etc. Of the total debts in these forms, what is the proportion of bad debts? Is that level comparable to the industry average ? These and other questions have to be examined by the treasury manager.

Secondly, what is the maturity pattern of such debts? Assuming that these debts are all due to credit sales, the maturity or due dates will reveal the spread of credit lines, period wise, weekly, monthly etc. Removing the estimated proportion of bad debts, what is the repayment or inflow schedule of moneys due. The bad debts losses are to be written off by the Management and trends in receivables are to be kept under constant watch and control. At the same time sales should not suffer. But promotion of sales through credits has to be kept under close study. As a marketing strategy, should the management encourage credit sales indefinitely ? What is the safe and prudent limit ? What alternative strategies can replace credit sales by say discounts, coupons, etc. Efficiency is judged by the proper spread of maturity of debts on the same pattern as the maturity of creditors.

Thirdly, the proportion of credit sales to total sales should be subject to close scrutiny and review by top management. Credit management and collection function should be kept under the same authority in a firm, namely, the Finance Manager.* Efficiency of collection of debts is judged by the ratio of credit sales to total sales which should be optimum, so that sales increase without increasing the credit risk to the firm.

The current ratio or quick ratio in the company has to be judged relative to others in the industry. The credits receivable and credit sales are part of the strategy of (1) Marketing and (2) Credit budgeting. These also reflect the management efficiency.

Credit budgeting involves the following elements.

(a) Proportion of total sales on credit.

(b) Cash discounts available on sales.

(c) Scrutiny of credit risk in credit sales.

(d) The component of loans and advances in current assets and the fixing of the optimum limit for them.

The company's credit management and sales strategy are closely linked. The policy of cash sales will not always succeed if the industry practices are sales on credit. Then the question of duration of credit comes up. The longer the credit period, the larger is the possibility of bad debts. But if the credit duration is unduly low, the sales and profitability may be low. An optimum mix should be the management strategy. This requires the joint efforts of marketing manager and finance manager.

---

* *Management of Working Capital* — Chapter VI Harbanslal Verma — Deep & Deep Publications.

To reduce bad debts but at the same time increase sales, duration can be reduced by proper policy of discounts on payments before the due date. Cash discounts can increase sales, reduce collection period, carrying costs and receivables. The policy of a company selling capital goods plant, project construction, exports etc., will have to be different. It has credit risks to be insured by EXIM Bank or ECGC.

More importantly, credit sales should be highly selective and discretionary. The clients are to be evaluated for creditworthiness and their integrity and dependability. In a service industry, credit sales are more prevalent as payment in terms of brokerage, underwriting commission and issue management charges etc., would all be on credit terms ranging from 3 to 6 months. So the receivables are generally higher in relative terms as much as loans and advances. Amounts receivable for services and advances paid to other specialists and suppliers may be generally high in the service sector.

Cash Vs. Credit Management

Cash and credit management are closely interlinked. Cash flows depend on the proportion of credit sales. Besides, the spread of maturity periods in receivables will decide the cash flows and their volatility or regularity.**

Cash as a proportion of current assets is generally low in a service industry like financial sector. In many cases it is less than 1% of the current assets, but in a mutual fund, where repurchase obligations arise on a daily basis or in a brokerage firm, the cash component may be higher. In a manufacturing firm, the cash component may at any time fluctuate from 5 to 20%. But in efficient finance companies, it ranged from 1 to 5%.

As referred to earlier the requirements of cash will vary from company to company within a given industry and from industry to industry. The activities and production lines and sales, level of sales, costs of production, credits given and taken and a host of other factors determine the level of required cash, by any firm.

Inventory Control System

In any control system, the minimum and maximum quantity levels are fixed by proper planning on the basis of past data and forecast for the future. The re-order point and economic order quantity are also fixed in the budgetary process.

The maximum quantity is the lowest level that the stock can be permitted to go, and still avoid possible shortage. Similarly, the maximum quantity is fixed beyond which it is a wastage to hold stocks. The re-order point consists of the average volume of use during the normal procurement time and an additional quantity for a safety net. Economic order quantity (EOQ) is the quantity which balances the costs of carrying a stock with the benefits of economies in order size. The bigger the order, the lower will be the cost of ordering. But the carrying costs will rise with the size of order. EOQ is that size which minimises the total inventory costs which include the buying or ordering costs and carrying costs. When these two costs, namely, ordering costs and carrying costs are equal, then we get an E.O.Q. But the companies have also to take into account the standard quantity of inventory which is used to replenish, when the balances drop to order point. The standard order quantity is similar to E.O.Q. at which orders are made to replenish the stock. This standard quantity is fixed on the basis of the rate of consumption per

** Bannerjee — Cash Management, The World Press Pvt. Ltd.

month, carrying costs, vendor's discount and risk of loss due to shortage, deterioration or obsolescence etc.

Normally, companies follow a range within which they keep the inventory and that is based on the past experience and on cost benefit analysis. Excess inventory is a wastage caused by poor purchase administration, poor materials management, of high discounts on large orders, expectations of scarcity and unwarranted prudence. The treasury manager has to set up a monitoring system for the quantity of stock, the order point, the re-order size, the flow of the stock during a period. The review period for the manager is the number of months within which E.O.Q. is exhausted. The planning of inventories should be to keep stock equal to a number of months requirement as calculated above plus a safety net amount.

Internal control and review of inventory is part of inventory management. The objective is to minimise costs and maximise profit. For this objective, the planning involves the fixing of minimum stocks to be kept always, the reorder point, E.O.Q. etc., after taking into account the size of E.O.Q., the practices in the industry and the distribution network strategy. To keep the carrying costs and order costs low and to secure the benefit of continued availability of stocks for sale, the purchase order system is designed by the management. During the regular periods, review and monitoring of the stocks is to be maintained through a regular reporting system on a weekly basis and internal control and audit is to be strictly enforced by the management.

Summary

This chapter sets out the management's role in setting out a financial plan both for short-term and long-term needs and then defines the short-term needs. In short-term finance, cash is the most important component and as such cash management, and the role of cash, and factors influencing the cash demand are set out. What is efficient cash management and the proper principles of cash management are also dealt with.

Sources and uses of cash and funds and the need for forecasting the cash needs and proportion of a cash budget are explained. The objectives of and the target of cash management are then explained. As part of cash management, liquidity mismatches, assets-liability mismatches and GAP analysis are needed. This is followed by a discussion of receivables management, payables management and the transaction period and its uses in estimation of working capital finance needed and for control of efficiency of the treasury operations.

Management of inventory and bank finance for inventory — working capital requirements and their estimation, norms for bank finance for working capital, methods of financing working capital, measures of efficiency in credit management, inventory control system for efficiency are all discussed in that order. The plan for short-term funds thus depends on the management of all items of current assets, current liabilities, transaction period, operating cycle, credit collection period, bills payable period, inventory financing methods and cash and credit management by the company, which are all functions of the treasury manager.

❑ ❑ ❑

10 LONG-TERM FINANCIAL PLANNING

(FACTORS INFLUENCING CAPITAL STRUCTURE DECISION)

1. Minimisation of Cost : The cost funds, raised has two components (a) cost of raising them like issue costs, administration costs, incidental costs etc. and (b) cost of servicing the capital, in the form of interest on debt and dividend on ownership capital. To minimise these costs, the management has to know the state of the market for raising funds, interest rate structure and the rates charged by banks and FIs and dividend expectations of investors. Preference capital has a fixed dividend of 14% or 15% and public deposits ranging from 9 to 11% at present. Along with the cost of issue and other incidental expenses and taxes and stamp duty etc. the cost of preference capital will come to around 18-20% and public deposits around 16-18%. Equity has no fixed dividend, as it is a variable dividend industrial security.

Although preference capital and debt instruments have fixed return on them, the cost to the company is different from that of return to investors.

To pay 14% on preference capital and debt, the company has to earn the following amounts, assuming a tax rate of 30% on net profits :

	Preference capital servicing	**Debt capital servicing**
	(30% tax rate)	(zero tax rate)
Earnings required	$= \frac{14 + 14 \times 30}{100}$	14 + 0
	14 + 4.2 = 18.2%	= 14%

The company has to earn profits of 18% to service preference capital and only 14% to service debt capital as interest on debt is a tax-free expense item, while dividends on preference capital as also on equity capital are taxable at the prevailing rates, applicable to corporate earnings.

2. Minimisation of Risk : The management should aim at a proper mix of debt to equity as debt increases risk to investors. Although debt is preferred due to its lower cost to the company, it increases risk to the company. The higher the debt relative to equity, the larger is the risk. This risk is called default risk or financial risk. But, if earnings are higher than the interest payable on debt, and these earnings are stable and growing and not volatile, the risk is lowered, and on the other hand, leverage can be provided to the equity by increasing the debt component in capital. Gearing or leverage is defined as the proportion of debt to equity in the total capital employed by the company.

The following table shows how earnings per share (EPS) is higher with debt financing :

	Equity Financing	Debt Financing
Earnings before interest and taxes (EBIT)	Rs. 8,00,000	Rs. 8,00,000
Interest at 18%	NIL	18,000
Earnings before taxes	8,00,000	7,82,000
Taxation at 50% assumed	4,00,000	3,91,000
Earnings after interest and taxes	4,00,000	3,91,000
Shares outstanding	90,000	80,000
E.P.S.	Rs. 4.44	Rs. 4.89

Note : Number of shares is first 80,000 with a paid up capital of Rs. 8,00,000. The company needs an additional capital Rs. 1,00,000 either by equity or debt. Then interest on Rs. 1,00,000 will come to Rs. 18,000 which is not there in the case equity financing. The new number of shares is 90,000 for equity financing and only 80,000 in the case of debt financing. EPS is higher on debt financing, as seen above.

Importance of Capital Structure

In long-term planning, the most crucial decision which affects the value of share of the company is capital structure. The net worth and profitability of the company are the variables influencing value of a share which has to be maximised by the treasury manager, through planning of long-term funds. The manager has to consider the various alternatives to increase net worth of the company and one of which is to provide the leverage to the equity holder through appropriate doses of debt.

A Real Case Study (Leveraged Structure)

Grasim Industries Ltd., has net worth of Rs. 1,664 crores and its debt was 1,769 crores. Its equity is Rs. 72 crores and reserves Rs. 1,592 crores — with such good financial position, it was able to raise long-term funds needed, for its new cement project and green field project through an NCD issue and Euro equity issue in 1994-95. Its leverage increased by the issue, which is shown below :

R.O.I. (Return on Investment) is profits after tax divided by average net worth is :

$$= \frac{182}{1380} = 13.2\%$$

The average net worth, i.e., average between end of the period and the beginning of the period is Rs. 1380 crores and net profits after taxes is around Rs. 182 crores. If Grasim is an unleveraged company, then total profits before interest and taxes are Rs. 482 crores. Removing corporate taxes (at 46.%) the post-tax profits are Rs. 260 crores. The R.O.I. for this is 260/2963 crores, assuming that the amount of Rs. 1583 crores is raised by equity, on top of its net worth of Rs. 1380 crores. The R.O.I. is 8.7%. Unleveraged R.O.I. is 8.7% while leveraged R.O.I. is 13.2% a difference of 4.5 points due to leverage of debt. The tax rate and other details were as in 1994-95, but for illustration, the date and year are irrelevant.

Capital Gearing (Leverage)

Low gearing means the equity share-holders are not paid an adequate or higher return because profits are swallowed up by high fixed charges on debt and preference capital. High gearing means that earnings are increased by use of debt capital or preference capital and after paying fixed income on the latter, the earnings per equity share will increase due to larger earnings. The condition is that rate of earnings shall be higher than what is paid on preference capital (14%) and on debt capital (18%). Thus, equity holders enjoy the leverage of trading on a larger capital with a given equity base, supplemented by borrowed funds.

Illustration of Capital Gearing

Type of Capital	Low geared	High geared
Ordinary Shares	Rs. 3.2 crores	Rs. 1.00
Preference Capital	Rs. 0.4 crores	Rs. 1.00
Debenture Capital	Rs. 0.4 crores	Rs. 2.00
Total Capital employed	Rs. 4.0 crores	4.00
Return paid to preference shares at 14%	Rs. 0.05	0.14
Debentures at 18%	Rs. 0.07	0.36
Total fixed returns	0.12	0.50
Total net profit earned (as % of capital employed 25%)	1.00	1.00
Net after deduction of fixed returns	0.88	0.50
No. of shares of equity (in crore)	0.32	0.10
EPS (Earnings per share)	Rs. 2.75	Rs. 5.0

The above tabular presentation and the calculation of earnings per share will show that high gearing will benefit equity holders, provided earning capacity of the company is higher than the return on fixed interest securities. The first case is of over capitalisation and second case is one of high gearing which resulted in a higher EPS.

In the former case, it is bad financial planning, as compared to the latter. Earnings in the above example is at a rate (25%) higher than the return on fixed income capital (preference shares and debts).

Average Cost of Capital

An important aspect of planning is to keep costs low.

Assume that capital structure of two projects or companies is given to us and that average weighted costs can be compared :

Take only one Company – say ABC Company				
Source **1**	**Amount** **2**	**Proportion** **3**	**After tax return** **4**	**Weighted cost** **5**
Equity	Rs. 4.00	40%	25	10.0
Retained earnings	2.0	20%	20	4.0
Preference Capital	1.0	10%	14	1.4
Debt	3.0	30%	18	5.4
	Rs. 10.0 Crores	100%		20.8%

Given the above data, then the weighted Average Cost of Capital is 20.8%.

ABC Company is having the above capital structure and its weighted average cost of capital is 20.8% and project giving a return above that rate of return will be accepted in the order of returns.

Cost of Capital

The cost of capital in investment decision-making and capital budgeting refers to the minimum rate of return, required by the investors. It is the weighted average cost of various sources of finance. The textbook definition of Soloman Ezra, M.H. Spencer etc. refers to the minimum required rate of earning or the cut off rate for capital expenditure or for an investment decision.

This concept is useful in capital budgeting decision, designing the capital structure or making any financial decisions, such as divident policy, capitalisation of profits, rights issue etc. This is also useful for evaluating the performance of management in financial field.

Specifically, there is a proper mix of debt, equity and other sources of finance, which will maximise the value of the firm and minimise the cost of capital. If the actual profitability of the project is higher than the actual cost of capital and the larger the difference between them, the better is the financial performance of the company. In capital budgeting decisions, following the net present value method, if the present value of expected returns from the investment is greater than or equal to the cost of investment, then the project is accepted and implemented, otherwise it is rejected. Implicit cost represents something similar to opportunity cost; it is the return lost by not-investing in the alternative opportunity. The explicit cost is the discount rate which equates the present value of future cash inflows with the present value of cash outflows.

Cost of Debt Capital

This is the rate of interest paid on debt, adjusted for floatation charges incidental expenses of servicing debt and incentives like giving a discount in the beginning or a premium at the end.

Kd = cost of debt

I = interest

P = Principal

Kd = I/P or I/NP (Where NP is net proceeds)

After tax cost of debt Kd = 1/NP (1-t) (where 't' is tax rate)

If the rate of taxation is 40% and 8% coupon rate debentures issued at par, issue proceeds are Rs. 1,00,000, then the cost of capital (debt) is :

$$\begin{aligned} Kd &= 1/NP\ (1-t) \\ &= 8000/100000\ (1-0.40) \\ &= 8/100 \times 0.6 = 0.048 \\ &= 4.8\% \end{aligned}$$

Cost of Preference Capital

It is normally a fixed rate, at present 14%. But the cost will vary with the conditions of issue — conversion facility, discounts given, or premium at the time of repayment etc.

Cost of preference capital KP

$$KP = \frac{D\ (\text{Dividend})}{NP\ (\text{Net Proceeds})}$$

The company, FINLEX issued (20,000) preference shares of Rs. 100 each at a premium of 10%; cost of issue is 2% per share fixed dividend is 14% for these shares.

The cost of preference capital is calculated as follows :

$$KP = \frac{2{,}800\ (d)}{20{,}00{,}000 + 2{,}00{,}000 - 40{,}000\ (NP)}$$

(Principal + Premium - Cost of Issue)

$$= \frac{2{,}80{,}000\ (D)}{21{,}60{,}000\ (NP)} = 12.96\%\ \text{Roughly } 13\%$$

In case preference capital is given at par or at discount, the net proceeds in the denominator will change and accordingly the cost of capital will also change. In the case of preference capital as also equity capital, tax is to be paid at the rate applicable to it, say at 40%.

Then the company will have to earn not 14% dividend payable but 19.6% so that tax is paid and after tax, a dividend of 14% is maintained to the preference share holders.

By estimating the cost of each of the sources and calculating the weighted average cost of capital of the project, planning for long-term funds has to be organised. With the availability of ECBs at lower interest rates now the cost calculus will have to be reworked. The calculation of weighted average cost of capital was already referred to. To arrive at the least cost structure of capital such calculations with various combinations of the sources of funds available to the company, have to be made and an optimum cost structure in tune with the expected return on the project has to be derived.

Estimating Long-term Needs

The long-term financial needs of each company vary depending on the nature of the industry, product cycle, stage of growth, project expansion, diversification and a host of other factors. As term finance is meant for long-term assets or gross block and related capital expenditure items, estimating of the long-term needs depend on the cost of the project. The banks give term loans on the basis of the projected cost of the project, for which company needs finance either as part of syndicated loans or a committed term loan, secured by fixed assets.

Estimation of project cost is on the following lines, in broad terms :

1. Cost of land for factory and other buildings needed
2. Cost of construction of the factory and buildings
3. Plant and machinery — indigenous and imported
4. Erection and incidental charges for machinery
5. Technical know-how and engineering fees
6. Arrangements for electricity, water, storage, railway sliding, pollution control, treatment of effluents
7. Equipments and miscellaneous fixed assets
8. Preliminary and new issue expenses
9. Pre-operative expenses
10. Interest on deferred payments and other charges
11. Provision for inflationary rise in cost and other unforeseen contingencies
12. Net working capital requirements.

Although some of the items, referred to above like interest payments and net working capital may appear as current items and not capital items, they are to be mentioned or required as a part of the long-term finance, as current operations and current income is not generated or is not enough for the initial gestation period of an year or two. Net working capital is of a long-term nature as it relates to the long-term portion of working capital.

Statement of Sources and Uses of Funds

When the total funds required for the whole project are estimated as shown above, the year-wise breakdown for 3 to 5 years, in the coming future is generally required to be given, in case of public issue in the prospectus and to the FIs and banks in case of term loans.

Take the example of an existing company (XYZ)

Estimated Projections	**Construction period/ initial years No. of years**				
	1	**2**	**3**	**4**	**5**
Source of Funds					
1. Internal					
Profits /Surpluses					
Depreciation funds					
Debenture redemption					
Reserve fund					
Capital redemption					
Reserve fund					
Development rebate reserve fund					

2. External					
Increase in share capital					
Equity capital					
Preference share capital					
Increase in debt capital (Public deposits)					
Debentures through public issues					
Term loans from FIs/Banks					
Increase in deferred payments					
Increase in lease finance					
Increase in bank's working capital limit					
Supplier's credit/buyer's credit					
Other sources					
Total sources					

	1	2	3	4	5
USES OF FUNDS OR APPLICATIONS					
I. Capital expenditure on new project; increase in fixed assets/expansion/diversification Normal repairs/replacements					
II. Decrease in term loans to banks/FIs					
III. Decrease in deferred payment for plant/machinery					
IV. Increase in current assets					
V. Interest on term loans and deferred payments, etc.					

Among sources of funds have to be added ADRs, GDRs or ECBs, depending on their feasiblity.

Dangers in Estimation

In the estimates made above, there can be dangers of over-estimation, which may result in wastage of funds, misuse and diversion. There can be underestimation which may lead to the shortage of funds and accompanying difficulties of delay in project execution, cost over-runs and the need for larger and additional funds. Both over estimation and under estimation are to be avoided by the adoption of scientific methods of calculation of estimated requirements. To provide for errors in statistical calculations or in projections, which are normal human errors, the company should provide 5% to 10% additional funds for such contingencies, in the beginning itself. But planning may lead to delay in commissioning of the plant and machinery and raise the costs of production and "Lower Profitability."

In long-term projection of funds there can be other dangers due to changes in external factors. The machinery may turn to be obsolete or the capacity planned becomes uneconomical or the market conditions for that product have changed, the Government's policy of allowing free import of plant may be reversed or the conditions of collaborators have changed and foreign capital goods are not available in time. All these events may scuttle the financial projections and result in delay in project implementation. The needed funds will increase and the former estimates will become invalid. Contingency provisions are therefore needed for all projects on hand.

Long-term financial plans are subject to many dangers as the period involved is long. Fixed assets once acquired cannot be dispensed with and become a dead weight. The planned estimates may go awry, if imported parts and machinery are involved due to change in rupee value (appreciation or depreciation), change in supplier's conditions, or any adverse developments in political relations in the collaborator's country). Even when there are no foreign collaborators or foreign capital goods, there are many internal factors which affect the financial projections such as the rapid inflation, leading to rise in costs, rapid technological changes, changes in market conditions and in Government policies. If the financial plan lacks flexibility and adaptation, it leads to many problems of stoppage of project work and rise in costs over the projected targets, leading to cost over runs, rise in unit cost of production and reduction in profitability over the projected levels, thereby lowering the share price of the company.

Capital Budgeting

Capital budgeting is a part of long-term financial planning. It relates to the capital expenditure on fixed assets or long-term assets of company. The main object of capital budgeting exercise is to plan and control capital expenditure, with a view to increase efficiency and reduce costs. Capital expenditure includes all expenditure on new plant, equipments, extension of the existing plant, replacement of worn out machinery and related to all assets of fixed nature and long-term nature. It also includes long-term core part of working capital or current assets like inventory of raw materials and finished goods. Sometimes, it comprises also deferred revenue expenditure on advertisement or brand development programmes or promotion of new product.

What are the Decisions involved in it ?

The basic features of capital budgeting are their longer gestation periods, high degree of risk and potentially large anticipated benefits. The budgeting exercise is a part of planning for long-term funds, with a view to increase the revenues and minimise the costs, so that the profitability of the company will increase. As the period involved is long, spread over years, there are more uncertainties and risks involves.

The types of decision involved are :

1. Accept or reject decisions.
2. Either this or that decisions or mutually exclusive decisions.
3. Capital rationing decisions with a cut off point for choice or projects.

The first category of accept or reject decisions are those based on the cost of capital and expected rate of return. If the project yields higher than the expected rate of return, it is accepted; otherwise rejected.

Mutually exclusive projects are the three alternative brands of printing machinery or two alternative technologies for manufacture of cement. If one is accepted as better one, the other is rejected automatically.

Illustrative Study (Case Study)

Baxi Ltd., is a company planning some project for expansion and diversification. Its expected minimum rate of return is 20% before taxation and its limit on capital expenditure is Rs. 1,50,000. Consider the table below for making a capital budgeting decision (Data given as estimated and for illustration)

(in Rs.)

Projects	Capital expenditure	Return on Investment (before taxation) %	Estimated savings (after taxation at 50%)
A	50,000	20	5,500
B	75,000	24	9,000
C	1,00,000	18	9,000
D	1,25,000	40	25,000
E	1,50,000	37	27,750
F	1,75,000	20	18,500

20% return and above is available on many projects, but the highest return of 40% is available on 'D' which gives a saving of only Rs. 25,000. The project E gives a return of 37% but a saving of Rs. 27,750. The choice may fall on project E, if the amount available for investment is Rs. 1,50,000. There can be other solutions also to this problem, which the readers can easily see from a reading of the table carefully.

Techniques of Capital Budgeting

The following are the normal methods of capital Budgeting :

1. Pay back period
2. Discounted cash flow
3. Internal rate of return method
4. Benefit cost index.

Pay Back Period: This is the method for measuring how quickly an investment can be recovered. The smaller the period of recovery, the better is the investment. Profitability also depends on the time period in which the investment can be recouped. The method considers the average rate of return likely to be derived.

Take the following example :

Projects are ranked in order of return below :

Project	Rate of return	Pay back period
1	20%	5 years
2	25%	4 years
3	15%	6.66 years
4	18%	5.55 years

The lowest pay back period is project-2 which is recouped in 4 years and this is accepted under this method of capital budgeting, if there are no other overriding factors.

Discounted Cash Flow (DCF): This method is based on the principle that money has time value and today's money is more valuable than that a year hence. In long-term investments, money values change substantially and hence the DCF method is most suitable. The formula for net present value (NPV) which tantamounts to the same thing as D.C.F. method is as follows :

$$\text{NPV} = \frac{A1}{(1+K)} + \frac{A2}{(1+K)2} + \frac{A3}{(1+K)3} \cdots \frac{An}{(1+K)n} - C$$

$$\text{or NPV} = \sum_{t=1}^{n} \frac{At}{(1+K)t} - C$$

Where A1, A2 ... etc. are cash flows at various time periods, K is the firm's cost of capital. C is the cost of investment proposed and "n" is the expected life of project.

If NPV as estimated by the above formula is greater than zero the proposal is accepted, otherwise rejected.

Example:

Project 'X' gives cash inflows of Rs. 900, 800, 700, 600, 500 in the coming five years if an investment is made for Rs. 2,500. The net present value of these cash flows at 10% discount factor (the factors are available as PVIF in published Tables) are worked out as is shown below.

Cash outflow Rs. 2,500

Year	Cash inflows Rs.	Discount factor	P.V. of cash inflow (in Rs.)
1.	900	0.909	818
2.	800	0.826	661
3.	700	0.751	526
4.	600	0.683	410
5.	500	0.621	310
PV of cash inflows Total Rs.			2725
Present cash outflows (Investment) Rs.			2500
NPV			+225

Since NPV is more than zero, it is accepted.

This method is more scientific based on time value of money and cash flows throughout the life of the asset. It helps the maximisation of the wealth of the company. But it has some disadvantages as the discount factor chosen makes all the difference. This method is cumbersome, when different amounts are invested at different times and cash inflows for each cannot be seggregated.

Lease Finance vs. Purchase: The NPV method can also be used to decide whether to purchase an equipment or lease it. Sometimes the tax saved may be an advantage on purchase as depreciation on purchase has a tax rebate. If NPV method shows that a project may be acceptable or a machine is worth purchasing, then another question crops up, whether it is worthwhile to buy it outright or lease it. The solution to this problem can be explained with an example:

Example :

D.C.F. rate of return available on the competing projects is 18%, life of machine is 5 years, cost of savings per annum is Rs. 7,00,000 prior to tax, cost of machine is Rs. 18,00,000. Alternative leasing terms are payment per annum Rs. 6,00,000 for 5 years. At the end of 5 years, the residual value of the machine is 2,28,000, corporate tax is 50%. If the machine is purchased outright, the effect on company's tax payment will be as follows :

Year	Savings	Additional Payments
1	5,40,000	–
2		2,10,000
3		2,32,500
4		2,49,500
5		2,62,000
6		3,00,000

The solution lies in finding out whether at 18% return net cash flows are more under leasing or under purchase. If the discounted rate of return from purchase is less than 18% it is to be recommended that leasing is preferable and funds available may be invested elsewhere.

Purchasing Option vs. Leasing Option

Year	Leasing cost saved	Tax saved	Residual valued at end	Total cash inflow	Cash outflow	Net actual flow	Discount factor at 18%	NPV
	Rs.	Rs.	Rs.	Rs.	Rs.	Rs.	@	Rs.
1	2	3	4	5	6	7	8	9
					Cost of machine (7=5-6)			
	–		–	–	18,00,000	-18,00,000	0.1	-18,00,000
1.	6,00,000	54,000	–	11,40,000	–	+11,40,000	0.85	+9,69,000
2.	6,00,000			6,00,000	2,10,000	+3,90,000	0.72	+2,80,800
3.	6,00,000			6,00,000	2,32,500	+3,67,500	0.61	+2,24,175
4.	6,00,000			6,00,000	2,49,500	+3,50,500	0.52	+1,82,260
5.	6,00,000		2,28,000	8,28,000	2,62,000	+5,66,000	0.44	+2,49,040
6.					3,00,000	-3,00,000	0.37	-1,10,000
Total	30,00,000	54,000	2,28,000	37,68,000	30,64,000	7,04,000	–	-4,725

Discount factors are taken from tables and the other data as given in the question.

Answer : Lease option is better, as NPV is less than zero, at 18% and therefore, the machine should be leased and not purchased.

Internal Rate of Return (IRR): Internal rate of return is that rate of discount, which equates the present value of cash inflows to the present value of cash outflows. It is also known as marginal efficiency of capital or marginal productivity of capital, or time adjusted rate of return. It is useful when the cost of investment and annual cash flows are known and only unknown factor is the rate of earnings on the project.

This rate is the same which makes NPV of investment equal to zero.

$$INV = \frac{E1}{(1+r)} + \frac{E2}{(1+r)2} + \frac{E3}{(1+r)3} + \frac{E4}{(1+r)4}$$

Where E1 E2 E3 etc. are net cash earnings in years 1, 2, 3 ... etc.

INV is the required investment.

E1 E2 ... etc. are known and r, the internal rate of return can be derived from the above formula. If r is equal to or higher than the cost of capital or the cut off rate the project is accepted. If r is the IRR and K is the required rate (or cost of capital), the proposal to be accepted, it should be having $r \geq K$

If the cash flows are uniformly the same every year, say C, then the factor to be located is F = I/C where I represents original investment. The factor so arrived at for the years 'n' can lead to the percentage rate of discount, for the relevant annuity tables.

Illustration of IRR Calculation: To pick up IRR which equates NPV to O is a matter of search with some relevant rates; take the following simple example :

ABC project has an initial outlay of Rs. 32,400. Its life is expected to be 3 years. The cash streams generated are as follows :

1st Year	16,000	Cash inflows
2nd Year	14,000	Cash inflows
3rd Year	12,000	Cash inflows

For calculation of IRR in this case, we have to try alternative rates say 14%, 15% and 16% etc. (The factors for these rates for 3 years are taken from tables).

Year	Cash inflow	Rate of discount 14%	PV	Rate of discount 15%	PV	Rate of discount 16%	PV
1.	16000	0.877	14032	0.870	13920	0.862	13792
2.	14000	0.769	10766	0.756	10584	0.743	10402
3.	12000	0.675	8100	0.658	7896	0.641	7692
PV of cash inflow			32898		32400		31886
Initial investment			32400		32400		32400
NPV			+ 498		0		- 514

From the above calculations the IRR is the rate which equates the NPV to zero or PV of cash inflows is equal to the PV cash outflows. The initial investment of Rs. 32,400 is equal to the PV of cash inflows at the rate of discount of 15% which is the IRR, in this case. The rule of acceptance of a project, as referred to earlier is that IRR should be equal to or higher than the minimum required cut off rate or cost of capital. The project giving this IRR is chosen for investment.

Benefit-Cost Ratio: Each project has some cash inflows and cash outflows. Benefits are cash inflows and costs are cash outflows. To derive this ratio, the present values of cash inflows are divided by present values of cash outflows.

$$BC_R \frac{\sum_{t=1}^{n} PVC_1}{\sum_{t=1}^{n} PVC_0} = \frac{\text{summation of present values of cash in flows}}{\text{summation of present values of cash outflows}}$$

BCR = Benefit Cost Ratio

The larger the cash inflows, relative to cash outflows the better is the project. If the benefit cost ratio is more than 1, then the project is accepted, otherwise rejected. This formula is very useful, simple and easy to understand.

This benefit cost ratio is also called the profitability ratio or index. Where PI is profitability Index and PVC_1 is present value of cash inflows and PVC_0 is the present value of cash outflows, the ratio to be calculated is the same as above.

$$P_1 = \frac{P_V C_1}{P_V C_0}$$

The rule of acceptance of proposal or otherwise is that if PI is greater than 1, the project is accepted and if PI is less than 1, it is rejected.

USE OF BREAK-EVEN ANALYSIS

(A) Use for Profit Maximisation

In forecasting sales, and estimating the funds, profits or inflows, break-even analysis is useful. The break-even point is that where profits are zero and price just covers the variable cost plus fixed costs and there is neither profit nor loss. In planning, if the break-even point is known, the profits can be maximised by-increasing sales and changes in prices. If price cannot be changed due to competition, then the sales and cost have to be adjusted to reduce the break-even point.

The chart below shows an analysis of break-even point to maximise the net worth (reserves and surplus).

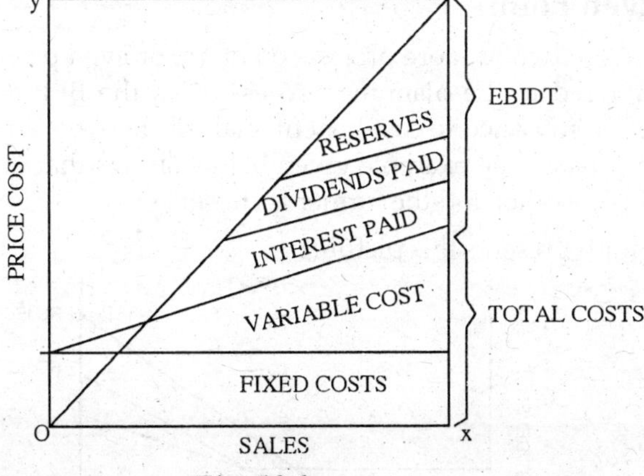

Fig. 10.1

By reducing variable costs, interest cost on debt, dividends and reserves can be increased. Assuming no tax, profits and surpluses can be increased by increased sales, increased price per unit and lower cost per unit. Planning for profit maximisation will have to take these factors into account.

(B) Use in Comparing Actual with Targets

The break-even analysis is also useful to control the operations, compute variation in profits budgeted and actual or sales budgeted and actual. It is possible that estimated cost is Rs. 1,000 but the actual is Rs. 1,500 and similarly the estimated sales are 5000 units while the actual are 4000 units. The impact of these developments on profits can be studied by the break-even analysis and corrections made during the year. This can be presented graphically as follows :

As a result of fall in sales and rise in costs the surplus/profits fell from AD to BC – Analysis of decline in profits shows that the fall in sales caused loss of profits = CD and rise in costs caused loss of profit = AB. Then corrective measure can be taken to increase sales or rise price or reduce costs. The planning and control process is helped by break-even analysis. The upward movement of break-even point (BEP) is bad and downward movement BEP is good. The extent of corrective measures and the direction in which changes are to be made in financial planning will be known by this BEP analysis. E is Budgeted Break-even Point and F is actual Break-even Point.

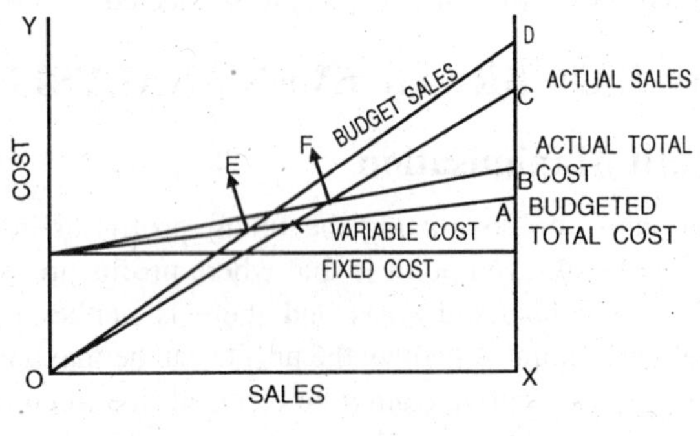

Fig. 10.2

(C) Use of B.E.P. Analysis is Choice of Investment/Projects (Break-Even Point)

If there are two or more projects on hand, or even proposed investments are being considered in the planning process, then the BEP analysis is useful. The projects can be subjected to cost-benefit analysis. Benefits are returns and costs are the total expenses. The example given below shows that one project gives more surplus than the other and the former is chosen.

The graph presents this picture :

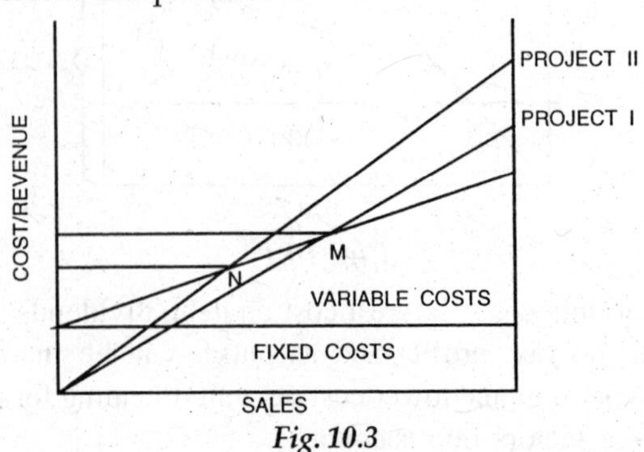

Fig. 10.3

Project-II gives an earlier break-even and larger surplus and hence project-II is preferred. Project-II is preferred to project-I on assumption that the amount invested in both the projects is the same, but the returns of flows of funds differ. The sound project covers the cost earlier and leads to larger profits. The benefits and cost analysis shows that project II is preferred to project-I. MN in the chart are break-even points. N is earlier and hence project-II is preferred.

Budgeting and Planning

Budgeting is a tool of planning of long-term financial needs. Both sources and uses of long-term funds are to be analysed. On the side of sources, cost of capital has to be considered and the method of calculating the weighted average cost of capital for a given capital structure and comparing the capital structures for the choice of the least cost combination have been referred to. On the uses side, the project to be chosen and the investment to be made are decided by a number of criteria like pay back period, NPV method, IRR method and cost benefit ratio. Most of them use the discounted cash flow method of estimating the profitability of the projects and the choice of the acceptable project is made on that basis.

All these methods are only rough and ready methods with an element of possible error. Leaving aside the statistical deficiencies, the analysis is sometimes faced with varying solutions, when experimenting with those methods. So the best lesson is that the theoretical tools, referred to above in this chapter should be used with caution and in practice, the investment proposals are considered on the basis of projected profitability and a number of other socio-economic factors or as per Government policy guidelines. In all cases however the commercial consideration of profitability is indispensable for planning of long-term funds.

Summary

After setting out what is long-term finance, its purposes and objectives, the chapter explains how a capital structure decision is to be taken. Sources normally available for long-term funds are then set out. Factors influencing the capital structure decision are the maximisation of returns, minimisation of costs and risks. The capital structure decision is important for the maximisation of profits and proper planning for long-term funds — nature and quantum.

The calculation of average cost and weighted average cost of capital is explained for the proper combination of different sources. The cost of capital concept with examples of cost calculation to the company is explained.

The method of estimation of long-term funds based on the sources and application of funds and dangers involved in any such estimation are set out. What is capital budgeting and how to take a capital budgeting decision is explained with examples. The techniques of capital budgetting, namely, pay back period, discounted cash flow, internal rate of return method, benefit cost index are some of the methods available to the treasury manager to be used in planning. To lease or purchase an equipment is a decision which is important to the company like the debt to equity ratio to provide the leverage. The use of break-even analysis in forecasting and planning and the tools of planning and budgeting are explained.

A Case Study on "Long-term Funds"

(Asean Industrial Structure Ltd.)

(New Project — An example of good planning)

History: This Company was incorporated in 1994 as a Public Ltd. Company with its Registered Office at Ahmedabad and Corporate office in Mumbai. The promoters are N.T. Vaishnav and his associates, who have experience in the field of project finance, corporate planning and merchant banking. The promoters had earlier promoted VMC Project Technologies, VMC Credit Finance Ltd., Internation Comptech Eng. Services Ltd. and Bhuvan Tripura Industries. N.T. Vaishnav is a qualified Chartered Accountant and his experience is mainly in the finance area.

Long-term Finance Planned

The long-term requirements of the proposed Asean Industrial Structures Ltd., are as follows :

Table 10.1

(Rs. in crores)

Uses of Finance		Sources of Finance	
Buildings	5.75	Equity Capital -	
Plant & Machinery	10.75	of Promoters	7.5
Infrastructure Project Support System	3.00	of Public (inclusive of M.Fs, F.Is, NRIs & OCBs, etc.)	17.5
Misc. Fixed Assets	1.50	Total Equity	25.0
Tech. Knowhow Fees	1.50	Share Premium to NRIs/FFIs	1.05
Preliminary Expenses	2.75	Leasing Finance	1.95
Contingencies	1.00		
Working Capital Margin	1.75		
	28.00		28.00

Note: Lease finance is to be provided by Gujarat Credit Corporation. There are the projections prepared by the company and not appraised by any FI as no loan from FI or bank is involved.

Table 10.2
Disposition of Funds Yearwise

(Rs. in crores)

Projections	1996-97	1997-98	1998-99
Fixed Assets	17.05	—	—
Infrastructure Project Support	3.00	—	—
Tech. Know-how	1.50	—	—
Increase in Current Assets	1.75	0.85	0.98
Taxation	6.95	10.00	12.58
Dividends	—	5.00	6.25
Use in Real Estate Business	5.00	10.00	14.00

Pre-operative Expenses	2.75	—	—
Supplier Credit for Turnkey Project	5.00	10.00	10.00
Infrastructure Project Support	4.00	4.00	6.00
Total	47.00	39.85	49.80
Opening Balance	—	5.41	3.62
Surplus/Deficit	5.41	(1.79)	0.07
Closing Balance	5.41	3.62	3.69

Objectives of the Project

1. The company will implement infrastructure projects through joint ventures in the area of express highways, Telcom, power ports, industrial parks etc. These will be implemented with the latest world technologies available through the collaborators abroad.

2. It will set up infrastructure projects engineering division to earn foreign exchange, by setting up projects abroad. These functions will be performed by the divisions.

   (a) Special infrastructure project group
   (b) Infrastructure project engineering export group
   (c) Project construction group.

Features of Financial Plan

1. There is no immediate pay off obligation to any debt holders, as no loans were arranged. The required current expenses, working capital and pre-operative expenses were all raised through equity only.

2. Due to deferred payment obligations the company has breathing time to develop profitability.

3. Lease finance is preferred to a loan due to its being off balance sheet item.

4. During the first year of its operations 1996-97, it does not pay dividend but provides for payment for turnkey project implementation fees, taxation, tech. know how fees, etc.

5. To earn profits on non-operative items, it has proposed to invest in real estate in Mumbai, Ahmedabad etc., to the extent of Rs. 5 crores in 1996-97, Rs. 10 crores in 1997-98, and Rs. 14 crores in 1998-99.

6. Promoters' stake is 30% of the enlarged paid up capital after public issue in Jan. 1996 for Rs. 25 crores.

7. As it is confident of public support, the public issue was not underwritten which saved some expenses. The project report was not drafted and appraised by any bank of FI, which again saved expenses. As it has not invited bank loan participation, it is free from managerial interference from banks. As working capital is also raised by equity for the time being it need not approach a bank for working capital which again saved expenses and there was no curtailment of its freedom in disposition of funds. By this pattern of finance chosen it has secured many advantages.

Advantages of the Plan

1. Initial interest costs or pay off are avoided as it has no debt component.

2. Equity base is kept high to have a large potential for leveraged borrowing in future.

3. By resort to lease finance, it has lease rentals to pay but no interference in its financial planning by banks/FIs, etc.

4. Working capital requirements and pre-operative expenses are covered in the public issue.

5. By resort to investment in real estate for capital appreciation it has lowered the tax rate applicable and yet provided for larger profit potential. As the operational profits may take time to realise, it has planned profits through non-operative methods to serve equity holders and pay dividends, in the second year itself. In the first year, it has planned to earn profits of Rs. 25 crores on which a tax is provided for at Rs. 7 crores. It has successfully tapped the investment potential of NRI and FFIs etc., from abroad and from MFs and FIs in India to a total extent of 44% of the project funds needed, as against 27% from the promoters. The public contributed only around 25% of the project finance with nearly 70% from institutional agencies; the project financing has made the capital structure mostly all equity based, less leveraged with high potentiality for future leverage and a large leeway and freedom for financial and managerial efficiency.

Planning for Long-term Funds

Case Study : Ramkish Tyres Limited.

(A Case of Poor Capital Budgeting)

Object : RTL was set up in 1989 for manufacture of tyres, tubes etc. It has an estimated capacity of 10 lakh tons of which actual production in 1994-95 was only 72000 tonnes (hardly 7% utilisation). It had started production in 1993.

Location :Factory location : Vijayanagaram, Andhra Pradesh.

Regional Office : Hyderabad.

Authorised capital Rs. 25 crores (raised from Rs. 15 crores).

Accounting Practices

When all companies close at March end of each year this company was still presenting accounts on the basis of June end figures. It has purchased some assets on hire purchase basis which shows continuing liability from the capital account. Depreciation is on straight line method as per the companies Act. Its inventories are valued at cost. Sales are only 52% of inventories, which is the most inefficient way of inventory management.

Its revenues are taken on accrual basis while its expenditure is on cash basis and no provision has been made for P.F. and gratuity of the staff. In fact, staff expenses along with power expenses worked to total to about Rs. 1 crore, which is half the total sale income of the company. An additional liability on capital account of Rs. 50 lakhs for remaining part of the contract was to be executed.

There was delay in payment of some bills, for which interest of Rs. 26.6 lakhs was paid, an extra burden on the company which is another example reflecting poor funds management. At least one thing which the company's management has showed was their commitment to the company by bringing in interest free funds into the company of Rs. 1.8 crores, arranged by promoters among themselves and their friends and associates. They were planning a rights issue for R.s 10 crores, and there was however, a contingent liability on account of bank guarantee of Rs. 18 lakhs.

The above accounting practices are not all above board and hence require a rearrangement by the treasury manager and is a fit case for analysis and planning.

For a project of Rs. 27 crores of gross block, only Rs. 14 crores of equity and Rs. 13 crores of debt sounds quite good. But what went wrong with its capital financing projections and cash flow projections ? Total dues as on 30-6-1996 were another additional amount of Rs. 13 crores. Including this in the total liability, equity of Rs. 14 crores has to be taken against total liability of Rs. 26 crores. This brings the total debt of equity to 1.9:1, a ratio which is not bad, by itself, if it has good earning potential, which is absent in this case.

Increasing Debt Burden

To run the full capacity 20 lakh tonnes of the plant, this company requires a minimum of Rs. 12 crores as W.C. Term loan and another Rs. 2 crores for increasing curing capacity — a total of Rs. 14 crores. This will increase the total cost of the project to Rs. 54 crores [original equity 14 + borrowed funds originally 13 + other liability 13 due to arrears of interest losses and other capital expenditure + fresh proposed borrowing 14.] As against Rs. 54 crores of needed funds equity base of Rs. 14 crores will constitute only 25% and it leads to a debt equity ratio of 4:1.

To obviate the high debt syndrome, they proposed to borrow abroad (Dubai Company) through issue of preferred shares FCB loan — which will be a loan of 3 years, afterwards convertible into preferred shares and a rights issue of Rs. 10 crores to Indian public and to its shareholders. What is the servicing capacity for these loans when its capacity utilisation is 7% and its inventories are twice its sales. It managed to have other income of Rs. 1.58 crores – almost equal to sale increase of Rs. 1.97 crores. The components of other income are not explained in the balance sheet but may be presumably through trading and capital gains. Its return on gross block/capital employed net worth etc. is zero and negative.

Its net sales to total assets is around 5% and to gross block, it is around 7%. Even if depreciation and taxation is not taken into account it has interest commitment due to increasing debt. Its earnings, including other income would be covered by debt servicing only. Its operating expenses have grown enormously from Rs. 8.2 lakhs in 1993-94 to Rs. 1.88 crores in 1995 a rise of 2.3 times while sale income itself has declined and taking total income, the rise is only 1.8 times. Its debt servicing capacity is zero, its capital liability has expanded enormously to Rs. 40 crores for which an equity base of Rs. 14 crores is inadequate and its debt servicing capacity is poor and cash accruals are inadequate. At the present rate the company will continue to be in red, as already its equity base was wiped out, the accumulated losses (6.4) plus arrears of interest (5.6) plus already incurred preliminary expenses (0.8) added to a total of Rs. 13 crores approximately.

Summary

Treasury Manager is concerned with long-term finance as well. Capital structuring; project planning, leasing option, sources and uses of funds, minimising the costs, planning and budgeting are all avenues, of cost minimisation and profit maximisation. These are all the financing decisions for solvency for long-term funds which are part of Financial Management and Treasury Management is also a part of the process.

Conclusion

The company's capital budgeting plan went haywire and its capital structure and project financing methods were faulty. Its project was delayed and sales and cash accruals were inadequate even to service debt and leaves no margins of profits. Its operations and sales strategies were all miscalculations. This is a case of what the fund manager has to avoid in his capital budgeting exercises.

Balance Sheet as at 30th June, 1995

Sources of Funds

(Rs. Crores)

1.	Shareholders funds share capital	14.2	
	Deferred liability	0.3	14.5
2.	Loan funds secured loans	19.7	
	Unsecured loans	2.5	22.2
	Total assets		36.7

Uses of Funds

1.	Fixed Assets		
	Gross block	24.0	
	(-) Depreciation	2.0	22.0
	Net block Work in progress	3.0	
2.	Current assets		25.00
	Inventories	3.7	
	Sundry debts	1.0	
	Cash & Bank balances	0.06	
	Loan/Advances	1.7	6.5
	Total current assets		
	Minimum current liabilities and Provisions	1.9	
	Net current assets		4.6
3.	Miscellaneous		0.7
4.	Accumulated loss		6.4
	Total Liabilities		36.7

Profit and Loss Account for the year ended June 30, 1996

(Rs. Crores)

Income :		
(a) Sale	1.98	
(b) Other income	1.58	
Total income (a + b)		3.56
Expenditure :		
(a) Materials	1.26	
(b) Expenses	1.88	
(c) Interest	2.87	
(d) Depreciation	1.04	
Total expenditure (a + b + c + d)		7.05
Profit before tax (loss)		3.49
Tax provision	Nil	
Current year losses	3.49	
Past accumulated losses	2.92	
Total loss carried to Balance Sheet		6.41

The above case studies on good financial planning and bad financial planning are only of historical importance and for illustration. Early in 21st century, with Close Scrutiny of SEBI and the responsibility thrust on Merchant bankers, such cases are not possible any more except in rare case of Scams in IPOs.

❑ ❑ ❑

11 INTERNAL TREASURY CONTROL

INTRODUCTION

All economic units have the goal of profit maximisation or wealth maximisation. This objective is sought to be achieved by a plan — short-term plan for working capital and long-term plan for fixed capital, which are explained in the preceding chapters.

These plans are implemented by incorporation of them in the budget in the form of activities and corresponding flow of funds and targets fixed accordingly for each level of activity. Control is a consequential step to see that the budget is being executed effectively as per the plan and goals are achieved thereby and actual results compared with results targeted. Control is thus part of planning and budgeting in any organization.

There are two aspects in the budget — one physical aspects and the other financial aspects, which are inter-related, physical activities are converted into financial flows and *vice versa*. Budgetary control therefore involves scrutiny of both these aspects as they are interlinked.

The financial plan should contain the elements of financial flows, corresponding to physical flows and norms are laid down for financial operations for the purpose of facilitating the internal control on them. In fact, control is a part of management function. Treasury control cannot be disconnected from management control.

Objectives of Internal Control

Briefly control is a process or processes of constant checking that operations are taking place as per the budget and plan priorities, and analyze the reasons for any divergence and take needed corrective action as and when necessary. At every level of management, the control aspect is necessary and that is what is called Internal Control.

Conceptual Background

Internal treasury control is a method of self-improvement. It is concerned with all flows of funds, cash and credit and all financial aspects of operations. From time to time and on regular basis, the internal treasury control is exercised on long-term financial targets and expenditures and short-term financial inflows and outflows and are reviewed from time to time if they are as per planned schedule or not.

The financial aspects of operations include (1) input financing, bills payable, trade credit, cash payments, etc. which are all as per the standards set for and the targets fixed (2) output financing in the form of inventory financing and bank finance for working capital and the gaps between inflows and outflows are met by planned recourse to low cost mix of financing.

The capital structure and changes if any needed and working capital financing and changes, if any, needed are all parts of the internal treasury control functions. The financial aspects of all operations, fixed assets management and current assets management have to be taken care in the plan and the control mechanism ensures that operations are carried on as per the plan and any deviations are reported regularly so as to enable the control mechanism to initiate corrective action. That chart attached will focus attention on the control function at various levels and operational financial controls, relative to operational controls.

Policy of Board of Directors (Top Management)

Internal Treasury Control	**Conceptual chart of Treasury Control**			**Co-ordination with Other departments**
	Fund Flows			
(a) Control on flows of long-term funds – capital structuring.	Own Funds Equity/Reserves etc.	Loan Funds Debt, debentures etc.	Other sources like deposits etc.	Top Management's strategy of planning-project Finances –
(b) Control on short-term funds – input financing.	Fixed Assets	Capital Expenditure		Production Management
(c) Bills payable, trade credits, each outflows etc.	Productive capacity Inputs of Labour, spares Raw materials etc.		Outputs of goods and services	Materials or purchase management
(d) Credit bills, bills receivable, inventory financing, working capital, Management Investments, funds flows, cash flow etc.	Operations in financial markets.			Sales or marketing Management
	Income - expenditure = profits Assets & Liabilities Mix Management			Operational results
(e) Control on output financing.				Financial results Profitability Evaluation

Chart 11.1

Elements of Treasury Control

The control aims at operational efficiency and remove wastages and inefficiencies and promote cost effectiveness in the firm. Financial control is exercised under different phases of planning and budgeting.

1. Setting up the targets or limits.
2. Laying down financial standards.
3. Evaluation of performance as per these norms or standards, such as standard costs per operation.
4. Reporting in a regular standard form and monitoring the financial aspects of operations.

The quarterly and annual budgets would set the targets for each department and financial standards are set out for each activity — say for raw material stocks, semi-finished and intermediate parts and final products — the stocking pattern — stocks at distribution network, standard order quantity, purchase norms, etc. Monthly budgets are evaluated by the performance sheets maintained daily and regular daily/weekly/monthly reports go to the financial controller. Reporting and evaluation go together and on the basis of the information system built over the past the budgets and plans are prepared for the next period.

More specifically, treasury manager has to plan cash flows and funds flow budgets. The objective is to maintain liquidity and solvency of the firm. Any deviation of receipts and payments have to be investigated and corrective action is to be taken. Alternative methods of finance and least cost sources are planned in advance.

Cash budgets and funds flow budgets are a reflection of the operation in physical form. Financial Controller aims at the profit maximisation through low cost finance and quicker turnover of funds. With quantity of cash or credit limited (M fixed) the velocity of M can be increased by which larger turnover and larger profits can be aimed.

Control Techniques

The control techniques are the following :

(1) Reporting and evaluation of information flowing from various departments through monthly reports on budgets or even weekly reports on operations.

(2) Ratio analysis based on Du pont system, which uses the Ratio of Return on Investment and Profit to Sales as tools of control.

(3) Use of charts on the flows, operations and on assets and liabilities from time to time and income and expenditure on a monthly basis are the other techniques of control.

Managerial Aspects of Control

Management is a wider term applicable to all financial aspects and operational aspects of production and distribution and sales. Management is a process which is to be exercised at various levels. Men, Machinery and Money are the three Ms that require a constant watch in the Management. Men may include labour, or technicians or even experts. Machinery encompasses the totality of field assets (gross block) which provide the capacity to produce a given level of output. The Money is the flow of cash and funds which enable men and machinery to produce the output by using the capacity of plant and machinery and distribution and sales personnel to sell the product produced and turn output again into money.

Management Control

Managerial system involves the control on these three 'M's. The crucial test of efficiency of Management lies in how they will organise : (1) Planning of operations (2) Executions of these operations (3) Co-ordinating the various levels and activities in operations and (4) Finally, controlling these operations with a view to achieve the targets of plan through the mechanism of budgeting. The functional aspects of Managerial process can be summarised as follows :

Management Process

(a) Planning & Goal Setting
(b) Organising the structure
(c) Co-ordinating the operations
(d) Controlling the operations

Levels of Control Process	**Control Process of**
(a) Top Management	(a) Men
(b) Middle Management	(b) Machinery
(c) Lower level Management (Supervisory level)	(c) Money

OBJECTIVES

Maximisation of Profits/ Wealth

Cost Minimisation & Return Maximisation

As Money is the lubricating mechanism for Men and Machinery, Finance Function is the most important function to achieve the goals set by the Top Management. These relations are set in a Triangle and top position is that of Finance function, as shown below.

Structure and Organisation

The structure and organisation of Internal Treasury Control is a matter of Top Management Policy. The objective of the organisation and the system of control that the top management adopts would determine the structure. The structure also depends on the nature of the business, the product of the industry, stature of the organisation etc. There is no uniform and rigid structural pattern suitable to all organisations.

The general system adopted by many organisations would entrust the internal Treasury Control to a special Audit Department or a Financial Controller or Chief Treasury Officer. For treasury operations the treasury controller is the Chief Treasury Officer directly reporting to the Board of Directors or the M.D. He is an executive of top management team responsible to help the Board with the plan of

Treasury operations, targets and objectives. Limits for expenditure for each level, and limits for inventory/stock etc. are set out. Chief Treasury Officer (CTO) is assisted by a Assistant Treasury Officer (ATO) incharge of Management Information System (M.I.S.) for reporting and evaluation. ATO is a co-ordinating authority and helps the CTO with data and information for decision-making and necessary to plan and prepare a budget for long-term and short-term funds in advance. The Top Management is responsible for fixing the targets — cost effective financial structure, cost structure, cost control and other methods of improving efficiency and productivity in the use of scarce resources of capital or funds.

The formulation of the inflows and outflow budgets is left to the Treasury Manager (Finance) and the budget on operations in the portfolio of Investments and Funds Management is left to the Treasury Manager (Investment). Thus, there are two wings of finance and investment in Treasury Management which will submit separate budgets, but as there are links between them, the co-ordination is attended to by the ATO. As the best method of control should emanate from bottom, it will start at the lowest rung of Divisional Heads or Departmental Heads which are the cost centres or profit centres or cost and profit centres. The results of their operations are compared to the targets fixed for each and reports should go from bottom to top. The results of the finance area and the results of the investment area are again co-ordinated by ATO.

As budgets are reviewed on a monthly and quarterly basis, continuous monitoring is done by the ATO and CTO and they organise Internal Management Audit or Materials Audit, Stock Audit, Stationery Audit etc. from time to time. Finally, the results of operations are incorporated in Income Expenditure Account and balance sheet of the company. The details are shown in the accompanying chart.

Chart on Structure
and Organisation of Treasury Control

Board of Directors
Managing Director
Chief Treasury Officer (CTO)
(Vice-President, Finance)
Assistant Treasury Officer (ATO)
(Co-ordinating & Controlling Authority)
M.I.S.

Treasury Manager (Finance)	Treasury Manager (Inv)
(Finance Manager)	(Funds Manager)
Responsibility Centres/Depts.	Market/Operations Depts.
Cost Centres, Profit Centres, Cost & Profit Centres.	Distribution Network
Results of operations	Results of Operations
Financial inflows and outflows	Profit booked/Losses booked

Income and Expenditure — Net profits
Measurement of Operations by R.O.I.
Balance sheet statement — Ratio Analysis

Role of Chief Treasury Officer: Plan targets are set by top management. Budget is accordingly prepared by each of the operational departments in consultation with the Treasury Manager (Finance) for the responsibility centres. The C.T.O. is responsible for all these planning exercises and for decision-making.

Chief Treasury Officer is the authority to formulate guidelines, standard costs and expected return for each activity. It is for the Asst. Treasury Officer to implement them through various departmental heads. He is helped in this process by the treasury managers, (now termed finance managers) who oversee the inflows and outflows for each of the responsibility centres and the profit centres. Expenditure limits and controls for each level of organisation and for each authority are set by C.T.O. The results of all profit centres including those of market operations are incorporated in Income Expenditure Statements.

Principles of Internal Control

First control should be at all levels of management and participation should be from all cadres of personnel. More important are specific levels of operations — ground level, divisional management level — middle management and at the top management level. The top level is also concerned with the strategic control, which refers to one aspect of plan objectives. Every organisation has some objectives or goals which are subject to flexible changes depending on the external and internal forces. The task of top management is strategic planning which is the process of deciding on objectives of the organisation, changes of these objectives and on the policies needed for achieving these objectives in the wake of changing environmental factors and the organisational structure which is necessary for this. Delegation of authority and responsibilities to various authorities is necessary part of the control system.

Secondly, in tune with the strategic plan, the top management aims at control, which is called management control. The function of the management control can be decentralised or centralised. The last type of control is the decentralised one which gives responsibility to lower level managers including supervisors to tune their operations to achieve the objective by reaching the targets, both in terms of quantity and quality. A margin of error and deviation from the targets (say by 10%) may be allowed due to uncontrollable factors, but the basic objective of control is to see that activities are in the direction of the plan and the budgetary targets are a guide. They keep the targets as goals, ensure that the resources are raised in the least cost method and that efficiency in the use of these resources is maintained at all levels.

Thirdly, for effective control, there has to be a system of building up of effective communications from top to the bottom and bottom to the top. The control will be effective if there is continuous and regular reporting of the performance against the targets from bottom to the top and the communication from the top to the bottom should be guidance on how to make changes or adjustments in manpower use or resource use, so that the targets can be achieved or the best performance can be reached. The reporting system is built up and communication is the basis of the reporting system for control purposes. Both monitoring and review of the plan targets are possible by a regular system of reporting. Review gives guidance to the divisional heads on the needed changes in the practices, or resource raising or resource use, so that efficiency and productivity are improved on a regular basis.

Fourthly, the control should be built on the Management Information System. This function involves the collection of data from all departments on their operations — targets or goals and their actuals setting standards for each level of activity, analysis of the operations and suggesting the methods of improving the efficiency and productivity. M.I.S. is a tool of top level management control and administer the standards for each level of activity. M.I.S. is the information base with research content which collects the information on the industry, on the competitors in the industry and the standards of cost and quality for each type of activity. It is the tool of taking decisions at top level and of implementing the plan.

Role of Controllership

The Controller is a top Management Officer who co-ordinates the control functions of all departments. The Controller is neither the Finance Executive nor the Accounting Executive. He is a management expert, with a background of finance, accounting, personnel and marketing. The Controller assists the top management in control and audit functions. He has the charge of Management Information System. The controllership concept is sometimes used in the service of Financial Controllers and sometimes compared to Accountant General or the Auditor General in Government. But in the reality, controllership involves all these functions of control on finance function, accounting function and audit function. Controller is the eyes and ears of the top management and is part of the organisational system for effective control mechanism. He helps the top management in strategic planning as he is incharge of M.I.S. which is the basis for taking decisions. He is the agency for collection of information and gets reports from departments, uses for analysis of variances and gives suggestions for improvement or mid-term corrections to the plan process. He is incharge of planning for control, reporting and interpreting and analysis of reports from operational departments, monitoring and evaluation of the plan process. He co-ordinates the departments in their plan process, in reporting system, payment of taxes and liaison with Government and Government departments etc., jointly with the other top executives.

Main Features of Effective Control

The effective control system should be supervised by the controller, whose functions were referred to above. The control system is facilitated by (1) Responsibility Accounting (2) Control by Exception (3) Automatic and Continuous Reporting and Monitoring and (4) Emphasis on feedback, which gives the information on the weakness and strength of the plan, reasons for variance of actuals from targets (5) Internal Audit function, physical verification of the assets, stocks and distribution network, protection to the assets through insurance etc.

Responsibility centres are given powers to self control and in the process the accounting function is also given to them to make each one of them a profit centre and their performance is accounted and evaluated on the basis of achievements versus targets. This is briefly what is meant by responsibility accounting and decentralisation of authority and responsibility.

Control by exception means that the control is exercised only in material or core functions and otherwise self control operates. Sample checks, physical verification and internal audit are confined to a small sample based on exception in this system of control.

The other features of the effective control system and the role of controller are continuous reporting and information collection, monitoring and review. Feed back reporting and internal audit check on selective basis are self explanatory and their use by the controller is expected to improve the operational efficiency of the organisation.

Physical Controls

Treasury has to keep a watch on the following variables for which physical verification may also be necessary

This verification is necessary for study of variances and he gets these reports from the departmental heads at regular periodical intervals.

(1) Stocks of raw materials

(2) Stocks of semi-finished goods

(3) Stocks of finished goods

(4) Stocks at various distribution centres

(5) Stocks to cash sales and credit sales

(6) Volume and value of output and sales

(7) Fixed assets and their state of maintenance, repairs and replacements

(8) Other assets, equipments, furniture tools and machines and dead stock verification

(9) Stationery and vehicles etc.

The treasury control involves a study of variances, to assess the extent of effectiveness of control on costs, expenditure control and on inflows and outflows. The physical verification and study of variances referred to earlier are very essential part of treasury control to improve the efficiency and productivity of the company.

Physical verification of books of treasury (Investments) and their trading operations is also necessary. The Treasury Manager (INV) is given limits for his operations which are subject to control on a regular basis. The reporting system wherever possible and audit of accounts and monitoring the trends and the developments in the variables relevant to the treasury operations, will help control.

Custodial Control and Insurance

The Chief Controller has the responsibility of preserving the fixed assets and current assets intact and maintaining them, through maintenance department. For this purpose, he has to organise from time to time checking of the custodial arrangements of the valuables, documents, trust deeds, mortgage deeds, agreements with collaborators, royalty agreements and other valuable documents. Although the company secretary has some statutory obligations to the company in these respects, so far as the treasury function is concerned, the treasurer has to organise the funds from FIs, Banks and co-ordinate with the Government departments, stock exchanges etc. In that process, he has custodial control on these valuable documents also. He has to coordinate with the Company Secretarial Department.

Insurance is also provided to all valuable assets and CTO will be responsible to see that the assets needing insurance are insured and that the insurance policy is current at any point of time. Fire, floods and other calamities and accidents do take place and these can be insured by the company. The control on what items to be insured and the currency of the insurance falls in the area of C.T.O.

Both custodial control and insurance control go together in some cases, as in the case of godown stocks, plant and machinery in some business concerns and factory and administrative building etc. C.T.O. will organise these controls through the respective departments.

Treasury Control on Market Operations

As referred to earlier, treasury function is concerned with finance and investment which are two sides of the same coin. While the finance can be visualised as related funds flows and cash flows and their control, investment function relates to investment and trading surpluses in funds, portfolio management of the funds and gap filling, in case of deficit through disinvestments. The process of investment and disinvestment and trading in financial markets are controlled by the following methods:

1. Setting the over all limits in each market and sub-market and individual limits for each of the instruments of trading. The limits can be in terms of expected minimum returns, maturity pattern and limits to trading in any scrip or in total in a market as for example — in terms of funds that can be deployed in ICDs, say 40%, Bill discounting (40%) and their short-term investments and bank deposits (20%) etc.
2. The stoploss limits for risk taking can also be set at 10% of the total funds deployed in each category.
3. Speculation to be limited to such overbought position or short sales which cannot exceed another 10% or even prohibited.
4. Similarly, currency positions in the forex market can be subject to overall limits for all currencies or limits for each of the currencies, subject to limits, the treasury is free to operate and his operations are evaluated in terms of net profits booked in any period. Limits to open uncovered positions and even post facto control on their operations are the common control methods on operators.

Effectiveness of Treasury Control

To achieve an effective financial control system, the Treasury Officer has to design the control with flexibility and accountability. The treasury heads in charge of the responsibility centres are given the powers in a decentralised manner. The power and authority is accompanied by accountability for the results versus the targets.

The control system is a method of self control for all the departments and treasury managers. The system of reporting should be simple and continuous monitoring of the operations under the budget is necessary. The control system should aim at the participation of all levels of personnel. Standard costs for each activity and budget targets are to be followed which is possible, if all personnel are aware of them and are informed such as of expenditure limits, standard costs etc. and are involved in the budgetary process.

Capital expenditure should be always accompanied by cost benefit analysis and alternatives to the proposed project and their ranking should be given for a scientific decision on acceptable projects. The departments concerned should be held responsible to the control on the operations and to make them profit centres. Profit evaluation from time to time as part of the monitoring and evaluation system of the plan, should be aimed for effective treasury control.

Control on Funds Flows — Significance

One of the methods treasury control is through funds flow analysis. It is a statement of sources and uses of funds derived from the comparative figures in the balance sheet and profit statement for the year in question and the preceding year. It indicates the quantum of funds short-term and long-term, and their cost contribution to the total funds used and how they are used for long-term purposes, fixed assets acquisition, long-term investments for short-term purposes — short-term assets, short-term investments etc. for the short-term wing, the bills receivables, inventories investments and how they are financed by trade credits short-term borrowings and bank credit.

Objectives of the Study of Funds Flow

The study of Funds Flow would indicate which transactions are financed by what source. When transactions take place, we need to know, whether funds moved or not and when they moved, in what pattern and how they moved.

Firstly, funds do not move when fixed assets are financed by issue of debentures or when the sundry creditors are paid in cash and both current assets and current liabilities are reduced by an equal amount.

Secondly, funds move when current assets are used to acquire fixed assets or *vice versa. It* is possible to acquire current assets by long-term funds by issue of debentures. Long-term assets can be acquired by short-term liabilities and long-term liabilities can be used for short-term assets or there can be conversion of short-term assets to long-term assets, without any change in liabilities or there can be conversion of long-term liabilities into short-term liabilities and *vice versa.* What the treasury control needs to watch is that fund flows are correct flows and the liquidity and solvency of the company is safeguarded.

Forecast and Actuals — Analysis of Variances

In the internal control mechanism, the treasury officer has to design a method of evaluating his forecasts in terms of the variance of the actuals from forecast. This can be done for any of the accounting variables like sales to inventories, bills receivables, loans, credits etc. period of credit given and period of credit taken, bills payable, purchase quantifies and their periodicity and other items of current liabilities.

In respect of these variables targets and actuals can be compared. The variances between actuals and forecasts can be studied for all the accounting variables or for the financial inflows and outflows. A few examples are given below:

Study of Variances

1.	Raw material and raw material mix	Material use variance	Material price variance
2.	Labour pay rolls	Labour efficiency variance	Wage rate variance
3.	Sales/Inventory Sales Mix and Inventory Mix	Sales to inventory ratio variance (physical)	Sales value to inventory value (Money terms)
4.	Variable cost overheads	Variable-cost to sales variance	Variable-cost to output variance.
5.	Fixed cost overheads	Fixed cost to sales variance	Fixed costs to output variances
6.	Man hour output	physical variance	Value variance

Quality variances and volume variances are also relevant for analysis and study.

System of Control of the Treasury — Accounting Control

(A) The system comprises of Financial Control through profit centre analysis — sales and cost or income and expenditure and profits of each of the responsibility centres
These centres (Departments or Divisions) are examined in terms of actuals versus targets and variances analysed for reasons and corrective measures are taken.

(B) Charting system involves the charting of all variables to be studied and analysed on the time trend basis, again in terms of actuals versus targets.

This chart can be designed on the lines shown below,:

Plan objective maximisation of net profits

Total investment/Fixed assets
Sales

Capacity Built
Operations

Capacity utilisation

Sales-minus costs

Current assets
Cash, Bills
Receivable
Inventory etc.

Net profits
Profit margin

Cost per unit, Margin of profits,
Selling expenses,
Administrative
Expenses etc.

Chart 11.2

Control of Efficiency of Men

	Actual	Target
1. Sales per man hour (or output)		
2. Pay roll per unit of sale		
3. Pay roll to sales/output		
4. Average sale per transaction		
5. Average cost per transaction		
6. Selling cost per transaction		

A host of such criteria can be designed depending on the nature of business market, products etc.

Control of Money Flows

Inflows or Incomes (Variables)	Outflows or Expenditures
Cash to sales	Sundry debtors to current liabilities
Credit sales/to total sales	
Bills Receivables to Bills payable	Average period of credit given by suppliers
Maturity of Bills	Average expenses to Average sales.
Average credit for customers	Total sales to working capital
Average holding of stock	Total profit to sales network

Management Audit

The top level Management can directly or through the Chief Treasury Officer arrange periodic Management Audits. It refers to an examination of the management policies set out and the extent of their implementation, effectiveness of the policy procedures, guidelines issued and the appraisal of the usefulness and effectiveness of the existing methods and procedures. From time to time as the market conditions change and production schedules and procedures change, it is for the foresighted management to see how effectively their management policies are working. It is for the top executives to appoint a special audit team for this purpose. This team will examine all the relevant data, hold personal discussions with Divisional heads, Departmental heads and with the Treasury Managers and assess the extent of effectiveness of the Management policies, systems and procedures etc.

Summary

Internal Treasury Control in any unit is part of the overall managerial control, as finance is the counter part of operations. The objective of Treasury Control .is to improve cost effective methods and to increase the profitability of the unit.

For this Treasury Control, the conceptual framework is designed, and how Treasury Control is to be effected along with operational controls is shown. The Top management is involved in it as this is part of Managerial function. A general organisational chart is designed to show how the Chief Treasury Controller is part of Top Management Team, by whatever name he is called, Vice-president (Finance or Treasury) or Director of the Board (Finance).

Elements of Treasury Control are the target setting, laying down the standard cost and norms for evaluation of performance by comparison of targets with actuals and study of variances along with continuous reporting and monitoring. Top Management sets out the goals, organisational structure and systems and procedures. Coordination and controlling is attended to by the Chief Treasury Controller.

The Principles of Treasury Control are :

1. Self Control and Control by exception.
2. Decentralisation and participative control.
3. Responsibility and Accountability go with the Profit Centres.
4. The control should be participative of all levels including the lower rung in hierarchy. Floor level Manager or Supervisor is also part of this control system.
5. Two way communication system, M.I.S. etc. are built and Reporting and Monitoring are continuous.
6. Physical controls, custody and insurance and Management Audit are part of this Treasury Control System.

❑ ❑ ❑

PART – III

OPERATIONS IN FINANCIAL MARKETS

12 FINANCIAL MARKETS – AN OVERVIEW

A financial market is one which involves the purchase or sale of financial assets or instruments. It has no geographical configuration but refers to demand for and supply of financial claims or instruments. A financial instrument is a claim on future money, or a security or promissory note or debt of one to another. It is a market where different types of financial products are exchanged for money and *vice versa*. Financial system is the generic term given to all activities in financial markets involving the use of money in relation to the real economy resulting in financial assets. Real economic activities and their relation to money leading to the emergence of financial system is set out in the chart below :

Macro Economic Activity (Chart 1)

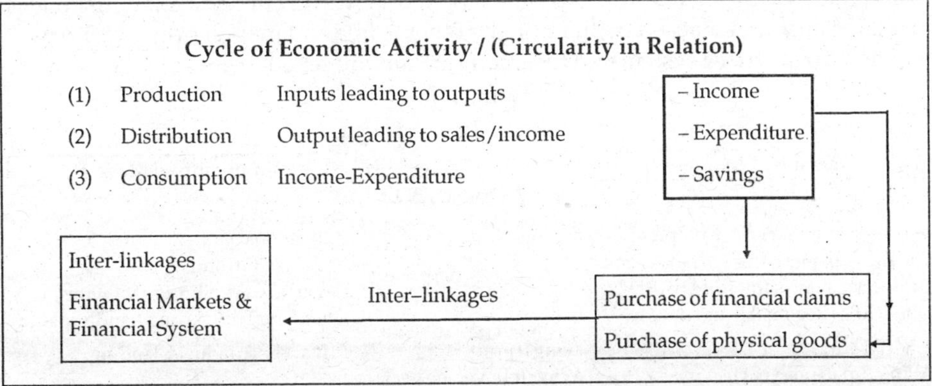

Production needs inputs which are supplied by land, labour and capital and enterprise. The rewards given to factors are incomes used for consumption. Distribution involves intermediation between consumption and production. Consumption therefore is possible through rewards to inputs in production which is used for consumption partly and partly for savings.

Interrelations between Financial System and Real System

In productive process, finance is an input needed for project finance or for working capital. Distribution also needs some investment which is finance for trade and business. Finally, consumption also needs some finance for meeting daily transactions to be met or for hire-purchase transactions or for just for meeting the short fall of cash on hand (temporary overdraft). All economic activities need finance and finance also leads to economic activities through savings of some for helping the investment of others or for expanding the productive capacity through larger investment. The last one involves credit creation by banks (M) which augments the savings of the various sectors of the economy and by borrowing and lending activity of financial institutions leading to the increase in the velocity of circulation of money (V). M stands for quantum of money supply and V for velocity of circulation of money. Both "M" and "V" together help financial transactions in Industry, Business and Trade (the transactions demand for money).

Similarly, savings and credit creation by financial system together help the growth of the economy, through larger investment. If there is a gap either temporary or permanent between income and expenditure, there is borrowing or lending, which leads to financial dealings. Again if there is a gap between investment and savings in the economy or of any sector of the economy, there is borrowing through credit and money creation by RBI, and lending by banks and financial sector.

What is Financial System?

Financial system emanates from the activities of money–borrowings and lending and buying and selling of financial claims. It arises out of the savings in the economy and credit creation by the banks and credit extension by the financial institutions.

In India, the financial system has two components, namely, the organised market segment, controlled by the RBI and the Government and unorganised sector or informal finance sector not controlled by the RBI and Government. While the first one is regulated and systematised by the RBI, the other is free and market oriented. The two regiments of financial system and their components are set out below :

Chart 2

FINANCIAL SYSTEM

Organised Market		Un-organised Market
	RBI/(Leader)/SEBI	
Banks – Commercial & Co-operative Financial Institutions – All India and State level bodies (FIs), NABARD and RRBs (Regional Rural Banks)		Indigenous bankers' money lenders Nidhis/Chitfunds Pawn brokers, Shroffs, Multanis Chettiars, Traders and Landlords etc.
Short-Term Wing (up to one year)	Long-Term Wing (above one year)	Private borrowing & lending.
Money Market	Stock Market and Capital Market	
Govt. securities Market which has both wings.		
NBFCs are now controlled by RBI.		

Constitution of Financial System

The Financial system, involves the creation of cash and credit and in the trading in the resultant instruments or claims on money in the markets which if they are well organised and controlled come under the organised markets. The markets are constituted by the demand for and supply of liquidity or trading in liquidity or conversion of claims on money into money and *vice versa*. This is also called exchange of money or cash for claims on money or *vice versa*.

The organised financial system can be depicted in the following Chart.

Chart 3

Cash	Credit	Lending & Borrowing	Claims on Money
Created by RBI	Created by Banks	Arranged by Financial Institutions	Bills of Credit Promissory Notes Traded financial Products and instruments, etc.
Money Supply (M)		Velocity of circulation of Money (V)	= (MV)

FINANCING OF ECONOMIC AND COMMERCIAL TRANSACTIONS

As seen earlier the organised financial system has short-term and long-term segments or markets. These markets can be set out as money market, (short-term) government debt market (both short and long-terms) and stock and capital market (long-term). While these markets are for domestic money, for the foreign money (currency and credit denominated in foreign currencies) we have the foreign exchange market or foreign currency market (Foreign Market).

Sectoral Analysis

Sectoral analysis of the financial system depicts the borrowing and lending activities of various sectors in the economy in tune with their incomes and expenditures. These are broadly reflecting the macro-picture of the financial system, depicted in the following diagram :

Chart 4

Savings (S)	**Investment (I)**	**Growth of G.D.P. (g)**
Net Saving Sectors – S>I – Lending (net)	Net Investing – (I>S) Sectors – borrowing (net)	
(1) Household Sector S>I	(3) Business Sector I>S	Economy
(2) Foreign Sector S>I	(4) Government Sector I>S	
Supply of Funds	Demand for Funds	
Buy IOUs or claims on Money.	Sell IOUs or claims on Money	
Financial Markets		

The larger the investment (I) the larger is the growth, *caeteris paribus*, given the capital output ratio. The growth (g) of GDP is a function of investment (incremental capital formation) multiplied by capital output ratio (K) where K is = Output generated/ (Capital Input used in the process) Incremental capital output ratio (K) is generally the term used for K and "K" multiplied by Investment (I), we can derive the growth rate of the economy.

Investment depends on savings where I>S, then the gap is filled up by borrowing. In the case of India total investment rate is about 26% while the saving rate for the economy is only 24% and the addition of about 2% is brought in by foreign borrowings.

Sectorally, household sector and foreign sector are net savers in India with income more than expenditure. Their excess savings are lent to the deficit sectors. The business (including corporate) sector is net investor with expenditure more than their income; so is the government sector. They are perpetually borrowers in India. The household sector's gross savings as percentage of GDP was between 20% to 24% over the last few years, while the private corporate sector's savings rate was around 3% to 4% and that of public or government sector was negative. The net short fall as between the savings of these three domestic sectors and the national investment is always met by foreign sector through inflows which ranged from less than 1% to 2% before 2001. Over the last few years, in the 21st century net capital inflow was negative, as there was a net outflow of capital in these years. It is normally around 2% over the recent past. Government and business sectors are the major borrowers in the financial markets as their expenditures are more than incomes and investment more than their savings. The lenders or suppliers of funds are household sector and foreign sector. Taking the corporate sector, they make new issues (borrow in the form of equity or debt). In the case of government sector, they borrow in the form of both short-term debt and long-term debt. Their new issues constitute the primary market and the trading in existing securities is called the stock market or secondary market. These two together constitute the capital market. Their issues of securities lead to the financial markets, namely :

(1) Money market for short-term borrowing.
(2) Government securities market for all government debt.
(3) Long-term borrowings of corporate sector.
PSUs, etc. in the capital market.

Chart 5

Overview of Financial Market — Instruments

Financial System's structure and operations can be set out as follows:

(I) Money Market — Controlled by RBI through DFHI (Discount and Finance House of India)

Players		Instruments		Segments
RBI	–	Inter bank call money	–	Call money markets
DFHI	–	Treasury bills (auction bills) of 14 days and 91 days to 364 days	–	Treasury Bill market
Banks			–	Commercial bills/paper market
FIs				
Mutual funds, Companies,	–	Commercial Paper, Private Sector Debt Instruments or Bills	–	Inter-Corporate
Brokers/Dealers etc.			–	Funds Market
		Certificates of deposits (banks) etc.		

There is one more market, namely, forex market. Domestic sector borrowings and lendings *vis-a-vis* the foreign Sector are reflected in the forex market, where currencies and credit instruments are traded in rupees *vis-a-vis* other foreign currencies like dollars, sterling etc.

Mode of trading is over the counter, telex, telephone etc. either directly or through brokers. Clearing facility is not there except that they can operate on their own accounts with the RBI. There is no organised market place, but geographically these market segments concentrated in the metrocities of Mumbai, Kolkata, Delhi and Chennai, in that order of importance. Bulk of the trade is in Mumbai and since 1993, these are traded on the National Stock Exchange (NSE) also.

(II) Government Securities Market is controlled by RBI, through Securities Trading Corporation of India (STCI)

Chart 6
Government-gilted Market

Players	Instruments	Segments
RBI, STCI	– S.G.L. Account Stock Certificates	– Primary Markets
Primary Dealers (PDs)		– Secondary Market of Central Government, State Government Securities
FIs	– Promissory notes	
Banks	– Certificates of Deposits	– Debt Market
PFs	– Bankers Receipts	– P.S.U./U.T.I. Bonds
Insurance funds	– Repos (Repurchase agreements)	– Dept. Undertaking's Bonds
L.I.C./G.I.C., etc. Finance Companies and Brokers/Dealers	– Switch operations	– Others
Manufacturing & Trading Companies.	– Government Bonds of various coupon rates and auction bonds of various maturities	

In this market, the operations are part of the stock market and traded quotations are to be provided by the stock exchanges. But trading can also take place directly without the intermediation of dealers/brokers. Trading is over the counter, through telephone, telex etc. RBI also deals in the primary market — new issues through underwriting and contributing the unsubscribed portions and in the secondary market through the S.T.C.I. RBI or S.T.C.I. trade only through P.D.s., licensed brokers/dealers or directly with the banks/FIs, etc. RBI dealings are mostly in switches or repos and less for cash. If it is in cash, they only sell securities for cash but do not buy from them except through Repos, or in special times to pump in money into the financial system or for LAF for banks.

(III) Forex Market (Controlled by the RBI directly or through authorised dealers in foreign exchange).

Chart 7
Forex Market

Players	Instruments	Segments
RBI	Currency	– Inter-Bank Market
Authorised Dealers	TTs, MTs, DDs etc.	– Indian Banks in Foreign centres
Money changers	Foreign bills for purchase, for negotiation for collection, foreign credits etc.	– Foreign banks in Foreign centres – Foreign banks in Indian centres
Foreign Banks, Indian Banks, FIs, Companies Exporters & Importers		– Bank dealings with the public RBI's dealings with Banks.

Risk management is very important in the forex market. The forex market is completely different from the domestic markets particularly in respect of risk–return characteristics. Firstly, the risk and uncertainty of interest and currency rates is more than in other markets. Secondly, the operations are complex due to influence of foreign multifaceted forces operating in the market. Thirdly, the calculations are complex due to the quotations in four decimal points for Rupee against Dollar and other foreign currencies and due to the cross currency quotations and arbitrage operations in the market. Fourthly, the speculative forces operate more here and profits and losses are also more in this market. Uncontrolled speculations and one-sided speculation is most risky. Fifthly, the existence of forward quotations, the forward premiums/discount provide both complexibility and also hedge against risk in spot deals or in forwards of various maturities. Sixthly, foreign exchange deals involve credit extension, conversion of rupees into other currencies and funds management in foreign currencies.

Conceptual Framework for Treasury Functions

In the above background of the brief description of financial markets in which the treasury manager has to operate, it is apt here to set out the conceptual framework for treasury function. As referred to in part I, treasury function relates to the management of cash, credit, short-term money assets and long-term finance and foreign finance, in a manner to subserve the goals of management and integrate the finance operations with production and other functions of the corporate or non-corporate units. The integration of these functions was already referred to in part I. Now to present the conceptual framework for the treasury function, we have to recapitulate the overall management function. Following chart depicts step No. 1 in such framework.

Any corporate or non-corporate economic unit provides some services or produces some goods for distribution to consumers and this process involves the use of finance in all operations down from the starting of the project preparation and implementation.

Chart 8 : Step (1)

Promoters & Directors		Finance Director
Economic Aspects		Financial Aspects
– Conceive a Project		– Conceive the scheme of least cost financing of the project
– Prepare a Project Report with input & output mix-Technology		– Prepare capital structure
– Implementation of the project	Long-Term funds for Capital Assets for project completion	Short-Term funds for Current Expenses during the pre-production stage and afterwards
– Building the capacity		
– Schedule of output and capacity utilisation.		

Chart 9 : Step (2)

Building up of Capital Structure

Equity	Loans from Banks/FIs			Equity or Loans from Collaborators	Debentures or Bonds
Promoters contribution	Public Issue through prospectus	Private placement and offer of sale	Rights (for existing company)		(for existing company)
	OFFER of sale (Bought out deals)			Public deposits (for existing company)	Foreign equity and debt (GDRs/FCCBs/ FCN/ECB)

The above chart depicts step No. 2 in the conceptual framework for the fund manager to design a least cost capital structure. Fund management starts with designing of the proper structure of capital and long-term funds. As capacity is being built, these funds have to flow in from a combination of the above sources, which give the least cost combination consistent with the product, manufacturing of the product or the nature of services rendered. During the period of pre-commercial production the above long-term funds are to be supplemented by some short-term funds, for revenue expenditure for salaries of staff, establishment expenses etc. which are normally provided in the project cost itself or through a separate funding loan from the bank.

During the pre-commercial production stage, the finance manager has to co-ordinate the drawing of funds as per the project plan and arrange funds flow to match the progress of the project and the forecast or as per projections given in the project report. He has to keep liaison with banks and financial institutions for arranging drawings in time and if necessary plan for additional funds during any period.

Chart 10 : Step (3)

During Operational Stage :		**Top Management**
Capacity utilisation	–	Input Financing
Production	–	Bills payable
Sales & other Income	–	Outflows
Cash & Credit Sales	–	Output Financing
Other Income	–	Bills Receivable
	–	Inflows
Working Capital	–	Inflows and Outflows of funds
Bank Finance	–	The gap
Planning budgeting & Control		Chief Finance Controller
Execution of the plan		Finance Manager
Financial Flows (excesses/shortfalls)		Operations for managing excess funds or/shortfall – Treasury functions
Investment		Funds Manager/Treasury Manager

Treasury Operations in Markets

The chart above presents the last step in the treasury operations and the conceptual framework for role of chief financial officer.

Role of Chief Financial Officer

In the finance function, there are various aspects, which require to be supervised and co-ordinated :

(1) These are planning and budgeting for long-term funds and short-term funds.

(2) Forecasting and projection of funds and identify the excess or shortfall and develop strategies to meet these.

(3) For shortfalls he has to plan for funds from banks or FIs, etc. and for excess funds he has to make investments and operate in financial markets.

(4) Monitors the operations, fund flows and fund management for the corporate units.

(5) Funds Manager operates the excess funds in financial markets and makes investment decisions. Investment decision and finance decisions are next door neighbours and go together. In particular while the earlier functions of planning and budgeting are looked after by finance controller (or Director, Finance), the later aspects of financial operations are taken care by the funds manager (for coordinating the inflows and outflows and arranging for bank borrowings etc.), but the treasury manager specialises in operations in treasury, namely, the investments in money market, in Government bonds, securities, treasuring bills and/or the foreign exchange and foreign currency operations and portfolio management etc. Investment operations are important for cash-rich companies also.

(6) Treasury operations and funds management are kept in separate hands or in the same hands, depending on the size of funds of the company,

width of operations, nature of the company and its operations and the extent of specialisation. In finance and investment companies these are generally kept separate. Similarly, investment and finance functions can be combined or kept separate depending on the extent of the operations and the need for specialisation or whether it is a bank, finance company or a manufacturing company. In banks, treasury functions are more important than finance functions.

Investment Decision vs. Finance Function

Funds management and treasury operations involve decision of investment and disinvestment in financial assets or instruments in various markets, referred to earlier. If there are excess funds and the company is cash rich but poor in profitability in operations the funds are to be invested judiciously in financial markets and if there is need for funds, management and control operations help and investments are converted into cash at short notice. Thus, conversion of cash into credit instruments and *vice versa* is thus part of overall funds management. Investment decision is thus a complementary part of finance function and both are next door neighbours. Treasury manager is mostly involved in operations in financial markets which involves both finance and investment decisions (referred to in an earlier chapter).

Investment decision is based on different criteria and principles slightly different from Financing decision. The former needs the expertise of capital market management and stock market operations and equity research, fundamental and technical analysis etc. But financing decision requires expertise in financial analysis and funds management to examine the alternative venues of financing and choose the least cost combination of finance. They need to do financial forecasting and budgeting exercises, as also the financing methods and arrange for the least cost financing of the fixed capital and of working capital. Besides, financing decision helps the company to meet the gaps between inflows and outflows and helps the production process to run smoothly and coordinate the marketing and production functions. Investment function helps the company to use its funds efficiently and maximise the returns. In case of many companies whose incomes from sales is to be supplemented it is the investment decision which helps. Both investment decision and finance decision are thus closely related and interlinked in the field of corporate finance for the Treasury Management.

Risk in Investment and Financing

Risk in investment is much more than in financing decision. One can take a wrong decision on financing method which leads to a rise in costs. But in investment decision the risk is more due to loss of interest or principal or both. A wrong investment decision may lead to loss of whole amount or any part of it. It is therefore a critical function in the finance area; risk is common in all investments, and risk is more in forex market as the foreign exchange rates vary widely due to everchanging international factors. The currency rates are subject to high speculative attacks which lead to highly fluctuating rates and funds invested can be completely wiped out over right in this market.

The investments in money market and Government securities market are also risky but subject to less risk than in the case of stock market (or equities) and as referred to earlier much less risky than in investment in foreign currencies. Treasury operations are therefore most risky, in general.

Risk management by proper hedge and cover of risk is necessary for the investment operations. It is in this context that investment functions becomes more critical for banks, finance and investment companies. For, manufacturing companies, financing function is relatively more important as the cost of finance has to be kept low and profit margins have to be increased. Broadly both investment and finance functions need to be taken care by the company.

Investment and Trading

Investment is purchase of securities or any financial instruments or claims of money. Companies keep some investments in short-term, some in medium-term and also in long-term assets. The investment and trading activities should be distinguished. As cash is required at short notice, investments in treasury bills, bills of exchange, commercial paper or other short-term credit instruments is necessary. Inter-corporate deposits or investments for a few days to a few months in UTI Units, PSU bonds etc. are examples of medium-term investments. Long-term investments are in equity shares, debentures, bonds, etc. including those in its subsidiary companies.

Trading means investment and disinvestment or buying and selling in above categories for the purpose of making capital gains or booking capital losses. Speculation is such trading for short-term gains. When some manufacturing companies are not making adequate profits, the finance manager will try to find alternatives of raising income. The funds manager or treasury manager will be given a role of profit generating centre in funds management or in treasury function in such cases. Some manufacturing companies combine manufacture with trading. Normally, manufacturing companies do not actively trade but keep investments of both short-term and long-term nature in the portfolio, to enable the company to improve its profits and generate cash at short notice from the existing investment portfolio.

Basically, treasury function involves both investment and trading. Taking open position in trading in stock market and in trading in forex market are examples of active trading, which is also called hedging or speculation. Investment aims at long-term gains and takes less risk while speculation is trading for short-term gain and most risky. Both for investment and trading, expertise is necessary for treasury manager to operate in those markets.

Financial Engineering (Derivative Markets)

Treasury Manager has to be conversant with financial engineering as a means of financing and as a mode of risk management. Financial Engineering is a multidisciplinary approach to the management of risk and return in treasury management or portfolio management. This involves the use of derivative financial products to decompose the standard financial transactions into their elements and then synthesise them into innovative cross structures to suit the requirements of the parties and preference of investors and the issuers.

Financial Engineering is thus the by-product of several factors which have grown in importance in recent years, namely –

(1) Development of many financial new products and OTC derivatives.

(2) Revolution in Information Technology.

(3) Financial deregulation and liberalisation and globalisation.

(4) Increasing volatility of the markets and need for risk coverage.

(5) Growing sophistication of Risk Management Techniques and their application to financial field.

(6) Application of scientific and advanced management techniques.

Financial Engineering Involves

(a) Multi-disciplinary discipline comprising engineers, mechanics and scientists.

(b) Adoption of derivative products like swaps, repos, and options and futures, options on futures, and futures on options etc.

(c) Decomposition into elements and recomposition of elements and

(d) Synthesis of new elements.

Recent Innovations Introduced

A Balance Sheet – Price risk transfers :

(a) Adjustable rate mortgages.

(b) Floating rate notes.

(c) Back to Back loans.

Credit Transfers (examples)

Loan Swaps.

Asset Sales without recourse.

Securitised assets.

Transferable loan contracts.

Liquidity enhancing transfers (examples)

Securitised assets instruments.

Securitised debt instruments.

Swap accounts.

Credit Enhancing transfers (examples)

Junk Bonds.

Zero Coupon Bonds.

Money Market Mutual Funds.

Equity Participating Financing (examples)

PCD, FCD, and convertibles, warrants, Loyalty Coupons etc.

Off Balance Sheet instruments (examples)

Futures, Options, Loan caps, Swaps, Repos, Forward Rate Contracts and Interest rate swaps and switches.

Letters of Credit (Examples)

Note Issuance Facilities, Guarantees, Sureties, Contingent liabilities.

Treasury on Line

The revolution in Technology brought about many changes in Treasury operations. Banks and MNCs have installed automation and software packages suitable to trading platform, electronic transfer of funds, automatic settlement and clearing system. By its role in dialing process it has increased the client base; easy access to data on prices, rates, negotiation, and striking deals in all market operations, whether it is equity or corporate debt or government debt of forex deals. Access is given to real time news, market reports, information and analysis.

All the above toots have increased volumes and speed of transactions, better price discovery and compliance with risk management rules of its top management of the Regulatory Authority or the government. They have made possible the operation of portfolio optimisation strategies, predecision tools and calculators, portfolio trackers, hedging and portfolio management tools, in trading and investment.

Negotiated Dealing System (NDS) introduced by RBI on a national basis has quickened the trading system in gilt edged market which increased the volume in turnover. The Clearing Corporation of India (CCI) offered online clearing system and automotive transfer of funds and guaranteed the settlements. The quality and quantity of trading in government securities market has increased thereby and ensured quicker and guaranteed settlement and clearing.

The integrated online system on the forex market facilitated 24 hour trading and handling of larger volume of foreign trade, remittances, exports and imports of corporates. The good corporate governance, investor grievance redressal and investor services, and performance of social responsibility and other corporate goals were achieved better by online and automotive control system made possible by electronic and computer based systems introduced by MNCs and banks.

In the forex market, there is a larger need for risk reduction, better discretion, credit quality, inventory pruning, and liquidity adjustment both at macro and micro levels. Role of interest rate differential, inflation rates, and liquidity condition influence the forex market more than other markets, although the same factors influence money market, equity market and debt market also.

Front office, middle office and back office are three levels at which online Treasury operates. The front office provides the client base better quality of negotiation, and quickening of dealing process. Front office owes profits to the Treasury through its operations. Middle office monitors to the top management the front office work and compliance with their guidelines, confirming the deals through contacts with the counterparties, ensures documentation, portfolio analysis and ensuring a MIS, for front office. Back office work relates to settlement and clearing and passing accounting entries and data collections processing and preservation. Adoption of STP or straight through process of all deals by automation and online system in Treasury was made possible.

❑ ❑ ❑

13 MONEY MARKET OPERATIONS

In this chapter discussion is centred on the money market and its components in India. Although short-term government securities market is a part of the money market it is discussed in a separate chapter.

Money market has no geographical constraints and relates to all dealings in money or monetary assets. J.S.G. Wilson defined the money market as a "centre in which financial institutions congregate for the purpose of dealing impersonally in monetary assets." This is giving too literal an interpretation of money market. In fact, money market is a wide term and encompasses a variety of transactions, instruments and institutions. Money market is a centre where borrowers and lenders of money and near money assets are put together. It may comprise a group of such markets for various types of money assets, characterised by relative degrees of liquidity or nearness to money. Such assets may be call money, treasury bills or bills of exchange etc. Secondly, although there are various centres of money markets such as Mumbai, Kolkata, Chennai, etc., they are not separate independent markets but are interlinked and related. Thirdly, in true sense of free and perfect competition, there should be only one price for each category of money assets, which would result from dealings of purchase and sale made on a purely impersonal basis and through blind economic forces.

Developed and Underdeveloped Markets

Indian money market is not well developed. Following the Vaghul Committee recommendations (1989), a number of new instruments have been introduced to develop the market. The essential characteristics of a developed money market such as the ones in London or New York are integrated structures between sub-markets, free flow of funds as between sub-markets or segments of the same sub-market, a high degree of specialisation with regard to dealings in instruments by various institutions and a single price for each of the instruments traded.

The Indian money market is characterised by lack of cohesion and full development due to the operation of some exchange controls in the economy despite some liberalisation recently and freeing of the rupee. Another important aspect of the money market is the dichotomy between the organised and unorganised markets. Unlike a developed money market, the Indian market is not characterised by a high degree of integration and cohesion.

The essential pre-requisites for integration are that there must be links between the several sub-markets and their relative prices for each of the assets traded and continuous contacts and relationship of borrowing and lending are maintained through the spill over flow of funds from one sub-market to another. Although the degree of risk and uncertainty varies from segment to segment and there are various frictions and hurdles to shiftability of funds such as costs of brokerage, commission, taxes, etc., which might explain to some degree the difference in prices between the sub-markets, there should be an essential unity of purpose in securing the highest return for funds and a general free flow of funds and information in the market. The integration may not be possible if there are special groups of institutions with separate standing and methods of operation and customers are attached to these institutions, each such group tending to be isolated from the others. This is the case particularly with the indigenous banking system in India.

Integration of this market with other sub-markets helps the siphoning off of the excess or short-fall in this market to others such as treasury bill or government securities market. Integration also aids the more economical use of cash by banks who are the major institutions in the market. In the recent years since 1992 reforms were started, there is a greater degree of cohesion and integration. The depth and width of the market is growing.

Integration and Specialisation

A well developed market would satisfy both the criteria of integration and specialisation. If the market is well integrated, the flow of funds between sub-markets will be free and quicker, increasing thereby the value of transactions. Specialisation is a natural result of the market, as the specialist is bound to emerge as soon as sufficient demand develops for his services. In India, the market is not specialised to the degree present in Western developed countries, as we do not have discount houses, acceptance houses or underwriting houses. The need for such institutions has not been felt and the volume of business did not warrant the emergence of such specialist houses which are being set-up now, starting with the underwriters being licensed and controlled by SEBI, and Primary Dealers in Government securities being authorised by the RBI, etc.

Modern discount houses have developed on the basis of the growth of bill business as in the UK. The merchants who were acting as intermediaries for those who wished to invest in bills began to evolve as dealers in bills themselves acting as wholesalers for the banks to buy and sell in retail.

Another example of the specialist institution is the acceptance banker who developed into acceptance houses doing the business of accepting a bill of exchange by lending its name for a client known or recommended to them, thereby facilitating negotiations. Acceptance business is very prominent in the London market by virtue of its acting as a financial centre for various parts of the world.

The trend towards specialisation is seen in the USA also in the development of firms for government securities dealings houses, namely, government securities dealers specialising in placement of private commercial bills and those concentrating on handling bankers acceptances and federal funds, etc. some securities firms specialise in acceptance business and some in bill business which are not developed in India.

Advantages of Mature Money Market

The advantages of a mature money market are multifold. The gaps between the separate sub-markets can be bridged by operators through arbitrage operations which lead to a single price for each category of assets. Secondly, it facilitates the profitable deployment of surplus funds of banking institutions. Thirdly, where money market is compact and integrated the control by the central bank would be easier. The central bank action would percolate quickly from one segment to another of the market and be more effective. The central money market may be developed alright but not properly linked with the periphery markets in the unorganised sector as in India. Alternatively, as in Thailand and a few other less developed countries, even the central money market is not well developed and the central bank's action may have to be direct and the traditional indirect instruments may not work. Fourthly, a developed money market helps promote certain attitudes and practices by bankers regarding the maintenance of minimum reserves and cash. Healthier practices by banks in this regard help control by the central bank. In addition, the central bank may exert its influence by consultation directly with the respective groups of interests in the market such as discount houses' association, accepting houses' association or foreign exchange dealers' association and this also facilitates operation of self control by SROs and the instrument of moral suasion by the central bank, will work better.

Sub-Markets

The call money market in India and Pakistan and federal funds market in the USA are examples of a sub-market dealing with near cash or overnight money. The demand comes from banks who fall short of reserves overnight or a few days and the supply comes from those who have got excess reserves with them. In India, this is called the inter-bank call market wherein funds are borrowed overnight for book adjustments by banks who fall short of the statutory cash reserves requirements. Brokers put through these transactions as between banks or the banks may choose to deal directly among themselves. In London and Paris, the discount houses who deal with bills wholesale require such funds for holding the bills. In New York such funds may emanate from government security dealers. Both in UK and USA as in India, the dealers in the market act as intermediaries for these dealings in inter-bank funds. Not infrequently the banks put through their transactions among themselves. In US banking, the need for such market is more than in India and the UK, where branch banking predominates and branch adjustments for excess funds can always take place. The federal funds market in US provides a mechanism for meeting shortage of funds. In some countries, where exchange control does not restrict their dealings abroad, the banks may depend more upon correspondents abroad for excess or shortfall of funds than in India.

In the inter-bank market in India, in addition to all banks, foreign and Indian, GIC, UTI, and LIC and many non-banks institutions also operate, mostly as lenders. RBI is the apex body for these institutions and acts as the lender of last resort to the market. In the inter-bank market, foreign banks are the main borrowers because by the nature of their operations they finance trade and operate in the market mostly with a narrow cash base. This sub-market is the most sensitive to changes in liquidity, as the stringency or surfeit of funds with the banks and the impact of the credit control operations of the RBI are felt here. As of now mutual funds, and many other institutions and high net worth companies in addition to banks and FIs are allowed to operate in this market particularly as lenders. Money Market Mutual Funds permitted to be set up by RBI are also allowed to operate in money market.

In the ultimate analysis, it is the readiness of the central bank to act a lender of last resort to the market that sets standards of liquidity to be kept by banks and their readiness to lend in turn. The integration of sub-markets also depends on the central bank acting as a lender of last resort. In a country like India with a seasonal ebb and flow of demand for bank funds either the banks keep excess reserves (which was true upto sixties in India) or have a ready recourse to the central bank. In the latter event, the central bank may impose discipline on the banks' operations. Generally, banks loathe the hegemony of central bank and hence prefer to keep excess reserves as far as possible. While some banks keep excess reserves, others can always borrow from them and thus the interbank market began to develop and thrive. The rate depends on the excess funds of the banking system as a whole and is regulated by the inter-bank agreement through the Indian Banks Association and DFHI set up by RBI in association with banks and FIs. The rate varies from day-to-day and transaction to transaction. The inter-bank agreement specified the maximum rate of 10 per cent in this sub-market, which was withdrawn in May 1989. Now, the rate may fluctuate freely depending on the market forces, and may fluctuate violently also due to excesses and deficits in banks' CRR.

In India there is a good bill market in which all banks, and particularly the big banks, discount approved inland and foreign bills. There is, however, no secondary market in bills as there are no further dealings in them except when they are rediscounted with the Reserve Bank, Discount and Finance House of India (DFHI) and Securities Trading Corporation of India (STCI).

Treasury bills constitute a separate segment of the market. These are of three months duration, issued on tap by RBI on behalf of the government for financing government investment and other expenditure. In addition, there are treasury bills of 14 days to twelve months durations. Mostly banks, UTI, LIC, etc., contribute to these bills in addition to government departments or agencies with surplus funds. These bills are now sold on auction basis, and interest rates are freed and the maturities may vary from 14 days to 364 days.

Bill Market in India

A bill of exchange is an instrument in writing containing an unconditional order by the market directing a specified person to pay a sum of money to the order or to the bearer of the bill. Such bills augment the instruments of financial transaction, supplementing the available resources in times of seasonal stringencies for the purpose of refinance from the Reserve Bank. They are a method of financing trade.

The Reserve Bank of India Act has provided for refinance to commercial banks through buying or rediscounting of bills of exchange or other commercial paper eligible for rediscount under the Act. This provision under Section 17 of the RBI Acts was meant to relieve the seasonal stringency in the absence of a properly organised bill market. Rediscounting of the Trade bills was left to the DFHI, IDBI, Exim Bank, etc. instead of RBI at present. The factors which affected adversely the growth of a bill market in india are the lack of uniformity in drawing bills, varying borrowing practices in different parts of the country with respect to bills, absence of distinction between trade bill and finance bill, high stamp duty, and popularity of cash credit and overdraft arrangements as a means of borrowing from commercial banks. In India there is a traditional attachment to cash transactions and neglect of credit transactions, which has also hindered the growth of a bill market.

INSTITUTIONAL STRUCTURE

At the head of the structure of the money market is the RBI which controls and regulates this market through Discount and Finance House of India (DFHI). The control extends to all those operating in the call money market mostly financial institutions, banks and mutual funds. More recently companies and individual units have been allowed to operate in the money market as lenders.

The commercial paper (CP) issued by companies for raising short-term working capital is being developed in India. The participation certificates (PC) issued by banks and financial institutions, the deposit certificates (CD) issued by banks and factorisation bills are the other instruments that are being developed in this market. The institutions operating in these markets are banks, development finance institutions like IFC, ICICI, and IDBI, investment finance companies like the LIC, UTI, GIC, etc., and other financial institutions and companies. In the inter-bank money market, however, only the LIC and UTI have been permitted to operate in addition to banks. In 1990, the GIC, IDBI, NABARD, mutual funds and other financial institutions have also been permitted to operate. In April 1991, the RBI allowed the entry of any entity with bulk lendable resources of Rs. 20 crores and above as also the money market mutual funds to enter the call money market as lenders. This market is being developed in India by the establishment of Discount and Finance House by the Reserve Bank in April 1988, in collaboration with the financial institutions.

There is no secondary market for many instruments like treasury bills, commercial bills, CPs and CDs, etc. Recently, schemes for the development of secondary market in commercial paper and for trading in certificates of deposits and participation certificates have been initiated by the RBI. In the money market, UTI units PSU bonds and some government and semi-government bonds are also traded.

DISCOUNT AND FINANCE HOUSE OF INDIA (DFHI)

The RBI is the leader and controller of money market and to perform these functions on her behalf, the DFHI was designed. The DFHI was set up by the RBI in April 1988 with a paid up capital of Rs.100 crores. This was supposed to oversee and supervise the money market operations. It can operate and intervene through the Bid and offer rates in the interbank market, treasury bill market, discount and rediscount of treasury bills, short-term commercial bills, commercial paper and other money market instruments. Of the paid up capital, Rs.51 crores was contributed by the RBI, Rs. 33 crores by public sector banks and Rs.16 crores by public financial institutions. Thus, DFHI is a public sector institution for the purpose of stabilising the money market through purchase and sale operations in the instruments of trading in money market.

Its sources of funds are the following:

(a) Paid up capital of Rs. 100 crores.

(b) Credit limits of Rs. 200 crores with public sector banks.

(c) Back up refinance lines with the RBI.

Its functions at present are as follows:

1. Operations in inter bank call money market.
2. Purchases and sales (through bid and offer rates) of treasury bills of 14 days, to 364 days respectively. (182 days treasury bills are now discontinued).
3. Discount and rediscount of commercial bills, certificates of deposit and commercial paper etc.
4. Buying and selling of government securities with banks and financial institutions.

For the treasury bills, commercial bills etc., it gives bid and offer discount rates as for example 364 days TBs 9.90% (bid) and 9.50% (offer) and for commercial paper it gives only one discount rate, say 10.75%. For government securities it quotes both buying and selling prices, at which it does business on a daily basis.

It can be seen from the Economic Times or any Financial Daily paper, that DFHI is buying and selling sometimes while at other times, it only buys. The operations are not dictated by commercial considerations but by the requirements of money market conditions and the RBI policy.

It was only in 1992, that the DFHI has started operations in the government securities market in addition to its operations in the money market. While the discount or rediscount rates are given in the case of money market instruments, actual purchase and sale prices as offered by the DFHI in the government securities market are published by the press, as released by the DFHI.

It should also be noted that DFHI is operating in crores of rupees in a variety of instruments both in the money market and the government securities market. Bulk of these operations are in response to the market conditions and to absorb the excesses of supply and demand.

NEW MONEY MARKET INSTRUMENTS

The excess cash balances of corporate units, banks and financial institutions flow into money market. But the money market has for long remained primitive and underdeveloped, confined to inter-bank call market and 91 days treasury bills. It was only since the publication of Chakravarthy Committee Report on the Monetary System (1985) that reforms started. Beginning with freeing of interest rates and raising the coupon rates on government securities, a new institution of DFHI was setup and new instruments of trading were introduced. Thus, treasury bills on auction basis were initiated for 91 days, and 364 days, respectively. The rates on them are determined by market forces. These come under government sector instruments.

For encouragement of bill finance by banks and to promote a secondary market in bills, the RBI has permitted the issue of negotiable usance promissory notes against trade bills discounted by banks. The government has waived the stamp duty payable on trade bill so as to encourage the secondary market in them.

The following new instruments are introduced in the banking sector and in the private corporate sector, during Nineties.

(a) 91 days participation certificates, involving no transfer underlying asset risk to the borrower but subject to a ceiling rate of 12%.

(b) 91 to 180 days PCs, bearing the full risk of underlying asset but subject to a floor rate of 14%. The floor and ceiling rates were abolished in 1995-96.

(c) Commercial paper : The companies with good credit rating say upto P2 are allowed to borrow through issue of commercial paper of 90 to 364 days at market determined rate of interest.

(d) Certificates of deposits of 6 months to 12 months, representing the deposits of the private sector in the banking system which are negotiable and tradeable.

(e) Factorisation Bills involving the inland bills receivables and supply bills payable to companies and banks converted into factorisation bills with or without recourse. These factoring and allied services are being provided by subsidiaries setup by banks, namely, SBI, Canara Bank, PNB etc. These bills are purchased by the subsidiaries mentioned above from the creditors and the funds are collected in due course from the debtors. These bills can be either with risk or without risk, involved in all debt collection.

(f) Forfaiting Bills : Foreign bills for discount and converting credit bills to cash.

Classification of Money Market Instruments

The instruments of money market fall under the broad heads shown below :

MONEY MARKET

Govt. and Semi Govt.	**Private**	**Inter Bank call Money Market**	**Inter Corporate Investments**
(a) Auction Treasury Bills of 14 and 91 days, and 364 day.	(a) Commercial & Trade Bills (b) Commercial paper (c) Certificates of Deposit	Inter Bank Loans, Deposits, Borrowings and Lendings.	Inter-corporate Loans, Deposits, Borrowing and Lending.
(b) Govt. Securities of short-term duration of upto one year.	(d) Participation Certificates		
(c) UTI Units	(e) Factorisation Bills. (Inland Trade bills)		
(d) PSU Bonds.	(f) Forfaiting Bills (Foreign Trade bills)		

Among the instruments more recently initiated, some beginning worth the name was made in respect of participation certificates and factorisation bills. Although more headway was made in respect of commercial paper and certificates of deposit, there is no secondary market in these instruments, as visualised by the RBI. The reason for this is that the holders of these bills keep them in their portfolio until maturity for two reasons. Firstly, many banks and financial institutions lack the technical expertise of proper portfolio management and secondly there was no well developed market for many segments of the money market. Till recently, there were no worthwhile avenues of investment open to the operators in the money market. Only over last few years, new instruments were brought into the money market and a secondary market is being developed in them along with financial deregulation and liberalisation of procedures in the market. The market is now open for a larger number of players and the volume of funds flowing into the market has since increased enormously. These developments were the result of recommendations of Vaghul Committee on Money Market Reforms and recommendations of Narasimham Committee on Financial Reforms.

Money Market Rates

The most liquid of the money market instruments, namely, call money has a rate which fluctuates widely from 1% onwards, as it depends upon the liquidity position of banks. The highest rate is probably on the L.C. bills of 90 days and non-L.C. bills which may go upto 19% or 20%. The tables below given various instruments of money market and their rates of return, yields to maturity and other details of duration etc. The main instruments traded in this market which can be seen from the accompanying tables are treasury bills, commercial bills and certificates of deposits etc. The expertise of management lies in selecting the right mix of assets consistent with the funds position of the company and market conditions. The Table below presents the data on the rates of interest on the major money market instruments.

Rates of Return on Treasury Instruments
(A Few Examples)

(as in March) (in % ages)

INSTRUMENTS	YEAR – LAST WEEK OR FORTNIGHT				
	1992	**1994**	**1996**	**1999**	**2005**
1. CALL MONEY RATE	30.63	6.38	10.87	7.69	4.72
2. 91 days Treasury Bill (Auction Cut off yield)	—	7.46	12.97	9.45	5.24
3. 364 Days T.B. Rate	9.27	9.97	13.12	10.27	5.63
4. Certificate of Deposit	14.5	9.60	17.13	11.50	6.34
5. Commercial paper	16.50	11.50	20.15	11.50	7.25
6. Minimum Lending Rate of banks (SBI)	19.0	14.00	14.5	12-13½	10.25
7. Coupon Rate on 10 year G.O.I. Loan.	11.0	12.50	14.0	12.25	6.11 – 7.06

Source : RBI Annual Reports of 2004-05 and earlier years.

The following table gives the indicative market rates for various government debt instruments. The yield on government paper represents the risk free rate of return.

Government Paper as in 2004-05 (March end)

Duration	Asset Description	Price (Rs.)	YTM (%)
91 days	Treasury Bills	98.69	5.32
364 days	Treasury Bills	94.70	5.61
5 year	12.29	NA	6.09
10 year Govt. Loans	11.50	NA	6.71

Source: RBI Bulletin, March 2006.

Magnitude of Turnover

The above tables present the data on the rates yielded on various instruments of Money market. The equally important indicators of this market are the magnitudes of turnover of the major instruments. The following table presents the data on turnover on daily basis in the recent years. The data shows the general trend of rising magnitudes of trade in major sub-markets of Money market, in which the treasury manager operates.

Table 13.1

(Rs. in crores)

Month—Daily Averages	Daily Turnover in Term Money market	Transactions in Repo market	Commercial Paper	Certificates of Deposits
April 2002	225	47,020	8,046	1,393
April 2003	604	41,815	5,994	1,485
April 2004	325	15,195	10,362	4,725
April 2005	661	12,174	15,598	16,602

Source: RBI Annual Reports

The RBI has been trying to develop the Term Money market and Repo market and with limited success. The fortunes in these markets varied from year to year depending on various factors uncontrolled by RBI. Turnover in Term market and in Repo market fluctuated, or declined due to the factors influencing them are the liquidity conditions with banks, and the RBI monetary and banking policy. The outstanding amounts in C.P.s and C.D.s showed however a consistent rise. Similarly the amounts involved in forex market through forward rate agreements showed a consistent rise. Commercial bills rediscounted by banks showed varying conditions due to liquidity conditions of banks and trade and commerce volumes involved (not shown in the above table).

Commercial Paper (CP)

The commercial paper is a new money market instrument introduced by the RBI in January 1990. A company with a net worth of more than Rs. 10 crores (later reduced to Rs.4 crore) can issue commercial paper. Its maximum permissible bank finance (MPBF) for working capital requirements should not be less than Rs.25 crores (later reduced to Rs.4 crore). It should have a current ratio of 1.33 : 1

and a credit rating of excellent (P1) (Plus) should be secured from the CRISIL (later relaxed to P2 only). A company should be listed on one or more of the stock exchanges and can be a FERA company or Indian company, which was later discarded by the RBI, making CP an independent instrument. The maturity period should be 3 to 12 months and the issue should be for a minimum of Rs. 1 crore (later reduced to Rs. 25 lakhs) and in multiples of Rs.25 lakhs (later reduced to Rs. 5 lakhs).

The secondary market transactions may be for an amount of Rs.5 lakhs and in multiples of it. The RBI's prior permission is required for each issue and the general permission is required for each company to enter this market, which was later delegated to the banks. The CP should be raised only for working capital purposes and less than 75% of the cash credit limit of the bank to the company. The company will have to bear the expenses of issue, commitment charges, stamp duty, etc. These are not permitted to be underwritten. The NRIs are permitted to invest on a non-repatriation basis. A company may enter into standby facilities with the bankers to ensure the meeting of the CP liabilities of the company which was later disallowed by the RBI making CP independent of Bank credit. The brokers can enter only in the secondary market trading as the issue is not permitted to be underwritten. Interest rates are free to be decided by market rates and banks are given discretion without reference to RBI. In 1996 the CP was delinked from cash credit limits of banks, as banks are asked to reduce this component of bank credit and increase loan component to corporate clients.

Certificates of Deposits (CD)

Only banks can issue the CD. It is a document of title to a time deposit. It is a bearer certificate and is negotiable in the market. The minimum CD should be for Rs.1 crore, later lowered to Rs. 50 lakhs and in multiples of Rs. 25 lakhs and further lowered to Rs. 5 lakhs, later.

It is issued by banks against deposits kept by individuals, companies and institutions and is marketable after 15 days. It can have a tenure of 91 days to 1 year. Banks are to observe CRR and SLR rules for them. These are permitted up to 1% of average aggregate deposits, later raised to 7% of average aggregate deposits. The Bank-wise limits were renewed in October 1993. They are issued on a discounting basis. No loans and no buy-backs are permitted and no duplicates are to be issued by banks. Banks cannot discount them or negotiate them. The burden of stamp duty did not allow the secondary market to develop. The reduction of maturity period of time deposits to 15 days was good for this market.

Certificates of deposits were permitted to be issued from 1991-92 by the all India financial institutions like IDBI, ICICI, IFC, etc. The maturity period for them may range from 1 year to 3 years and aggregate limit for such issues by them was fixed by RBI from time to time. There is no ceiling interest rate on them. The interest rates vary depending on the liquidity conditions in the market.

Commercial Bills

The Commercial Bills market did not develop in India due to prevailing cash credit system of credit delivery. In order to encourage Bill Culture, the RBI advised banks in October 1997 that atleast 25% of inland credit purchases of borrowers should be through Bills. Absence of a secondary market in bills has also affected the development of the market for bill finance.

With a view to developing the bills market in India, the interest rate ceiling of 12.5% on rediscounting of commercial bills, along with the interest rate ceilings of 10.5-11.5% on inter bank term money and 12.5% on inter bank participation. Certificates were withdrawn since May 1, 1989. The success of the bill finance scheme will however depend on the extent of financial discipline of the borrowers, which has to be encouraged.

Term Money Market

The RBI has been attempting to develop the Term Money Market in India, which was absent due to prevailing restrictions on banks. As early as October 1993, RBI permitted many public FIs to borrow the term money of 3 to 6 months from the market within the limits stipulated for each institution. In April 1997 banks were exempted from maintaining CRR and SLR on liabilities to the banking system, subject to the condition that the effective CRR and SLR on total demand and time liabilities would not be less than 3% and 25% respectively. In April 1999, the RBI clarified that there was no restriction on the maximum period for which repos can be undertaken so as to encourage the time money borrowed from the market. The banks and FIs are now free to borrow term money from the market.

Participation Certificates

As in the case of certificates of deposit, participation certificates are also issued by banks for periods ranging from 3 months to 6 months extended later upto a maximum period of one year. All the instruments are as per the recommendations of Vaghul Committee Report on money market instruments in India. Essentially these are instruments for participating in the advances by a bank in need of funds by other lender banks and FIs. Two types of such certificates are being developed.

1. 91 days PCs involving no transfer of the underlying asset risk to the borrower but subject to a ceiling rate of 12.5%.

2. 91 to 180 days PCs bearing full risk on the underlying asset but not requiring statutory reserves unlike in the above case and subject to a floor rate of 14%.

The stipulation relating to fixation of interest was withdrawn in October 1993. Subsequently, lending and borrowing rates of banks have been freed from RBI controls, except for lendings below Rs. 2 lakhs.

The first one is unsecured debt, but securitised for the purpose of negotiation and development of secondary market. The second one which may extend upto one year is more risky and carry a higher return.

MANAGEMENT IN MONEY MARKET

Conversion of cash into short-term instruments of money markets to utilise the surpluses of cash for earning positive return and conversion back into cash to meet liquidity need is the main objective in money market operations. The management of such activities of investment has to balance between the opposing objectives of liquidity needs on the one hand and income earnings on the other. This requires expertise and experience. Besides, the selection of proper instruments among treasury bills, commercial bills, intercorporate investments commercial paper etc. involves a critical choice, as that should enable the manager to maximise returns without sacrificing the needs of liquidity. Should he use his funds in bill discounting investment in commercial paper or other avenues of money market? In this selection process, he has a clear direction of the period for which he can spare the funds, risk he can take and the return he can expect or aim at.

In the process of management of funds, the treasury manager thus has to have a perspective of;

1. Return aimed at,
2. Risk prepared to take, and
3. Time duration of investment.

Money market provides a buffer between cash or liquidity and long-term high return investments in the stock and capital market.

In portfolio management also, the manager has to keep a proportion of funds in money market instruments. This proportion depends on the objective the fund, growth versus regular income or various combinations of these ob tives. Once the proportion allotted to money market instruments is chosen, the major task is the allocation of the allotted funds into various instrum within money market depending upon their risk-return characteristics.

The basic principles of management would apply in respect of investme money market also. Cost effectiveness and maximisation of returns are the ob tives that the management aims at. These objectives can be achieved by a prop choice of the instruments bearing in mind their characteristics. Besides cash excess of requirement should be used profitably and the return of funds shou be in excess of the inflation rate or a positive real rate of return.

The money market instruments are classified under the category of goverr ment instruments, inter bank call money, corporate instruments PSU bonds an UTI Units etc. The risk on government and semi-government instruments is lower, but their return is also low compared with the investments in the corporate sector. Thus, treasury managers aiming at higher returns concentrate on bill discounting, commercial paper, certificate of deposits and intercorporate deposits. But a judicious combination of investments in call money for higher returns and in the treasury bills for quick liquidity would be necessary for a balanced investment. The choice above depends on the environmental conditions, opportunities, returns and risks.

TREASURY FUNCTIONS IN COMPANIES

The role of Treasury Function is to manage funds in an efficient manner, so that the operations in the area of finance are facilitated in relation to company's manufacturing and Trading activities. The treasury function is thus supplemental and complementary to the finance management functions. For the purpose of performing this role, the treasury manager operates in various financial markets, including the inter-corporate market, money market segments, etc. Treasury function is a handmaid of finance function.

More recently, with the growth of capital market and investment activity the role of treasury was expanded to make it a profit centre in each corporate unit whether it is a manufacturing company or finance and investment company. Traditionally the role of treasury has been to support the manufacturing function. More recently importance of treasury has increased due to liberalised financial markets and market oriented economy. The profits in manufacturing and trading activities can be increased by the treasury operations and secondly, where manufacturing activity is weak, or loss making, for some reasons, treasury is expected to create profits, so that the overall profitability of the company is improved.

During 1992 to 1994, when the companies raised money from public through new issues, they collected funds much in excess of the needs, for manufacturing activity. The excess funds were entrusted to treasury managers to improve profitability. The cash rich companies also resorted to this practice of using the treasury for making extra profits for the company. But during 1995-99 when the finance markets were depressed, the finance function was at a low gear and treasury function became more critical for banks and companies.

inancial Borrowing by Bonds or GDRs

Another such area of excess funds is from foreign borrowing. Some high edit rated companies with good track record can borrow abroad at cheaper es of 5 to 10% including the cost of issue and brokerage etc. Such brisk inflow unds was seen in 1993 and 1994. These funds flowed into stock market, money rket, and forex market, wherever the returns are higher despite the guidelines their disposition, there is a time gap between the inflow and their use in the ceptable avenues say from 30 to 90 days during which an astute treasury anager can almost double the money by rotation of such excess funds, in oreign markets.

An expert treasury manager should not however be greedy, because he can see the high risk avenues and is not lured by high returns, if they are going to sink him in trouble. He is shrewd to see the red signals. At the same time he has to take calculated risks and hedge them where necessary, because in the context of high risk-high return scenario, he cannot maximise the returns, if he is afraid of risk. But his prudence and expertise tells him how far to go and where to stop.

In the boom conditions of 1993-94 many good companies like Videocon were reported to have defaulted in ICD market. In such times the ICD rates will soar to 40 or 50% when particularly money market conditions are tight as in October-November 1995 when call rates soared to 130%. These conditions do occur although infrequently but even so prudence and proper risk management are necessary for treasury function.

HOW TREASURY CAN BE A PROFIT CENTRE

Treasury Manager uses the extra cash or funds in the company to lend and to deploy in various segments of the money market lending inter-corporate market in discounting bills or certificates of deposits or commercial paper etc. In the inter-corporate market (ICD) many times, collateral is taken for lending for short periods of 15 days to a few months and that is the major market for the majority of treasury managers.

The Treasury Manager trades in the interest rate differentials and maturity differentials of various instruments. He will shift funds from one to the other, depending upon the maturity and interest rates (or yields). He has a given maturity pattern required for the company, depending on the anticipated excess outflows compared to inflows in any period or any special need like the advance tax payment, interest or instalment payment to banks and FIs etc.

Example of Operations

To give an example; some funds (say Rs.50 lakhs) are required 30 days hence and another Rs. 1 crore two months hence and another Rs. 2 crores three months hence thetreasury manager looks out for counterparts in other companies in need of funds and places Rs.50 lakhs with two or three companies for periods ranging upto 30 days with or without collateral depending on the risk of the other company. There is the inter corporate deposit which will give him a return of 10-15% for that period. Next he places Rs.2 crores in commercial paper of 60 days at a return of 6 to 8% or alternatively rotates Rs.2 crores in inter corporate market at higher rates, if he has good customers. The funds which are free for 3 months are used for badla financing at a rate of return of 15 to 20% provided he has contacts with stock broking firms. If none of these avenues of yielding instruments are possible, he may keep money in bank instruments of certificates of deposits (6 to 8%) or in discounting bills of 90 days at rates of 15 to 20%. Some bills are available even [illegible] 30 to 60 days and contact with bankers is necessary for the purpose. The fun[illegible] managers in banks, financial institutions and other companies are to be the cont[illegible]act points for treasury operations. Fund placement needs expertise of high order with good acumen, quick decision and good contact points. He is constrained by [illegible] available opportunities and requirements.

Treasury operations need expertise, because in his operations he has to shift quickly from low yielding to high yielding avenues and from one market to another. He has to catch opportunities quickly and take decision on the spot and act immediately. The operations may also involve borrowing from cheap sources and lending at higher rates. Suppose the company has deposits from public, which have just flowed in and not used for working capital. The treasury manager uses them for lending at 20% for 30 days while he pays interest on deposits at 15% — a clear Profit of 5%. Including the casts of servicing, administration, brokerage etc. the margin of profit may come to 2-3 percentage points even so, such opportunities abound in plenty for a shrewd treasury manager.

NEW INSTRUMENTS INTRODUCED

After the introduction of economic and financial reforms a number of new instruments have been introduced in the capital market. Some of them are relevant to money market operations, as well, although they are meant mainly for capital market, as some of them are tradeable.

(1) Zero Coupon Bonds (ZCBs): For the first time Zero Coupon Bonds of five year maturity were floated on an auction basis for a notified amount of Rs.3,000 crores on January 17, 1994 by the Government. The main characteristics of these bonds are that no interest is paid periodically, but sold on auction basis and not at fixed price of Rs.100, as usual and that they are redeemed at par of Rs.100 at the time of redemption. These are attractive to issuers as there is no cash outflow until maturity. They are suitable to some investors as they have lock in of funds for a period and when they receive a lump-sum at the maturity, they are subject to capital gains tax which is lower than income tax. The government received Rs.1624 crores at so many overwhelming bids and cutoff point was taken as Rs.53.90 to get Rs.100 at the end of 5 years.

(2) Secured Premium Notes (SPN): For the first time, these were issued by TISCO with a detachable warrant and redeemable after 5 years. The warrant attached therewith assures the holder the right to apply and get allotted equity shares, provided the SPN is fully paid up like ZCB, no interest will be paid until maturity. Unlike ZCB, the holder will have the option either to get the par value plus the premium after the lock in period or get the conversion into equity as exercised by the holder after a specified period or at the time of redemption. The SPNs are sold at par of Rs.100 and redeemed at the end of 4 to 7 years at a premium, if they are not converted into equity earlier.

(3) Non-Convertible Debentures (NCDs): With detachable warrants, but with a coupon rate, the holder of NCDs with detachable warrants is given the option to buy a specific number of shares from the company at a predetermined price, at the end of 3/5 years. If the shares are not applied for through surrender of warrants the company will be free to dispose them of and the holder of NCD will get interest and repayment of principal at maturity. Reliance issued such NCDs with warrants to UTI in 1991-92.

(4) Zero Interest Fully Convertible Debentures: These are having face value of say Rs.100 and no interest will be paid during the period, but at the end of the lock in period, conversion into equity is given at a predetermined price and extended automatically and compulsorily. L&T has issued these FCDs, of a similar nature.

(5) Equity Shares with Detachable Warrants: Fully paid equity shares are sold to the public with detachable warrants to induce the investors to accept the shares. The detachable warrants are tradeable as they are listed on a stock exchange. The investors benefit, if the warrants can be sold at a good price which is the case if the company is doing well in terms of profitability of operations. Returns on these instruments are higher than on regular equity shares.

(6) Fully Convertible Cumulative Preference Shares (equipref): Equipref has two parts — part A and part B. Part A is convertible into equity compulsorily and automatically at the time of allotment. Part B will be redeemed at par or convertible into equity shares or repaid at par at the time of maturity after the lock in period of 3 to 5 years. During this period it is paid a fixed dividend. Conversion is at the option of the holder and if conversion is opted it will be lower than market average price-average of the high and lows during the preceding six months prior to conversion. These were given by L & T and Blue Blend, etc.

(7) Preference Shares with Warrants: Each preference share carries a fixed dividend and a certain number of warrants, what will entitle the holder to apply for equity shares for cash at a premium. These preference shares are not transferable for a period of 3 years and between 3rd and 5th years, warrants can be converted into equity in one or more stages at predetermined rates. If the holder fails to convert, unsubscribed portion will lapse and will continue to be a preference share entitled to a fixed dividend.

(8) Secured Zero Interest Partly Convertible Debentures with Detachable and Separately Tradeable Warrants: It has two parts — part A is convertible into equity, at a fixed rate at the time of allotment and part B is non-convertible to be redeemed at par, at the end of the specified period. Part B has detachable warrants which are tradeable. But if held by the holder it will entitle him to a specified number of shares at a price to be worked out by the company.

(9) Fully Convertible Bonds with Interest (Optional): These bonds/debentures do not carry an interest upto first six months and after that, the holder will have the option to be indicated in the beginning itself to apply for equity at a premium. Interest is payable, if conversion is not opted at a predetermined rate.

(10) Floating Rate Notes/Debentures: These are instruments of debt of short duration say five or six months, extendable upto 5 years, carrying no fixed rate, but the rate is 2% above the Bank Deposit rate of two years and above — say if the deposit rate is 12% the floating rate is 14% and so on. UTI and ICICI have issued these for institutions/companies. The floating rate Bonds of 3 years to 5 years are also issued on the same terms. The SBI had issued them in 1993 first. Interest is payable half yearly at the rates adjustable to the Bank rate or Bank deposit rate of 2 years and above and conversion into equity is also offered in some cases.

(11) Naked Debentures: These are unsecured debentures and are issued at a fixed interest rate by only high credit rated companies, for fixed years 5 to 7 years. The public may not prefer these securities and hence mostly aim at corporate and institutional investors.

(12) Debentures or Equity with Loyalty Coupons: If the investor continues to hold atleast for two/three years, the loyalty coupon will entitle him with a fixed amount of equity for equivalent amount. There is no market for loyalty coupons and there is no option to investor, except that he may decide to sell or not to sell before the lock in period, depending on his needs.

(13) Discount Bonds (DBs) and Deep Discount Bonds (DDBs): These are bonds at a discounted value (say at a price of Rs.35) for a par value of Rs.100. DDBs are issued by IDBI, with a maturity of 25 years at an issue price of Rs.2700 with a maturity value of Rs.1 lakh at the end of 25 years. DBs are generally issued for 5 to 7 years. These are issued by SBI, IDBI etc.

(14) Capital Indexed Bonds: These Bonds are linked to capital values, or inflation Index, as measured by WPI or CPI. They are issued with a face value of Rs. 100 or Rs. 1000 and have a maturity period of 5 to 7 years. These are issued generally by government and semi-government and are open to corporates, individuals, and institutions.

Other Money Market Instruments

PSU Bonds, UTI units and treasury bills are also traded in money market. Acceptance business and bill discounting is developing in India as well. Money market is kept open now to corporates, individuals, MFs, etc., if they have surpluses above a specified amount to operate and lend. ICD market with many variants with or without collateral is developing in India. Deposit certificates of banks, participation certificates, to which a reference was made earlier are developing faster due to security of funds with banks. With freeing of interest rates on deposits of companies and of banks, deposits of above one year, there is keen competition for short-term funds of less than one year and for one to three years. The fact that restriction on NRI to lend in India is removed in Sept., 1996, may lead to more short-term funds to flow into India.

The treasury operations in the new instruments and in short-term money market funds assume all the importance due to the recent liberalisations. The RBI has been encouraging the growth and widening of the money market in India by granting entry into market to new bodies agencies, corporates etc. and by promoting the growth of money market mutual funds.

MONEY MARKET MUTUAL FUNDS

The RBI has been exhorting the banks to set up money market mutual funds (MMMFs) to participate in the money market operations time and again since 1992. But banks have ignored the offer, as the time was unsuitable for them. Finally some banks have setup MMMFs, after 1996.

MMMFs have been launched successfully in many developed countries, as they have well developed money markets and the short-term rates are attractive enough for investors. The operations of MMMFs in these countries have grown over the years. But Indian conditions are different and short-term money rates are lower than long-term rates except in the case of call money rates which may fluctuate from a low of six per cent to any high rate. The RBI has its own reasons for asking MMMFs to be set up and operate in money market, namely, that wide fluctuations in call rates can be narrowed by the funds mobilised from public by these MMMFs through their operations in markets and channelling them into the money market.

Specialising in Mutual Funds

In many developed countries there are specialised mutual funds as for example, for investment in real estate or in gold and other metals or for any industry group like electronics etc. One such example of specialised mutual funds is money market mutual funds, which will pool the savings for investment in the instruments in the money market. In the Indian conditions, money market is lacking in the width and depth and MMMFs are expected to help provide better liquidity and act as a vehicle of development of various segments of money market. From the point of view of Investors, they are expected to provide a window of short maturity investments with better returns.

The launching of the MMMFs and their schemes depended on (i) the availability of extra savings/resources from public (ii) preference for the type of short-term assets which money market provides (iii) width and resilience of the market to provide avenues for investment on a large-scale by these funds and (iv) the extent of returns available on these market instruments.

MMMFs Regulation

It was decided in October 1999 that RBI will cease to regulate the Money Market Mutual Funds and that SEBI will take over the regulation of them like other Capital Market Mutual Funds. MMMFs, registered with RBI will have to seek SEBI registration from October 1999. The banks and Public Financial Institutions, which floated MMMFs were asked not to offer Money Market deposit accounts. If the banks want to operate MMMFs, they have to set up asset management company with an investment of Rs. 10 crores. Besides, they have to follow the trust structure, necessary for setting up of mutual funds, as per the SEBI guidelines.

This change was necessitated to bring all the MMMFs on par with Liquid Funds, floated by regular mutual funds. They will no longer be required to observe a lock in period of 15 days, as hitherto, under the RBI guidelines. Uniformly all mutual funds are brought under a single window control of the SEBI. The deposits of banks are insulated from the deposit accounts of MMMFs which separates banking business from the mutual fund business.

The banks will have to set up separate outfits of a mutual fund and observe all the SEBI guidelines, if they want to operate any schemes of Money Market Mutual Funds. They have also to take prior permission of RBI before approaching SEBI. This is a healthy development in many ways as the SEBI can now regulate on an even level all the mutual funds, whether they are operating in the money market or capital market. Secondly, banks will have to separate their Money Market Mutual Fund business and follow the regular Mutual Fund route to operate any schemes of deposit accounts for money market operations. Control will also be strengthened and the growth of MMMF business will be on healthier grounds. It has been decided to allow cheque writing facility to gilt funds and to those Liquid Funds' Income Schemes of Mutual Funds, which predominantly invest in Money Market instruments upto not less than 80% of their corpus, subject to the same safeguards, as prescribed for MMMFs. The RBI has also issued operating guidelines in this regard.

The MMMFs could be set up un the private sector or public sector, by banks, FIs, foreign institutional agencies of foreign security firms with an Indian partner. But all of them were regulated by the RBI before October 1999. But after that, the regulation of these has come within the fold of SEBI. Besides, they have to conform to all SEBI guidelines with regard to Mutual Funds and Asset Management Companies.

The SEBI and RBI have come to an agreement in January 2000 with regard to the regulation of the Debt Market Segment in the capital market. The RBI and the Government desired that the sole agency of regulation of all segments of the capital market should be SEBI only. In this background, the control of money market funds has come to be vested in the SEBI.

RBI's Perspective

The RBI policy statements have made it amply clear that their objective is to make money market segments grow in depth and width and iron out undue fluctuations due to scarcity or surfeit of funds, by allowing these MMMFs to operate in the money market.

The RBI expects that they would bring in funds when necessary to provide liquidity to the market and take them back for better returns after 30 days of lock in period. Even among the instruments of money market, not many have returns of more than 8 to 10 per cent and not many are well traded. The most popular can be commercial paper and treasury bills with rates varying from 6 per cent to 8 per cent. In the call money markets, rates may fluctuate widely from one per cent to 100 per cent or so but that will be for a few days only in a year and if there is a lock in period of 30 days as the RBI stipulated, there may not be many takers for these schemes. This lock in period was removed by Jan. 2000.

Scope for Mutual Funds

Having seen the lacklustre performance of the Indian mutual funds one wonders whether there will be any investors in MMMFs except corporates. If these funds set up in USA and other developed countries succeeded and set the pace of growth of other mutual funds, the picture was the reverse of that in India today. Money market returns are higher sometimes than those on capital markets in these countries, while in India barring the highly fluctuating call rates, the rates on money market instruments are lower than in the capital markets. Barring the exceptional periods like the bearish phase, the returns on stock markets are higher than the maximum rates of 10 per cent on money market instruments. Similarly, the returns in the money market which have higher interest rates ranging upto 100 per cent in the unorganised sector will be exceptions rather than the rule. If that is the normal interest rate structure in India, how investors prefer money market returns to stock market returns? Then, where is the chance of individual investors to participate in such schemes? Particularly, in the scenario of 1996-97 investors were very choosy and scared of many scams in capital market and mutual fund schemes.

Money Market Access

Earlier to June 1995, only public sector's general mutual funds were allowed to operate in the money market, for lending in the call/notices money and rediscounting market instruments. The facility was extended later in June 1995 to private sector mutual funds which are licensed and approved by the SEBI, as it will promote liquidity in money market.

Public sector banks and institutions were allowed to set up money market mutual funds to operate in the money markets, as per the earlier policy. This policy of MMMFs was first announced by the RBI in April 1992. After four long years, no single MMMFs registered or set up. The market perceptions differ from those of the RBI policy makers and the reasons for making this scheme a non-starter were the interest rate structure in India and the inopportune time of its announcement when the money market conditions were unfavourable and interest rates in the short end of the spectrum were low.

The situation is different later in that there is liquidity crunch in the money market and the prevailing rates are attractive for investors, but not for individual investors whose hard-earned savings needed returns more than the inflation rate of 8 per cent and a premium on them — in total return of 15 per cent. Even the capital market mutual funds do not provide this return. But the corporate sector, which is normally satisfied with a return of even less than 20 per cent but prefer shorter maturities, may be interested in these MMMFs but these corporate investments in MMMFs were excluded by the RBI in their policy statement. This restriction along with a restriction of lock in period of 30 days would make it unattractive to companies, insurance and pension funds etc. But individuals may not be interested in them although it is kept open for them.

ELEMENTS OF NEW POLICY FOR MMMFs

Under the relaxed new policy for MMMFs, the RBI has permitted the private sector mutual funds also. It has also dispensed with the earlier limiting floor on the size of the mutual funds and the investment limits on individual instruments. But the limiting factors which still remained are: (i) it should be confined to individuals and not corporates and (ii) there should be a lock-in period of 46 days for the scheme, which were also removed in mid 1996, and the lock in period was brought down to 30 days and later removed.

Earlier, there was a stipulation that the minimum subscription size for an MMMFs should be Rs.50 crore. Besides, the earlier guidelines *viz.* only 25 per cent of their funds in treasury bills, 30 per cent in call and notice money, a maximum of 15 per cent of the fund should be in commercial paper and 20 per cent in commercial bills at any time, etc. were removed. While removing the maximum investment limits for MMMFs in respect of CPs the RBI has, however, retained the MMMFs exposure to CPs by any individual company to a maximum of 30 per cent of the total resources raised by the fund.

As regards the instruments of investment, these remained unchanged as before, namely, the treasury bills, dated government securities with an unexpired maturity of upto one year, call and notice money, commercial paper and certificates of deposit. The MMMFs cannot have any investments in Inter-corporate deposits or bonds floated by public sector units and debentures issued by private corporate sector.

It is clear from the above guidelines that the RBI wants them to develop the debt market of the government and supplement the funds of banks and financial institutions through such contributions to commercial paper and certificates of deposits etc. What they are intended to do is to widen the money market and help the cause of liquidity of banking and financial system.

But, by excluding the corporates as investors and eliminating their access to the PSU bonds, debentures of corporates and intercorporate deposits, the MMMFs are deprived of excess funds of corporates and their investments in corporate debt. These limits were also withdrawn later in 1996.

The RBI has also allowed the NRI investors to repatriate dividend income abroad but not the principal amount, which will not therefore encourage any large investments from NRIs also.

The constraints to growth of MMMFs in India, under the present policy guidelines are thus needed to be relaxed. The market in bill discounting is not large and is concentrated with banks. The inter-corporate funds market is however developing well so far, and with recent liberalisation of the limit for such investments upto 30% (including subsidiaries), this market will develop faster than before.

By January 2000, many restrictions on MMMFs were removed or relaxed, the regulation of these funds was passed on to SEBI. They have to be set up as Trusts and they can even have schemes or liquid funds based on gilted securities with a checking facility if there is a tie-up with a bank. Accordingly, the MMMFs began to expand their activities in the 21st century. They were expanding in the area of Liquid Money Market funds and gilted funds during 2000 to 2006. As the general MFs were also allowed to operate in the Money market and gilt edged securities, it is difficult to separate the role of each of these categories of MFs. But as the growth of the assets under these schemes is substantial, we can surmise, the MMMFs should have played a catalytic role under these schemes to expand and deepen the money market in particular. The treasury operator has to keep in mind these areas of recent development before he operates in the Money Market. It may be mentioned in this context, that net assets under the liquid and gilted fund's of MFs has grown to Rs. 58,634 crores by 2004-05.

Conclusions

To conclude, the chapter sets that the details of the money market, in which the Trends and features, composition of the sub-markets, constitutents, institutional structure and instruments operated upon are set out. It provides the necessary background for the treasury manager to operate in the money market.

❑ ❑ ❑

14 GILT-EDGED MARKET OPERATIONS

Introduction

Gilt-edged market is a market for government and semi-government securities. These are issued by the government through the RBI to the public, which in this case are banks, FIs, PFs, institutions, companies etc. Since 1992 these securities are auctioned and the discount on sales determines the rate of interest. The issues with fixed coupon rate as before, are confined to issues in the State Government borrowings or even discontinued in the case of Central Government issues.

These securities are promissory notes of the government representing their borrowings from the public to meet the gap between their income and expenditure or their capital expenditure. This market is captive in nature because the Law requires some institutions to invest a proportion of these funds in government and semi-government securities. Such institutions are banks, financial institutions, finance and investment companies, provident funds, pension funds, trusts etc. As the interest rates on these securities are low and they are for longer periods of 5 years and more, the individuals and partnerships etc., are not interested in them. More recently with the raising of interest rates on them nearer to market rates, some institutions and companies are getting interested in them. Banks have to invest in them a minimum of 25% of net demand and time abilities. PFs and insurance companies have to invest 30% to 50% of the total funds and NBFCs up to a minimum of 15% of the total funds in Central and State Government guaranteed bonds. LIC has to invest 75% of its funds in government and semi-government securities. This has been recently relaxed by the government.

Form of Securities

The securities are issued at present in the form of stock certificates and Promissory Notes. If they are stock certificates, they are registered with the RBI banks and financial institutions are permitted to hold these in the SGL account with the RBI instead of taking them in physical stock certificates. For transfer after buying and selling, if they are held in the books of SGL of the PDO of the RBI, their book entries would be enough to effect the transfer. Otherwise, these stock certificates are not transferable by mere endorsement as in the case of SGL books of the RBI and can be transferred by executing transfer deeds, as per the requirements of Law. The RBI has been encouraging the bankers now to hold them in Demat form, when the transferability becomes easier and quicker in respect of traders on NSE.

The RBI is a banker to government and as such debt management is a responsibility of the RBI and banks and RBI holds the bulk of the public debt of the government in the form of these securities. Only a small proportion of it is held by insurance companies, PFs etc. The holders of these securities do not operate in this market for portfolio management purposes except for in the case of foreign banks and SBI. The secondary market has now become active and trading in that market is growing in volume and value.

Components of Gilt-edged Market

In the gilt-edged market, as in the case of Corporate Securities there are two sections, namely, Primary Market and Secondary Market. The chart below shows the details of these markets.

The Primary Market is a wholesale market where RBI is the underwriter and allots the securities to the applicants on behalf of the government. Many of these are sold now on auction basis and allotments are made to those whose bids are above a reasonable level set by the RBI. On the same basis, the RBI sells the Repos (or Repurchase Agreements) of government securities to the institutions, banks, etc. to meet the market demands. The interest rates are decided by the discounts quoted in these bids and these are market related rates.

CHART I

PRIMARY MARKET	GILT-EDGED MARKET	SECONDARY MARKET
	RBI	
WHOLESALE MARKET (System of primary dealers as wholesalers and market makers)		RETAIL MARKET (The operations of primary dealers)
BANKS, FIs, LIC, GIC, PFs, OTHERS	DFHI/STCI (of RBI), BROKERS, BANKS, FIs, PFs, Etc. (OTC)	
UNDERWRITING BY RBI.		
Issue of Certificates and their servicing	OPERATIONS OF RBI	
	DIRECT with BANKS FIs, PFs, Etc.	INDIRECT through Licensed Dealers
		BANKS, FIs, PFs, etc.

Note: RBI is in both the segments; in the first as the underwriter and original subscriber and in the second as the retailer or dealer through the open market operations.

In the primary market, RBI sells those securities to banks, financial institutions, PFs, Pension Funds, dealers etc. RBI as the underwriter of the Central Government Securities makes up any shortfall in subscription for them. But in the case of state Government and Semi-Government securities it arranges for subscription in full through use of its good offices with banks, but does not directly subscribe to them.

In the secondary market, which is a retail market, trading is over the counter. Main operators other than the DFHI are banks, FIs, PFs, companies, etc. The RBI operates only in central government securities through the DFHI and STCI who may deal directly with banks, FIs, etc., or indirectly through the brokers who are authorized to deal in this market by the RBI.

Both in the primary and secondary markets, RBI has set up institutions to deal in these markets as market leaders, namely, DFHI and STCI. The underwriting activity of RBI is shared with a class of primary dealers who are authorized to be market makers by the RBI in the gilt-edged market.

The main features of primary market in the government and semi-government securities are set out below.

Primary Market Operations

1. New loans to be issued are decided by the government in consultation with RBI, as to the terms of issue, maturity cut off yields or coupon rates, etc.
2. The RBI acts as underwriter and contributes to the loans unsubscribed by the public; It is issue manager and Registrar. This work is now shared partially with a class of primary dealers.
3. The timing and conditions, the amounts involved are discussed by the RBI with banks and FIs, and sometimes prior commitments are enlisted from major banks.
4. The floatation of loans is effected throughout the year depending on the conditions of the market and requirements of Government.
5. The timing and amount of loans are adjusted as to the availability of bank funds and SLR requirements.
6. The loans are contributed in terms of cash as also conversion of existing maturity loans.
7. The loan certificates are issued in the form of Promissory Notes or Stock Certificates and the issue of bearer bonds was discontinued since a long time. They can now be held in Demat form also.
8. The amounts required to be borrowed by the center and state governments are indicated in their budgets before the year starts and well before the borrowing operations are initiated leaving sufficient time for RBI to plan the issue, depending on the needs of the government and market conditions.

Secondary Markets in Government Securities

The government securities market is a part of the overall stock market, although trading does not take place in the trading ring of the exchange. The market is a captive market confined to banks, FIs, PFs, etc. This is an over the counter market (OTC), with trading by telex, telephone, etc. The RBI conducts open market operations to stabilise the market and help the institutions, banks, etc. operating in the market. Only since the 80s the interest rates in this market have been raised to more realistic levels in tune with the market trends. The operations in the market still continue to be confined to banks and FIs, and PF and Insurance companies, either directly with the RBI or through brokers in the market. Even today the market is limited in terms of the number of players and the brokers who act as intermediaries. The secondary market in gilted securities is operated on both SGL account with the RBI or directly in the wholesale debt segment of the NSE. The secondary market in SGL accounts started in Sept. 1994. The volume of these recorded a growth of 55% by 1998-99, and has been growing further in the 21st century.

As referred to earlier, the trade in this market is effected in person, telex, telephone, etc., among banks directly or through the brokers. As such, it is called over the counter market. In the proper trading with the RBI, called open market operation, only licensed brokers authorised by the RBI and now primary dealers authorised by the RBI are permitted to deal with the RBI. These brokers are expected to report the prices of securities dealt with by them to the stock exchange. The RBI does operations with brokers or directly with banks, financial institutions and other players in the market. The securities are quoted in major stock exchanges and NSE and trading in NSE is reported regularly. The RBI conducts open market operations in selected central government securities, which is published on a daily basis on all working days. Repos and switches and cash sales are allowed by RBI in these securities upto some limits and in treasury bills also. RBI operates either on out right purchase or sale basis or on the basis of Repurchase agreements (Repos).

Role of Yields

In order to appreciate operations in government securities, understanding of yield is necessary as yields have a major role in these operations.

Coupon Rate and Nominal Yields: Yields are an important determinant of the demand for these securities. These are various types of yields which are discussed below:

Nominal Yields: Coupon rate is the rate of interest payable per annum per Rs.100/- of face value. If the purchase price is different from the face value then the return is (coupon rate ÷ purchase price) × 100. This return is called the nominal yield.

Real Yields: Nominal yields deflated by the Index of inflation rate, such as WPI or CPI will give real yields, which reflect the true purchasing power of the return on these securities.

Net Yields: Nominal yields adjusted for tax rate or payment of relevant taxes at which tax deduction at source takes place will give net yields.

Current Yield: Coupon rate is the rate at which the bond carries interest. This is the nominal yield payable on the face value of the bond regularly and remains unaltered, say, for example, the [13.4% Loan 2000]. State loans carry a higher coupon rate than the Central loan for comparable maturity to compensate for the larger risk involved in the former.

$$\text{Current Yield} = \frac{\text{Coupon rate} \times \text{face value}}{\text{Cost (Market price)}}$$

Redemption Yield: (Yield to Maturity – YTM)

This takes into account the price paid for the bond, length of the time to maturity and the coupon rate of the bond. This is the yield which the holder gets per annum if he holds it until maturity and is the same as current yield if the bond is purchased at par (Rs.100). Redemption yield = current yield + or – (minus) average annual capital gain or loss (for the bond purchased at a discount or premium as the case may be).

The gilt-edged yields have no role in determining the amount of funds borrowed or on the responsiveness of the public to the borrowing programme. For, the former depends on the projected outlays of the government in the various annual plans and budgets and the latter on liquidity requirements imposed on banks. As the gilt-edged market is an isolated and captive market, the linkages of these rates to other interest rates in the markets have for long been indirect and weak. The dichotomy in rates in the government securities and other securities existed for long, but constitute a levy on the holders of government debt for the benefit of others and the loss on such investments has to be made good by higher rates to the non-government sector. There is thus no feasibility of insulating completely the gilt-edged market from the rest of the money market. Only since the last few years, namely, 1992, the gilt-edged rates have been approaching the market rates through a system of auctioning of securities.

Commercial Banks' Operations

Although Banks, LIC, GIC, are all bound by Law to invest a proportion of their deposits or funds in government and semi-government securities in the primary market, they start operations in the secondary market immediately thereafter for disinvestment or

(a) to adjust their portfolio of these securities to net outflows of funds.

(b) to improve their yields and

(c) to adjust the maturity pattern of their holdings to suit to the new issue of government securities and net outflows of funds.

Generally, the portfolio management of commercial banks involves a compromise between the maximising of return and minimising of risk. The investment portfolio of the banks is influenced by the various economic factors such as monetary policy, credit regulations, the outlook of the interest rates etc. Banks are generally unwilling to hold securities of long-dated maturities as they are sensitive to the risk of fall in the capital value although, in more recent years, they are holding them for yield consideration. If interest rates are likely to rise, banks will shift from medium to short and *vice versa*. From the banks' point of view, long-dated loans are not an ideal type of investment, as they are likely to have greater fluctuations in the capital values and bank funds are mostly short-term in nature. Banks give support to long-dated loans first although they may disinvest them soon after in favour of high-yielding state loans and short dated loans. But PFs, pension funds, LIC, insurance companies, etc. prefer investment in the long-dated loans for yield purposes. They acquire them as and when funds accrue to them by purchasing them from the banks in the open market or the RBI.

Banks' operations in government securities market are presently not motivated by considerations of a profit centre for the treasury in this market or all the markets together. The expertise of banks has been not been traditionally in the field of portfolio management in the investments. Only recently, the treasury function in the markets has become a separate unit of profitability or profit making and emphasis is laid on the needed expertise for efficient portfolio operations in this market. As shown in the chapter on commercial banks' treasury operations, banks' operations are aimed at adjusting the maturity yields on their portfolio or avoid capital losses, imminent on their portfolio due to changes in coupon rates and yields on fresh issues, from time to time.

Banks and Gilt-edged Market

Banks and financial institutions are required to invest in government securities by statutory requirements. For example banks, have to invest as per SLR upto 25% of net demand and time liabilities in government and semi-government securities. The contributions to the new securities floated are, therefore, only from banks and financial institutions, trusts, PFs, etc., who have surplus funds or are required by law to invest in these securities. Due to the controlled rates of interest on these securities, these are not attractive for the general public to invest or hold. There is, therefore, no secondary market in the government securities. But banks, financial institutions, and PFs trade in these securities to take advantage of the differences in prices between the primary and secondary markets, and to gain in yields or to secure a maturity distribution that they desire to have.

The portfolio requirements of investors are determined by the maturity pattern and yield pattern of their existing securities. They operate in the market to take advantage of the price and yield differentials. The price differential may exist due to the adjustments taking place between the primary and secondary markets in securities representing trading at wholesale and retail levels. The price differentials may also be due to the distance factor as between centres or due to the regional disparities in industrial development. The registration charges or stamp duties in each State in respect of government securities are different; besides, regional disparities may exist in industrial development leading to differences in PF accruals and hence in the demand for government securities as between the states.

Brokers and the Markets

Brokers do not enter the initial issues market as the issue of government securities is underwritten in a monopolistic manner by the RBI. This system is replaced by repos during the reforms since 1992. The government has removed this monopoly condition and kept open this market to brokers as in foreign countries. These are called primary dealers (PDs) referred to later. Secondly, most brokers do not act as dealers in government securities due to lack of financial backing to hold these securities. They mostly act as intermediaries between trading banks, financial institutions and PFs, etc. The brokers deal with the RBI as per the prices fixed in their buying and selling lists. Bilateral and triangular switches are put through with the banks by the RBI for which brokers act as intermediaries. The RBI fixes quota for each bank for these switch deals, with a view to preventing the banks from unloading low yielding bonds on the RBI. The financial institutions and PFs are permitted to buy from the RBI their requirements of securities in terms of maturity and yields. There is a selected list of brokers called approved list of brokers of the RBI in each centre with which the RBI deals in government securities. The approved list is very restrictive in the sense that only a few with a proven record of government business and a large turnover in addition to their reputation for credit worthiness are enrolled as approved brokers. Their profit is limited in the market due to low margins but operations are attractive due to larger turnover.

YIELD CURVES

What is Yield Curve ?

Yield Curve reflects the relationship of yield to maturities. The yields of securities may differ with respect to the term to maturity. The relationship varies from country to country and period to period, depending upon the interest rate structure, risk and uncertainty in the market, and host of other factors. Normally, in the case of gilt-edged market, where risk of the issuer is negligible the remaining risk is only related to term to maturity. The yield should increase with increase to maturity upto a point and after that it appears to flatten and even decrease. Thus, the yield curve declines at the long end in case of increased demand for such maturities and decreased supply or in times of long-run certainty of the trends and short-term uncertainty.

Theory of Yield Curve

There are three types of theories to explain the yield curve, namely, the expectations, liquidity preference and preferred habitat theories. According to the first theory, when expectations of future interest rates are lower, then long rates would flatten or decline. When the future expected interest rates are higher, the yield curve slopes upwards (JR Hicks, F. Lutz and B. Malkiel are associated with this theory). The expected future rates as compared with the present rates will determine the yield curve.

According to Keynes' liquidity preference theory, the liquidity preference of investors is for short-term more than long-term. The savers prefer present cash to future claims. So the longer term maturities will have to yield higher according to this theory, as investors have to be prompted to invest in larger maturities only through higher rates of interest or yields. (Keynes and Hicks).

According to preferred habitat theory, there are different classes of investors in the market whose preferences vary widely. Thus, LIC, pension funds, insurance funds will prefer long-term investments rather than short-term investments. On the other hand banks and companies prefer shorter maturities as their funds are of short maturities and liquidity preference make them prefer short periods. But the fact is that the demand and supply forces vary as between the short end and long end of the maturity spectrum and the resultant yields will be smaller yields in the short run and yields will rise with increase in maturities in respect of those classes of investors like banks and companies. But long-term yields will rise or fall depending on the supply and demand forces for these maturities, from LIC, GIC, pension funds etc.

In each segment of the market say 1 to 5 years or 5 to 10 years and above 10 years, the yields are decided by a combination of factors, mostly by demand and supply factors, for each segment of the gilt-edged market. Thus, yield differentials exist as between loans of the same maturity, as also of different maturities.

How to Operate on the Yield Curve

The RBI generally prepares its own curve on the basis of non-market rates, but their own rates, namely, the rates quoted by them on select securities at any point of time. The yield curve so developed is used for fixation of cut off yield for accepting bids by the RBI. The cut off rate is slightly adjusted either side depending on the amount they would be able to raise at that cut off line. The higher the amount they could get in auctions, the lower will be the devolvement on the RBI. So there is no rule or a fixed standard on how the RBI will fix the cut off point. The treasury manager has therefore to assess the existing liquidity in the market and forecast the expected subscription and the likely cut off point of the RBI. On the basis of his own judgement and assessment of market forecast, he has to make his bid in the auctions. Similarly, in his day-to-day operations in government securities, he should plan for yields, consistent with a maturity pattern suitable for the needs of the bank or the company. Besides, whether too much capital gain or capital loss which will result from these operations is justified or not has to be judged by each bank. This has to be based on the tax planning and the tax bracket, into which the banking company falls, and they are top level decisions.

Maturity and Asset Liability Mix

The fund manager has to keep all these points in his mind in these operations. He has to be prompt in his actions and alert to the market changes and base his forecast on the basis of good research component. He should be prompt in keeping scope for buying high yielding securities and at the same time adjust the maturities that the capital loss will be minimum. For, the longer the maturity, the larger will be the capital loss, for a given rise in yield. He should also avoid asset liability mismatches and more assets should not be of long duration when liabilities are of short-term. Assets can however be short, when liabilities are mostly of long-term nature.

Example of Yield Curve

Funds manager in gilt-edged market has to know how to draw an yield curve and interpret it. RBI's offer of new loans or cut off point of accepting bids in auctions will depend on the expected yield curve. The rates on different maturities will be at or lower than the market rates except when the RBI wants to raise upwards the yield curve itself as under the recent reforms. Anticipating the rates to be offered by the RBI consistent with the yield curve, the funds manager has to offer the bid in the auctioning in the primary market.

In the secondary market yield curve will be useful to operate at different levels of maturity in the market. Thus, the yields on the treasury bills at present range between 6.5% to 7.5%. Yields on short-term government securities will be in the range of 7 to 8%. The finer points in decimals count for the decisions in this market as the opeiations are in crores of rupees. The treasury or the fund manager can gain upto a crore if he purchases Rs.100 crores of securities at a lower price in decimals (in paise 10 to 90 in a rupee). But a lower price means a higher yield, which in turn leads to capital depreciation on existing securities. The first guideline on valuation of securities is to be marked to market up to 75% of the total securities as at end March 2000. Now the rule is 100%, and the principle of marked to the market will lead to a large capital loss in the portfolio of the government securities.

The RBI cut off point sometimes will be higher than the market rate for two reasons.

(i) When the amount they want to raise from the public is larger and their own devolvement should be lower and

(ii) When they want to push up the yield level in general.

The funds operator will also face a trade off in that if he purchases more securities at a lower price; there will be saving in present expense but his portfolio will lose in capital value. If he purchases at a higher price, he will lose in the present juncture but there will be capital gain on his existing portfolio.

The law of the market is that government who spends more and borrows, will have to pay more *Ceteris Paribus,* in terms of cost of borrowing and similarly bond holders who are avaricious in raising yields, will lose in the depreciation in old securities in their portfolio. There is thus a trade off for both government and the bond holders in this market.

As the discussion so far and the later pages on RBI's open market operation (OMO) will show, yields can differ in decimal points for the same maturity. The yield curve given below for example is typical and is not smooth upwards sloping, the funds manager has to draw his own charts for both treasury bills and Government securities, based on his own perceptions of how the RBI is going to act in OMO and in cut off points in the primary market. The funds manager can gain only on a correct perception of RBI in operations, quick changes in maturities and yield, by continuous operations in the market. The graph below depicts the yields in gilt-edged market as in 1996 and 1999. The yield curve as in March 2006, has shifted down and ranged from 6.5% to 7.5% and then flattened off. (not shown in chart).

Treasury Operations of Government Debt

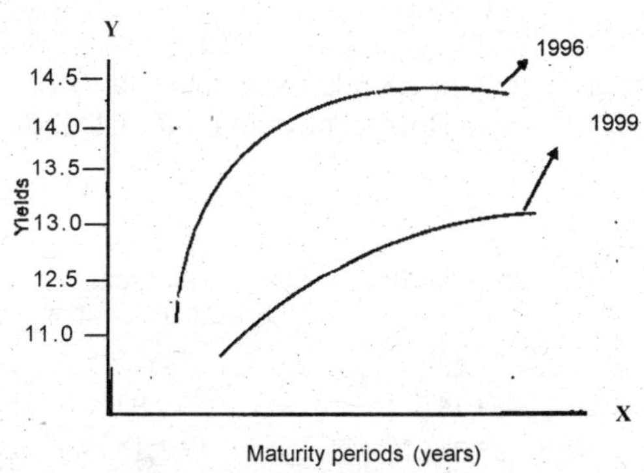

Emerging Trends in the Market

It will be seen from the Graph that the 1999 yield curve is flatter than the 1996 curve due to expectations of lower interest rates in 1999.

One can see from the RBI policy announcements that they wish to develop the market as shown below:

I. Government borrowing needs are forecasted in the budget.

II. RBI plans the different trartches of borrowings at different time periods in the year and its own contribution to finance government deficit is to be minimal but has now stopped altogether.

III. Opening of the auction on fixed day and the operations at this level will take off through PDs, planned by RBI for which reference is made later in the Chapter.

Growth of Auction Market

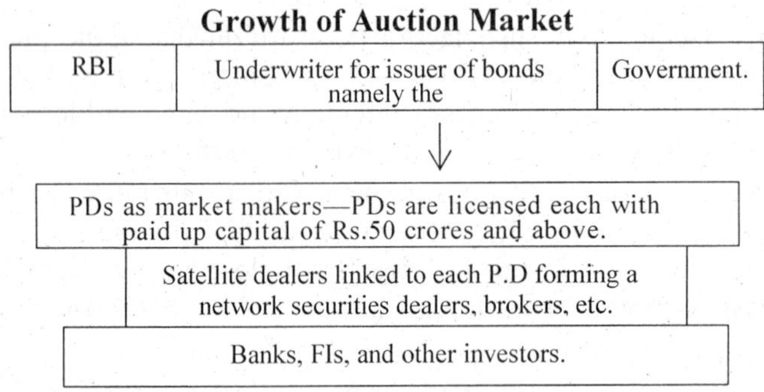

IV. Growth of the Secondary market operations.

IV. Growth of the Retail Market through MFs and Banks.

Investor Base

Banks and FIs are expected to have their clients' orders booked for purchases and sales in these bonds. Continuous trading on the basis of orders for portfolio management is anticipated in future. Companies and investors can be the clients for the main traders among the banks. It is as if the banks and financial institutions can do retail business for finance and investment companies, NBFCs and individual investors. Non-availability of scrips should not be a deterrent, to their participation, as the banks and their fund managers can pass the entries in pass books for these dealers which can be converted into cash, as the need arises for these clients. This system will mobilise excess funds of clients for trading in government securities.

Every year, the government spends more than its income both on capital and current account taken together. Both centre and states together had the deficits as shown below :

Rs. in Crores

Year	Revenue Deficit	Gross Fiscal Deficit of Centre	Gross Fiscal Deficit of States
1997-98	46,449	88,937	44,242
1999-2000	54,147	79,953	80,223
2005-06 (BE)	95,312	1,51,144	1,07,041

Source: RBI Annual Reports.

Gross fiscal deficit is the excess of total expenditure including loans, (net of recovery) given by them over revenue receipts (including external grants) and non-debt capital receipts. This gives an idea on how much government sector borrows from other sectors, including the RBI. The methods of borrowing include external finance and internal finance, in the form of market borrowings, small savings PF, special deposits, reserve funds, etc. and RBI credit (called the conventional deficit) which is now stopped. The RBI credit is defined as variations in 91 days Treasury bills issued to and held by RBI adjusted for changes in government cash balances with RBI. Of these, market borrowings constitute about 47% of the total fiscal deficit or finance required by the government. Market borrowings lead to internal public debt, which constitutes the government securities market. Total internal debt of the centre now stands at Rs. 14,06,525 crores as at the end march, 2000, accounting for about 40% of the GDP of the country. Such is the importance of government debt market in India. In fact, domestic liabilities of Centre and State in total constituted about 79% of GDP as at end March 2006.

Public Debt Management

RBI is held responsible for public debt management of the government under the Public Debt Act, 1944, replaced by Government Securities Act, 2004. It does this

1. by underwriting and subscription to new issues, not subscribed by public.
2. by use of OMO as a technique of purchase and sale of government securities to control the liquidity and the interest rate structure.
3. by use of SLR and CRR as the method of controlling the liquidity of banking system and their contributions to government debt.

On purchase list, securities which are quoting around par value will be there, so that the sellers will not lose any amount but secure liquidity from RBI. These purchases are mainly for cash. Some purchases used to be there on a switch basis before April 1992. Switch operations being neutral has no impact on liquidity and hence given up. They are replaced by repos, as a method of controlling liquidity. The sale list would depend on the availability of its stock in ample measure with the RBI on its own investment account. Secondly, it depends upon the demand aspect, namely, whether high yielding ones are required or short-term securities are in demand in the market.

Aggressive OMO is reflected when a high yielding security is put on sale. On the other hand, when the coupon rate and YTM are not attractive, the policy is one of defensive nature or passive stance is indicated.

RBI's Policy Initiatives

The RBI has started since 1991-92 a number of non-conventional methods of raising debts, with concurrence of the government, namely, the auction sale of government securities, funding of treasury bills at fixed coupon rates and their sales through auctions. Issue of low coupon dated securities on auction basis and other changes in open market operations through repos, etc. have been adopted by the RBI since 1992. Market related rates of interest have resulted thereby – some borrowings continued to be at a fixed coupon rate and some repos on auction basis. In 1994-95 a six year maturity loan was offered on tap at 11.64% and in 1995-96 one 10 year maturity loan was given at 14% coupon rate, in addition to all other methods of borrowings referred to above. The weighted average yield rates began to fall from 1997 onwards. It was 12.01 in 1997-98 and 11.86 in 1998-99. The objective is to elongate the average maturity period and secure market related interest rates. The policy of lowering the interest rates and the interest burden of the Government prevailed in 1999 and 2000.

Secondary market is being developed through the following mechanisms :

1. Offer of market related rates (referred to earlier).
2. Transparency of deals through SGL account and through NSE, whereby the yields and prices are flashed to the public on a daily basis.
3. Payment and settlement system is rationalised by adoption of DVP (Delivery versus payment) for those deals where buyers and sellers have accounts with SGL of RBI.
4. Adoption of a system of primary dealers (PDs) for acting as wholesalers and market makers.
5. Liquidity in the market is to be imparted through STCI or DFHI. Lack of information and competitive environment is missing in this market, which is reflected in high rates, paid for treasury bills and for medium term government securities at one stage in 1994-95. Secondary market can develop on quick and easy access to information and that can be provided through bid and offer rates of PDs, as initiated by RBI.
6. Integration of sub markets is another pre-requisite for development of a secondary market in government securities.
7. Valuation of securities should be on a marked to market basis which at present is provided for 75% of the portfolio of the holders of government securities (introduced since 1992). The full portion of the portfolio is now valued on marked to market basis, as in the case of some private sector banks.
8. Lastly, the interest rates in the primary and secondary markets should be related and signals from one should reach the other. There should be free competition, free flow of information and a mature system of price determination, in addition to integration of all segments of the market and rational pattern of yields developed in the process. RBI has entered into an agreement with government that there will be automatic and compulsory funding of treasury bills, when the ceiling of Rs. 9000 crores is reached. The RBI follows its own pattern of fixing the rates on new issues independent of the rates in the secondary market. Its argument is that the market rates on a few deals or a couple of deals do not reflect the total market and that rates should not rise or fall too much as they will result in capital losses or capital gains to the banks on the existing securities in their portfolios. Banks are not operating in this market actively due to earlier unattractive rates and lack of public interest in them. Besides historically, this market was developed on the basis of compulsion on the part of banks and financial institutions based on the statutory requirements with regard to their investments. Now the RBI is exhorting banks to operate in the secondary market on behalf of their corporate and individual clients by inducing their demand on the basis of the present attractive yields on government securities. Early in the 21st century, banks FIs, MFs and corporates have been operating in the secondary market for yield and duration adjustments and for portfolio management.

Problems in the Secondary Market

This segment is not well developed in India as banks have been used to deal with RBI and other banks, only when it is absolutely necessary, but portfolio management in treasury debt was absent in India to any significant extent. Banks and FIs keep their investments in government securities as per the statutory requirement and not by volition. The element of voluntary dealings will enter in if the yields on government securities are attractive as at present and treasury operations are made profit centres. For this, portfolio management in banks and non-bank corporates has to be encouraged, which is being done through liberalisation, privatisation and globalisation under various economic reforms in the country.

First to make these securities attractive, market determined rates are offered on them, when they are sold on auction basis from the year 1992-93. Secondly, funding of treasury bills into government securities is also made at market related rates. Thirdly, the government offered an issue of 5 year zero coupon bonds for Rs. 3,000 crores in 1993, out of which an amount of Rs. 1,624 crores was realised. These are some of the methods of non-conventional borrowings.

Besides, there is the conventional method of borrowing, through offer of loans with coupons and dated securities. Thus, on June 8, 1995 the government issued 10 year stock at 14% maturing in 2005 for a total amount of Rs. 1,000 crores. In the same year, it has sold securities on auction basis for Rs. 5,209 crores and by funding of treasury bills for Rs. 2,388 crores and by zero coupon bonds for Rs. 5,000 crores. Thus, of the total government borrowing, conventional borrowing (net) was Rs. 4,298 crores (40%) and other medium and long-term borrowing was Rs. 6,585 crores (60% of the total in non-conventional methods). The state government loans are offered on the conventional basis of coupon rates only.

Secondary market operations are encouraged by flexible interest rate policy, institutional strengthening in gilted marketing system and through various reforms referred to earlier and introduced by the Government.

Open Market Operations — RBI

As part of the debt management policy of the RBI, it operates in the gilt-edged market to buy and sell government securities on cash/switch basis. These operations directly affect the reserve base of the banks through an increase or decrease in the cash with banks or the public. These operations are designed to bring about a proper change in the size, composition, ownership and distribution of the marketable debt of the government, as well as to influence the prices and yields on these securities in tune with the interest rate and credit policies of the government and the RBI. Although these operations have a monetary impact, they were not used for the support of monetary policy as such. The government debt requirements and the cost of such operations influence the debt management policy in India.

Open market operations are conducted only in selected Central Government securities, whose stocks with the RBI are adequate for these operations to be conducted. These operations have both monetary impact and debt management effect, although RBI aims more for the latter.

The reason for confining these operations to the central securities is that these are held by the RBI on its own investment account and can be used as backing for the issue of currency. Very few are conducted on cash basis while the majority are on a switch basis. The general trend is that there are more sales of securities than purchases to help curtail the liquidity with the banks and financial institutions as part of the anti-inflationary drive of the monetary policy. Only in a few exceptional years, there were net purchases which helped the augmentation of reserves of the banks.

After the reforms in the financial sector started, many changes were noticed in all the markets, including the gilt-edged market. These policy changes are referred to elsewhere in this chapter. The most important change, so far as the RBI and OMO are concerned is to effect the monetary control through changes in CRR and SLR. In fact, RBI's open market operations can reduce the liquidity much more effectively, in the banking system, than increase in CRR of banks. The OMO is very flexible and amenable to operations on a daily basis, which is not possible in the case of CRR of banks. The RBI has therefore been using the OMO for monetary control starting with the other reforms in government securities market since 1992.

Monetary Control through OMO

Monetary control of RBI on banks is partly through interest rate, which in the case of India is the refinance window which is not of much use due to varied rates of refinance charged by RBI — one rate for export refinance and another for repos, another against government securities or treasury bills and yet another for discretionary or penal refinance. Secondly, the RBI operates monetary control through OMO. Policy initiatives taken during the last few years to facilitate efficient open market operations in gilt-edged market are the following :

1. Shift to market related rates of interest through adoption of auction system of selling government securities.
2. Proper institutional structure, developed through DFHI; STCI and primary dealers and mutual funds etc.
3. Payment system is changed to delivery versus payment system for SGL operations.
4. Transparency in operations and Demat form of trading.

Primary dealers would be actively used in OMO and IPO and transparency of these deals is ensured through transactions in SGL account which are published by the RBI and STCI on daily basis. Deals through NSE are also published regularly.

The OMO is scheduled to influence the liquidity by purchase and sale operations. It should not effect adversely the main borrowing performance of the government; it should on the other hand, help the floatation by pumping in liquidity through repos or repurchase deals just before the new issues are made by the government.

Transparency in deals and publications of all transactions on a daily basis is arranged for all deals in SGL account and for NSE deals. An extract of such publications on a particular day can be had from the Financial Dailies. The deals struck are of Central government and state government securities, treasury bills and repos. On similar lines, data of NSE are also made available to public on the internet and the press.

Repos

For the first time in 1992-93, the Central Government raised its entire market borrowings through the auction system. Bids were invited and market determined rates were used for allotment of securities and deciding the cut off point for accepting bids. The cut off yields are based on the discounted prices for a par value of Rs. 100.

The first auction sales of repurchase agreement (Repos) for central government's dated securities was made in Dec. 1992 to even out short-term liquidity in the banking system with a fortnightly make up period. These repos are for periods ranging upto 14 days, as the fortnightly reporting of CRR requires the support of repos. These repos are used for sale of government securities with the agreement to buy back within a maximum period of 14 days.

These repurchase agreements are abolished to pump in funds by the RBI to impart liquidity to the call money market. Repos were thus delinked from the Money market. For liquidity purpose RBI purchases securities first with the agreement to sell them back at the end of the period. In Nov. 1995, the repos are made for not less than 3 days and not more than 14 days, so that funds from repos are not used for overnight call money among banks. In the case of repos used in government securities market RBI first sells them to repurchase back at the end of the period to facilitate liquidity for short periods in the banking system.

Switch Quotas

A system of allotting annual switch quotas by the RBI was prevalent since 1973, mainly to enable financial institutions and banks to improve yields in the gilt-edged market, in the investment portfolio of banks. This quota enables a bank to switch with RBI, one maturity loan against another maturity loan.

Reform in the Gilt-edged Market

The system of switch quotas was dispensed with in April 1992 as it did not encourage the banks to depend on the market. In order to force them into the market and develop a secondary market in government securities, the RBI gave up this system.

Since 1992, the RBI has been offering for sale only a select number of central government scrips, which it gives in its list, instead of giving all the scrips in its portfolio, for its operations. Certain scrips are kept in the list for cash for providing total liquidity for at least a few scrips in central securities. These are some of the reforms in government securities markets adopted since the financial reforms started in 1991. After April 1992, 182-day treasury bills were discontinued, but in their place, the auction of new instruments of 364 day treasury bills on a fortnightly basis was introduced. Another step towards active debt management operation by the RBI was the introduction of an auction scheme for issue of 91 day treasury bills for a predetermined amount. The interest rate is definitely higher than the fixed discount rate of 4.6% as used to be for long before. With this, there will be no short-term government paper at a fixed rate of interest. After this, 14 day treasury bill on auction basis was introduced and time money and term deposits of a minimum of 15 days were introduced to widen the depth of the market.

Changes After Securities Scam (1991-92)

The scam was attributed to the nexus of bankers and brokers in the unholy process of misusing some of the loopholes in the practices of banks in the guise of portfolio operations in Government securities. Thus, the practice of using Banker's Receipts (BRs) in Government securities trading was misused and forged documents and wrong entries have been the mechanism through which the scam took place. The fact that RBI's supervisory functions and banks' own internal control system were lax and defective has aided the scam operations.

The effect of scam on banking is manifold. It was in the investigations of SBI's Annual Accounts that scam came to light first. Many Indian and Foreign Banks, N.H.B., Canfina and a host of other institutions were involved in losses. Of the banks, Bank of Karad was totally submerged in the scam and was wound up. The public confidence in banks was shaken and their deposit growth decelerated.

Board for Financial Supervision (BFFS)

The remedial action has been initiated first by the RBI itself. Its internal supervisory and organisational matters received first attention. A supervisory Board called the Board for Financial supervision was set in RBI in collaboration with the government. The Board will devote exclusively to supervisory functions in the Financial System. The PDO of RBI is also revamped and computerised for better transparency and quicker service.

For the Securities scam centering on trading in Government Securities through Banker Receipts (BR), the RBI has been blamed by the Joint Parliamentary Committee. After that, the RBI has initiated a number of measures like streamlining the operations through BRs, strengthening the public debt office of the banking department at the level of regional offices of RBI, setting up of a strong supervisory system for banks, etc.

On top of these measures, the RBI has set up a Securities Trading Corporation of India, for the purpose of trading in government and semi-government securities. Earlier it has authorised the DFHI to trade in government securities also in addition to money market instruments. The DFHI has neither the manpower expertise nor the resource base for this purpose and hence the STCI. Gradually DFHI will be given over to market constituents, for which the RBI has started its disinvestment in DFHI.

So the present proposal is to set up an agency for trading actively in government securities market with a view to activate and if necessary stabilise the market. The captive market in government securities among banks and FIs at present will be broad based to attract the general public, at large. Accordingly this STCI was set up with a broad based ownership with a paid up capital of Rs.500 crores, contributed by RBI, cooperative and commercial banks, mutual funds, financial institutions, etc. to supervise and develop the gilt-edged market on a wider base in India.

Securities Trading Corporation of India (STCI)

The STCI was set up in May 1994 and commenced operations in June 1994. The entire authorised capital of Rs.500 crores was issued and fully paid up March 1995. The objective of its operations is to develop vibrant secondary market in gilt-edged market and to help the RBI to implement its policy in public debt management. To further strengthen the institutional structure of the government securities market, a system of primary dealerships was initiated and six primary dealers were licensed in 1996. The STCI will operate both in treasury bills and government securities market. Borrowing and lending in the call money market is also a responsibility of the STCI, in addition to DFHI. During the first year of its operations, namely, 1994-95, its turnover dealt with was Rs.39,361 crores in the government securities market.

It can deal with the banks and financial institutions and public on the one hand and the RBI on the other. It can do repos deals with RBI through treasury bills and government securities. It can operate in call money market also to absorb the excess of supplies or demand. During Oct.-Nov. 1995, when the call money rate touched a new peak of 130% and there was acute stringency of funds, the STCI operations helped to ease the rates down to around 25%.

System of Primary Dealers

A system of primary dealers was introduced by the RBI in gilt-edged markets in 1995. Primary dealers in government securities in most advanced markets like the United States of America, Canada, the United Kingdom, France and Australia, are usually a select group of securities firms. They act as market makers for the securities. They are approved either by the central bank of the country or the Treasury.

Primary Dealers serve a number of purposes such as the following:

(i) Help placement of government securities in primary issues by committed participation in auctions;

(ii) Provide active secondary market in securities by giving two-way quotes;

(iii) Act as conduit for open market operations by the central banks; and

(iv) Provide signals to central banks for market intervention.

Primary dealers enjoy certain privileges like maintenance of clearing balance with the central bank and participation in clearing, facility of borrowing bonds/funds from the central bank, operating switches with the central bank, right to participate in securities auctions and access on an exclusive basis, to open market operations.

The Reserve Bank announced on March 29, 1995 guidelines and procedures for enlistment of primary dealers in government securities market. The broad features of the guidelines are :

(a) The eligibility is based on the considerations that primary dealers should have strong capital base and dealers in securities. Thus, subsidiaries of scheduled commercial banks for all-India financial Institutions and a company incorporated under the companies Act, 1956 dedicated predominantly to the securities business in particular to the Government securities market and having net owned funds of a minimum of Rs.50 crores will be eligible to apply for primary dealership.

(b) A primary dealer will be required to have standing arrangement with the Reserve Bank based *inter alia* on the execution of an undertaking to (i) Have a commitment to bid for a minimum amount in Central Government dated securities and treasury bill auctions during a year and to maintain success ratios of 33.33 per cent and 40 per cent respectively, (ii) Underwrite accepted bids against notified amounts, (iii) Offer firm two-way quotes for government securities, and (iv) Achieve an annual turnover of not less than 5 times in government dated securities and 10 times in treasury bills. These would ensure that they are committed to market making and are consistent and successful in their participation in auctions.

(c) The primary dealers shall maintain the minimum capital standards on risk weighted basis. Risk weights have been prescribed for government securities to take care of position risk arising out of dealing in securities. While in other countries such requirements have been prescribed as 'margins.' In India risk-weighted system has been used to make it harmonious with capital adequacy standards for non-banking financial companies.

(d) The Reserve Bank would extend to primary dealers facilities like current account/Subsidiary General Ledger (SGL) account and liquidity support linked to bidding commitments, freedom to deal in money market instruments and a favoured access to open market operations. These are vital for effective functioning of primary dealers.

(e) Primary dealers would be subject to the Reserve Bank regulation. They would be required to submit periodic return as prescribed by the Reserve Bank and to provide to the Reserve Bank access to all the records, books and documents as may be required.

Unfortunately the above guidelines are too stringent and RBI does not provide refinance or liquidity to PDs with the result that there are not many takers for the scheme by the end of 1995. However with some liberalisations six primary dealers were registered with RBI by Sept. 1996, which has since increased to 17 by 2006.

Earlier Reforms in Gilt-edged Market

Chakravarthy Committee Report on review of the working of the Monetary System (1985) has recommended a number of reforms, in the monetary system and in government securities market. In particular, it recommended that the government should refrain from borrowing from the RBI as it might increase the monetary expansion but the deficits of the government budgets be financed from the open market borrowing at market rates.

Thus, treasury bills of 91 days, 182 days and 364 days have since been sold on auction basis which led to market interest rates on these instruments. Subsequently Narasimham Committee (1991) also recommended the reduction in S.L.R. of banks and allow market related rates on government securities. Thus, rates of discount are determined by conditions of market liquidity. Not only banks continued to be participants but individual investors, corporate bodies, trusts, local bodies etc., became active participants in the market due to more realistic rates of return on them.

The DFHI was given powers to operate in government securities market, as market stabiliser or jobber, giving bid and offer rates in some securities. The reduction in SLR of banks lowered their demand for dated securities but the market related rates, higher than before at 12 to 14% began to attract non-bank institutions and other agencies into this market to trade.

As referred to earlier, the RBI has also introduced the auction of repos with the objective of stabilising the liquidity and absorb the excess or make good deficits in liquidity in the market. The market related rates on repos and the free play of market forces on them have helped to strengthen and activate the government securities market.

Financial Reforms and Gilt-edged Market

Gilt-edged market is closely related to reforms in the banking sector, as the bulk of the demand for government sector securities arises out of the banking sector Following the Narasimham Committee recommendations, the SLR and CRR of banks have been reduced from April 1992. With the gradual reduction in SLR in stages, the effective SLR is reduced to 31.5% and CRR to 12% (as at end sept. 1996) and further to 25% of S.L.R. and to 10% of CRR by Jan. 1997. The freeing of their lending rates and other liberalisation measures boosted the financial markets.

Following the securities scandal of 1991-92, some further reforms were introduced in 1992, Banker Receipts (BR) in Government securities are not permitted where the SGL facility is available. In cases where BR is permitted, it is only for ready deals. Ready forward deals through BRs are prohibited in government securities, treasury bills etc.

Effective from June 22, 1992, RBI issued new guidelines for dealings in Government securities for banks and brokers. All inter-bank ready forward deals are prohibited in Government securities, PSU bonds, UTI units. Where SGL facility is available, all deals should be put through the SGL only. Bank receipts in lieu of physical certificates only for ready deals under certain specific conditions such as delivery from another centre, or where allotment advice is there but certificates are not issued etc. Where there are no stocks with the SGL, no deals are allowed and banks should make sure of their position in the SGL. No ready forward or double ready forward deals are permitted in any securities or bonds even for a client's account or in Portfolio Management System. The operations in SGL, the transfer forms and the procedures have been streamlined to eliminate all malpractices of short sales or wrong entries.

The banks have been advised to strengthen their internal control system. The reporting and monitoring has to be supervised by qualified inspectors and auditors. The top management is held responsible for inspection and monitoring. Similarly, restrictions have been imposed on the deals to be put through by the brokers and business is to be distributed through as many brokers as possible.

The rates on Government securities were enhanced to make them market related rates. With a view to developing an active market in Government securities, the dependence of the Government on the market is increased and its dependence on RBI and banks reduced. The system of auctioning of Government securities was introduced in 1992 to allow the rates to reflect the true market conditions. The Central Government securities were sold on auction basis in respect of 5 year and 10 year loans in June and August 1992 respectively and this practice continued, as referred to earlier.

The RBI reforms in government securities market, the setting up of STCI and the licensing of some primary dealers to act as market makers in gilt-edged securities have helped to reform the market. The PDs as also the commercial banks are expected to develop the secondary retail market in gilts, whose rates have now become market related rates. The streamlining of RBI's depts. and of practices and procedures have also strengthened the market. The banks and corporates have now started operating more frequently than before due to the provisioning requirement, of banks, capital adequacy norms to be adjusted for risk bearing assets due to the need for supervision of depreciation on gilted portfolio of current nature on banks' investments. The retail market in gilts is expected to be developed soon following these reforms.

RBI MANAGEMENT OF GILT-EDGED MARKET

RBI as Agent of Government

RBI is entrusted with the operation of Government Debt Management Policy as a banker to the Government. Management of Government debt is part of monetary policy and also of broader economic policy. Government debt arises out of Central government budget deficit and their borrowings from RBI, banks and financial institutions and others. RBI is a banker to governments both central and states in India.

Reforms in this policy started way back since 1985, when PSUs were allowed to borrow directly from capital market through bond route rather than through budget provision. This start gathered movement with financial reforms which were initiated following the Chakravarthy Committee Report.

Primary market in Government debt or securities involved the role of RBI as a passive manager before 1991. It had no control on the volume raised through adhocs, treasury bills, volume and maturity structure of Government securities. Both medium and long-term debt predominated and skewed in the direction of debt of 15 years and above. The creation of adhocs to finance the government expenditure and short-term debt of government were all dictated by the exigencies of the government policy. The RBI is an underwriter of all the government issues, particularly of centre, and manages their borrowings and debt.

In the secondary market, the government securities trading remained a narrow and captive segment. The coupon rates were low without any relation to growing market rates. The demand is generated for these securities through RBI's monetary policy and the use of S.L.R. and open market operations. Bank rate and other instruments were not effective due to nature of debt instruments and term structure of their yields.

Government debt measured by gross fiscal deficit reached a high of 6.1% in 1980-81 and 8.3% in 1990-91 and reduced to 5% to 6% during 1996-97 to 1999-2000 and further to 4% by 2006. The monetary policy was mainly oriented to facilitate government debt operations and their requirements.

Initial Reforms

The committee on the monetary system (Chakravarthy Committee 1985) and the working group on money market (Vaghul working groups 1987) provided the initial guidelines for reforms. The measures initiated since then included the following:

1. In addition the existing 91 day treasury bills, 182 days treasury bill were introduced to act as a short-term borrowing method in Nov. 1986. These bills were sold on auction basis upto April 1992 when they were replaced by 364 days treasury bills which were also sold on auction basis.
2. Coupon rates on Government securities were raised in stages from a low level of 6.5% in 1977-78 to 11.5% in 1985-86 and the maximum maturity reduced from 30 years to 20 years. The coupon rates for 5 years were kept at 10% and for 10 years at 10.5%. In 1996-97, the coupon rates ranged from 13.5% to 13.85%, which were lowered to 11-12% by March 2000 and further lowered to 5.6 – 7.5% by March 2006.
3. The Discount and Finance House of India (DFHI) was setup in April 1988. It was intended for operations in money market, particularly in treasury bills and impart liquidity for all other instruments in money market so as to develop the secondary market in them. It was later allowed to operate in government securities market also as buffer between the RBI and other market participants. Later the operations in government securities were taken over by the Securities Trading Corporation, setup in May 1994 (STCI).
4. A number of new instruments were developed to provide depth and width to the money market and gilt edged market through the certificates of deposits (CDs), Commercial paper (CPs) and Inter-bank participation certificates (PCs), B Floating Rate Bonds, etc. The ceilings on inter-bank Call money (at 10%) inter bank deposits and bills discounting were removed in 1989. To further develop the Call and notice money market, in addition to LIC, and UTI which acted as lenders only from 1971, GIC, IDBI and NABARD were also given entry into this market in May 1990. Later on, even mutual funds and any economic entity with a minimum funds of Rs.20 crores was given entry into the money market as lenders of their surplus funds.
5. Flexible Debt Management Policy was pursued.

Reforms After 1991

The recommendations of Narasimham Committee on Financial System's Reforms (Nov.1991) became the basis of further steps in the reform process. The important steps are as follows:

1. Shift to market related rates of borrowing by the Government, and to improve liquidity in securities.
2. Shift from direct controls by the RBI to indirect controls and open market operations.
3. Innovations in market instruments.

4. Phased elimination of auto monetisation of the Central Government budget deficit.
5. Development of secondary market in government securities with yields comparable to market related yields.

RBI Measures Include the Following

1. Reduction of S.L.R. for banks from 38.5% in 1992 to 31.5% by 1994 and C.R.R. from 15% to 10% by end January 1997. The incremental CRR was abolished and incremental SLR was fixed at 25% on NTDL. As at end 2005 the CRR and SLR stood at 5% and 25% respectively.
2. Adoption of Auction System for fixing the market determined rates for treasury bills and government securities since 1992. The 91 day treasury bills were sold on auction from January 1993 and 364 day treasury bills replaced the existing 182 day treasury bills since then and were issued on auction basis and RBI does not participate in these auctions. Slowly the market absorption of Government debt was increased and RBI's own participation was reduced to negligible proportion. But there can be devolvement on the RBI as the under-writer. The 182 day treasury bills were reintroduced on April 1999 on an auction basis and were abandoned later in May 2001 but were reintroduced in April 2005.
3. Shift in Maturity structure of Government debt of long-term to medium and short-term debt upto 10 years.
4. The cutoff rates in auctions are emerging slowly as bench mark yields in interest rate structure India.
5. The market became responsive to interest rates and yield curve.
6. Auctions have helped the banks to develop skills of anticipation of yields and led to competitive pricing of securities, both in the primary and secondary markets.
7. Discounting of switch operations in O.M.O. and realistic pricing of securities, introduction of repos and setting up STCI promoted the development of secondary market.

Repos and Listed Securities

RBI provided repos on auction basis from Oct. 1992 and reverse repos facility was offered to DFHI and STCI to provide liquidity support to these institutions. Both fixed rate repos and auction based repos continued.

Repos used to have a minimum of 3 days and a maximum of 14 days which were removed in 1999. Repos with RBI and with other banks and FIs continued to be used.

Flexibility in listing and pricing of securities in RBI purchase and sale operations under O.M.O. is ensured. The daily list of RBI for purchase on cash basis and sale of securities was changed in a flexible manner. Switch operations gave way to repos operations.

Innovative Government Debt Instruments

1. Issue of 14 day treasury bills and auction based issues in addition to the fixed rate issued continued.

2. Conversion of 91 day and 364 day treasury bills into dated securities and at the option of holders.
3. Controlled sale of bills on tap basis at prices determined in auctions.
4. Zero coupon bonds were issued by the centre in January 1994. Which became attractive due to their special features of no reinvestment risks and with tax advantages. There is no TDS collected on income from TBs and Government securities.
5. Auctioned securities made on instalment payments — partly paid stock.
6. Phased elimination of automative monetisation of central government debt. Role of adhocs was reduced and they are phased out and by an agreement with the government first for limiting the resort of adhocs to a specific amount and later replaced the facility by ways and means advances as in the case of state governments. The agreements was originally made with the Government in September 1994, and phasing out took place by 1997-98.

The phasing out of these adhocs by ways and means advances from 1997-98 was announced in the central budget for 1997-98.

Pre-requisites for development of a secondary market:

(a) Transparent system of trading, introduced through computerised trading through brokers on N.S.E. and of S.G.L. deals.

(b) Secured systems of settlement and payment insured through DVP (which means delivery versus payment) both under SGL and on NSE deals.

(c) Promotional measures to increase the instruments for trading and institutions eligible for trading.

(d) Inter-bank repos facility and ready forward deals among banks, with DFHI and STCI to improve liquidity in the market to be effected through SGL in Mumbai only.

(e) Refinance facility provided against government securities to banks in excess of their S.L.R. to a limit of 90% of excess holdings since October 1992 was withdrawn in 1996 due to improved liquidity among banks following the lowering of incremental S.L.R. of banks to 25%.

(f) Valuation of investment portfolio. Those of approved securities are bifurcated into current and permanent. Starting with 70:30 of permanent and current categories in 1992-93, the ratio was brought down to 60:40 in 1995-96, 50:50 in 1996-97, and to 25 : 75 in 1999 - 2000 and the entire amount was marked to market from 2003.

Guidelines were given for the use of BRs and the use of the services of brokers to avoid any misuse of them.

System of Primary Dealers

A system of primary dealers to deal in wholesale and to act as underwriters in gilt-edged securities was adopted by RBI in March 1995 and in 1996 there were already 14 of them licensed to be primary dealers and their number stood at 17 as in 2006. Those who are regularly dealing in them and with a minimum net worth of Rs.50 crores are eligible to be primary dealers. They are given underwriting commission and liquidity support, by the RBI.

The primary dealers should bid for a minimum amount of dated securities and for treasury bills and offer two way quotes for government securities and widen the investor base through an annual turnover of not less than five times in gilts and not less than ten times in treasury bills. A system of network dealers to deal in retail was also being implemented by the RBI. Their functions are being expanded.

Nature of the Markets

Gilted market is mainly over the counter telex and telephone. Primary issues through the RBI is notified in the press. Secondary market trading is firstly between RBI and banks and primary dealers, DFHI and STCI and authorised brokers. More recently the RBI dealings with and through brokers were drastically curtailed. Besides banks were encouraged to deal directly or through NSE member brokers from June 1994. Dealings through S.G.L. operations are continued and delivery versus payments and transparency in dealings are insisted. Demat form of holding gilted securities and trading in them is being encouraged.

Centre's Internal deficit reached a level in 1990-91 of 31% of G.D.P. As at end March 2005, it was around 40% of GDP and debt service ratio was around 38% of revenue receipts.

Total Central borrowings are composed of the following items.

Dated Securities and Market Loans

91/364 day treasury bills are called short-term market borrowings. 182 day bills were stopped in 1992 and reintroduced in May 1999. 91 day treasury bills are both on tap and on auction basis and in the form of adhocs from the RBI. These adhocs are phased out in 1997-98 and ways and means given are below the line item and do not constitute market borrowings; other long and medium-term borrowings of the centre included funded treasury bills into dated securities, and new instruments like zero coupon bonds, and partly paid stock, etc.

Auction sale of Government securities include: those sales started since 1992-93 and devolvement on the RBI declined and completely stopped with PDs, taking over this job from the RBI.

Price based auctions were introduced in May 1999 through 11.19% GOI stock 2005 and 12.32% Stock 2011. Many new instruments of issue were introduced, later on.

Data on Yield and OMO.

The table below presents the State on Central Government yields and OMO of RBI.

Table 14.1

(in Rs. Crores)

Year	Weighted Cut off yields (in %ages)	OMO Net sales (Rs. in crores)
1991-92	11.78	3,444
1995-96	13.75	583
1999-00	11.77	35,370
2000-01	10.95	19,324
2002-03	7.34	53,780
2003-04	5.71	41,849
2004-05	6.11	2,899

Source : RBI Annual Reports.

It will be seen from the table that yields have first risen upto 1995-96, to be in tune with market related rates, and then fell steadily, as the RBI interest rate policy was to keep them low, relative to the inflation rates, and to be aligned with the global rates. Lower rates were also required to spur the investment growth for a sluggish economy, noticed during 2001-03.

The OMO of RBI have been net sales but no consistent trend, as they are guided by the needs of the market and liquidity requirements of the economy. The fact that they are net sales through out, except for a few ad hoc years, shows that the RBI has been absorbing the excess liquidity in the system to keep prices and inflation stable.

So far as to secondary market in gilted securities is concerned, firstly its turnover is increasing after NSE trading was started. Secondly, outright transactions in the government securities was only about Rs. 12 lakh crores, as compared to Repo transactions in them at around Rs. 27 lakh crores — a total of Rs. 39 lakh crores in 2004-05. It will be seen that Repo transactions predominate accounting for about 69% of the total transactions in secondary market in government securities. This market is being developed to increase the depth and width by measures referred to earlier in this chapter.

❑ ❑ ❑

15 FOREX MARKET OPERATIONS

An important part of the activity of treasury management is funds management in forex market. This market deals with exchange of currencies and dealings in foreign exchange.

Foreign exchange as a subject refers to the means and methods by which rights to income and wealth in one country's currency are converted into similar rights in terms of another country's currency. It involves the investigation of the methods by which the currency of one country is exchanged for that of another, the causes which render such exchange necessary, the forms in which such exchange may take place and the ratios or equivalent values at which such exchanges are effected.

Such exchanges may be in the form of one currency to another or of conversion of credit instruments denominated in different currencies such as cheques, drafts, airmail transfers, fax and telegraphic transfers, cable transfers, bills of exchange, trade bills, banker's bill or any promissory notes. It is through these instruments and foreign currency accounts of banks that the banks are able to effect such exchange of currencies or claims to currencies.

Every exchange of goods and services as between countries is having corresponding exchange of remittances involving two currencies as depicted in Figure on next page:

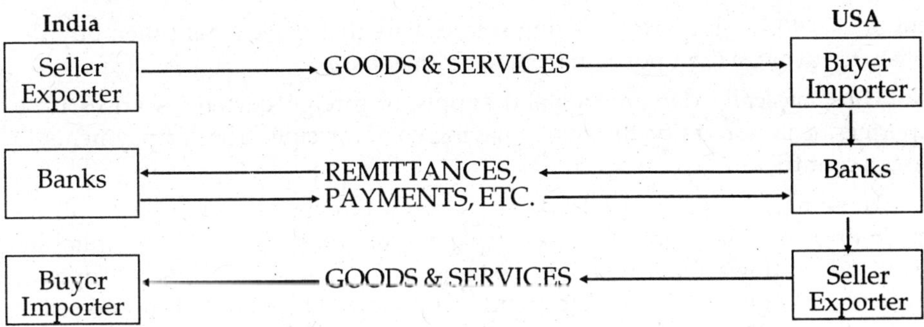

Fig. 15.1

No currency will be physically exchanged as it is not a legal tender in any country other than that in the issuing country. So exchanges take place through book entries and / or through credit instruments by banks. The instruments through which exchanges of currencies take place are Telegraphic Transfers (TTs), Mail Transfers (MTs), Demand Drafts (DDs), Cheques, Bills of Exchange, etc. In the absence of banks, the buyer-importer who has to pay in dollars has to hunt for an exporter seller who received an equivalent amount of dollars from the foreign importer. Banks facilitate such transactions by acting as intermediaries between buyers and sellers or importers and exporters.

International Financial System and Foreign Exchange Market

One of the important components of the international financial system is the foreign exchange market. The various commercial and financial transactions as between countries result in receipts and payments as between them. Such receipts and payments involve exchange of one currency for another. Thus, rupee is a legal tender in India, but an exporter in UK will have no use for these rupees. He, therefore, wishes to receive from the importer in India only in pound sterling. Then the importer will have to convert such rupees into pounds in that transaction. The foreign exchange market provides facilities of such operations.The demand for goods and services from one country to another is the basis for demand for currencies in the exchange market. Such merchandise and invisible trade items constitute nearly 70-80 percent of the total transactions in the market. Conversion of currencies is also necessary for short-term capital flows or long-term investment in financial or physical assets of another country. It will thus be seen that the services of the exchange market are necessary not only for trade transactions but for any financial receipts or payments as between countries. Any receipt and payment of foreign cash, coins, claims in currencies or credit instruments involve a foreign exchange transaction.

There is, as for any other currency, a market for the rupee. If an Indian bank buys dollars, it will pay rupees for dollars and transactions are an export or an import, inward or outward remittances or any similar transactions between Indian residents and foreign residents. An exporter in India receives dollars from say, USA and he surrenders the bill of exchange along with other documents to his bank. The bank would have bought that currency from the exporter. The bank has since been on the look-out for selling those dollars in the foreign exchange market for those in need of dollars. Let us say, an importer in India importing from the USA is in need of dollars to pay to the exporter. Another bank is approached by the importer with a demand for dollars and the former must have sold dollars to the importer. Having sold dollars that bank would then buy the dollars to cover up their position from the former bank.

Thus, basically demand for and supply of foreign currencies arises from exporters or importers or the public having some receipts from or payments to foreign countries.

These may be due to (i) Trade transactions of exports and imports. (ii) Invisible payments and receipts for example, travel, transport, etc. (iii) Capital inflows and outflows for investment hedging and speculation. These receipts or payments may give rise to foreign credit instruments which banks buy and sell at specified rates. There are different rates for buying and selling in which an interest element is included and quoted by the banks if the bill or promissory note or any instrument of exchange is not a demand or sight bill but a usance note involving some period to run to maturity for payment. Even in the case of sight bills, some grace period of 2 days and transit period of 10 to 20 days are allowed as fixed by the Foreign Exchange Dealer's Association, depending upon the place on which it is drawn and interest element for these periods also included in the rate quoted by banks.

Banks generally cover up these positions in currencies by corresponding purchase or sales from other banks. Such a market as between banks is called inter-bank market. There are reputed brokers who act as intermediaries for banks in these transactions.

Bank's Purchase and Sale

Every foreign exchange transaction involves a two-way conversion — a purchase and sale. Conversion of rupees into dollars involves purchase of dollars and sale of rupees or *vice versa* depending upon the angle from which we are looking. If it is looked at from the country having rupees (India), then the transaction looks as follows:

(a) Sale of rupees for dollars (importer) — conversion of home currency into foreign currency.

(b) Purchase of rupees for dollars (exporter) — conversion of foreign currency into home currency.

An Indian banker has to keep his account in rupees, he buys and sells foreign currencies like any commodity for money (Indian rupee).

Instruments Traded

In addition of conversion of foreign currency notes and cash for domestic currency notes/coin, a number of instruments of credit are used for effecting conversion of one currency into another. These instruments are discussed below:

(1) Telegraphic Transfers (TT): A TT is a transfer of money by telegram or cable or telex or fax from one center to another in a foreign country. It is a method used by banks with their own codes and correspondent relations with banks abroad for transmission of funds. As it involves the payment of funds on the same day, it is the quickest means of transmission of funds. As there is no loss of interest or capital risk in this mode, it enjoys the best rate for the value of receipts.

(2) Mail Transfers (MT): It is an order to pay cash to a third party sent by mail by a bank to its correspondent or branch abroad. It is issued in duplicate —

one to the party buying it and the other to the banker — correspondent or agent abroad. The amount is paid by the agent bank to the third party mentioned therein in the transferee country by its own cheque or by crediting the party's account. As the payment is made after the mail advice is received at the other end, which will take a few days, the rate charged to the purchaser is cheaper to the extent of the interest gain to the seller bank. MT rates are cheaper than TT rates.

(3) Drafts and Cheques: Draft is a pay order issued by a bank on its own branch or correspondent bank abroad. It is payable on sight but there is always a time lapse in the transit or in post between the payment by the purchaser of the draft to his bank and the receipt of the money by the seller in the foreign centre. As in the case of MT, there is risk of loss of the draft in transit, delay in effecting payment to the beneficiary and loss of interest during the intervening period. The rate charged by the bank for this is less advantageous to the buyer of the draft than in other modes.

(4) Bills of Exchange: It is an unconditional order in writing addressed by one person to another, requiring the person to whom it is addressed to pay certain sum on demand or within a specified date. If it is payable on demand it is a sight bill and if it is after a period, it is a long bill or a usance bill. Such bills can be banker's bills or trade bills. Bank bills are drawn on a bank abroad. While the bank bills carry better rates due to their greater security, the trade bills drawn on private parties may not fetch good rates. Sight bills are paid on sight but allow a transit period of 10 to 20 days for which interest is lost. In the case of usance bills, the purchase price is adjusted on the basis of maturity date of the bill for the interest loss, adjusted in the rate quoted for such a bill.

Segments of Foreign Exchange Market

There are four major components of this market, depending upon the level at which transactions are put through:

1. Banks with the public. 2. Inter bank deals. 3. Deals with the correspondents and branches abroad. 4. Deals with RBI.

Basically, the exchanges involve no physical exchange of currencies except in small denominations when travellers and tourists carry them across national borders, but through exchange of credit instruments or book entries in the books of banks in various centres. The banks are linked together by phone, cable, telex, post or other means of communication. The transactions are put through directly by the banks or through the brokers located at various centres where these transactions are concentrated like Mumbai, Kolkata, Chennai, etc. All the dealer banks in foreign exchange in India have an association called Foreign Exchange Dealers' Association.

Exchange Rate Mechanism

As in the case of any commodity, there is a price for any purchase or sale of a currency. Such a price in the exchange market is called the exchange rate. This is defined as the number of units of one currency that will be exchanged for a unit of another currency. The exchange rate of any currency can be expressed in two ways — one in terms of the number of foreign currency units against a given unit of domestic currency (thus, Rs. 100 = £ 1.7900 pounds as indirect method) and the other in terms of the number of domestic currency units against a given unit of foreign currency. (Thus, 1 pound = Rs.85.24 as direct method as at mid July 2006).

It is pertinent to ask what factors normally determine the exchange rate in the market. *Prima facie*, if the market is free and rates are allowed to fluctuate, the exchange rate would depend on the supply of and demand for a currency. Thus, taking dollars *vis-a-vis* rupees, the rate is determined by the demand for dollars and supply of dollars in relation to the rupee. Those who demand dollars are primarily importers from the USA to India who have to pay the US exporters in dollars. Similarly, those who supply dollars are primarily the exporters to USA who are paid in dollars by importers in USA.

The rate of exchange is determined at any moment by the forces of demand and supply of a currency which in turn depends on the demand for and supply of commodities and services as between India and the USA. They also depend on arbitrage and interest rate speculation, currency speculation and short-term capital flows if these are permitted. This can be represented diagrammatically as follows:

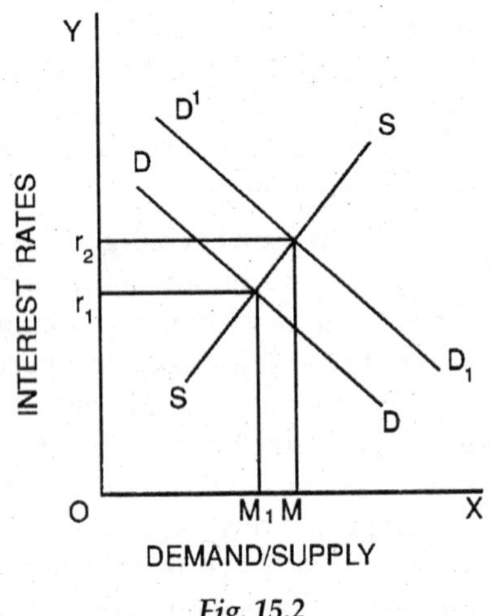

Fig. 15.2

Given the supply (SS), if the demand increases from DD to D_1D_1 the rate will rise from r_1 to r_2 and *vice versa*. A rise in the rate for rupee means more foreign currency units are surrendered for a given unit of domestic currency.

Purchasing Power Parity Theory

The basic factors which determine the exchange rates are the intrinsic purchasing power of the currencies in their own domestic economies. In the era of paper currencies, which are not backed by gold or gold exchange standard, currencies of different countries are not based on their intrinsic worth in terms of gold, but in terms of what Prof. Gustav Cassell, the renowned classical economist, called the Purchasing Power Parity Theory. According to this theory, exchange rates are determined by what each unit of a currency can buy in terms of real goods and services in its own country. The rate of exchange is the amount of currency which would buy the equivalent basket of goods and services in both the countries. Such an exercise in real world is based on comparisons at two periods of time, with one year as the basis of comparison, but no absolute comparison as between two currencies is possible as the pattern of goods and services produced varies from country to country. It is assumed that the base year prices in both the countries are at equilibrium and the exchange ratio at that time represents the ratio of their purchasing powers. Thus, if the base period exchange rate is 1:1 a doubling of prices in the domestic economy of B with A's prices remaining constant, would lead to a new exchange rate of 1:2. This ratio would set the bounds or limits to day-to-day fluctuations in the exchange rates, based on the supply or demand forces for each currency.

This theory of Gustav is criticized on the ground that the quality of good and services in both the countries is not the same and that a comparison of them is not realistic. The markets are not free due to trade and payment restrictions such as tariffs, quotas etc. Besides the base period exchange rate may not be equilibrium rate which distorts the comparison of their purchasing power parities at the current period. The index number technique used for such comparison is also criticized as defective due to changes in the composition of goods, their qualities over periods of time etc. etc.

Spot and Forward Rates

If an importer is paying on receipt of documents, then he can buy dollars spot and the bank sells him spot dollars. But if the importer agrees to pay three or six months hence, his demand for dollars might arise only after three or six months hence. These dollars are called forward dollars and the market is the forward market. The existence of a forward market provides cover or hedge against fluctuations in exchange rates. This exchange risk falls on the banks who are buying or selling dollars forward. The banks in turn can pass on the risk to the central bank of the country or to a foreign bank at another centre, or a correspondent bank abroad.

Just as banks are buying and selling spot, they also do business in forward currencies. Corresponding to the spot rate of exchange, there is a forward rate for various periods. If any bank succeeds in matching forward purchases with forward sales of the same currency, it avoids 'taking a position' and assume no risk; if they do not match, the bank may have an uncovered position which it may cover with another bank which has a contrary position. If it fails to cover with a bank, it may still do so with the central bank of the country or with a correspondent bank abroad. If a bank takes a position uncovered, it may take a calculated risk in the hope that the rate may move in his favour or he has failed to secure a proper cover in which case he would adjust uncovered position against a spot deal or against a future sale or purchase.

Currencies purchased or sold in forward would be subject to the influences of interest rates at home and abroad. A forward currency will be at premium (higher than the spot expressed in foreign currency per domestic unit quoted as Rs.100 = $4.75555), as at end June 1991. Later rates were quoted as $1 = Rs.31.3283 in June 1993, and $1 = Rs.35.79 in Oct. 1996 and Rs. 44.61 at end March 2006. If interest rates abroad are higher than at home, the premium (or discount) will depend on interest rates and expectations of interest rates and exchange rates. Forward premia for U.S. dollar is 15 to 20 paise per month at one stage of turmoil in Oct.-Nov. 1995 speculation. The forward premia was also high at the time of South East Asian financial crisis during June-Aug. 1998 with 9-10 percent per annum for 3-6 months forward. During 1999 and 2000, with falling interest rates in India, the premia fell to 3-4 per cent per annum for 3 and 6 months forward.

Speculation and hedging operations are taking place in free markets to take advantage of interest rate and exchange rate differentials. In the case of India, such hedging and speculation are not possible as banks are not allowed to take position in any currency beyond the minimum working balances to be kept in various centers. In a free foreign exchange market, short-term capital flows take place to take advantage of interest rate differentials and will be quickly reversed, leading to instability in the exchange rates. One-sided speculation is also very destabilizing which generally the central bank of a country would not allow unchecked. Controls on capital account, particularly to counter such destabilizing short-term flows, are in tune with the spirit of the International Monetary Fund. Speculation on a limited scale and if it is on both sides of purchase and sale is healthy and welcome to keep the balance in the market and absorb the excesses of demand/supply of currencies in the foreign exchange market.

Arbitrage

When foreign exchange markets are free to fluctuate, the exchanges rate of a currency should be the same in almost all the centers. Thus, if the dollar rate per sterling is different in New York and Frankfurt, the funds would flow in either direction to take advantage of the rate differential. It is, however, possible that slight differentials might be still there due to carrying costs of moving funds from one place to another, brokerage and other costs. Such operations in terms of movements of funds from one center to another are called arbitrage operations.

Such operations can take place only if there are no exchange controls in both the countries and if funds are free to move. Thus, if either New York or Frankfurt is subject to exchange restrictions involving central bank supervision of funds inflow and outflow and ban on free movements, arbitrage cannot take place and differentials in rates between two countries might exist.

Arbitrage is not limited to two centres or two currencies alone. Three-point and multi-point arbitrage can also take place if the respective currencies are free. Thus, in a three-point arbitrage, the dollar-sterling rate and the dollar-franc rate are considered and the cross rate between sterling and franc should be in conformity with the above two rates. Otherwise, three-point arbitrage can take place by moving funds from dollar to franc and franc to sterling and back to dollar from sterling. Suppose the dollar-sterling rate is 1 pound = $ 2.80 and franc 350 = $1 and pound = 1020 francs. Starting with $100, one can buy up pounds, move from pounds to francs and thence to dollars back, making a gain of about $5 per $100 in the above example. Thus, arbitrage can take place as between centres or currencies at more than two centres and currencies at a time. Such arbitrage operations may be for gain in exchange rate differential or in interest rate differential as between centres. The former are called currency arbitrage and the latter interest arbitrage. An operation of simultaneous purchase and sale in each of the two markets to take advantage of interest differential is called interest arbitrage. Such deals are put through as swaps or forward deals.

The operations in the foreign exchange market are exposed to a number of risks which are difficult to foresee and forecast. These risks may be credit risks arising out of lending to a foreign borrower whose credit rating is not known for certainty. Secondly, there may be currency risks of trading in a currency whose stability and strength is known to fluctuate. Thirdly, there are country risks involved in lending to a country whose political and economic strength may be unpredictable and is uncertain. Fourthly, there are risks of illiquidity due to mismatch between current assets and current liabilities with the result there may be sudden need for borrowing and difficulties may arise in securing funds at short notice. Lastly, the dealers sometimes take risks by exceeding the limits of prudent trading in a currency with the result that they may find it difficult to cover the transactions and incur losses in such a position. Such risks are more marked in international lending and borrowing and in foreign exchange and currency markets. Further details of risk are discussed in a separate chapter. Indian banks are free to cover their risk and do trading in foreign currency markets at present.

Indian Foreign Exchange Market

In India there are many commercial and co-operative banks who are authorized to deal in foreign exchange called authorized dealers and are eligible to operate in the foreign exchange market. However, not all co-operative banks are authorized to deal in foreign exchange. These banks cover their open positions in currencies in London through their correspondents or branches abroad or in India in the inter-bank market. The published figures on the amount of inter-bank transactions and on account of merchant transactions are available in RBI publications with a time lag. These are published under the heads of spot, forward and forward cancellations in merchant deals and spot, swap, and forward in the interbank market. However, banks finance thousands of crores of foreign trade, and put through crores of foreign remittances and a host of other purchases and sales. In the process of such purchases and sales directly with the public, the authorized dealers would have various currencies which they try to dispose of by matching demand with supply in the inter-bank market. It is only the unmatched net requirements that are purchased from the RBI, or excesses sold to the RBI. The data on RBI purchases and sales are available month-wise in the RBI Monthly Bulletins and Annual Reports. There are also authorized money dealers, who exchange foreign money to Indian money and many hotels and departmental stores accept foreign currencies.

Exchange Dealers

The foreign department of every bank draws up a position sheet for each currency daily in which purchases and sales of the currency are recorded. As the banks generally avoid taking any exchange risk by keeping uncovered balance, they try to cover their position by the end of the day. When the purchases exceed sales, the credit balance is plus (or long) and overbought. This is to be covered by equal sales of that currency. When the sales exceed purchases, the debit balance is minus/short or oversold position and is to be covered by equivalent purchases. These sales and purchases would include both spot and forward, import bills or export bills negotiated or purchases clean sales or purchases (other than through bill, namely, by TT, MT, cheques, drafts) BC sales or OD sales, etc. Banks are now permitted to fix their own prudent norms for taking positions in currencies by the Top Management.

Before entering into the inter-bank market, the banker decides how much to cover and what is the outstanding balance position in his books. Banks operate in the inter-bank market through the foreign exchange brokers. In every important market centre, some brokers operate in these dealings. The banker keeps some minimum balances in all his Nostro accounts to meet the customer-needs as they accrue. The more exactly he synchronizes the delivery dates of his purchases and sales, the greater is his profit. The finer the rates he quotes, the better in his position. The better he foresees the trends in exchange rates of currencies and interest rates in various centres, the more efficient he is and the better is his profitability.

In the inter-bank market, banks put through the dealings of purchase and sale of currency through authorized brokers. Brokers in each centre are in contact with other centres in India and in foreign countries for effecting matching transactions in various currencies. In all centres, export bills, import bills and various remittances are daily purchased and sold by banks. Imports give rise to payments abroad and purchase of foreign currencies. As the bulk of the imports in India is on government account and the SBI keeps the account of the public sector undertakings and of government, the SBI enters the foreign exchange market mostly as a buyer of foreign currencies. Exports are more concentrated in the private sector in which all banks are involved in varying degrees. Hence, sales of foreign currencies in the exchange market are more evenly spread among the banks in india. Many times, brokers cannot match in the local centres for odd currencies like Austrian shilling or Nigerian naira or Libyan dinar, which are to be put through in a more sophisticated market like London or Singapore.

In India, some financial centres are more developed than others in the foreign exchange market. Thus, Mumbai, Kolkata and Chennai are more developed than others. Some of the foreign exchange transactions being seasonal, the markets are also seasonal.

RBI and Exchange Market

The RBI operates in the market as the last recourse agency. The RBI purchases and sells sterling spot and buys and sells forward sterling upto six months but since June 1966, forward sales have been stopped. Since the abandonment of convertibility of the US dollars in 1971, the forward cover for a longer period was felt necessary due to greater exchange risk and it was provided by the RBI upto 9 months at a rate of 0.005 pounds per month fixed and extendable up one year in total, at a nominal charge of 0.0075 pounds per month for the extended period.

The other currencies in which the RBI started operations during the seventies are dollars, DM and Yen. The RBI started purchase spot and forward dollars from July and August 1966 respectively, and with brief interruptions from August 1971 to October 1972 and February 1973 to September 1973, the RBI continued to purchase spot and forward dollars. Similar purchases of DM and of Yen were started from March and May 1974 respectively. The period of forward cover was upto three months initially but was extended upto six months from September 1975. Thus, the RBI provided cover for 4 currencies which are our major trading partners, namely, sterling, dollar, DM, and Yen. The Bank purchased and sold spot pound but bought forward Sterling and bought dollar, DM and Yen both spot and forward.

The RBI was operating in four major currencies, namely, UK Pound, US $, Japanese Yen and DM. Early in 1987, the RBI has started selling spot US Dollars with the result that it used to buying and selling of two currencies, UK Pounds and US $, in addition to its purchases of DM and Japanese Yen. It has also adopted recently the practice of changing the rates quoted by it in the course of the day if the conditions in the market warranted it. The RBI used to quote both the spot and forward rates in the currencies it transacts with the banks and in Asian Currency Units (ACU) on a daily basis.

The RBI was providing cover for a fairly long period of upto 10 years in respect of long-term contracts for engineering exports and construction projects.

Since November 1975, the RBI has also offered the cover to ADs against exchange rate fluctuations in respect of deposits received in foreign currency from non-residents. Most of the facilities which the RBI offers are intended for exporters in terms of cover or purchase and sale. This is justified in view of the national importance attached to exports. But they have not offered similar facilities for importers for two reasons. Firstly, bulk of the imports into India is by the government or public sector agencies who do not need such facilities. Secondly, the inter-bank market is designed to develop to provide cover as and when needed by the importers in this regard. The RBI is maintaining itself as a last resort institution in foreign exchange as in domestic finance. The policy of RBI in this regard is very flexible and designed to promote self reliance by banks and greater resort to the inter-bank market. The RBI has, however, responded to emerging situations in the foreign exchange market quickly and promptly. Since rupee convertibility was launched in March 1992, RBI is publishing a reference rate around which it operates in the market to stabilize the rate of exchange of rupee in terms of US dollar.

RBI Operations

In the background of this historical perspective, the latest position is presented below:

The RBI stopped giving forward quotations and forward purchases and sales since october 2004. The RBI now gives reference rates only in spot U.S. dollar and Euro — the two major trading partners. The Asian Currency Unit [ACU] and other foreign currencies are not quoted now. While the ACU has lost its significance due to rupee being made fully convertible on current Account, since March 1994, the quotation for other major currency are left to be given by FEDA, as indicative rates. These are given of the cross currency rates by FEDA, to be adopted by the banks themselves. The ADs are now free to fix their own daily rates, based on FEDA rates.

The RBI does open market operations only in U.S. dollars, involving mostly net purchases. The earlier methods of aiding exporters through providing forward covers through banks and/or subsiding interest costs of exports were all given up. Similarly, the foreign exchange risk cover for NRI deposits with ADs was also withdrawn, due to lower international interest rates and lower importance given to those deposits following the greater role played by ECBS and private trade credits.

During the years 2004 to 2006, the foreign exchange market remained stable but with slow depreciation of the rupee from Rs. 43 to 46. As in mid July 2006, the rupee was quoted at Rs. 46.17 to Rs. 46.27. The forward premia over the spot rates was also lower in 2006, as compared to earlier years. The total turnover in the forex market was no doubt rising, particularly in the last few years in the 21st century, but constitutes still less than one percent of the global forex turnover.

Floating vs. Fixed Exchange Rates

In the post-Smithsonian era, after 1973 the currencies have been on various types of floating systems due to the abandonment of the convertibility of US dollar. Single float, joint float, managed float etc., are examples of such floats. The system of fixed exchange parities (par values) was given decent burial following the breakdown of the Bretton Woods system in August 1971.

Floating rate is a rate which is allowed to fluctuate freely according to supply and demand forces. Such float is a free float if no intervention takes place by the central bank of the country. In the real world, some degree of intervention exists which leads to a managed float. Such managed floats are either single or joint. Dollar, Sterling and Yen were floating with varying degrees of intervention within a band of 2.25 percent on either side and they are single floats. The European Common Market countries (West Germany, France, Belgium, Netherlands, Luxemburg, Ireland, Denmark and Sweden) are under a joint float within a narrow band called "Snake in the Tunnel." The new IMF policy is to keep relatively stable exchange rates within a wider band of fluctuations. Indian rupee is kept relatively stable with the help of a basket of currencies, upto July 1991, when the rupee was devalued and LERMS' was adopted later.

Factors Influencing Forex Rates in India

The following are the more important factors influencing exchange rates :

(1) Demand and supply factors for each currency, spot and forward
(2) Special debt service payments of the Government through the SBI
(3) Imports payments for bulk purchases of oil, fertilizers etc. by STC
(4) Tax payments and call money rates in India
(5) Banks resource position in rupees due to CRR and SLR
(6) RBI policy, reference rates and its regulations relating to Forex Market.

Present Exchange Rate System

With the initiation of economic and financial reforms, in July 1991 far reaching changes were introduced in the foreign exchanges policy and exchange rate management. FERA was diluted and banks have been allowed greater freedom of lending and lending rates have also been freed. Foreign exchange release is mostly left to the banks, for many purposes, subject to an upper limit for each purpose. Rupee was made partially convertible first in 1992 followed by full convertibility on current account, inclusive of invisible account in March 1994. The era of full-fledged controls on foreign exchanges has ended with these reforms.

During 1992-93 to 1994-95, there was some semblance of stability in the Rupee due to large foreign investment inflow to offset the outflows on account of trade deficits. There was a high degree of volatility in March-April 1995 and a major turmoil in October-Nov. 1995, depreciating the rupee *vis-a-vis* to dollar by about say 18% which is partly due to the dollar weakness *vis-a-vis* the DM and Yen on the one hand and weakening of the rupee strength due to a larger demand for dollars for import payments, service payments, etc. Basically Rupee could not be sustained of the old rates due to higher inflation rates in India *vis-a-vis* her trading partners. The Rupee fell to Rs.35 per dollar in Nov. 1995 and the RBI had intervened heavily to keep it at that level, but later it began to slide down further to Rs.46 by end of 2000, reflecting the weakness of the rupee. The swap premia and forward premia widened to 15-20 paise for 3 months basis. Banks have been asked to cover their risk abroad, but bring funds due for exports and remittances but delay the import payments and other outflows. They can take exchange risk overnight upto Rs.15 crores and submit daily return on their position. The overnight limit of Rs.15 crores was later given up and banks are given freedom to fix their own prudential limit. The reporting is for control on any speculative positions by banks. Although banks are free to operate in cross currency positions also, this should not lead to over speculations, but confined to hedging.

Need for Hedging

With increasing liberalization and free flows following deregulation in the foreign exchange market there is need for hedging and cover for exporters and importers and banks have to provide this, by dependence on foreign markets. The need for well developed forward market with hedging facilities through derivatives like futures contracts, swaps, options including cross currency options is being met by the market itself. The RBI wants the market to develop itself with all its segments, without support from RBI. The details of risk management are set out in a separate chapter.

Case Study of a Foreign Department of ABC Bank

ABC Bank is a nationalized bank, whose name is withheld, as the objective of the case study is only to provide information. The organization of the International Banking department is as shown below: (Position as in 2002)

AGM **Commercial and Industrial Dept. (C & I Dept.)**

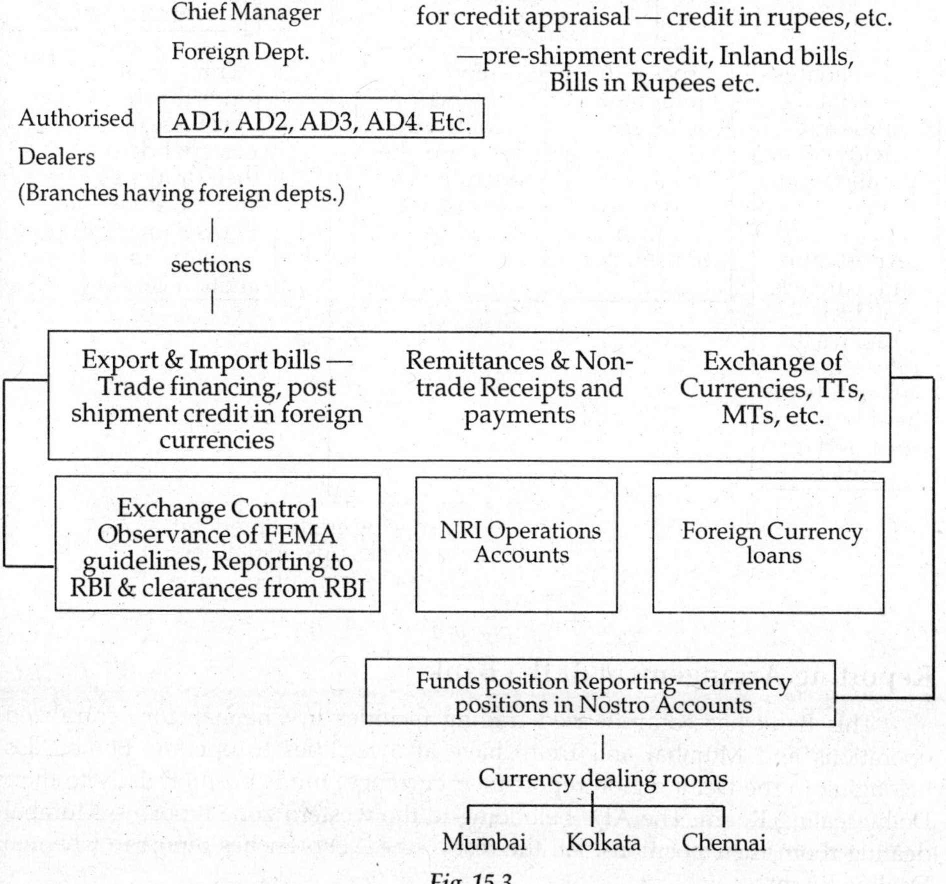

Fig. 15.3

DEALING/TRADING ROOM STRUCTURE

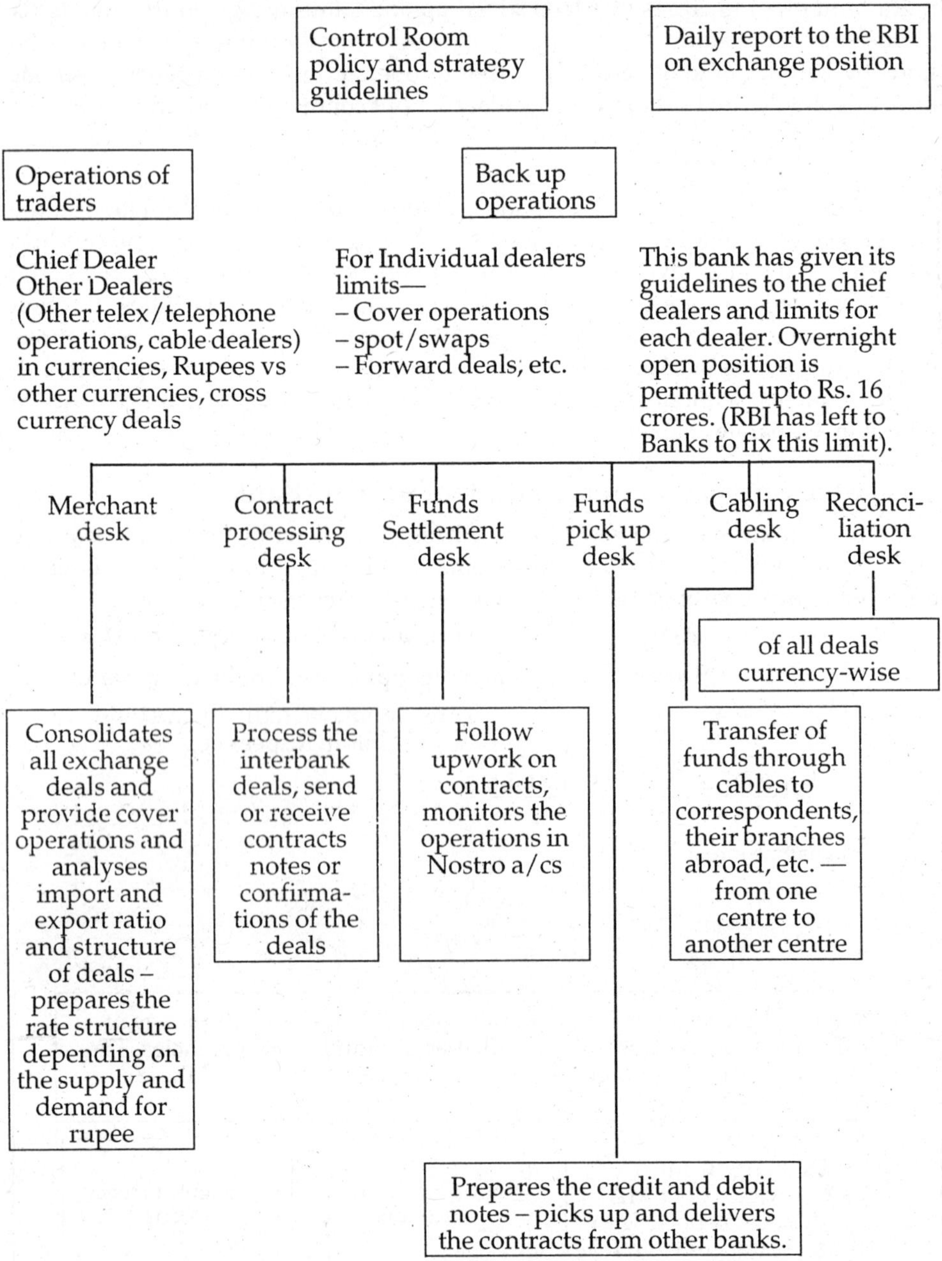

Control Room policy and strategy guidelines

Daily report to the RBI on exchange position

Operations of traders

Back up operations

Chief Dealer
Other Dealers
(Other telex/telephone operations, cable dealers) in currencies, Rupees vs other currencies, cross currency deals

For Individual dealers limits—
- Cover operations
- spot/swaps
- Forward deals, etc.

This bank has given its guidelines to the chief dealers and limits for each dealer. Overnight open position is permitted upto Rs. 16 crores. (RBI has left to Banks to fix this limit).

Merchant desk — Consolidates all exchange deals and provide cover operations and analyses import and export ratio and structure of deals – prepares the rate structure depending on the supply and demand for rupee

Contract processing desk — Process the interbank deals, send or receive contracts notes or confirmations of the deals

Funds Settlement desk — Follow upwork on contracts, monitors the operations in Nostro a/cs

Funds pick up desk — Prepares the credit and debit notes – picks up and delivers the contracts from other banks.

Cabling desk — Transfer of funds through cables to correspondents, their branches abroad, etc. — from one centre to another centre

Reconciliation desk — of all deals currency-wise

Fig. 15.4

Reporting Arrangement of the Bank

This Bank has computerised trading facilities in Chennai, for centralized operations and Mumbai and Delhi have also facilities to operate. Some ADs belonging to the Delhi region report their currency/funds position daily to their Delhi dealing Room. The ADs belonging to the western zone report to Mumbai dealing room their positions. All the rest of the AD branches report to Chennai Dealing Room.

The bank has some correspondents in each important international centre, in addition to its own branches in selected countries. In these foreign offices and correspondents, they are keeping their Nostro Accounts, through which their credits and debits in currencies are passed.

This bank is very conservative and dealers are instructed not to exceed their limits and not to indulge in speculation or be a party to the speculative positions taken by its client exporters and the companies with export earnings. The bank has an over all limit of Rs.16 crores, permitted by its Head office guidelines. Subject to this over all limit, individual dealers are given the limits in their transactions, to take open positions or risk of currency rate changes.

As a standing instruction, the hedge deals and cover operations abroad are allowed but mostly through their own branches abroad. Only if absolutely necessary, they are permitted to take cross currency positions. Otherwise all the deals are through dollars and rupees and the cover is in dollars.

The foreign branch of an authorised bank (say at Hongkong) has also foreign exchange dealing functions say for illustration.

The Dealing Room is headed by a Chief Dealer who is assisted by an officer in the Bank.

The following are amongst the major functions performed by the Dealing Room :

(1) Quoting, negotiating and fixing rates of exchange for larger-sized customer transactions involving purchase or sale of foreign currencies.

(2) Preparing of the list of 'Card' rates for various foreign currencies *vis-a-vis* HongKong dollar that may be applied to transactions in respect of which there is no need or scope for negotiation of the rate of exchange-small-value purchase sales, commissions, interest etc.

(3) Arranging cover against purchase/sale of foreign currencies from/to customers.

(4) Trading on own account i.e. purchase/sale of foreign currencies for sale/purchase against profit.

(5) Mobilisation of required foreign currency funds either by swapping Hongkong dollar funds or by borrowing from other banks.

(6) Borrowing and/or lending in the Hongkong Dollar Market for maintenance of the Minimum Cash Balance with the Local Monetary Authority or meet any other local Exchange Control Rules or Central Bank Guidelines.

(7) Accepting customer forward contracts for purchase/sale of foreign currencies and arranging cover against the same where possible and necessary.

(8) Placement/conversion/transfer of surplus Nostro account balance and Vostro account balances as well as necessary funding of Vostro and Nostro accounts to meet drawings on those accounts.

(9) Maintaining of rate scan record.

(10) Sale and purchase of Government securities.

(11) Use or investment of surplus funds.

The foregoing functions are to be performed within the frame-work of limits, guidelines and policy prescription laid-down by the management such as the following :

(1) Transient day-light limit for the maximum uncovered position in each major foreign currency.

(2) Overnight limit for uncovered open position in each major currency.

(3) Aggregate Gap Limit (AGL) and Individual Gap Limit (IGL) in respect of mismatched maturities of each month.

(4) Customer-wise limits for forward contracts.

(5) Counter-party exposure limit.

(6) Forex and Money Market limits fixed by other Banks for our Bank.

RBI Policy applied to Banks

RBI continued to delegate more and more powers to ADs in dealing in the forex market and in effecting receipts and payments.

RBI has now been publishing the reference rate of rupee against dollar on a daily basis. The RBI is dealing in buying and selling of Rupee for the dollar only both spot and forward and now only spot. On the basis of the RBI's Reference rate, Foreign Exchange Dealers Association (FEDAI) is giving the rates for banks, but banks are free to adjust their rates depending upon their currency positions.

\$ 1 = in Rupees

Examples of RBI and FEDAI Rates

	RBI Reference Rate	FEDAI Rate
March 4, 1994	31.3800	31.3790
Sept. 30, 1996	35.7600	35.7550
Nov. 30, 1999	43.4100	43.4050
March 31, 2006	44.6100	44.6000

In the forward exchange market, RBI allowed free functioning following the current account convertibility of the rupee since March 1994, particularly after deregulation of lending rates in Oct. 1994. The swap premia seemed to adjust to real interest rates, i.e., interest rates adjusted for inflation rates. Another factor affecting the swap premia is the call money rates in the respective countries.

RBI has been persuading banks to develop forward market in India by dealings with interbank and in foreign market. There is however need to develop foreign exchange derivatives for providing hedge through forward contracts, swaps and cross currency options. It is possible to develop rupee based options if international quotes for rupee are available which is not the case at present.

Currency Deals

Right now, the quotations are called direct quotes. The principle the banker follows is to give two-way quotes based on "give less and take more." The spread between the buying and selling rates is the banks' profit. The interest component for any period is shown separately from the currency position. The spread depends on the cable cost, brokerage cost and administrative cost leaving only a small margin of profit to the banker.

If the quotation is $1 = 35.750 – 35.780, then the banker is prepared to buy dollars at Rs.35.750 and sell dollars at Rs.35.780. Here the principle is buy low and sell high. Let us take a quote of $ to pounds say pound = $ 1.5200 – 10; the quoting bank wants to sell sterling at $1.5210 and buy at $1.5200. The price of dollar to D.M. 1.5810/20 means that for every dollar, the quoting bank will pay 1.5810 DM and would receive 1.5820 DM for dollar. In the quotation, the bank always wants to gain.

In some banks the dealing rooms are located also in Chennai and Bangalore. In fact foreign banks concentrate their deals mostly in Mumbai, while SBI had its Central Dealing room at Kolkata. The largest component of inter-bank market operations is concentrated in Mumbai.

SPOT TRADING OPERATIONS

This bank has classified the trading operations as shown below:

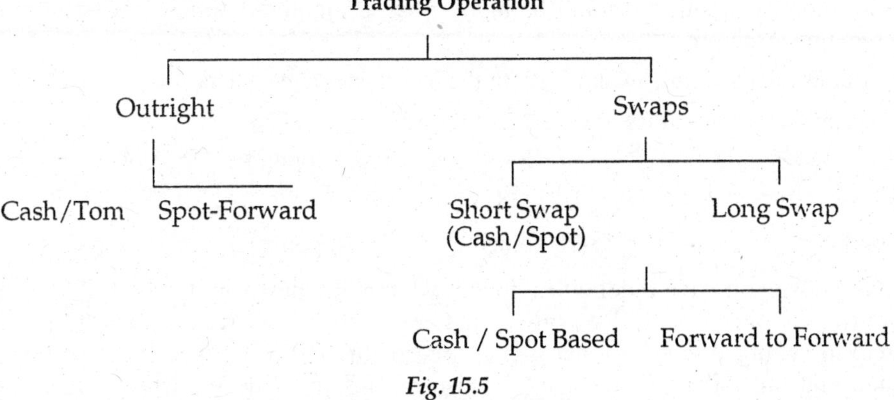

Fig. 15.5

Spot is settled on the same day (cash), value tomorrow (tom) and forwards (beyond spot date), spot deals are less risky while forwards are more risky. The forwards may be for a few months.

Spot Trading has two types of deals:

1. ***In and Out Trading:*** The number of deals are many but the profit / loss in each is minimal. Minimal exposure and minimum risk is involved in this.
2. ***Position Trading:*** There will be a fewer deals with large exposure being held for some time for profit to be booked.

The portfolio dealer in foreign currency has to go in for a judicious mix of these two strategies. Examples of these two strategies of the trader in Mumbai is given below.

For in and out trading the exposure, pound 1 million

1 million pounds bought @ 1.5270, sold 1.5272, profit : 2 pips

1 million pounds bought @ 1.5274, sold 1.5277, profit : 3 pips

and so on; he made 10 deals, each with a profit of 2 to 10 pips. For 10 transactions of million 1 pounds, he has made a profit of say 20 pips, exposure is only pound 1 million in total.

In position trading, the trader takes a big exposure of $5 million hoping DM will improve against dollar. He sells $3 million first at DM 1.5840 and if the trend assumed is correct, he sells another $2 million at DM 1.5780. When the DM rose to 1.5700, he sells all the DM for dollars back to make profit on his total position. Say the average sale price of dollars is 1.5780 and now purchase price is 1.5700. He made a profit of 80 points for dollar, which is a large amount, for deals involving millions of dollars.

Cross Currency Deals

Dealings in forex market depend on the availability of rupee funds as also the foreign funds. Therefore, the surplus funds or float of the banks are used for the dealings *vis-a-vis* the foreign currencies.

In India, premium or discount depends on the demand and supply position and not much on the interest rates. Movements in the spot currency rates also influence the forward premium or discount. Suppose, a large import payment in dollars is due 3 months hence, the premium for 3 months is higher than 6 months premium because of demand and supply factors, although in terms of interest rate gain, 6 months premium should be higher than 3 months premium as per normal interest rate structure.

Let us take a simple example, with the help of some past data.

Suppose the pound Rs. rates are as follows

	$ - Rs.	Rs. — pound	pound - $
Spot.	31.25 -28	47.50 -53	1.5260 -70
1 month	15-20 points	13-16 points	36-32 points

Suppose you have a deficit in pound, what is the best way to cover it? Rupee is at discount over pound. If we buy pound or sell pound, we receive less (13 paise). Instead of going directly to sterling, if we go through $ - rupee route and $ to pound. and on dollar, we receive 15 paise by this method. We bought spot $ at 31.28 and sold one month forward at 31.43 (discount added 31.28 + 15). Then take the pound - $ forwards 36-32 pound is at a discount and dollar at premium. Here we sell spot dollar at 1.5270 and bought one month forward dollar at 1.5234 (36 points deducted from spot rate (1.5270 - 36).

Combining the above two deals, we bought $ at 31.28 and sold at pound 1.5270 to acquire pound. The spot £ at 47.76 Rs. (31.28 x 1.5270). We sold forward $ at 31.43 and bought forward $ at 1.5234 for pound. We sold one month forward pound at 47.88 Rs.(31.43 x 1.5234).

Thus, we bought spot pound for 47.76 Rs. We sold one month forward pound at 47.88 Rs. We gained 12 paise in this swap deal. Whereas we would have lost in direct deals as the rupee was at a discount on pound.

Mismatch — Need for Matching

In export and import deals and other purchases and sale deals, the dealer gets short dollar purchase 1,000 million — not covered. Forward dollar sold 2,000 million — not Matched. If the purchases and sales of the same currency and the same maturity are done on the same day, they are said to be matched. Otherwise matching is to be done through inter-bank deals or with foreign branches and foreign correspondents abroad, so that open position is minimal. The uncovered oven position in any currency overnight should not exceed Rs.16 crores as per the bank's own guidelines. The cover can be through swap — spot to forward or forward to forward. However, risk matching or risk reduction has to be adopted by the dealers through any derivative products.

When you expect premium to go up or swap differentials to rise, pay now and receive later — sell now and buy later. When you expect premium to come down in any currency, buy now and sell later.

Forex Management

If we have extra Nostro funds keep them in call market in that currency and earn some interest abroad. If German interest rate (6%) is higher than in US rate of 4% buy DM spot and keep in the call market at the higher rate of 6% in Frankfurt and convert back to dollar by selling forward DM one month to three months hence; here the currency rate expectations play a major role. If the DM is becoming dearer and its interest rate (6%), higher than in New York (4%) then the above operations in funds management will earn profits. Such operations should maximize profits with minimum risk.

Similarly, payments are due to come to India in $ three months hence from US. Three months dollars will be in demand. So buy spot dollars and keep earning interest in Europe at 6% more than in US and sell them to those needing dollars three months hence.

There are a host of other methods of gaining in forex market due to interest rate differentials and expectations regarding them and exchange rate changes and their expectations or cross rate differentials in exchange rates. The RBI has allowed the ADs to go in for interest rate hedges in foreign markets. The object is to develop the market for hedges and for derivatives in India.

Derivative Products

One of the methods of risk coverage by the treasury manager is the use of derivatives, either in the bond market or in the forex market. The risk in the cash market can be hedged in the derivatives market. An example of such deals in the forex market is the forward contract to cover the risk of currency fluctuations in the spot contract. Swaps and options are other examples of risk covering instruments.

Forward Contracts

It is a contract for delivery of foreign currency at a specified future date at a fixed exchange rate. Only genuine trade and invisible transactions can be covered in India, as per RBI guidelines. These forward contracts for foreign currency can be delivered at a fixed date or within a specified range of dates and penalty provisions may be laid down for breach of contract by either party. These depend on the terms of the approved contracts, usage and practice.

Swaps

A swap is a deal in which a bank buys specified foreign currency and sells the same at different maturity dates, like simultaneous purchase of dollar on spot and sale of forward dollars of the same amount. Here the risk is possible due to adverse movement in exchange rate, which is covered by prior fixing of the rates. Forward to forward deals is the purchase of two months dollars, followed by a sale of three months dollars. Swap deals are used as a tool to cover arbitrage operations, namely, buy in Frankfurt and sell in London of the same currency (dollars), swaps are also required to cover a mismatch in forex deliveries to the genuine clients of the bank. Use of swaps or even repos for speculative purposes are not permitted by the RBI. Arbitrage of risk cover and genuine matching of demand and supply are permitted by RBI. Repos are repurchase agreements, which have been already explained in an earlier chapter. Repos can be used to buy and sell foreign exchange involving forward contracts.

Options

Currency options are contracts with a right to buy or sell a stated currency without any obligation, at a fixed rate on a future date. If the future rate moves against the expectation, the holder of the options can exercise the right to buy or sell. For this right to cover the risk, the party has to pay a price called premium under the American options. The customer can exercise the option at any time during the currency of the contract but under the European contract, the option has to be exercised only at a specified date mentioned. As it is only a right, but no obligation, it need not be based on genuine transactions and may lead to speculation. The writer of the option is under an obligation to sell for a buy option and to buy for a sell option.

Futures

While forward contracts can be entered into by any parties outside the stock exchange or in any organized system, the futures contracts are regulated by a proper authority with fixed terms, involving an obligation to buy and sell or give and take delivery. A currency future contract is an agreement to buy or sell a foreign currency at a fixed amount at a stated price or rate at a specified future time. The obligations rest on both the parties and their deals are regulated and supervised by a properly constituted authority.

FOREX MARKET

Linkages with Call Market

In the Indian context, with developing forex market following the freeing of rupee for conversion and convertibility on current account ensured since 1994, a number of loop holes in the system have been noticed. One of such is the non-availability of a good derivative market to hedge the risks in the spot market and forward markets.

Due to inadequate linkages between domestic market and foreign market foreign inflows have been adding to liquidity to domestic markets and a co-ordinated monetary policy and foreign exchange policy could not be followed, as curbing of excess liquidity in the domestic economy led to higher interest rates and dichotomy between the interest rates as between markets led to higher arbitrage operations as between markets.

In a tight liquidity market, operators convert spot dollars into rupees and buy forward dollars. This would bring some pressure on forward premiums. Although these premiums are mostly influenced by bulk purchasers like ONGC, and FCI, SCI, etc. one month forward premium climbed and fell in tandem or tune with the call money rates.

The cash reserve ratio has changed only in Jan. 1997, and as the RBI is contemplating no changes in December there will be no further fall in interest rates, which is indicated by the RBI fixing the cut off yield on 2000 loan at 13.55% as against the market expectation of 13.40-50%. The maintenance of higher yields on the government bonds is indicative of policy initiative of the RBI reflecting no further fall in interest rates for the time being. The inflation rate has stopped falling and that government budget deficit is likely to remain high also indicate as no further fall in the interest rates. Since 1997, when CRR was 10%, there were many changes in CRR and stood at 5% since Oct. 2004. Call market conditions also changed. Inflation rates remained stable at around 4% only since 2001-02, but exchange rate changes took place independent of interest rate expectations and inflation rate expectations due to international factors.

Indian Forex Market

Indian Foreign Exchange Market has limited freedom, as some of the operations and particularly the Capital Account are still controlled. The RBI is the controlling authority along with the Ministry of Finance, Government of India. The RBI can directly or indirectly intervene in the market for purchase and sale of foreign currencies, particularly U.S. dollars and RBI reference rate is given in U.S dollars. The Foreign Exchange Dealers Association of India (FEDAI), also gives guidelines for banks, in the form of cross currency rates margins, charges etc. More recently, both RBI and FEDAI have voluntarily reduced these controls and individual banks, are now freer than before in fixing the margins, spreads, charges etc. in foreign exchange deals. The RBI wants to encourage the banks to take up challenges of globalised markets, and learn to manage the risks in forex deals. The derivatives, markets, forwards, futures etc. are being developed with less or no controls of RBI. The interlinkages as between interbank forex market and interbank domestic call market on the one hand and as between spot and forward exchange markets on the other are being developed.

Data on Forex Market

The data on Forex Rates of major currencies and cross currency rates along with the RBI reference rate are available in the Financial press as well as on the RBI websites, on a daily basis. These are also published by the RBI in their Monthly Bulletins and other publications.

The RBI operations of purchases or sales in Forex Market are also available in the RBI publications. Presently RBI is making purchases and sales, on spot basis in U.S. dollars only. The data on RBIs foreign exchange reserves, forex turnover and sales both in spot and forward are also published by the RBI.

Besides, Trade weighted exchange notes — Real Effective Exchange Rates (REER) and Nominal Effective Exchange Rates (NEER) of the Indian rupee are compiled and published for the RBI in their bulletins under the following heads: (1) REER and NEER with export based weights of 36 countries. (2) REER and NEER with Trade based weight of 36 countries with 1993-94 as base year — Indices (With Base 1993-94 = 100). (3) Indices of REER and NEER of the Indian Rupee with Base 2003-04 (April-March) = 100 is the latest series of data, published by the RBI with 6 currency based weights.

These induces with Trade based weight of 6 countries which are major trading partners of India reveal the extent of depreciation of the rupee, compared with the base year, namely 1993-94 or 2003-04.

FEDAI is also giving out the Indicative Rates of major currencies in which Indian banks are dealing in the Forex Market. The nominal exchange rates are not adjusted for inflation and the methodology of compilation of NEER and REER is published in RBI Bulletin of July 1998.

The data on Fonward premia as against U.S. dollar are published on a daily basis in Financial Press, while the monthly averages are published by the RBI, in their Hand Book of Statistics. The data on turnover value in U.S. dollars for merchant transactions and for inter bank deals, effected in the Indian Forex Market are available in the RBI Bulletins. It will be seen that inter bank deals are nearly 3 to 5 times larger than those of the merchant transactions.

Foreign Investment flows under the heads of Direct investment and Portfolio Investment are published month-wise and year-wise in the RBI Bulletins. FII investments in the stock and capital markets are published by the SEBI on a daily and monthly basis. There are thus a comprehensive data base on foreign Exchange deals and Forex Market with RBI, Government, SEBI and FEDAI to make any analysis needed to take policy decisions for Treasury Management.

Global Interest Rate Swaps

With a view to further develop the Forex Market, the RBI has allowed the companies exporting and importing interest rate swaps in global markets. Permission was also granted to banks to develop derivative products to meet the requirements of hedging the risk of export and import trade.

RBI has also recently permitted banks to seek global rate swaps. Interest rate swaps are simply exchange of interest payments from a tied rate system to a floating rate system and *vice versa,* depending on the requirements. If the bank offers floating rate on FCNR deposits and loans are given at a fixed rate, then the risk of fixed rate has to be hedged with a floating rate swap for fixed rate receipts, from clients.

Foreign banks operating in India have already entered with their counterparts into such swaps on behalf of Indian corporates who are permitted to hedge their risk. It is reported that dollar interest rate swaps also accounted for 34% of the total outstanding deals at the end of 1995, followed by Yen and DM and French Franc etc. There is a huge global market in such swaps to which Indian banks have been permitted to enter in (1996). Interest rate swaps which were allowed for companies to hedge earlier are now kept open for banks as well to be operated in the global market. This is a further step of globalisation of Indian forex markets.

Euro-bond Markets

Indian Banks and foreign banks in India are allowed in both Euro-Currency and Euro-Bond market. This is an international market for borrowing capital by any country's Governments, corporates and institutions. The centre of activity of

** Interest Rate futures were allowed in India since June 2003 on the NSE. But the attempt did not succeed at all, afterwards.

borrowing and lending is London and Europe. But borrowers and lenders come from all over the world. There is an Asian dollar market also.

The currency market is far short-term funds and the bond market is a long-term funds market. Banks of multinational character called international banks or investments banks organise these transactions. The supply of deposits in dollar or other convertible currency comes from the exporters with foreign currencies, mostly in dollars and countries with balance of payments surplus with the USA. Although called Euro dollar, it can be Asian market (Asian dollars), Gulf market (petro dollars), etc.

Origin

Developed since the 1960s following the huge surpluses of U.S. dollars to countries other than U.S.; the reasons for the off shoot of such dollars outside U.S.A. are the following:

(1) Continued deficits in Trade payments of U.S.A.

(2) Use of such surpluses outside in London and Europe.

(3) Lack of funds in the Capital markets of New York and London for the traditional borrowing from natural capital markets.

(4) Regulation "Q" in U.S which controls the rates in U.S. Time deposits.

It is a telephone and telex market and called the OTC market and thus depends upon the infrastructure for financial services like tele communications, telex, phones etc.

As referred to earlier, while bonds refer to long and medium dated securities or debt, the Euro-Currency notes refer to short dated debt of a few months to an year.

Magnitude of Trade

In 1987 the Euro-bonds were 150 billion dollars, while the same in 1964 was 500 million dollars only. The magnitude of the market now runs into billions and trillions of dollars depending on whether it is in dollars or pounds, DM, yen etc. These are mostly fixed rate issues, warrants, convertible and floating rates notes or bonds etc. The borrowers and the issuers of Euro bond loans are banks and other financial institutions, corporations, Government and semi-Government bodies and Supra national organisations. Investors in this bond market are central and commercial banks, Government agencies, international financial organisations like ADB, IFC, etc., and investment and pension funds, insurance companies and corporations are also in this market.

Market Features

1. Both investors and borrowers are well-known names in the international markets.
2. These loans are unsecured and no Government guarantee either, only credit-worthy borrowers are generally approaching this market.
3. Country's credit rating and borrowing party's credit rating are being looked into. Standard and poor or Moody's ratings are popular for assessing the credit worthiness of borrower and its country.

Regulations

This market is functioning outside the countries and is offshore in nature. No regulation of any national and international nature exists. SROs regulate the investment industry. Thus, the market practices in the secondary market trading are based on the rules laid down by Association of International Bond dealers.

Some parent companies and some foreign Governments do guarantee the interest and payment of principal. The mode and time of payment is provided in the agreement itself and stricter controls are exercised in the collection of interest, although these rates are lower than those on national bonds of any country. Many countries notably USA and Germany removed the withholding tax to attract bond market to the national bounds. The Euro-bond market has been kept out of the jurisdiction of any nation.

Magnitude and Terms of Issue

The maturity period ranges from 5 to 7 years and an Indian Company (Reliance) issued a 100 year bond in this market. Issues of 10 to 20 years are normally possible and popular issues are for about 5 years. The size of the bond issue varies from a few millions to a few billions of dollars.

Bearer Status

These bonds are negotiable and transferable as they have the bearer status. There are no restrictions on transfers, and the right to receive interest and payment of principal is with the bearer of the bond. The bonds are printed on special security printing paper and terms and conditions are printed on the back of the paper. There is also authentification of the individual bonds by the staff of lead manager. The security and safe custody of the bond and the avoidance of fake certificates are all the responsibilities of managers to the issue and banks dealing in the market.

Instruments Issued and Traded

1. ***Fixed Rate Bonds:*** Here the company gets say a 10% coupon bond for a maturity of 5 years.
2. ***Convertibles:*** Issuers of bond are eligible for conversion into shares of the company after a date at a fixed conversion price.
3. ***Floating Rate Notes:*** This coupon is changed every 3/6 months depending on the LIBOR or any other standard rate laid down in the agreement.
4. ***Swaps:*** Interest rate swaps such as borrowing at fixed rate but swapping for floating rate and *vice versa* is possible.

Currency swaps can be depicted as shifting of one bond of dollars into some other currency, either as fixed rate or at a floating rate. The documentation involved in such deals should show the following details :

(i) Mechanics of Issue,

(ii) Loan Syndication,

(iii) Issuers,

(iv) Lead Manager,

(v) Co-Managers, etc.

UNDERWRITERS

B.O.D. (Bought out Deals)

Bought out deals refer to those transactions, which take place, when the bond manager offers the issues at a specified price. Paying agents in different centres are appointed in various commercial centres in different countries.

Lawyers and Auditors are needed for proper documentation of offer circular and prospectus and preparation of the agreement and signing of the same before the money is released to the borrower. There will be an issue of Tombstone in the press at the end of the issue. The fees are paid to all these parties: bond manager, Co.Manager, underwriters, solicitors, lawyers, auditors etc.

Euro Bond Clearing and Settlement System

Buyer and seller exchange the notes what they owe to each other: These contain the details of the buyer, the number securities and the seller and the money he is due. All the trades are automated and transactions in primary and secondary markets are kept in the form of book keeping entries in the books of traders – before automation, contract notes were issued to the parties to the trade. They are checked manually and transferred to computer system for matching and confirmation.

ACE System

$$\text{ACE} = \frac{\text{Automated confirmation entry}}{\text{Trade details}}$$

Rules of AIBD and their code of conduct will apply to these entries.

AIBD = Association of International Bond Dealers.

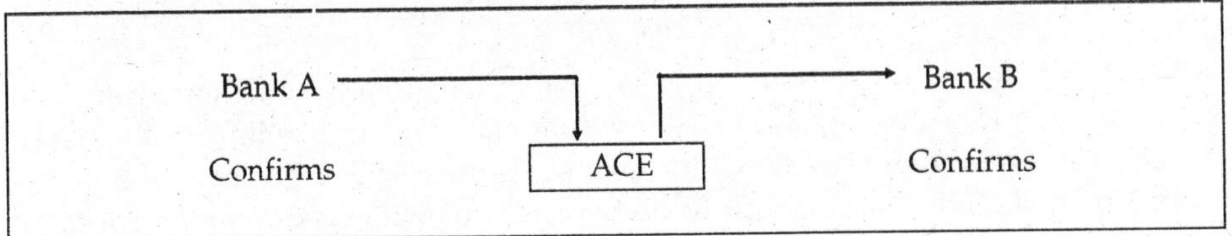

The Confirmation Contains all the trade details

Trading on the Yield Curves

The following examples show how trading on yield curve leads to gain in spreads which can be got through swaps, switches etc.

Deals in Two Loans

Take two loans: **1.** One year loan 9.19% **2.** 3 year Loan 10.51%

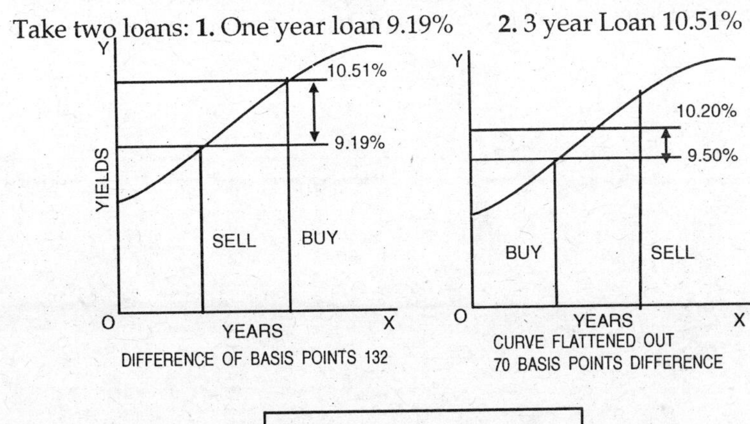

YIELD GAIN 132-70 = 62 POINTS

Fig. 15.6

By combining these two deals through switch, you gain 132 basis points and lose 70 basis points respectively, but a net gain of 62 basis points is got in the switch/swap operation.

INTER MARKET SPREADS

Anamoly in yield spreads (Deals)

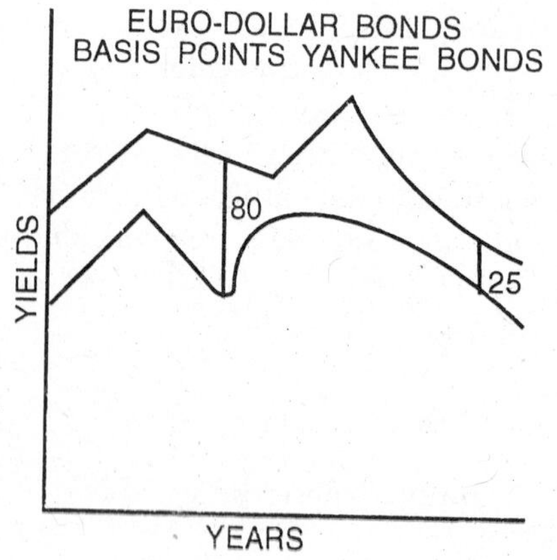

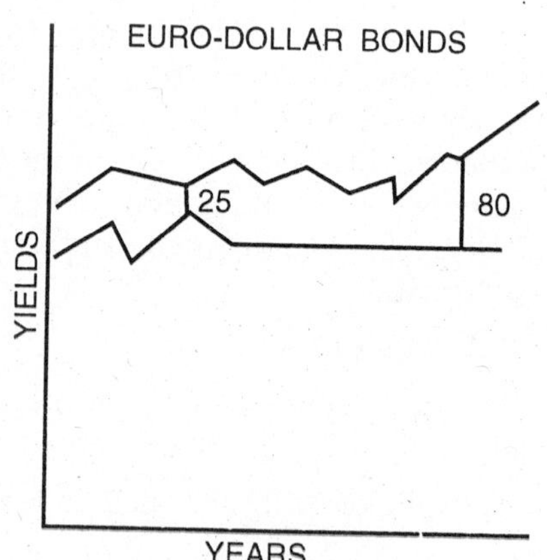

Fig. 15.7

In this case, we take advantage of Inter-market spreads, which are different, as can be seen from the charts above. By buying in one and selling in the other, one can gain the difference in spreads as basis points, which in deals of millions of dollars, make for a large profit to be booked, but with accompanying foreign exchange risk.

Conclusions

In conclusion, the Forex market is more complex and the operations in the various segments of the market, the instruments and methods are fraught with more risks and consequences that only expertise and experience of the Treasury manager can help in their operations. The Indian forex market is developing fast and it has great potentiality for becoming a high profit centre, but with a high risk profile.

❑ ❑ ❑

16 BANKS' BALANCE SHEET ANALYSIS

Corporate Balance Sheet analysis was discussed in chapter 6. Banks' Balance Sheet is different and hence a separate treatment in this chapter. Unlike manufacturing and trading companies, the balance sheet of public sector banks, shows no data on paid, up and reserves separately as also bad and doubtful debts. Tax provision and depreciation provision and other contingencies are not shown in Income-Expenditure Statement and Profit and Loss Account. It is understood that from the year 1996-97 the RBI has changed the format for balance sheet and income-expenditure statement of banks to provide for greater transparency. The private sector banks and listed public sector banks however publish all the details as per the requirements of law and listing. Agreement with the Stock Exchanges. The RBI had issued guidelines to disclose in the bank balance sheet the following items from the year ended March 2000 — Maturity pattern of loans and of investments, foreign currency assets and liabilities, changes in NPAs, maturity pattern of deposits and borrowings, lendings to sensitive sectors, etc. As per the proposals with regard to NPAs, classified as standard, sub-standard and doubtful and loss assets all will be shown separately as schedule 9 of the balance sheet. All advances will be shown on a gross basis and provisions made for each of the category of assets will be shown separately and deducted from the gross figures, to arrive at the net figures. All disclosures of provisions and contingencies are to be shown separately as in the case of any type of Joint Stock Company.

In the Profit and Loss Account also, banks will provide break up of provisions and contingencies for each of the categories separately, say for bad debts, taxation, depreciation etc. The variations in provisions or changes year-wise, changes during any period and transparency of these data will provide a better picture for analysis of investors and public and will ensure that Indian bank's balance sheets are in tune with the international standards and one can compare Indian banks and foreign banks on the basis of similar standards. These disclosures would help financial planning and analysis, which are vital for Treasury operations, particularly when they are done on quarterly and monthly basis.

The RBI publishes consolidated Balance Sheet data of Scheduled Commercial banks in Macro terms once a year with a time lag. This is analysed below for illustrative purposes.

BRIEF BALANCE SHEET DATA
All Scheduled Commercial Banks
Macro Balance Sheet of Banks (2004-05)

As at end March 2005

LIABILITIES		ASSETS	
To Capital and Reserves	1,49,435 (6.3)	Cash & Balances with RBI	1,18,087 (5.0)
To aggregate deposits (public)			
(i) Demand Deposits (inclusive of SB A/c)	6,79,539 (28.9)	with Banking System	96,204
(ii) Time Deposits	11,57,447 (49.1)	(includes call money)	(4.1)
To borrowings (From Banking systems)	1,68,316 (7.1)	Investments	8,68,135 (36.8)
		Approved securities	7,15,194 (30.3)
		Non-Approved Securities	1,52,941 (6.5)
To Other Liabilities & Provision	2,01,244 (8.5)	Loans & Advances	
		Loans Overdraft (long term)	10,61,594 (45.1)
		Bills Purchased Discounts (short term)	89,544 (3.8)
		Fixed & Other Assets	1,22,418 (5.2)
Total	23,55,983	Total	23,55,983

Note: Percentages rounded up.
Totals in both columns may not add up exactly due to rounding up.
Figures in paranthesis are the percentages to total.

Data have been reclassified so as to roughly coincide with short term, medium and long farm funds. Capital & Reserves are long term funds (6.3% of total) used for building fixed and "other" assets (5.2%). Demand Deposits and Borrowings from Banking system accounting for short term funds, repayable on demand (36% of total sources) are used partly for cash, Balances with RBI and banking system (9.1%), Bills purchased and Discounted (3.8%), which are both short term, and partly for medium term Investments in approved securities (which are convertible into cash at short notice (30.3%). Short term funds are not adequate to finance only short term assets and they have to be rolled over and used for medium term purposes. For some medium term purposes, short term funds and provisions might have been used. The medium term funds of time deposits (49%) are used only for loans and advances (48.9%) on the Assets side, which are mostly medium and long term in nature.

Thus, even by the crude analysis, made above there is no matching of assets and liabilities, maturity wise. If this is so at macro level it will be more so at micro level of individual banks. It is a well known fact that banks deal mostly with short term funds, but the public confidence in them enables them to venture into medium and long term uses. Roughly two thirds of the Aggregate deposits are Time deposits, which are of one to 5 year duration. But they are used for long term investments and loans and advances (37% + 45% = 82%) of the total assets, although aggregate deposits contribute only 78% of the total labilities. There is thus a disproportion is asset allocation, from the available sources for the banks. This calls for caution and extreme care in the Treasury operations in banks, as they have to bring about the matching of assets and liabilities and arrange for short funds management. The interest sensitive assets and liabilities are to be seggregated from those of interest insensitive items and matching of each of those categories has to be aimed at.

The above example gives a macro picture of mismatches, lack of proper financial planning as there are misallocations among investments and loans and advances. These will be more in individual banks, at micro level due to lack of the needed expertise and experience in Treasury operations, which are vital for banks.

The macro data does not give segmental breaks downs, and seggregation of interest sensitive and insensitive items, and separate breakdowns of Bad and doubtful debts, etc. The Treasury managers in individual banks have therefore an enormous task of building the necessary information systems (MIS) for financial planning and analysis, and for sourcing the needed shortfalls and utilising the excess in any of the segments or sectors.

The Bank's Management of Treasury thus encompasses :

1. C.R.R. and S.L.R. observance and compliance.
2. Active bonds/debt management trading strategies within the S.L.R. quota to book capital appreciation and depreciation and avoid capital losses on the "current" portion of the investment portfolio, which has to be marked to market values.
3. Active trading in government and similar debt to make investments an avenue of commercial profits to the bank. The interest rate and yield gains along with the capital gains should be aimed at by the treasury to make this a profit centre by itself.
4. Matching of the inflows and outflows and of assets with liabilities and their maturity distribution so as to ensure efficient funds management and secure the least cost combination of financing the capital finance and working capital funds which is a finance function. These objectives can be secured by efficient financial plans, productive use of surplus funds, and efficient investment operations in the financial markets, keeping in view the need for short-term liquidity and long-term solvency. Both cash management alongwith ALM and risk management are involved so as to protect the solvency and liquidity of the bank.

Maturity Classification

The short-term assets of banks should be the major concern of banks as their liabilities are mainly short-term and banks are short-term financial institutions. Leaving aside cash and balance with RBI which account for 5% of the aggregate deposits of all scheduled commercial banks as at end March 2005, the short-term assets comprising balances with other banks, money at call and short notice advances to banks and other short-term assets are working out to 8% of liabilities to public other than commercial banks and RBI. Of these short-term liabilities in the form of demand deposits, borrowings, participation certificates etc. worked out to 17% and short-term assets referred to above constituted 13% of them inclusive of cash and RBI balances. These do not take into account the short-term liabilities to the banking system as these details are not available in published data. RBIs advances to banks were recently reduced considerably due to excess liquidity conditions with banking system.

CRR or cash reserve ratio was 5% and investment deposit ratio worked out to 37% at end March 2005, leaving only around 58% of the aggregate deposits to be used for loans and advances. Even here 39% of advances are flowing for low earning priority sector advances, in the case of Indian banks, which leads to low returns and low profitability. Of the total liabilities of banks of Rs.23,55,983 crores at end March 2005, term deposits worked out to 63% of the total, which can be used for investments and advances by banks.

The pattern of deployment of funds in investment is such that they are distributed maturity-wise and more in short-term maturities than in medium term and very little in long-term gilted securities. Banks prefer short and medium securities and high yielding State Government and Semi-Government securities. The maturities are so arranged, that every year, some funds are due for repayment to enable the bank to contribute to the fresh issues made by the Governments every year. They are normally distributed for maturities of 1 to 10 years and very little over 10 years, but banks have funds of maturities of 5 years and less.

As regards advances, the forms in which funds are lent and their relative importance are as follows:

As at end of March 2005

(Figures in Rs. Craves)

	Types of Credit	Percentage to Total Credit	
(1)	CASH CREDIT OVER DRAFTS	4,37,060	38%
(2)	TERM LOANS	6,24,534	54%
(3)	INLAND BILLS FOREIGN BILLS	89,544	8%
	PURCHASED & DISCOUNTED	11,51,138	100%

The distribution of advances for short duration loans is in the form of over-drafts, cash credit and bill finance, which together account for about 46%. Medium term loans like packing credit and term loans account for 54%. This is in tune with the maturity-wise inflow of funds through savings and demand deposits, borrowings from banking system and other short-term funds.

Asset-Liabilities Matching and Banking Spreads

A major function of treasury is to match the structure of liabilities with that of assets. In the matching of assets and liabilities of banks, one aspect is the net return on them which is the difference between the average return on assets and the average cost of liabilities. In the case of banks, the major liabilities are deposits and less important are their borrowings from FIs, other banks and RBI. The deposit component varies from bank to bank, some depend more on notice deposits, some more on short-term deposits while others have long-term deposits, but a few may have many NRI deposits and institutional deposits.

The average rates on deposits and lending were estimated for various Indian banks as follows:

	Indian Banks (Examples) Year 2004-05	**Deposit Rate (average)**	**Lending Rate (average)**	**Spread**
1.	Canara Bank	4.01	6.86	2.85
2.	Bank of India	4.00	6.35	2.35
3.	SBI	4.02	7.05	3.03
4.	Dena Bank	4.32	7.18	2.86
5.	Bank of Baroda	3.65	6.79	3.14

Note: Average deposit rate is interest expended as per cent of total assets. Average lending rate is interest income as per cent of total assets.

The spread varied from a low of 2.35% in the case of Bank of India to a high of 3.14% in the case of Bank of Baroda. The highest is in the case of IOB (3.64) (not shown above).

These spreads reflect, firstly the efficiency of treasury operations and secondly the constraints of Government and RBI regulations regarding priority sector lending, NPA and the structure of deposits. If lending is mostly consumer credit, the returns may be as high as 20-25%. So is the case of lease financing, hire purchase etc. If a bank like SBI has most of its consumers of high credit rating, P.S.U. and Government undertakings, the average return is the low.

The average costs on deposits and returns on lending were estimated for foreign banks, also in the same fashion.

Year 2004-05

Foreign Banks	**Average deposit rate**	**Average lending rate**	**Spread (%)**
BNP Paribus	3.08	5.99	2.91
Deutsche Bank	2.84	3.63	0.79
Citi Bank	2.22	6.52	4.30
Bank of Tokyo	1.39	5.02	3.63
HSBC	2.31	5.83	3.52
Standard Chartered	2.97	6.69	3.72

In the case of foreign banks, their structure of deposits is completely different as they do only selective banking and not mass banking. Their deposit rates are lower than the average for Indian banks and their lending rates are substantially higher than the average rate of the Indian banks. Foreign banks portfolio of assets and advances portfolio are concentrated in high yielding consumer credit, foreign credits, foreign trade financing which are in general more lucrative than working capital and term loans granted by Indian banks. Besides, priority sector lending with very low rates of interest is small at 20% for foreign banks as compared with 35-40% or more for public sector Indian banks and private sector banks.

Sources and Uses of Banks

The banks have a float of inter-bank assets/liabilities of around 3 to 4% and aggregate deposits of 88% of total assets. RBI refinance has been reduced drastically in more recent years and it stood at around 1% of the aggregate deposit liabilities. Leaving aside the CRR requirement of to 5% from 2004, kept by them the banks are free to use their funds for investments and advances. Investments in Government, semi-government and approved securities constituted 30%, which is in excess of the requirements 25%. The trading in the excess government securities and even within the SLR quota is not efficiently managed by banks at present, barring the foreign banks. In fact, the aggregate cash deposit ratio was 6.4% and investment deposit ratio was 47.3% as at end March 2005, which are both higher than the minimum requirement. Obviously some banks, if not all, are responsible for this inefficient management of funds, among banks. (See Table on all SCBs, given above) There are making Investments, outside the SLR.

Generally, advances are more remunerative than investments due to the fact that interest rate, on government and approved securities are lower, despite the recent upward adjustment of those rates to the market related rates, which are definitely higher than the erstwhile controlled rates. But as for example in 1994 to 1996, investments turned out to be more remunerative than advances due to liquidity crunch and sharp uptrend of interest rates in money market and capital market instruments. The freeing of interest rates since 1994 has been responsible for a change in the banking investment scenario.

But very few banks, are yet taking advantage of trading in Money Market and gilt-edged markets. Banks have also been reluctant to enter into these markets due to the traditional fear of losses, conservatism and caution, which was imbibed by them, due to RBI's controls for decades. Besides, the large proportion of Gross NPA 5.2% of Gross Advances in 2005 in the credit portfolio of banks has also been a deterrent to many banks to venture into new and untested fields. The frequent changes in RBI policies and the bitter experiences with the scam related episodes in some banks and lack of decentralised decision-making process in banks have also been attributed as the reasons for the banks not taking full advantage of trading in the money and capital market. Even in the gilt-edged market, which has been their monopoly for years, they are still not active, barring a few Indian banks and all foreign banks.

Leaving aside investments as required under SLR (say 25% at end March 2006) their short-term assets with banks and others stood at around 8% while their short-term liabilities in the form of savings deposits and in the form of demand deposits 15% in respect of commercial banks as at end March 2006. The above data proves adequately, the inertia and inexperience in proper investment management among banks. (See table on next page)

Sources and Uses of Funds
(All Scheduled Commercial Banks)
2005-06

Rs. Crores
At end March 2006

LIABILITIES (Sources)	Rs.	ASSETS (Uses)	Rs.
From Banking System	75,165	Cash in hand and balances with RBI	140,160
From Public			
Aggregate Deposits	21,09,047	Money at cell and short notice	13,619
Aggregate Deposits plus Borrowings	23,80,973	Balances with other Banks/Advances to Banking System	40,773
Demand Deposits 15%	3,64,640		
Time Deposits 73%	17,44,409	Total Current Assets	54,392
Other Borrowings 12%	2,71,924		
From RBI	1,488	Investments	7,17,454
Grand Total	24,57,626	Advances (Bank Credit)	15,07,077
Cash ratio	6.6%	Total	24,19,083
Investment Deposit Ratio	34.0%	Other fixed assets	38,543
Credit Deposit Ratio	71.5%	Grand Total	24,57,626

Source : RBI Bulletin, May 2006.

In the above data, paid up capital and reserves are not taken into account and these may account for about 6% of total assets/liabilities and are used for fixed assets and other assets. Current Assets inclusive of balances with RBI are 72% of the current liabilities to the Banking system. Borrowings from RBI are very small and are only emergency borrowings. Liquidity of banks is good due to good coverage of current liabilities to banking system by current assets. Solvency is good due to high capital adequacy ratio (CRAR of 12.8%) which is above the stipulated minimum and low level of NPAs at 5.1% an 2006 as against 10.4% in 2002. Advances and Investments are covered to extent of 9.3% of aggregate deposits of public and other borrowings in 2006.

The emerging picture of the above ratio analysis shows that the banking system has improved in capital Adequacy norms, and has sound solvency and liquidity conditions. The banking operations are based only on the confidence of the public in the banks and on the liquidity of their operations, so that the public funds with the banks are safe and their cash demands are met as required. This is the macro picture but the treasurer is interested in the micro picture of the individual bank, with which he is concerned.

Sources and uses of funds of a bank have to be analysed for planning the least cost combination of sources and arranging for shortfalls in sources to be met or excesses of funds to be utilized for maximizing profits. One of the vital functions of treasury management is to make financing decisions and the other is investment decisions and these are facilitated through financial planning, forecasting and financial analysis, referred to in the earlier chapters.

The treasury management in banks is not well developed due to various historical factors. The traditional conservatism of banker is one such factors. The controls by the RBI and the Govt. on banking operations through the B.R. Act is yet another factor. The CRR and SLR on banks has been another hampering factor curbing the independence of banks due to overregulation by the RBI. Besides, the captive nature of gilt edged market and undeveloped nature of the money market Debt market and forex market, in which the treasurer is supposed to operate, have also been responsible for making treasury operations redundant.

Things have changed since the initiation of financial reforms in the Nineties deregulation and globalization trends in financial markets have opened up the potentiality for treasury operations in banks. Now treasury operations are an essential part of banking operations.

Profitability of Banks

Net profits of public sector banks as reflected in the ROA (Return on Total assets) stood at 5% in 2004-05 due to reduction in the effective average cost of deposits. These average costs for the nationalised group went down. The reduced costs are attributed to the reduction in the deposit rate ceiling and a change in the composition of deposits in favour of savings and demand deposits. The average return on investments went up after 1993-94 while the average return on advances declined. But the banks' performances are in favour of increasing the use of funds in CRR and SLR, due to lack of manpower expertise for proper treasury management in banks, and inadequate professionalisation and decentralisation, except in the case of foreign banks.

The proportion of sub-standard and doubtful assets of SCBs was brought down from 9.2% in 2002 to 4.5% in 2005. There was also an increase in the number of banks which have reduced their NPA from 5 to 10. Even so, high ratio of NPA and the need to book depreciation on current portion of investment portfolio for market operations are also inhibiting factors to Indian banks to pursue active treasury management.

The asset-liability mix is also not properly managed by banks in India. One of the indicators of efficient management is the spread between interest income over interest expenditure. The return on assets (ROA) is only marginally positive at about 1% for all public sector banks. Net profits of all SCBs declined in 2004-05 as compared to the preceding year.

If we take the spread between interest income and interest expenses as percentage of total assets, it will be seen from the table below that the spread is meagre at 2.2% for all banks in general, but higher for private sector banks and foreign banks. It was as high as 4.0% in respect of foreign banks.

Table (For 2004-05)

	Public sector banks	**Private sector banks**	**Foreign banks**
Interest income as % of total assets (Return on funds)	7.5	6.5	7.2
Interest expense as % of total assets (Costs of funds)	5.7	3.0	3.2
Spread/gap	1.8	3.5	4.0

The banking practices and investment management strategies, particularly with respect to operations in financial markets are thus, definitely more efficient in the case of foreign banks as compared with Indian banks.

BANKS AND FOREX MARKET

Factors Influencing Forward Premiums

Banks' treasury operations also extend to forex markets. The supply and demand for forward dollars and expected interest rates and currency rates will influence forward premiums. The RBI made an arrangement that dollar supply will be enough in the market. The FII inflows and external commercial borrowings were higher. The foreign reserves were about 141 billion dollars adequate to meet any contingencies (at end of 2005). FIIs were expected to invest more than 14 to 16 billion during 2004 to 2006. India met comfortably the external loan repayment liabilities (1.6 billion dollars of India development bonds) and those of Resurgent India Bonds.

In November 1995, the forward premiums were as high as 17% and reached a peak of 26.81% on March 26, 1996; the RBI has sold forward dollars. Importers covered their positions by buying forward dollars. Exporters who were anticipating further fall in rupees, during that time did not sell forward dollars. There was only buying pressure at that time, which led to an increase in premium to as high as 26-30%. This has come down to 5.49% for 6 month forward in April 2002 and further to 1.48% by June end 2005. To ensure that there is sufficient inflows, the Government liberalised the rules for borrowing abroad through ECB and GDRs and gave encouragement to inflows of foreign funds for investment in India. It was also laid down that GDRs will not come under 24% of ceiling for FII investment in Indian companies after conversion. The ceilings for foreign direct investments was increased in Telecom I.T. and for some infrastructure projects etc. In this context, the RBI expects that there will be sufficient supply of dollars to keep the forward premiums low. The inflow of foreign funds due to RIB in August 1998 eased the tightness in the forex market. Besides, the Government liberalised the entry of FDI, which led to larger inflows in 1999.

Following the recent liberalisation for the inflow of funds and for development of the forex market, the Government has relaxed the guidelines further in 1999 - 2000. Corporates are now allowed to use improvised derivatives like range forwards and ratio forwards for currencies other than rupee.

Range forward option involves the simultaneous booking of a call and put options at different strike prices. They can choose the strike prices to make up front premium cost zero. This will provide the hedge for currency movement in either direction.

A ratio range forward is a combination of call and put options at different strike prices and for different amounts in a ratio of a call to put, in order to bring the up front cost to the desirable level.

Cross currency options and plain vanila options have become expensive as there is no flexibility for them. By using the range forwards, they can reduce the hedge costs, as these derivatives are flexible, and structured to the requirements which are specific to companies.

The corporates can now use improvised range forwards, ratio range forward, subsidised collar or band for securing a zero cost hedge or for securing the hedge at lower costs.

The corporates are expected to exercise options at an agreed band of strike prices and the writer bank has also a limited risk of currency volatility. Corporates are however not permitted to speculate in the use of derivative products, as per the RBI guidelines. Similarly, banks are permitted to hedge in foreign currencies but not for speculative purposes.

Currency Derivatives for Banks

Forward contracts and future contracts are frequently used in foreign exchange deals by corporates and banks. Financial futures are contracts for simultaneous right and obligation to buy/sell a fixed quantity of a foreign currency at a fixed future date at a rate agreed upon. It is different from forward contracts in that it is for a standard amount, with the standard dates for maturity, say March, June, September and December and a regular trading place. On the other hand, a forward contract is flexibly agreed for any amounts, for any maturity as mutually agreed upon between the parties and traded over the counter or by telex and telephone.

Currency Futures

Currency futures are used for hedging against any adverse changes in currency rates. An importer desiring to make payments in sterling to a London exporter will hedge by buying sterling in currency futures market, if he thinks that sterling will appreciate in the coming months, when his payment is due. The contracts being for specific amounts, he buys the number of contracts required to roughly match with his required amount of sterling. Alternatively, he may buy dollars in futures and convert dollars into sterling at the time of payment due. He will do so, if he thinks that dollar will become stronger than sterling in the coming months, and because RBI reference rate is given in terms of dollars.

Interest Futures

Another hedging tool is the interest rate futures contract. If a borrower has his interest rate linked to LIBOR his risk lies in the possibility of rise in LIBOR. The traded 3 months deposit rate can be used for hedging for 6 months on a rollover basis If each contract is for one million dollar, he will buy 10 contracts for 10 million dollars of the loan at an interest rate of say 5%. If the LIBOR interest rate goes beyond 5%, he will gain; otherwise he will lose only the contract price paid by him, but his risk is limited and known.

Treasury managers in banks use interest rate hedges for protecting themselves from fluctuations in interest rates. A contract for 100 dollars can be bought say 94.50 for three months hence. If a banker has funded a three months fixed interest rate loan, by borrowing in the inter bank market, the banker would hedge against a rise in interest rates beyond the rate at which he borrowed. The price of interest futures will move in sympathy with forward interest rates, implicit in spot interest rate structure, for different maturities, as spot and future rates are linked through expectations and arbitrage operations. Interest Futures were allowed to be traded since June 2003, on NSE, but they could not take off in a big way for trading purpose.

Forward rate agreements are contracts between say a banker and a borrower, the former guaranteeing to the latter, the LIBOR, rate at an agreed future date for a fixed amount. If he is a depositor, the LIBID rate is used. If as an example the agreed future rate is 9% and the actual rate is 10%, the bank will reimburse the party the difference of 1%, but if the actual rate is 8% then the borrower will have to pay the banker the difference.

In making such forward rate agreement or any other forward contract the bank involved itself in asset liability mismatch, due to its dealings with customers. The bank will then hedge them in the inter bank market or with the foreign correspondents. As the futures are for specified dates and for standard contracts, forward contract agreements both for currency and interest rate swaps will provide a better venue and flexibility for hedge operations of banks.

Under currency swaps, the counter parties agree to exchange specific amounts of two different currencies followed by repayment of these over a time in instalments reflecting interest and principal. Under the interest rate swap, the streams of interest payments of different character are periodically exchanged as shown below :

1. Exchange of floating rate for fixed rate (coupon swaps).
2. Exchange of one bench mark of floating rate for another say from LIBOR to T.B. rate (Basis swaps).
3. Exchange of fixed rate flows in one currency to floating rate flows in another currency (cross currency interest rate swaps)

Swaps are a useful method of liability management of banks with a view to reduce the costs and structure their liability profile best suited to their respective cash flows. The counter parties among banks, exploit their respective capabilities in the different markets to reap comparative advantages to both. A larger premium is demanded for fixed rate than for a floating rate and for low credit rating country/company than for a high credit rated country/ company.

Currency Options

Some of the important currency options can be set out here for illustration. A call option is a right to buy with no obligation, while a put option is a right to sell with no obligation.

> ***Cap:*** Major banks offer an insurance service to cover fluctuations in LIBOR in the form of a CAP or a ceiling level during the currency of a loan. The bank will for a fee agree to reimburse the customer in the event of LIBOR rising above the CAP.
>
> ***Collar or a Band:*** If the bank insures the party against a cap and a floor, that is called a band or collar. This is equal to a simultaneous purchase of a call option and a sale of a put option on the LIBOR. The fee charged by the bank will depend on the volatility of rates, period of the contract and the party's own relations with the banker etc.

The bank in turn hedges the cap commitments, through liability management, by an issue of F.R.N. of its own with a cap on LIBOR. If the FRN issue without a cap is attracting a spread of 1/8 % above LIBOR, the bank will have to pay say 1/4% of above LIBOR, if it is with a cap. The bank will not take a risk, with a liability mismatch or an uncovered option, given by it to its customer.

Tunnel option is a simultaneous purchase of call and a sale of a put (or *vice versa*) at different strike prices in a manner that the bank covers its commitment to its customers, with different maturities. A "knock-in" option is a call option on say the pound at a strike price 1.50 dollar, but exercisable only if the spot rate is above 1.55 dollars. On the similar lines a contingent option can be taken, for a call to be exercised only on a contingent event of say the rise of LIBOR in pound goes beyond 6% corresponding to "knock-in" option, there can be a "knock-out" option also, if the call option lapses due of its falling to say 1.45 dollar per pound, for the exercise price of 1.5 dollar per pound. There can be many varieties of such options in the derivative markets.

In India, the derivative markets are being developed by the RBI and options on Rupee are not written. RBI has now permitted hedging strategies to be used by corporates to promote the exchange market in rupees. Companies can enter into options for their tender bids and sell them back to the ADs during its tenure and enter into a fresh one without prior approval of the RBI. Exchange control rules are amended to allow exporters to transfer goods from one buyer to another buyer, when the goods are shipped or at foreign centres, provided the cost is not lower than 10%, of the original indent and such transfer and realisation of export proceeds are not delayed beyond six months from the date of shipment. A number of other measures were taken by RBI to develop Forex Market.

Conclusions

To sum up, the bank's Balance sheet and Income and Expenditure statements are to be analysed for the purpose of planning and budgeting which are necessary for treasury operations. Firstly, asset-liability matching has to be attempted. Secondly, cost and return analysis has to be made to widen the spread and profitability of the banks. Thirdly, sources and uses of funds and cash have to be planned so as to meet the deficits with least cost combination and utilise the surpluses to maximise the profits. Maximisation of profits and minimisation of costs are aimed at by the treasury. Lastly, banking operations in Forex market and the factors influencing the forward market and the tools available for risk reduction in Forex market are broadly set out for the treasury to function effectively.

❑ ❑ ❑

17 TREASURY MANAGEMENT IN COMMERCIAL BANKS

Treasury management is a crucial activity in banks and financial institutions, as they deal with funds, borrowings and lending and investments. By nature of their activity, they earn their profits through operations in money and near money claims. They, borrow from the public, in the form of deposits which along with other borrowings constitute their liabilities. Their assets are mostly in the form of loans, advances and investments. As their liabilities are mainly of short-term and medium-term nature, funds management becomes critical for ensuring a proper match of assets with existing structure of liabilities in terms of maturity and of returns, and costs so as to optimise, the profits, or income consistent with maintaining their liquidity and solvency. Commercial banks being the creators of credit have an additional responsibility of maintaining their image of creditworthiness, responsibility, safety and integrity to the public. This makes their funds management activity more important than for other institutions and corporations. Besides, the market constraints and RBI regulations also impose statutory and operational limits, within which banks have to function.

Non-performing Assets and Capital Adequacy Norms (CRAR)

From end March 1996, all banks should have achieved the CRAR of 8% of capital to risk assets. So far the Government have given around Rs.12,000 crores to many public sector banks to strengthen their capital base (1996-97). The Banking Companies (Acquisition and Transfer of Undertakings) Acts 1970/1980 were amended in July 1994 to allow them to have public share contribution upto 49%. Since then, the banks have strengthened their capital of either Tier I on Tier II and reached a level of 12.5% by end March 2006.

NPA is defined as a credit facility in respect of which interest has remained due for past two quarters from end March 1995 onwards. Banks were required to classify their advances into 4 groups:

Standard, sub-standard, doubtful assets and loss assets.

Provisioning for sub-standard and doubtful assets was stipulated at 30% and loss assets at 100%. The provisioning for NPAs of less than Rs.25,000 in amounts has been kept at 10% from the year 1995-96 onwards.

Commercial banks are expected to observe capital adequacy norms and income recognition for any extension in their loan portfolio which in most cases attracts 100% risk coverage. Thus, there are limits to which banks can expand their credit portfolio and next to credits, investments portfolio assumes importance, as it is major earner of incomes for banks. Thus, there is need for professional expertise in the management of bank's investment portfolio, which is also constrained by SLR requirements.

CRR

Next to credits and investments, banks are obliged to keep a certain proportion (now 5%) of their net demand and time liabilities in the form of cash with itself and balances with RBI. The minimum to be kept in this form is 3% as per the statute and the RBI is empowered to vary this ratio, for purpose of monetary control, but it will pay interest on the additional reserves beyond 3% at a rate determined by itself (now withdrawn). For any reserves kept beyond 5%, which is the present requirement, RBI will not pay any interest.

SLR

Under Section 24 of the Banking Regulation Act of 1949, banks are required to keep liquid assets (called SLR) in the forms of cash, and balances with RBI in excess of CRR requirement, gold and unencumbered approved securities. These unencumbered approved securities include Central and State Government securities, Treasury bills of 91 to 364 days and bonds of public financial institutions, Municipal and local bodies, State Electricity Bonds and any others as notified by the Government.

In addition to the above approved securities, under Section 19(2) of the Banking Companies Act, 1949, Banks' investments may cover bonds of PSUs, Units of UTI, shares and debentures of companies and money market instruments such as commercial bills, commercial paper, certificates of deposits of other banks, etc. As per the RBI's present guidelines, there is no restriction on amount of investments in PSU bonds and UTI units. But there is a limit of 5% of incremental deposits of the preceding year to be invested in shares and bonds of companies including those devolving on them as part of their underwriting activity.

At present, the SLR requirement is 25% of NTDL in aggregate and 25% of the incremental deposits of banks. Within these constraints, the investment portfolio of banks has to be managed with a view to maintain income and profits and yet maintain sufficient liquidity and solvency and observe the RBI norms for SLR, CRR, capital adequacy and income recognition, etc.

Investment Function

Each bank is expected to prepare a detailed investment policy statement in the beginning of each year and submit it to the RBI after getting it approved by its

Board. This investment policy should lay down the overall investment objective, guidelines for conducting the transactions in securities, investment policy with regard to each category of securities and classification of securities under "current" and "permanent" for the purpose of depreciation provision and trading in securities. Submission to the RBI is now dispensed with and powers have been vested with the Board of Directors of banks.

Normally, the objectives of investment policy are as follows:

(a) comply with the SLR requirements

(b) ensure adequate liquidity

(c) earn maximum income possible and increase the overall return on the total portfolio.

(d) book capital gain or losses, so as to minimise the tax liability and maximise the after tax profits.

(e) adjust the maturity of securities to be in tune with the maturity pattern of deposits and borrowings

(f) ensure a proper match of assets with liabilities and avoid any mismatch of assets and liabilities in terms of maturity and returns or yields.

In general, banks first attempt to fulfil the requirements of SLR. Even within this requirement, banks can plan the choice of securities, central, state and government generated bonds. Trading within the requirement is confined to central Government securities in respect of operations with RBI. This is in the form of switches and repos to banks and FIs for adjustment of yields and maturities to the desired pattern. Purchases and sales of Government securities are made with STCI, primary dealers licensed by the RBI and NSE brokers. Normally banks deal with other banks directly, and if they deal through the brokers, they should be NSE brokers. Brokers are asked to quote on "net to us" basis, i.e., to pay and receive the exact amounts as per the rate quoted in the contract without any deduction towards brokerage. The brokerage is paid separately and the amount should not exceed 5 paise per Rs. 100 of contract.

The practices of foreign banks and Indian banks vary with regard to the organisation, functional delegation and market operations. Even among the banks of Indian origin, there is no uniformity in practices and procedures. In many banks, decisions are centralised while actual operations are delegated to the funds managers. The well-organised markets for funds management exist at present in major commercial centres like Mumbai, Delhi, Kolkata, Chennai and Bangalore where these operations are conducted.

Bank dealings in approved securities in investment portfolio are conducted either in primary market or secondary market. In primary market, the bank may underwrite a part of the public issue or make an application for firm allotment in the case of the private placement and send bids in RBI auction of gilts or T.Bs. In all such cases, the finance department of the Bank will put up a note with details of the available excess funds, costs and benefits of the proposed investment and secure the approval of the competent authority, namely the Board, before it is passed on to the Funds Management cell in the centres where operations are executed. In the secondary market trading is done by the treasury manager under guidelines given by the Head office under the competent authority, as may be delegated by the Board. Generally, sale and purchase transactions in government securities are done through transfers in the SGL account with the RBI, where both the parties have SGL account. Transfers among the parties in the case of non-government securities are effected through the BRs issued (Banker's Receipts). These BRs are in accordance with the format, prescribed by IBA and deliveries on BRs are obtained within a reasonable time. The RBI has laid down the guidelines as to the use of BRs and transfer forms for transfers in the SGL Account. Trading in govt. securities and TBs in the secondary market are allowed on NSE, through their dealers.

Planning Investment Portfolio

The planning department does exercises on the budget for each year in advance for all funds inflows and outflows, estimates deposits, borrowings and other sources of funds and lays down the pattern of their utilisation. The amount of money allotted to credit portfolio, and investment portfolio are set aside after making necessary allotments to CRR and SLR requirements. The investment portfolio within the SLR and outside SLR is segregated. The budgets as approved by the Board are passed on to the RBI for information and record. The budget allocations are adjusted from time to time to changing conditions in the economy and the financial sector and reviewed quarterly and half yearly. The allocations made in SLR and outside SLR are utilised as opportunities arise.

The funds department or finance department coordinates with the accounts department for effecting operations in funds in the investment portfolio. The investment decisions on allocation of funds in various asset categories or instruments are the prerogative of the board of directors and sometimes these powers of taking decisions are delegated to various levels of functionaries at the central office to improve operational efficiency but subject to some limits.

All the operational results and data are reported to the Controller simultaneously for monitoring and control. The treasury or money management in banks starts with an analysis of the flow of deposits, their quantum and maturity structure. The cost of funds through deposits and borrowings and other liabilities is estimated to arrive at the average cost of the liabilities and maturity pattern of these liabilities. Then to suit these inflows, the outflows are planned and expected average returns from each of these categories of outflows, namely, credit and investment accounts after allocating the required funds, for CRR and SLR requirements.

Thus, the planned budget is the starting point of the operations of the investment cell or funds department. The finance and accounts department of the central office co-ordinates the operations and provides the back office accounting and recording support.

Funds management involves the allocation of funds for CRR and the daily cash balances position. All the branches report the cash balances and/ or the balances with the RBI in the respective centres on a daily basis. The telexes of these data are consolidated in the central office funds department and telexed to RBI on a daily basis and get the confirmation from the point of RBI.

Each branch reports to the local office which consolidates and reports the balance sheet data on a weekly basis called weekly abstract and return under Section 42(2) of the RBI Act, now on a fortnightly basis.

In every bank, there are some big branches which account for the bulk of the deposits inflow and explain the major changes in the demand and time liabilities of banks. The Zonal offices are normally asked to submit the details of the items in the above return from these identified big branches, on a daily basis, in order to enable the bank to maintain the required CRR on a daily basis. All branches submit the weekly return giving the daily balances and balances with other banks, counted for purposes of SLR. The CRR is required to be maintained on a daily basis in such manner that atleast 85% of the CRR obligation is kept on any day and the average for the fortnight maintains the 100% of the CRR requirement. These data are reported once in a fortnight to the RBI by the finance department calculated on a daily basis. The data on identified major branches is used to maintain CRR on a daily basis. The report for each fortnight contains the details of NDTL and required cash balances. Actual holdings and excess or shortfall on the average to be maintained on a daily basis, are also reported. These are finalised and sent on a daily basis every fortnight within 12 days from the last date of the last fortnight to the RBI. The levels required to be maintained for CRR are generally observed by borrowing if necessary from the inter-bank market.

Operations in the Secondary Market

As per the RBI norms, banks are expected to classify the portfolio of approved securities into current and permanent category. The component classified as current category is used for trading operations in the secondary market. The component titled permanent category is expected to be held by the bank until maturity and hence not tradable. For classifying the securities into current category, all approved securities are judged and assessed in terms of maturity, current status regarding valuation, prospects of trading in securities and the active market for them.

Judged by the above criteria, treasury bills, short and medium-term gilts which have an active market are put in the current category besides all non-approved securities like shares and bonds which are also part of the current category. Depreciation in respect of current category has to be provided for as per the guidelines on yields furnished by the RBI, for every year for each of the maturities of securities and maintain capital adequacy norms after depreciation provision.

In addition to the above norms of RBI, each bank has its own internal norms for the management of current component of approved securities and non-approved securities in the investment portfolio. Since capital adequacy norms are to be adhered to, current component is so adjusted that depreciation is the lowest and all long-term securities are included in the permanent category as capital depreciation will be more for every unit rise in yields in their case. Thus, the banks may choose to limit their involvement in gilts of short and medium-term nature and put a ceiling on the investment portfolio at 25% or so of the capital or networth, as depreciation or capital losses are less in their case.

The investment account like any other account is maintained on the principal of double entry book keeping. The bank's investment portfolio under the current category has to be valued at the cost or market price whichever is lower. As depreciation will erode the profits and reduce the networth, a careful planning of the investment strategy is needed to keep the depreciation low, minimise the costs and maximise the income from the investment portfolio of a bank.

The bankers in general give due weights to important criteria like the maturity of securities, yields, and composition of instruments.

From the banks, point of view, their desired pattern of investment depends upon the existing pattern of their deposits. Short dated securities with maturity upto 3 years and medium dated securities of 3 to 7 years are most ideal for holding by banks. Financial institutions and insurance and provident funds prefer investments of medium-term with maturity of 3 to 7 years and long dated securities of above 7 years, as that suits their long-term nature of funds. In times of falling interest rates banks may be willing to purchase long dated securities, but they are not desirable for a prudent investment strategy. In times of rising interest rates, short and medium-term securities are preferred. The decisions with regard to purchase and sale of securities are influenced by various factors like general economic outlook, expected interest rate changes, tax concessions available, supply of securities and their yields etc.

Yields are another important factor for banks to make investments. Banks prefer to have good yields and avoid depreciation. Their objective is to maximise income by having high yielding securities, consistent with the maturity they wish to hold, namely, in the area of short and medium-term periods. They therefore undertake swaps and switches for shifting from low yielding securities to high yielding securities even within the SLR portfolio.

With regard to the composition of the investment portfolio, the proportion they hold of various categories of assets, namely, of short-term assets like treasury bills, bills of exchange discounted, commercial paper, etc. and medium-term central securities, state securities and guaranteed bonds and non-approved securities etc. is decided by the bank's strategic plan of investment. Each bank has generally its own criteria for choice of assets; for example, foreign banks prefer foreign bills, high yielding commercial paper and trading in bond market for which they have the expertise. Smaller banks in India prefer to hold short and medium-term securities of state governments and central government and high yielding guaranteed bonds within the SLR limit. Their trading in secondary market is limited to their market contacts and manpower expertise. Bigger Indian banks like SBI operate both in the primary and secondary markets and in money market and gilt-edged market. They have decentralised system of decision-making subject to certain internal guidelines of prudent investment in various sub-markets, such as debt market, gilted securities and PSU Bonds and others.

BANK MANAGEMENT OF FUNDS

One of the old private sector banks namely Tamilnad Mercantile Bank has the following features.

Table 17.1 – Financial Indicators

		2003-04	2004-05
(1)	Interest income as % of Total assets	10.56	9.13
(2)	Interest expended as % of Total assets	6.33	5.01
(3)	Net interest margin as % of Total assets	4.23	4.12
(4)	Provisions & contingencies as % of Total assets	1.75	1.64
(5)	Operating expenses as % of Total assets	2.31	2.22
(6)	Net Non-Performing Assets (NPAs) as % of Total Assets	2.06	1.37
(7)	Net Non-Performing Assets as % of net advances	5.00	2.74
(8)	Capital Adequacy Ratio	21.07	19.74
(9)	Net profit as % of Total assets	1.59	1.47

(10)	Interest income to working funds	—	9.49
(11)	Non-interest income working funds	—	1.26
(12)	Operating profit to working funds	—	3.23
(13)	Return on Assets	—	1.47
(14)	Profit per employee Rs. lakhs	—	3.60

It has a branch net work at end March 2005 of 173 and ATMs of 22. It has a business turnover of Rs. 8,490 crores and foreign exchange merchant turnover of Rs. 3,076 crores during 2005-06. It is a relatively smaller bank with a regional sweep of operations, but has substantial foreign exchange operations. The non-interest income, which refers to its Treasury operations, is small, at 1.26 % as a percentage of working funds.

TREASURY INCOME

As published by the RBI, the data on the Scheduled Commercial banks in the trend and progress of banking in India, does not give data on Treasury operations separately. The only item of non-interest income as percentage of working funds, bank wise, is available.

As at end of March 2005, non interest income as percentage of working funds is low at around 1-2 % for nationalised banks and private sector banks, but it is relatively higher for foreign banks in India, with the highest ratio at 24% for Sonali Bank, followed by 12.05% for JP Morgan Chase Bank.

The low percentage of income does not truly represent the importance of these operations or their magnitude in banks. The data on the magnitude of operations in Treasury are not published by the RBI. Many banks, both nationalised and private have had on line trading in government securities and in the Forex markets. For even a small bank like Tamilnad Mercantile Bank Ltd., the foreign exchange merchant turnover for 2005-06 was as high as Rs. 3,076 crores.

Some individual banks, say PNB, which is a listed company, publish segmentwise results. Thus they give breakup of Treasury and banking operations separately. The data published by PNB for 2005-06 are given below for illustration.

(in Rs. crore)

Particulars	Treasury		Banking		Total	
segment wise details	2005-06	2004-05	2005-06	2004-05	2005-06	2004-05
Segment Revenue (External)	4,241	4,326	6,574	5,809	10,815	10,135
Segment results before provisions & for contingencies	1,315	1,476	1,797	1,636	3,112	3,112
Segment results after provision contingencies	448	1,453	1,823	857	2,273	2,311

Segment wise, Treasury and Banking operations are the two major segments reported by bank. The data shows the low importance of Treasury segment in the total operations of banks. The details as published by Karnataka Bank are shown on next page.

(Rs. in crores)

Particulars	Treasury		Banking operation		Total	
	2005-06	2004-05	2005-06	2004-05	2005-06	2004-05
Revenue	220	295	965	766	1,185	1,061
Result (Profit/Loss)	12	82	284	183	296	265

Source : www. karnatakabank. com

The details of the State Bank of Patiala are presented below :

SBP – Data

Audited segment wise details for year ended March 31, 2006

(in Rs. crores)

	Particulars	Year ended 31-3-06	Year ended 31-03-05
Segmental Revenue			
(a)	Treasury	991	1,058
(b)	Other banking operations	1,818	1,432
(c)	Total	2,809	2,490
Segmental Results (Profit/Loss)			
(a)	Treasury	–20	–122
(b)	Other banking operations	476	514
(c)	Total	456	392
Segment-wise Assets			
(a)	Treasury	14,390	14,643
(b)	Other banking operations	26,616	16,401
(c)	Total	41,006	31,044

Source : E.T. Daily, May 10, 2006

Treasury constitutes about ⅓rd of the total business or assets of bank, as seen from the above tables.

BACK OFFICE SUPPORT AND ACCOUNTING

Back office is part of the Treasury Dept. to support the front office of funds management.

Treasury managers execute deals and pass deal tickets in triplicate. The original copy is kept with the fund manager while the second copy is sent to the other party of purchase and sale and the third copy goes to the back office. Deal sheet is prepared at the back office and checked with the confirmation notes sent by the other parties to purchase and sale. Any discrepancies are ironed out and corrected copies are sent to the controller of accounts department periodically. These are also audited from time to time.

The back office maintains portfolio accounts under the head of gilts, approved securities, bonds, CPs, CDs, etc., Security-wise details are kept by them. Those eligible for open market deals, repos, and those eligible for refinance from the RBI etc. are kept in separate accounts in order to facilitate investment decisions and operations.

Back office (1) prepares the funds position, (2) allocates the funds for treasury bills, (3) put in auction bids with the RBI after the survey of the market views on the cut off interest rates for 91 days and 364 days TBs respectively. As only export bills are eligible for RBI refinance at present their accounts are kept separate. (4) back office arranges for physical custody of certificates at various centres, (5) collection of interest on dividends, (6) income and presentation for redemption etc. (7) reconciliation of SGL account with RBI with their own accounts of purchases and sales of government and approved securities is another function of Back office. All the centres having physical custody of certificates have to certify their holding on a quarterly basis. The inspectors and auditors are also sent for physical verification of these certificates. Security custody and after deal services relating to income, dividends, bonus, etc. are all the responsibility of the Back office.

The Back office has to coordinate with accounts department on the one hand and planning department on the other. Once the targets are set and available funds are earmarked for various classes of investments, decisions on yields, maturity and composition of assets are advised to the funds department by top management. The investment position for SLR purposes and beyond SLR for trading purposes are set aside for operational guidance. The investment in money market involves funds management and watching of short-term assets and liabilities with a view to keep the liquidity position intact and still earn returns on their assets.

The operations in call market and treasury bill market are in particular guided by the bank's cash position, funds inflow and outflow and their asset liability mismatch. The inhouse norms of prudence in investment in treasury bills, short-term gilts, bonds, etc. are laid down by the Board and implemented by the finance department through their treasury managers.

The investment management in banks is guided by norms of caution and utmost prudence. The guidelines for SLR investment and non-SLR investments are separately set out. Trading in the secondary market takes place both in the SLR and non-SLR components as the bank has to minimise the capital depreciation on their holdings in the current component of their investments of gilts, PSU bonds and others to avoid erosion of their capital base.

The Back office has to perform the functions of accounts, correcting and reconciliation of accounts, arranges payment and receipts for all deals put along by funds management cell (FMC). Physical custody and verification of certificates and all related functions are performed to support the front line operations in the FMC. The excess funds position or the shortfall in CRR or SLR are all monitored and watched by the central office for advising on the necessary actions on the frontline and the controller for monitoring and surveillance actions to be taken in regard to the investment portfolio of the bank, by the Treasury manager.

The RBI issues the telex messages to all banks on a daily basis on the bid and offer rates of the securities open to repos, switches and swaps and DFHI rates for dealing in treasury bills, commercial paper and other bills and government securities. With a view to ensuring transparency, data on all the deals on the SGL Account, volumes and prices of securities are released by the RBI, STCI, and DFHL. The transactions on NSE are also flashed during the trading time by electronic display on their terminals in the deal rooms of funds managers. Besides the daily financial papers carry the prices of bonds and approved securities and non-approved securities. The deal rooms keep in constant touch with the market operations and their counterparts in other banks through telephone and telex communications. But the decisions of what to buy and the prices etc. are decided by the central office investment cell. All accounts and operations are also reported to the controller for information and post facto control on the investment operations and review at quarterly and half yearly intervals, and keep constant surveillance and monitoring on funds management by the treasury manager. This brief account of treasury operations and control is based on the practices of some Indian banks and the practices may change from bank to bank and among the foreign banks in particular.

Conclusion

The outline of the content of Treasury Management is set out in this chapter with reference to banks. Although this context varies from bank to bank, all banks in general have to observe CRR and SLR, plan the inflows and outflows, financing and investment operations of the Treasury. The major policy guidelines of the Board of Directions have to be implemented through the Treasury Department by the Top Management. Capital Adequacy norms, income recognition and a host of other guidelines of the RBI have to be observed. The Treasury Department's operations through Front office and the support of the Back office, Accounting and Controllership functions are all allied and have to be co-ordinated by the Top Management Team.

❑ ❑ ❑

18 RISK MANAGEMENT IN MARKET OPERATIONS*

All financial markets and operations in them are risky due to volatility of rates, uncertainty of return and repayments. Such risks are more in Forex Markets, when the Indian rupee became fully convertible the risks in the foreign exchange market have become more pronounced and the need to take risk or protect oneself from these risks has become crucial. Many countries have already made their currencies convertible on current account and some are in the process of doing so. In the context of such scenario of free foreign exchange markets, uncertainty of currency rates and their volatility has made it imperative for the dealers in foreign exchange to expose themselves to the risks. Risk is inherent in the foreign exchange dealings due to the following reasons :

1. Currency rates and exchange rates fluctuate more widely.
2. Trade across countries involve dealings with parties — exporter or importer — who are unknown and whose creditworthiness is uncertain.
3. Foreign dealings also involve countries whose credibility and creditworthiness is not certain.
4. Interest rates and foreign and domestic factors influencing those markets are more complex and more unpredictable.

Many countries are having political and economic problems, racial and communal riots or other disturbances and there is no certainty about their economic and financial policies and their willingness and capacity to repay the loans and service them through their exports and inward remittances. Economic fundamentals may be bad and inflation and other problems of the country, such as unemployment, poverty, low rate of growth or no growth in the economies etc. may

* Detailed Treatment of Risk Management is available in Author's Book "Financial Economics", Part - IV.

be rampant in these countries, when they may default in their external obligations, as in the case of some African and Latin American countries. Their capacity to borrow on commercial lines will be poor and they depend on donations, gifts and concessional aid from Governments and international bodies. They are not in a position to service and repay the debts to foreigners.

Exchange risk is also due to fluctuations in the rate of exchange in conversion of one currency into another and likely changes in interest rates which might effect the forward rates. Forward cover of any currency which the banks provide will take into account the possible changes in interest rates, inflation rates and their expectations. Besides, exchange risk will also depend on the economic strength of the country and its foreign reserves, as the volatility of the exchange rate depends on them.

Risk in Money and Gilt-edged Markets

Treasury Manager is exposed to risks in all his investments, as investments are all risky. The degree of risk varies from instrument to instrument and market to market. Risk and uncertainty go together. Risk is variability of return, possibility of loss of principal or capital losses etc., while uncertainty is lack of certainty of any outcome and the nature of the outcome.

Risk arises from Treasury operations in markets due to the following reasons :

(i) Market and demand changes.

(ii) Interest rate changes.

(iii) Purchasing power changes and

(iv) Government policy changes, and sovereign risk.

The above are called systematic risks which are not controllable and external to the unit.

The following risks called unsystematic risks arise out of the internal factors of the company.

(i) Business risk involving competition, fall in demand, increased costs and lower profit margins etc.

(ii) Financial risk due to uncontrolled rise in debt, incapacity to service the debt, inefficient financing of capital structure, wrong asset liability mix, financial stringency and incapacity to borrow due to poor current ratio.

(iii) Credit risk and default or Insolvency risk due to inefficient management, poor financial planning and difficulty of servicing creditors.

Treasury Manager can foresee some of these emerging trends if he is efficient and can take corrective steps, say in arranging right degree of leverage, proper financial structure of capital, planning for proper assets liability mix, safe current ratio, synchronising receipts with payments and by arranging proper maturities for both.

General Guidance for Risk Reduction

Basically, treasury manager can reduce some risks through proper planning and forecasting, referred to earlier. As risk is inevitable, he has to plan the correct degree of risk, which the company or the bank can tolerate. After making the investments continuous monitoring, revision and corrective measures are needed to reduce the risk. Thus, if interest rates rise, maturity pattern of existing bonds portfolio should be changed to reduce capital losses and acquire some high yielding bonds. Similar measures are necessary for changes in business conditions, cost of credit and availability of credit or other policy changes.

Besides, he has to diversify into a basket of investments with varying degrees of risk instead of putting all eggs in one basket — some treasury bills, some commercial paper and inter-corporate investments can be grouped together. In the graph below, risk- return scenario is depicted, so that he can choose a combination which gives a risk tolerable or manageable but with maximum return possible and by the use of Beta technique, adopted in risk management in portfolios.

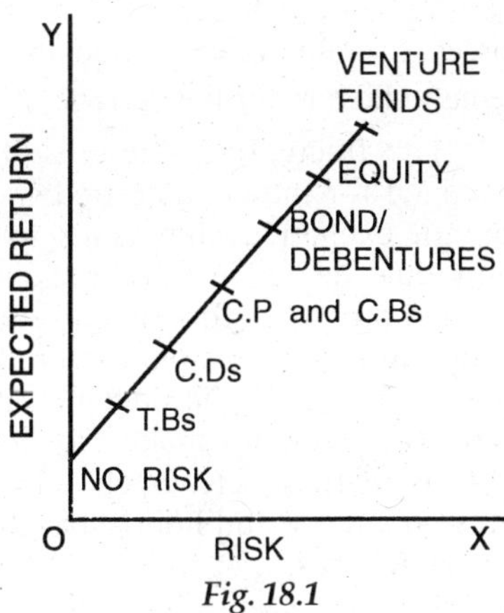

Fig. 18.1

By diversification and choice of investment — suitable to their risk tolerance, the market investment risks can be managed by the Treasurer, through proper Investment and Portfolio Management.

Strength of Currency

Exchange risk depends on the strength or weakness of currency which in turn is a reflection of the strength of the economy. Thus, a country whose productivity is low and its competitive strength in international markets is poor cannot export enough of the domestic products abroad and its foreign exchange earnings will be poor. Such a country will have a week currency and its rate of exchange will be uncertain.

A strong country's currency like US $ or Japanese yen will have good export performance resulting in trade surplus or good inflow of foreign funds for investment because of its high productivity, low costs of production, latest technology and good investment climate, leading to high rates of growth of output, employment and income. So economy, its strength and its rate of growth and its competitive strength along with a host of other factors will influence the currency rates. The exchange risk is thus dependent upon an array of economic and extra economic factors which will lead to an unpredictable rate of exchange. The risk and uncertainty of exchange rate is a multi-dimensional phenomena and requires an expert to fend and manage the risks involved. Genuine trade and investment require a stable and fixed exchange rate which is not possible in free and competitive world, where trade and receipts and payments abroad are all free and market determined. There is thus, need for risk management for all dealings in foreign exchange and particularly so, for exporters and importers.

Exchange Risk Defined

Exchange risk simply means that the rate at which a currency is exchanged for another currency may be uncertain and the amount that an exporter receives in domestic currency or an importer has to pay in terms of domestic currency will be unpredictable and uncertain. Similarly, if funds are transmitted from one country to another, the amounts to be sent or to be received will not be certain, if exchange rates are not fixed. But in the present global economy, free market forces operate to determine the exchange rates depending upon the supply and demand factors for the currency.

The fluctuating rates result in uncertainty and risk, which will have to be managed for the genuine traders and investors in foreign countries and dealers in foreign exchange and banks in India. Under free market forces operating, no individual dealer in foreign exchange can influence its price, but the supply and demand pressures for any currency in total lead to its appreciation or depreciation. The totality of receipts either for exports or inward remittances or inflows of funds will decide the demand pressure while the supply pressures emanate from those who have to make payments outside for imports, outward remittances or outflow of-funds etc. Such demand and supply pressures influence the exchange rates on a daily and hourly basis and from time to time and lead to uncertainty, in exchange rates.

High Exchange Rate Risk in Forex Market

Foreign exchange rates being freely determined, the following factors influence the exchange rates and enhance the risk in particular:

1. Hot money flows are between countries and currencies will take place to secure advantage of short-term economic and political factors or disturbances or fears of such developments leading to changes in currency rates and interest rates. This happened during June - July 1998 in the South East Asian economies like Thailand, Indonesia, Malaysia etc.
2. Speculative attacks on currencies in anticipation of exchange rate changes and interest rate changes through short-term flows or funds. One sided speculation which takes place in countries without capital account controls is possible and is destabilising.
3. Exchange rate volatility emerges out of erratic fund flows as between countries, short-term flows of funds in either direction and inflows of funds followed by immediate reversals, etc.
4. Freely fluctuating exchange rates across countries do sometimes lead to erratic movements of rates on either side, unless countervailed by central bank of the country to offset such excesses.
5. Present international monetary system under the IMF imposes the burden of adjustment on the deficit countries to change their exchange rates rather than on the surplus countries. In the absence of proper adjustment on both sides, balance of payments adjustment is delayed and partial with the result that exchange rates remain uncertain and fluctuating and, sometimes even unpredictable.
6. Limited powers of IMF to discipline the surplus countries also lead to partial adjustment or lack of adjustment as between currencies of countries with the result that currency rates may fluctuate very widely and require central bank intervention to stabilise the rates.

Basically, exchange rates as between two currencies should reflect the true fundamentals of the concerned countries, such as domestic purchasing powers, relative strength or weakness of the economies, in terms of their productive power and trends in output, employment and income. In the absence of stabilised and equilibrated rates, the actual prevailing rates may fluctuate widely with demand and supply Pressures. In order to avoid such destabilising fluctuations in rates, many developing countries maintain exchange and trade controls to reduce such risk and promote trade and investment in their own countries.

The risks in foreign exchange market in India are of the following nature and include transactions in both trade and non-trade items of balance of payments :

1. Risk of creditworthiness of the other party in trade in concerned countries.
2. Risk of credit control and exchange control in countries, which have them.
3. Risk of economic and political policy changes in the other country.
4. Risk of interest rate changes in the respective countries.
5. Risk of loss of goods shipped in transit or theft, damage, or destruction.
6. Risk of market changes in the concerned countries or changes in the costs or in duties or levies imposed by the trading partners on others.
7. Risk of war or epidemics, or riots or any untoward events affecting trading relations as between the trading partners.
8. Risk and uncertainty of exchange rates of one currency against another.
9. Risk and uncertainty due to changes in forward rates for the currency following the changes in interest rates as between countries.
10. Risk of changes in cross currency rate for any unpredictable changes in the currency markets and in foreign exchange markets.

Foreign exchange markets are very sensitive and volatile as they are influenced by all and sundry developments in economic, political, social and financial factors among the countries. Events across borders and domestic and international forces operate on the markets to force volatility in rates and lead to attendant risks in the exchange markets.

Exchange Rate Management in India

The rupee was devalued twice in July 1991 and the depreciation of the rupee continued in the free market thereafter. The rupee dollar rate was Rs.17.1274 in March 1990 which fell to Rs.32.3727 since March 1994 when current account convertibility was introduced by the Government. Later the rate fell in stages and stood at Rs. 43.62 in Feb. 2000, Rs. 46.10 in Feb. 2006.

After the structural reforms undertaken since July 1991, the rupee exchange rate management assumed all the importance and attention from the RBI and the Government. The Liberalised Exchange Rate Management System (LERMS) introduced in March 1992 was a step in that direction of a freely convertible rupee at a future date. Under this system, rupee can be freely converted at free market rate upto 60% of exports, while official rate still prevailed for the 40% or rest of the exports. This system called Liberalised Exchange Rate Management System (LERMS) helped to stabilise the rupee and the official rate remained unchanged except for a downward adjustment of 1.12% in the rate effected on December 4th 1992. The market determined rate remained also stable and the spread between the official rate and the market rate remained in a narrow range except for short and extraordinary periods.

The experiment with limited convertibility was successful and the Government was emboldened to launch the full convertibility on Trade Account in

March 1993. Since then there was unification of the dual exchange rate into a single floating rate which imparted considerable strength to the rupee. Now the external value of the rupee was determined by market forces fully. As this is on the trade account, it only meant that the ADs did not have to surrender to the RBI the exchange proceeds at fixed rate as before. The exporters can sell their earnings at the free market rates to the banks and the importers have to buy the same from banks at the prevailing market rates from time to time.

Since mid-January 1995, the RBI has banned the rollover of forward contracts, and as a step in the direction of liberalisation, allowed the customers to book forward contracts in any permitted currency. Now the companies will have to book forward contracts matching with their foreign exchange exposure. This facility to hedge in any currency given to corporates will permit the corporates to take positions in currencies and develop the foreign exchange market and the forward market in particular. This facility was later extended to banks also to help them to develop the forex market through proper hedging abroad and by developing derivative products for risk management.

Full Convertibility of Rupee

The experiment on convertibility on Trade Account proved a success in the sense that no untoward fluctuations in the rupee rate were noticed during 1993-94 with the result that the Government has announced in March 1994 the full convertibility on Current Account also which means that all invisible receipts and payments have to be effected at market related rates. Thus, not only trade items but all invisible items or services are paid and received at the free market rates since March 1994.

In the Budget 1994-95, the Government of India have also announced a package of further measures to promote and facilitate exports; exporters are allowed to retain 25% of the foreign exchange earned in dollar denominated accounts abroad. Export Oriented Units (EOUs) are permitted to retain even upto 50% of their exchange earnings in dollar terms abroad. These measures would help reduce conversion costs in payments abroad for their import requirements and other service payments. In October 1997, certain moves in the direction of capital account convertability were initiated by the RBI. The RBI gave greater freedom to add for their operations on the Nostro accounts, maintenance of FEECAs by exporters and their use and even release of foreign funds, for joint ventures and foreign investment by exchange earners.

The foreign exchange receipts and payments are now freer than before under all current account items, particularly for travel, tourism, medical expenses and education. The Government have introduced amendments to the FERA and replaced by FEMA in the year 2000 to do away with many controls on foreign investments in India, inflow of foreign technology, employment, etc. India is now on a path of full convertibility of the rupee on both current and capital account. Preparatory to that, foreign investment in equity of Indian companies is permitted upto 51%. Much of this investment Which requires to be cleared by the Government, Ministry of Finance, Investment Division has been flowing into priority sector industries. Foreign direct portfolio investment has been freely allowed without limit and foreign financial institutions and foreign security firms have been permitted by the SEBI to operate in the Indian stock and capital market.

Multilateral Investment Guarantee Agency (MIGA)

The MIGA is an international agency set up in 1988 for the purpose of promoting and encouraging the flow of foreign direct investment. It offers investment insurance and advisory services for foreign direct investment in developing countries. It provides protection to international investors against losses arising out of non-commercial risk of currency transfers, expropriation, war and civil disturbances. It provides promotional and advisory role to Governments in framing and implementing foreign investment policy. India signed the MIGA convention in fiscal 1992 and with this the member countries who signed this convention increased to 85. India has also opened up bilateral negotiations for extending the investment guarantee with other countries for promoting the foreign direct investment in India. Thus, it has entered into bilateral guarantees with many countries, including the U.S.A. Russia, among others.

FERA Liberalisation

FERA companies which are companies incorporated in India but in which non-resident interest is more than 40% have now got freedom from many restrictive provisions under Sections 26(7) 28, 29 and 31 of FERA. FERA companies are now permitted to do the following :

1. to borrow money or accept deposits from persons resident in India.
2. to acquire any undertaking, carry on any trade, commerce or industry or purchase shares of any company.
3. to allow trade marks of theirs to be used by any person or company.
4. to accept any appointment as agent or technical or management adviser.
5. to acquire hold, transfer any immovable property in India.

All FERA companies are now treated as Indian Companies. The FERA is now replaced by FEMA in 2000 with less emphasis on controls but more on facilitation of all inflows, investment, etc.

Trade and Exchange Risk

In dealing with international currencies, risk is inherent in both trade and finance. These risks arise out of dealings as between countries.

1. in terms of exchange of goods for money.
2. in terms of sale of services and payment thereof in foreign currencies.
3. lending and borrowing in foreign currencies and
4. capital inflows and outflows from foreign countries. Risks arise out of all these transactions and due to unpredictable market related forces which determine the supply and demand pressures on foreign currencies. Demand and supply for currencies emerge from corresponding demand and supply for goods and services and needed receipts and payments to and from abroad.

The instruments involved in foreign trade and in foreign exchange dealings have also a component of risk in them. Briefly these instruments are :

1. Currency dealt with in small quantities and involve loss or theft or cheating for counterfeit notes, etc.
2. M.T/T.T/D.D/Cheques, etc. risk is in transit loss, time in transit and delays involved, etc.

3. Commercial and trade bills: bills of exchange and other foreign trade bills and documents have risks involved in the parties, drawer, drawee, and the goods involved in these bills. Sight bills are having a grace period during which payment can be delayed. Usance bills have a period to maturity of 30 to 180 days usually. These bills and documents are given to banks for collection negotiation or outright purchase, which are again full of risks. The risks arise out of defective documents, time for waiting, problems with goods in transit, shipping or airfreight, etc. party risk and country risk and risk of default or non-payment. Besides, there is the currency risk during the conversion of foreign currency into domestic currency and *vice versa.*

How to Manage Risk

The corporates and importers have to bear some risks. Some risks like party, country and currency risks are passed on to the banks, ECGC and EXIM Bank. Insurance agencies cover some risks like those in transit time, shipping and airfreight, etc. Banks in turn pass on some risks to Central Bank of the country, or cover them with foreign correspondents, international markets or inter-bank market.

Exchange Rate and Currency Risk

Exchange risk is determined by free flow of demand and supply forces for one currency against another, credit risk, country and client risk can be insured with ECGC but currency is not insured by anybody including the RBI. The banks and customers have to bear this risk for trade and payments.

Besides, the demand for a currency is also influenced by the hedge and speculative forces. The forward rates are at discount or at premium depending on the current interest rates and expectations about them, present rates of exchange, expectations about their movements, future arbitrage and hedge deals and short-term speculative flows of funds etc. Some discussion on forward rates is reserved for later paras.

TYPES OF EXCHANGE RATES

The exchange risk depends on the type of rate. In this context, it is relevant to know the types of rates which are common in the foreign exchange market. The major types are set out below:

1. ***Spot rate:*** the rate for immediate exchange of currency or receipts. Thus, the rate for exchange of currency notes, TTs, MTs, cheques, and DDs which are clean and unaccompanied by documents is called the spot rate.
2. ***Forward rate:*** the rate for delivery of currency at a specified future date.
3. ***Short rates:*** the rates for short periods of 30 to 90 days.
4. ***Long rates:*** the rates for long periods of 90 days and above.
5. ***Telquel rates:*** the rates for broken periods of 15 days or 45 days etc. The risk varies with the rate dealt with. The longer the period of rate, the larger is the risk. The telquel rates are generally higher than for rounded periods of 2/3 months due to more work involved in such deals and the deals with documents carry higher risk than clean credits or instru-

ments, for the simple reason that there may be more risk in documents. Similarly, the forward rates are having more risk than spot rates.

Risk also varies with the country and the currency in which the instruments are drawn. The political and economic factors, stability or otherwise of the political system and economic policies and a host of non-economic factors play a role in deciding the risk and the rate charged.

Forward rate is generally at a premium due to larger risk involved in it. It is assumed here that the rate is quoted in direct method say $1 : 1.58 DM. The forward premium will indicate the larger number of DM per dollar to be given in each transaction. Applying the principle of "buy high and sell low" for the indirect method of quotation, as in the case of rupee until August 1993, the forward rate for the rupee will be at a premium in the sense that more rupees are to be given for a dollar. Take an example, say $1: Rs. 43.6200 for TT buying spot. The forward premium for one month is 10 points which means that the rate will be $1:Rs. 43.6210 for one month forward and so on. This means that you have to give Rs. 43.6210 for buying a dollar forward, one month as against Rs. 43.6200 for spot buying. If you are selling dollars you will only get Rs. 43.6190 for dollar forward.

Arbitrage and Speculation

In addition to the financing of the genuine trade and payments on merchandise and invisible trade account, banks do finance capital flows of both short-term and long-term. Funds move in and move out for hedging and speculation as between currencies. While sometimes the hedging transactions help to stabilise the rates, the same cannot be said of the speculative flows of short-term nature. The excesses of such flows destabilise the exchange market and lead to violent fluctuations in exchange rates. The greater the volatility, the larger is the risk in foreign exchange market and premium on forwards will go up abnormally. Arbitrage is dealing in foreign exchange to take advantage of the differences in cross rates as between centres or currencies or as between quotations in two or more centres. Thus, if dollars are cheap in one centre and dear in another centre, arbitrage takes place to buy in the cheap centre and sell in dear centre with the result that rate quotations will tend to get equalised as between centres. Thus, to an extent, arbitrage has a stabilising influence on the foreign exchange market.

Types of Risk in Foreign Exchange

There are different types of exchange risks in the foreign exchange market which are set out briefly below :

1. ***Credit risk of customer:*** Credit / rating by international banks and international credit rating agencies will help reducing this risk. In India, ECGC and banks do take this risk for the exporters.
2. ***Country risk:*** This is different slightly from the currency risk and arises out of the policies of economic and political nature and their external payments position and their export earnings to service the foreign creditors, convertibility or otherwise of their currencies, etc. The country risk is also in many cases covered by ECGC or Exim Bank.
3. ***Currency risk:*** This risk arises out of the volatility or otherwise of the currency and its strength or weakness in terms of other currencies and interest rates and relative degrees of inflation in the respective countries which influence the exchange rates. It also depends on the hot money

flows and speculative short-term flows as between countries which will destabilise the exchange rates. The currency risk is generally covered by banks on the guarantee of the ECGC.

4. ***Market risk:*** Risks of commodities, their quality and the change of Government policies or taxation etc. are borne by the exporters or the ECGC in some cases. It will thus be seen that some risks cannot be avoided or passed on by the exporters and in fact many more risks are to be borne by the importers than by the exporters as any government generally wants to encourage exports from the country.

5. Unforeseen calamities wars, riots, perils of air and sea etc.

6. ***Special risks of importers:*** In India both exporters and importers face risks of foreign exchange market, referred to above, but risk coverage to exporters is more than to importers. The reason is that the Indian Government has to enable exporters to compete effectively with their foreign counterparts, where exporters get many facilities, particularly credit at low rates of interest and lower tax rates.

The RBI cannot now impose controls as FERA has been liberalised but it has been entering the market to stabilise the rate and more recently it has been announcing a reference rate for U.S. dollar and Euro for its operations, to stabilise the market. FERA is fixing the rates for major currencies around which banks are free to operate in the Indian foreign exchange market. Banks continue to cover the currency risk and EXIM Bank provides the credit and country risk cover for long duration export contracts and deferred payment contracts, project exports etc. EXIM Bank also provides refinance for approved projects and schemes to the concerned banks. ECGC extends the risk coverage by insurance of country and party credit risk — for banks to lend to parties of unknown credit rating. But banks and firms are allowed to keep funds abroad and take risk in currencies and even trade in foreign currency markets upto limits set by the managements of each of the banks. They can hedge, swap currencies, enter into arbitrage deals, secure forward cover abroad, and even take open positions in currencies. Options and futures are also open to banks and firms to cover their risks and trade in the markets for hedge purposes.

Options for Treasury Manager

Purchase of Foreign currencies from exporters and through inward remittances payments abroad and remittances.	Sale of foreign currencies for importers and payments outside.
1. Type of currencies highly well traded Franc, Yen, etc., which are convertible currencies.	Like Dollar, DM, £, Franc, Yen, etc.
2. Not, well traded and internationally not readily accepted.	Like Dinar, Riyal, Baht and Rupiah etc.

In the latter case, the treasury manager will cover the deal immediately by reversing the entry through the London or Frankfurt markets. In the case of the former currencies he has the following options :

Options for Treasury Manager in Convertible Currencies

Take an overnight open position. High risk return scenario.	Swap one currency for another from weaker to stronger. Hedge the currency position risk-full coverage.
Outright purchase/sale to reverse the entry.	Future option or futures contracts.
Hedge operations executed in the following segments. (a) Forward to forward (b) Inter Bank Market in India (c) Foreign Bank Branches	Hedge operations take the form of hedge for one currency by another to hedge of spot to forward or forward to forward.
(d) Central Bank of the Country.	Foreign correspondents. Foreign Banks and in Foreign markets.

Illustrations

An Indian importer has to pay $ 1,75,000 for some equipment imported for his factory and the terms of payment are.

1. Immediate deposit of $ 50,000
2. Payment of 2nd instalment at the end of 3 months — $ 50,000
3. Final payment at the end of delivery — 6 months hence $ 75,000

At the prevailing spot rate he buys dollars at the current rate of Rs.43.64 per $ at end March 2005 and makes a payment of Rs.21.82 lakhs (TT rate) plus the bank charges and other incidental charges. This is at the spot rate of $ to Rs.43.64 for TT selling. For instalment of $ 50,000 at the end of 3 months, he can keep open the options and see the position of the rates at the end of 3 months, or take a hedge, of buying forward dollars three months hence, at present. The 3 months premium 15 paise per U.S. Dollar (the rate is 43.64 + 0.15 = 43.79) and an amount of Rs.21.90 lakhs is used to buy forward dollars three months hence for $ 50,000. The six months forward premium for a rate of Rs.43.64 is a premium of 29 paise, for import payment which leads to a payment of Rs.32.95 lakhs, for buying 6 months forward dollars of $ 75,000. Suppose the rates have fallen and /or the premium has fallen, he will lose and if the premium has gone up he will gain by this hedge. Depending on his perception of trend of the rupee rate he will either cover the payment or not. Therein lies his expertise.

Similarly, an exporter is due to receive Rs. $ 1,75,000 and if he thinks that rupee is depreciating, he will keep his funds in dollars or exchange for other strong currency like yen or DM where he can keep the funds with relatively higher interest rates.

Suppose the Indian interest rates are 12% and U.S. interest rates are 6%, he will gain 6% p.a. by keeping his funds in India. On the other hand, if the extent of depreciation of rupee can compensate more than the loss of interest of 6% he will keep his funds in dollars until they are used.

The other alternatives open to importers and others who have payment to be made abroad are : (a) Swap the spot dollars for forward or (b) Take an option (call option) in the form of a right to buy dollars at a price three months hence if it exceeds Rs.43.64 (at the present premium for three months of 15, spot rate will lead to a 3 months rate of Rs. 43.79). An exporter due to receive funds can similarly keep open the position of $175,000 to be received three months hence or hedge them by buying forward rupees at the present time. TT buying is 44.20 and premium for 3 months is 14 with the result that he gets Rs.44.06 per dollar three months hence ($ 175,000 x 44.06 = Rs.77.10 lakh). If on the other hand he kept open the position and rupee depreciated to Rs.44.30 at the end of 3 months he would have got an amount of Rs.78.05 lakh — a profit of Rs. 95,000.

In a similar manner, an importer can also gain if he buys dollars in spot for $175,000 by paying Rs.76,63,250 outright and keep the dollars in US. or Europe where the interest rates are high provided he expects the rupee to depreciate further.

In the futures and options markets the dollars or other foreign currencies are quoted if there is a well developed market. Thus, the premium to be paid depends on the expected movements of currency rate, inflation rates and interest rates. If a 3 months option for dollar is cheaper than swapping or buying outright forward dollars, then the funds manager has to adopt the least cost method of payment abroad out of all the methods open to him.

Similarly, an exporter or trader who is to receive dollars may prefer to trade in them abroad, gain interest for the month that he cannot use them and then make use of them for payment abroad at the needed time.

By taking any of these options he may gain or lose depending on the actual moments in currency rates and interest rates and his expertise in correct forecasting. The forex market traders deal in a number of currencies for buying and selling, but match them as far as possible and keep an open position only in currencies, which are strong in their opinion, which may appreciate but not depreciate in rates. He will lose if his expectations prove wrong and for this a limit of stop loss order is given to him, namely, 10% of the total volume of funds traded by him. These limits are left to be decided by the bank managements only as per the guidelines of the RBI.

In case he gets some less traded currencies like Saudi, Riyal, Kuwaiti Dinar or Norwegian Kronor or Malaysian Ringit he covers them up immediately in foreign markets as it is not possible to cover them in India and they are risky to hold.

Treasury Management

Treasury manager operating in forex market gets a funds statement from all branches and regions early in the morning. He has before him a statement of all currencies held by the Bank — the amounts and maturities.

The Foreign Departments of Banks has to undertake the following operations.

1. Import financing 2. Export financing 3. Bills for collection and negotiation 4. Guarantee or giving confirmation 5. Conversion of foreign currencies to rupees and *vice versa*, etc.

All branches which undertake foreign operations has three aspects in their operations.

(1) ***FERA Operations:*** Reporting to RBI of all transactions branch-wise.

(2) ***Credit Angle:*** Provide Rupee finance after credit appraisal and assess their foreign credit requirements. This involves the same principles as observed in project appraisal in rupees and extension of term loan, cash

credit and advances. The C&I Department of the Bank will take care of it.

(3) ***Funds Operations:*** For each bank the foreign currency operations are concentrated at the head office, say calcutta for SBI and at Mumbai for Bank of India, and for many other banks and at Chennai for a few banks, like SBH or Indian Bank.

It is this funds manager's function which is vital in the forex market. The trader in currencies takes an open position and if professionally handled he can make it a profit centre.

Currency Dealer

Treasury manager has to trade in currencies in various forms. He covers the open position in some currencies, which are weak in the inter-bank market in India or with correspondents abroad. He allows open positions in some strong currencies upto permitted limit of say 10%. Risk is being limited by such operations.

For trade related demand and supply for currencies, either spot or forward currencies are sold or purchased and net positions are covered up as shown above. Similarly, the demand for and supply of currencies are not for trade but for non-trade transactions like royalty payments, travel and transport etc. As at the end of the day, the quantum of all foreign currencies are tallied with transactions, which are effected by the Back Office.

The net positions in currencies, as held in our nostro accounts abroad and vostro accounts of foreign correspondents with themselves are tallied. These nostro and vostro account balances are the amounts available for trade by the treasury manager, on the next day.

As referred to earlier he hedges the currency and country risks by swaps options and futures or in some cases takes a calculated risk for profit which may land him in losses also. A treasury operator, who will not limit his losses with a stop-loss order or is over ambitious may get into troubles due to sudden adverse changes in currency rates and interest rates abroad. A prudent and cautious operator can gain in these operations but limit his losses to a point. Therein lies the expertise of treasury operator in forex market.

Market Makers in Foreign Exchange Market

A market maker is one who takes the risk and gives a two-way quotation for any currency — bid and offer rates — and deals in given currencies. As the RBI deals only in dollars, the banks who act as market makers, which are generally foreign banks, concentrate deals in dollar but quote cross currency rates such as dollars to sterling or dollars to yen etc. The market makers are generally prone to take positions or hold uncovered currency holdings in strong currencies such as dollar, yen or DM as their rate fluctuations are minimal and risk is lower. The risk manager in a company or in a bank, plans his holdings of uncovered currencies into a diversified portfolio, to reduce risk and maximise returns. He may invest in short-term assets or money market instruments of countries whose currencies are strong. Such currencies are unlikely to fluctuate violently and the degree of volatility will be low normally. Both interest rate volatility and exchange rate volatility are taken into account for taking any risk or cover a risk.

A market maker has to forecast not only the currency rates but the interest rates in the respective countries, which will influence the forward rates. He may cover the risk in some currencies but keep open positions in others. He takes calculated risks to maximise his returns. Leaving the uncovered positions, he may cover others by the following methods :

1. Swap forward to spot, 2. Swap forward of one maturity to another maturity 3. Swap one currency against another of same maturity or a different maturity, 4. Buy spot for future liability, 5. Buy strong currency and sell weak currency, 6. Buy forward of one maturity against sale of another maturity or of another currency and a host of other techniques.

Market makers in the foreign exchange market are authorised dealers and the Reserve Bank in the last resort. In markets of well developed countries, the Central Bank intervention is minimal and the market making is left to reputed foreign exchange dealers and international banks. Swaps are one method by which they cover their risks. Swap is exchange of one maturity to another and forward deals are another mode of hedge against risk. Some treasury dealers take to cross currency options and perch their funds in strong currencies abroad. In the absence of international quotes of rupees, no rupee based options can be introduced in India.

Risk in Forward Market

As referred to earlier forward exchange rates are more risky than spot rates. These refer to rates which are quoted for the currencies for delivery in one month to six months ahead. During 1991 to 1994 the exchange markets were undergoing many changes due to the ongoing reforms in India.

During major part of 1994 following the full convertibility of rupee on current account, forward markets turned more volatile and listless conditions prevailed in the spot market. Forward market stabilised during 2002 to 2006 and premium came down drastically.

The forward market is generally influenced by many factors in addition to spot market conditions, as the following examples have shown:

(a) Perception regarding U.S. dollar rate and Indian non-resident rupee exchange rate against dollar and in general currency markets.

(b) Current position and forecast of domestic and foreign money market conditions.

(c) Arbitrage, hedge and speculative deals effecting the market.

(d) Currency risk manager's strategies of the proportion of forward cover effected to total exposures.

Forward market cover was as high as 18% in 1992 just at the time of introduction of partial convertibility of the rupee in February 1992 but fell to less than 10% by February 1994, when the rupee gained in strength. Since June 1994 RBI discontinued its swap window and forced the treasury managers to go for interbank deals. The exporters and importers are able to cover their forward risk with the banks for their receipts and payments, but in times of currency stability such covers are less in demand and the traders choose to take some risk themselves. Similarly, the currency manager will also keep some open positions. Since 1995 companies and banks are allowed to trade in currencies and in forward exchange. The currency risks of short-term of 3 to 6 months are generally lower. The currency risks, involved in medium and long-term foreign exchange exposures of companies are unpredictable and difficult to cover. But these risks are high in India at present. The earlier practice was of covering such risks by Exim Bank and medium-term forward market. Now banks as well as firms can keep foreign currencies abroad and trade with the attendant risks. Without reference to RBI, Banks are permitted to provide exchange facilities to their clients, depending on their needs since July 1995. The factors of interest rates and money market conditions are important determinants of forward market. The banks started covering their positions of exposure under FCNRA Scheme, when the market was volatile. But FCNRA Scheme was phased out during 1993-94 as there was no need for it as it involved a currency risk coverage.

The risk of currency manager is higher or lower depending on a host of factors. The proportion of risk covered by him to total exposure will depend on his perception of money market rates in India and abroad and volatility of the currency markets and a number of financial and non-financial factors. When the US dollar interest rates are high, exporters prefer to keep their earnings abroad. If the rupee dollar rate is stable, exporters can take a view on the future exchange rate and lock in a forward to forward swap arrangement with banks to obtain a better cover on their receivables. The forward market is however illiquid beyond 6 months as the banks find it difficult to foresee the coming trends.

The risk that the currency manager takes will vary from manager to manager and from the conditions in the money market and currency market. He generally covers his risk by taking forward to forward cover by adopting appropriate swap techniques and calculated risk management through diversification and proper investment strategies. The currencies in which he takes a position should be stable as US dollar or DM or Yen. The same can be said of the currencies held abroad by firms and companies in India.

Hedge cover of exchange risk for the trader is common. Besides, banks resort to currency Swaps, options and futures in foreign currencies to cover their exchange risk. The risk manager generally keeps an open position only in strong currencies, which are likely to be less volatile. Highly volatile currencies are generally less traded and their risk invariably covered. But the cover rates are also higher, generally.

Need for Forward Market

The recent attempts of the RBI to develop a rupee exchange market and a forward exchange market were already referred to. The companies are in a position to trade in the market and take position in currencies which need not be in the currency in which their foreign trade contract lies. They can keep foreign exchange earned abroad and trade in the currencies permitted by the RBI. The foreign currency option market is also expected to be developed due to these measures, taken recently by the RBI, as also the forward exchange market in India. Sodhani Committee's recent recommendations for developing the Forex Market (1995) are referred later.

Derivatives for Taking Foreign Exchange Risk

Huge external debt of the government and the repayment obligations through the normal channels of foreign exchange market creates an undue burden on the rupee. The exchange risk involved in this burden can be managed by taking an insurance policy against adverse fluctuations. The government should transfer the risks associated with exchange rate volatility to international markets, at terms attractive enough depending on the country's creditworthiness. It is securitising the debt of the government at market determined rates.

The derivatives available are discussed earlier, namely, futures options, swaps and forward rate agreements in which banks operate in foreign centres openly and freely, but in India, the RBI regulations are not completely removed for companies, banks and other institutions to develop these markets in India to hedge their risk. The present liberalisation process allowing hedges has however set some limits also so that the freedom to operate is still constrained.

The exchange crisis of Oct.-Nov. 1995 and in June-Aug. 1998 in India led to more controls on foreign dealings, changes in monetary policy etc.

(i) CRR was reduced to ease liquidity crunch (ii) Nearly $ 2 billion dollars were pumped into the market by RBI from its reserves (iii) Banks were asked to report forex transactions on a daily basis in a format given by RBI ensure that overnight exposure of any bank is not more than Rs. 15 crores, surcharge on import credit was also imposed by the RBI. The premiums for three months forward has come down to 15 paise and so are the premiums for one and two months respectively from the high levels, which ruled at more than 25-30 paise at the crisis time in Nov. 1995. Since that time the RBI was more cautious but liberalised the restrictions later as the situation improved. But the rupee depreciated from Rs. 31 to $ to Rs. 36 per dollar. A similar episode was witnessed in Dec. 1997, when the rupee fell further to Rs. 39.5 per $; due to turmoil in forex markets in Asia and India.

Need for Derivative Markets

The risk of fluctuations in exchange rates which will now be more frequent under the free market rate system should be hedged. The commitments of the government for its debt servicing can be planned well ahead and the risk of variability is passed on to the international markets. The risk premium will generally be higher in times of high volatility in the market as in Oct.-Nov. 1995 and in latter episodes of Nov.-Dec. 1997 and July-Aug. 1998. In this context, derivative market need to be developed in India for adoption of proper techniques of risk management.

When the government moved to the acceptance of Article VIII status of IMF Article of agreement in August 1994, RBI, made a number of sweeping changes in FERA. ADs were given a wide variety of powers and discretion to release foreign exchange and trade in the exchange market upto certain limits without reference to RBI particularly during 1996.

Some of these liberalisations were reversed during the foreign exchange crisis of October-November 1995, when the rupee fell steeply from Rs.31.4200 at June end 1995 to Rs.34.74 in mid December 1995. At one stage in October 1995, the rate fell to as much as Rs.35.85. The first round of rupee depreciation during August-September 1995 was by 6.9% and the second round of depreciation was steeper at 11% in October 1995. There was in all a total depreciation of 18-20 % over one year, since 1994. There was further depreciation of the rupee during subsequent years 1996 to 1999, particularly due to East Asian currency crisis in 1998, on top of a crisis in December, 1997 and a general slow down of the economic growth and the rupee to dollar rate fell to Rs. 44.20 by March 2000 and Rs. 47 by March 2001.

The method by which RBI met this challenge was (1) to support it when the rate fell below a level, which according to them is justified by real economic factors and (2) to announce a number of measures to increase the inflows by exporters and reduce the outflows due to import payments and offering higher rates on deposits of NRIs etc., (3) announce a reference rate of rupee in terms of dollar and monetary and credit measures to support the rupee.

Sodhani Committee Report (1995)

This Committee has come out with two reports — one on the details on various schemes and incentives available to NRIs and the other for development of active exchange market system. The major recommendations are set out below.

NRI investments are not freely flowing in due to the following constraints, which have to be removed, namely, administrative red tape, tax hurdles, government interference, rampant corruption, infrastructure and inadequate access to bank credit by NRIs.

The time taken for allotment of new issues to NRIs is very long; despatch of certificates or statements should be faster and there should be quick transfer of shares from one to other and for payment of dividends etc. The issue of shares to NRIs by company is to be left free without prior permission of RBI but the companies have to report the holdings of NRIs and the details of those holdings as per the committee recommendations.

NRIs should be free to buy not only in new issues but from existing shares from Indians directly. Only the ADs should have the powers to scrutinise and effect the payments. These should be no lock in period for shares, in sick units, acquired by NRIs, OCBs and they should be brought in on par with all FFIs. All these recommendations are implemented in stages since October 1996.

As regards the measures for the development of Forex Market, the following are given as a few examples :

(1) To increase the number of participants by inclusion of companies, and merchant exporters.

(2) To allow the ADs to lend and invest or borrow abroad and to allow them to keep cross currency positions abroad.

(3) To allow developments of modern products and derivatives such as futures, options etc.

(4) To develop proper accounting practices and disclosure standards for such operations.

(5) Companies and exporters can keep funds abroad and take positions.

(6) The RBI and tax authorities should clearly bring down their requirements and relax their controls and formalities regarding the abolition of withholding tax on derivative transactions.

(7) Legal and regulatory framework should be simplified and even reduced.

(8) Risk management techniques should be expanded and developed through the introduction of futures and other derivative products.

(9) RBI's attitude should change from regulatory angle to developmental angle.

These measures are yet to be implemented. Although the wording of the Sodhani's report is different from the words used above, the substance of the Report's recommendations are set out here. The most important pre-requisite for developments of the forex market in India is the reduction of controls and restrictions, delegation of more powers to ADs and expertise in RBI and banks to be improved and banks to be empowered to deal with risk management techniques and for development of derivative markets. The government and tax authorities should be either liberal or free such foreign transactions with a low withholding tax of not more than 10% as applicable to FFIs in some respects at present. The treatment given to NRIs by banks has to be the same as of residents and OCBs and NRIs should be treated on par which is now implemented. The role of the treasury manager in banks and companies, therefore becomes critical, needing a multi disciplinary expertise, in the forex market, as it is more volatile and complicated by national and international factors.

Interest Risk Management

So long as the interest rates were fixed by the RBI and the Government, the interest rate risk did not crop as a major factor of risk to banks and corporates. Deregulation of interest rates and leaving them to market forces gave rise to a system of volatility to interest rates and yields. Some liabilities of banks and corporates have become interest sensitive, which led to greater burden on them to manage asset-liability mismatch and risk of interest rate changes. The changes in these rates will lead unpredictable variation in the spread between the lending and borrowing rates and profit margins.

Risk of interest rates is due to their movements in either direction and volatility in them led to changes in the margin of spread, which is the basis of their income. This will sometimes erode the profits and lead to uncertainty of incomes.

Risk Measurement

Risk measurement is basic exercise needed for risk management. Gap analysis measures the mismatches between the rate sensitive assets and liabilities. Interest rate risk is measured by calculating the gaps between the time intervals between maturities of liabilities and assets, and cash inflows and outflows as revealed in the balance sheet data. Each item in the balance sheet of banks generates some cash flows. These will suffer due to change in interest rate until their maturity or repricing the assets is possible and reinvestment will change. There is a gap between the interest sensitive assets and liabilities. Any asset or liability which has a price is interest sensitive. Similarly, if interest rate is fixed on any asset or liability this will lead to a risk due to change in interest rates. There is a gap between interest sensitive assets (RSA) and interest sensitive liabilities (RSL). These gaps have to be observed and a watch is kept on them period wise say monthly or quarterly. The gap is positive, when RSA is greater than RSL (RSA > RSL). The gap is negative when RSA is less than RSL (RSA < RSL). Positive gap, will benefit from rising interest rates and negative gaps will benefit from falling rates. When short-term interest rates rise, interest income rises more than interest expenses because more assets are repriced. The spread will then increase.

The gap concept is only an elementary measure of the interest rate risk. Gap report only reflects the time difference between repricing of assets and liabilities but fails to measure the entire impact of a change in interest rate. For getting the entire effect of interest rate changes, net present value analysis of all cash flows, both on assets and liabilities side is necessary and application of duration concept is also necessary for managing interest rate risk.@

Risk Mitigation Process

Entering into Forward contracts is one method of mitigating the risk in Forex market, due to uncertainty of exchange rate. This is resorted to by exporters and importers with banks and banks in turn in the interbank market. Forward contracts can be entered into for any expected inflows or outflows from foreign countries, for invisibles, services, remittances for fees, royalties, travel, tourism etc. As per RBI guidelines, entering into forward contracts or cancellation or early deliveries are permitted, if they are backed by genuine commercial, or trade transactions. Hedging in futures or forward markets is allowed in India at present, as a risk reduction measure. But trading in futures for speculation is not allowed; so also cancellation and early deliveries are not permitted for speculative purposes. They are only allowed by merchant traders to limit losses or avoid possible losses due to cancellation of underlying trade contracts or rescheduling of deliveries by buyer or seller or a possible default of the counter party.

Sometimes cancellation and early deliveries are resorted to book profits and speculative gains which are against the RBI guidelines. The FEDAI has also laid certain guidelines for ADs in respect of forward contracts, either for merchant transactions or interbank deals. Rules Nos. 7 and 8 deal with the cancellation and early deliveries of Forward Contracts. The ADs are not advised by their top managements to do such deals for speculation or taking positions in currencies for gains from changes in premium in Forward markets.

Forward premium in March 2005 was 2.28 percent per annum for one month contracts. The rupee Dollar rate in March, 2005 in spot market was Rs. 43.82 per US $. This gives an actual monthly premium of 8 paise per month. On this basis of expectations of rise or fall in this premium amount, speculative positions are taken by merchants, treasurers and banks.

DERIVATIVES ON NSE

Use of derivatives is a method of risk management. The derivatives can be Nifty Futures and options or stock futures and options. The data relating to the derivatives set out as follows :

Underlying Instrument – Index or Stock

Type of Trading Cycle,

Contract size,

Expiry date,

Price steps,

Base price, Daily settlement price, Price Bonds,

First day of Trading.

Last day of Trading.

@ See author's book on Investment Management, Chapter 35.

The Daily Financial Press gives out the data on prices and volumes, such as price, open, high, low, and close and data or volumes – open interest, no. of contracts, etc.

In derivative trading, there is need for good accounting standards, as there are fallacies and pitfalls in such accounts, leading to defaults and payment difficulties for many companies in the past. Derivative trading is highly speculative and treasurer has to take extreme care in risk management through derivatives.

There is need for greater transparency good financial reporting, and preparation of Financial statements and Balance sheet should be fair and correct. The FAS 133 is being used as fair and transparent which means that contracts have to be marked to market value and are reflected in the Balance sheet, not as off Balance sheet items but as part of Balance sheet. The internationally accepted principles of Accounting (GAS) have to be adopted in the financial reporting of derivative trading, for successful treasury management.

INTEREST RATE RISK MEASURES

1. Gap or *Mismatch Risk:* This gap will rise when assets and liabilities will fall due for repricing at different times. A floating rate issue will reduce the risk to zero, as there is no gap or time for repricing. Mismatched repricing periods of assets and liabilities is a form of risk.

***2. Net Interest Position* Risk:** If a bank has more assets, on which interest is earned than liabilities on which it pays interest then the bank has net interest position which leads to risk. But, when interest rates rise, the bank with positive net interest position will gain.

3. Basis Risk: Interest rates of any two instruments will not change by the same degree or percentage. Both borrowing rate and lending rate will not change in the same degree or proportion, which causes risk. This is the change in interest rates by basis points which will vary from instrument to instrument. The differences in basis point changes will lead to an additional risk. Thus, rates on deposits of some maturities will change while some lending rates only are changed.

4. Repayment or Withdrawal Risk: If interest rates fall, there is a possibility of some borrowers repaying the high interest loans and if interest rates rise on deposits; old deposits may be withdrawn and new deposits are kept at high interest rates. As interest rates rise and fall, the banks are exposed to some degree of risk as customers exercise the embedded options, inherent in their deposits and loan contracts. The larger the interest rate changes in quantum and more frequent these changes are, the greater will be the risk to the bank.

***5. Yield and Price Change* Risk:** With change in interest rates, yields and prices of fixed income securities change in inverse relation. Prices fall when yields rise and *vice versa.* A bank having a large component of long-term loans, a rise in yield will lead to fall in prices and hence depreciation and loss of capital value. Yields curve risk arises when the yield curve varies as between different securities and of differing maturities. Changes in yields result in price changes and such frequent changes upset the planning for income and profits. Price risk along with reinvestment risk should be looked into. The differences in the timing of interest cash flows for reinvestment between assets and liabilities may create a further risk.

How to Cope with Interest Risk

Obviously it is better for the bank to manage its balance sheet items to have less interest sensitive assets and liabilities. They have to resort to floating rate liabilities and flexi-debt instruments. Bankers can also vary the gap in tune with interest rate changes on the basis of forecasts.

The portfolio composition should be constantly reviewed and changed in tune with the change in interest rates. The one method of doing it is to get the duration of its loans to match with the duration of deposit or match the cash inflows with outflows as exactly as possible.

The banks have to reduce asset sensitivity, after maximising the discretionary funds.

Extend investment portfolio maturities, increase short-term deposits and borrowings to suit to lending or investment pattern, increase fixed rate lending of long-term or adjustable rate loans.

The banks have to reduce sensitivity of liabilities.

Increase longer term deposits and borrow on flexi-rate basis but sell fixed rate loans.

More recently banks and financial institutions are opting for flexible rate loans or loans adjustable to basic deposit rate of one year and above. Banks can adopt strategies like matching long-term assets by equity own funds and match repriceable assets with similar repriceable liabilities and resort to options, futures, and various combinations of them to hedge interest rate risk by swaps for principal as well as flows of interest payments. More important, banks have to scrutinize the credit delivery system, improve the quality of assets and reduce the NPA (Non-performing Assets).

Asset Liability Management (ALM)

Asset liability management can be defined as the process of adjusting liabilities to meet loans and asset demand, liquidity needs and safety requirements. It should take care to ensure the following :

(a) An active management of liabilities or deposits.

(b) Ensuring bank profitability.

(c) Securing the long-term operating viability.

ALM is management of funds wherein the discretionary element is properly used, by increase or decrease the interest sensitive funds. It should ensure that bank rates are competitive on both liabilities and assets. Besides, regulatory factors should be favourable to enable the company to change the composition of assets in tune with the maturity composition of liabilities. These factors require a good secondary market, interest rate deregulation, and competitive market free scenario.

Instruments for ALM

1. Use of CDs and active primary and secondary market in them as the interest rates on them are freed.
2. Another instrument for use, where interest rates are freed is call and notice money which banks can use.

3. Since 1988, inter-bank participations certificates are used for adjusting liabilities with flexibility of rates offered and minimum costs and maximum return.
4. Float or liabilities in the process of collection or cash and credit in the process of collection.
5. Refinance from RBI and IDBI etc.

Banks discretionary funds should be maximum in order to enable them to make proper ALM Bank-wise data showed that SBI and its associate banks are having maximum discretionary funds.

Objectives of ALM

1. To maximise the income, and control risk exposure.
2. Liquidity should be ensured and the spread between return and costs should be maximum.
3. Bank interest income minus interest expense should be termed as gap which should be maximised.

Spread Management

RBI will fix a minimum rate or maximum rate on deposits and loans and subject them to these guidelines. The banks should have a large component of interest sensitive assets and liabilities which is possible with big size banks. If a small bank has predominantly retail deposit mix of fixed interest rates, it needs to aim at fixed rate earning assets and maintain as much spread as possible between return and costs.

Disintermediation reduces the low cost funds for banks and deregulation of interest rates puts pressure on banks and spreads may be reduced. Liquidity pressures due to deregulation and disintermediation can be managed effectively by big sized banks. Interest sensitivity is measured by changes in interest rate on the concerned assets or liability divided by the change in RBI refinance rate. GAP=RSA – RSL, where RSA is in the rate sensitive assets RSL is the rate sensitive liability.

Traditional Gap Management

Banks first fix the length of the plan horizon, of say 3 months, then the estimates of return and risk for pursuing various alternative programs of borrowing and lending should be set and finally the bank chooses that programme with a stable net interest income. The gap is the excess of interest sensitive assets over interest sensitive liabilities; incremental gap is worked out by taking one year, divided into quarters and maximum insulation of net interest income is achieved by making the incremental gap equal to zero. Under the traditional approach, banks would have their net interest income immunised from interest rate changes.

Examples of interest sensitive assets are short-term investments in securities, Treasury bills, CP and CD etc.

Examples of interest sensitive liabilities are instruments of CDs and ICD and volatile call money, notice money term deposits, short-term debts are all rate sensitive.

Rate Adjusted Gap

Different parts of assets and liabilities will respond differently to change in interest rates. Each asset and liability item of balance sheet should be multiplied by its corresponding rate change ratio, namely, RSA/RSL. After those adjustments if the rate adjusted gap is zero, then interest income of a bank is considered to be fully immunised to market rate changes.

Maturity mismatches can be offset by lengthening or shortening either of assets or liabilities. Liquidity problem can arise at any point or period. Hence, it is necessary to be prepared to adjust continuously both the assets and liabilities.

Liquidity needs of banks arise due to :

1. Meeting the contingent liabilities.
2. Non-receipt of expected funds inflows.
3. Non-renewal of deposits or withdrawal of funds.
4. Profits may change either in investments or in advances side.

The source of liquidity may arise from any one or more items both in assets and liabilities. Bank should be prepared to adjust on both sides of the balance sheet.

"AL" MANAGEMENT FUNCTION

The existing scenario may change due to quality changes in loan assets investment opportunities funds, growth, regulatory directives, Government policy changes or overall state of the economy. It is necessary to set up a A.L. committee and A.L. managers as per RBI guidelines. Performance budgeting is to be adopted and executed. This committee continuously monitors the changes affecting the assets and liabilities, spread between the assets and liabilities, maturity, distribution of the assets and liabilities. Credit, investment and funds departments, should be coopted for the work in A.L. committee. Credit management committee, Investment management committee and Liability management committee will coordinate with the objective of making performance cost effective and achieve profit maximisation.

PROFIT PLANNING APPROACH

Performance budgeting aims at profit maximisation. This is a part of overall planning approach. This involves the balance sheet management and all items of assets and liabilities. In other words it tantamounts to A.L. Management. Credit, investments and fund managements are involved in this exercise. Non-funded business is also involved in profit planning and maximisation of profits. The steps in profit planning are the following :

Fix a plan horizon say one year, identify the key areas for effective cost control and for fixing targets. Then, the bank has to prepare a profit plan for each operational profit centre and arrange for a co-ordinated approach. To implement the plan, the appropriate strategies are set out and operated which will be followed by monitoring, review of performance and mid-term correction and changes in both assets and liabilities and their mix.

The discretionary components of both assets and liabilities should be isolated and profit planning through changes in deployment of funds or sources should be resorted to - Non-SLR component and current portion of investments and advances to trade and industry outside the priority sector, SSI etc. could be manipulated under strategic management techniques.

Profitability can be improved by adjusting the above discretionary components of both assets and liabilities. Profitability is contingent upon stable spread or margin. The bank should maximise the spread in respect of fixed rate funds. In respect of interest sensitive items, maturity changes and for duration changes along with the changes in the mix of investments and advances will help promote the growth of profits. This is part of the overall asset liability management operations by the banks. ALM is a risk management technique particularly with respect to interest rate changes. As treasury operations involve risk management, ALM planning, budgeting etc. are all closely related to treasury management.

Some Techniques of ALM are the use of the Derivatives

I. ***Ready Forward Deals (Repos):*** These are part of investment operations of banks. Ready forward deals are buy back arrangements or repos transactions. It is a transaction with commitment to buyback, or reverse the deal, buying with selling or selling with buying of treasury bills or any other investments.

Example: BOI has excess security of X and IOB wants to purchase it say for a short period of 14 days. BOI is a seller and needs money. IOB is a buyer and has excess money. BOI is borrower of funds and IOB is buyer of security.

II. ***Double Ready Forward Deals:*** When a bank sells a security to another bank on a ready forward basis and simultaneously purchases some other security on ready forward basis, it is termed as the double ready forward deal. BOI will sell some security X to IOB, but BOI does not have X, so, it borrows X from Ind bank in exchange of Y security. The BOI enters into buy back agreement with IOB in X security. In this, three parties are involved and two transactions took place. Hence, it is called double ready forward deals.

III. ***Switch Deals:*** If one bank exchanges or switches one security X for another security Y, then it is called a switch deal for the same amount.

Some of the factors which influence the above deals are current yields, differences in maturity, appreciation and depreciation, profit or loss on security and voucher (interest warrant) loss or gain etc.

RBI Guidelines on Investment Policy

1. Each bank should lay down the investment guidelines and get it approved by its Board separately for operating on own account and on behalf of clients, as custodians or agents.
2. Since June 1, 1994, any bank can enter into ready forward contracts in TBs Or in such dated central government securities as approved by RBI and the government and these transactions should be done through SGL account only.
3. All double ready forward deals in TBs, and government securities are prohibited.

4. The double ready forward and ready forward deals among banks are prohibited in P.S.U. bonds, units of UTI and approved securities either on own account or clients accounts.
5. If SGL accounts are there, for both buyer and seller, the deals should be done through SGL account only. These are to be done on SGL transfer forms approved by the RBI signed by two officials of the bank. Penalties will be imposed if any bank issues sale order without having securities in SGL.
6. Bankers receipts (BRs) are generally prohibited for banks to deal in Government securities. In the case of other securities BR can be issued for ready transactions only, when allotment advice is given but physical certificate is not yet received. The security is in some other centre or was lodged for interest receipt for which there is proof.
7. BRs cannot be issued for less than 3 days and more than 30 days.
8. Banks cannot issue BRs covering the transaction under PMS of clients or brokers and BRs are to be executed on the forms approved by the IBA for the purpose.

Banks have to keep seperate accounts of the transactions of client PMS and their own. (PMS is Portfolio Management System)

Records of SGL transfer forms issued should be maintained and these records, should be tallied and reviewed at quarterly intervals with the books of PDO of RBI. The internal audit department, should periodically audit these accounts of BRs and ready forward deals. The banks have also to report to their top management these accounts on a weekly basis.

Dealing Through Brokers

If deals are put through brokers and not directly among the banks then that should be done through member brokers of N.S.E. only. Although a broker will not reveal, the name of the dealer, the contract note should indicate the name of the counter party. After that, the bank should deal directly without any further role to play by the brokers. The banks should have a panel of approved brokers and record should be maintained of the deals done through each broker and no disproportionate part of the business should be done through any one or a few brokers.

Audit Review and Reporting

Banks should undertake half yearly review of these transactions at end Sept. and end March and put up these reports to their Boards within a month from end September and end March. A copy of these review reports of auditors should be sent to RBI also.

Current and Permanent Categories

Investments in permanent category are long dated and are held upto maturity. These are carried in the books, at book value and the difference between the acquisition cost and redemption price should be considered as accrued over the period still outstanding to maturity.

Investments under current category are short dated securities, treasury bills and other approved securities. These are carried into the books at lower of the cost or market value. These are meant for trading and booking profit or loss. The carrying value of securities under current category should be revalued at market prices on a quarterly basis. The gains or losses on this account should be put under the head of "Trading of debt securities" and the net amount under this head should be taken to income statement. Each time a security is acquired, the bank should demark it as for current category or permanent category. The transfer of any security from investment account (permanent category) to trading account should be done with the prior approval of the Board of Directors of the Bank and should be properly documented. The potential loss or gain due to such transfer arising from the difference between the acquisition cost and the market value as on the date of transfer should be properly accounted.

Banks have also to observe the norms of income recognition and follow the classification of assets into standard, sub-standard, bad debt and loss making assets. As per this classification provision has to be made for loss of depreciation and the capital adequacy norm of 8% of risk assets which is now 10% should be observed by all banks. They should also reduce the NPAs by proper planning and strategy, from the present level of 17% for scheduled commercial banks.

Conclusions

Treasury Management involves operations in Financial Markets, which are exposed to many risks. Hence Risk Management is an important component of its functions. Operations in money and gilt edged market are less risky than in Forex Market. Changes in prices and yields and maturity mismatches are some of the major problems in money and gift-edged market. But interest rate risk, purchasing power risk currency and exchange rate risks are some of the top risks in Forex Market. In the capital market systematic and unsystematic risks prevail.

Risk Management involves are attempt at risk measurement and plan for various combinations of risk reduction methods through derivative products and proper investment management. This chapter has set out various risk reduction methods.

❑ ❑ ❑

19 IMPACT OF TREASURY OPERATIONS

The object of this chapter is to investigate the feasibility of measuring the impact of the treasury function on the corporate unit. As the treasury operations are mostly concentrated in the banking sector in India and it is in a *nebulous* stage in the other sectors of the economy. This study is concentrated on the banking sector in a micro sense, in the background of macro picture.

In the banking sector, the major *treasury* operations are in the portfolio management, although in a wider sense, the treasury function purvades most of the activities of the banks. Taking the narrower definitions of treasury function, the discussion in this chapter is confined to portfolio management in scheduled commercial banks.

Theoretical Framework

The major theoretical models that seek to explain the portfolio behaviour of commercial banks are set out below.

(1) ***The Accommodation Model:*** The accommodation principle states that banks try to meet the legitimate needs and credit demands of commerce, industry and agriculture of the economy. It postulates that the social objectives which the banks have to fulfill lay in meeting the credit and investment needs of the country. This model is more suitable for the nationalized banks in India after 1969.

(2) ***Profit Maximization Model:*** This is the classical model based on the principle of marginal costs and benefits. The optimum holding of any asset is attained when its marginal return equals to marginal costs. The totality of interest and non-interest income net of the total costs of deposits and borrowings is taken into account. The spread between unit

income and unit costs should be maximum so that overall profits are optimized for the bank. This approach is more suitable for banks in developed countries and private sector banks in India.

(3) ***Risk-Return Approach:*** The modern economic thought, based on the Markowitz model of portfolio theory, has postulated this approach as applicable to commercial banks. Risk minimization through adoption of a *Beta* measure and maximization of return are pursued by banks. Domestic and international asset diversification is aimed at. The utility or profit has to be maximized with a constraint of given level of risk. Under this NPAs are to be kept at nil or negligible level and the free competitive environment should enable banks to spread their discretionary funds to maximize returns with a proper risk management *strategy* to keep the risk of the lowest level possible. International banks adopt this approach in some form or other.

(4) ***Stock Adjustment Principle:*** This principle postulates that banks, have *a desired level* of each balance sheet item and they adjust the stock of each variable on both assets and liabilities side to be as near as possible to the desired levels. The desired stock is set by the banking principles of prudence, safety liquidity, solvency etc.

(5) ***Environmental Adaptations:*** Lastly, the portfolio of banks is to be adjusted to the environment, that they face – the statutory and regulatory requirements and social and economic constraints. If the portfolio of scheduled commercial banks is analysed in the above background, it will be seen that banks gave top most attention to the RBI Policy guidelines and Government's Social Policy objectives. Very little attention is paid to the pure business principles, and no treasury objectives were pursued in India so far as public sector banks are concerned after the nationalization of banks in 1969. The focus was on social banking and pursuit of accommodation principle in portfolio management. The lead bank scheme and the setting up of regional rural banks in the seventies led to the pursuit of branch expansion and consolidation of banks. The subsequent trends reveal some structural changes in banks strategy of investment.

STRUCTURAL CHANGES

Firstly, the period 1970 to 1990 saw the siphoning off of funds of banks by RBI and the Government through rise in CRR and SLR. The CRR is raised from 3% in 1970 to 15% in 1990 and SLR was raised from 28% to 38.5% during the same period. These factors led to building up by banks of the liquid assets and Govt. and semi Government securities. Efficiency and profitability took back seat and the prime driving force for banks' investment strategy was to meet the immediate statutory requirements and provide the needed funds to the government sector and loans and advances to specified priority sector categories of agriculture, SSIs food credit, fertiliser credit, weaker and neglected segments of the society like traders, artisans etc. In this process the proportion of non-performing assets has increased due to the neglect of credit standards and poor appraisal of projects, profits and profitability suffered, as also the criterion of efficiency.

The period of eighties was a phase of transition to deregulation and liberalisation. The rise in interest rates of government borrowings, introduction of new investments in the money market an Institutional *Strengthening*, following the reports of *Chakravarty Committee* and *Vaghul Committee*. The banks became conscious of yield considerations in investment strategy and became more active in investment in money market and Government debt market during the eighties.

The third phase of nineties saw a sea change in the environment of the financial sector following the economical and financial reforms initiated by the Government since 1991. Banking and foreign exchange controls were relaxed in stages, interest rates were freed from controls of RBI and Government to a large extent following the Report of Narasimham Committee I and II,on financial and banking reforms CRR and SLR were lowered and Government and semi-Government bodies were forced to borrow from the market rather than depend on the RBI and banks, greater reliance was laid on market and price mechanism, liberalisation, privatisation and globalization.

Capital adequacy norms, prudential norms, income recognition and provisioning for bad and doubtful debts, restructuring of banks etc. were provided for during this period. The CRR was brought down from 15% to 10% of incremental net demand and time liabilities while the CRR on outstanding net demand and time liabilities continued to be at 9%. The SLR was brought down from 38.5% in 1990 to 25% of NDTL. Thus, the statutory pre-emption of bank funds was brought down from 63.5% in 1990 to 34% in 1999. The banks were free to use the rest of the funds at their discretion.

At the beginning of the new Millennium since 2000 banks faced a new environment of global markets, free competition, and market oriented economy, free interest rates, free rupee on current Account in the forex markets deepening and widening of the financial markets institutional strengthening, and expanding net work of instruments and avenues of investment along with liberalised policies of the RBI and Government. In addition to credit risks, the banks have to face interest rate risk, currency risk,liquidity risk, market risk and a host of other risks. The CRR was brought down in stages to 5% by 2004 and SLR was kept at 25%. During the period 2000 to 2006 there was more deregulation of banks and discretionary funds kept with banks was as high as 70% of the aggregate NDTL.

Need for Regulatory Frame Work

It is in this context that there was a felt need for proper regulation of banks so as to avoid bank insolvency and failures following the whole gamut of risks that they face now. The Second Narasimham Committee Report came out at this time in April 1998, which recommended *inter alia* prudential norms for banks operations, capital to risk weighted assets ratio (CRAR) to be fixed at 10%, introduction of free and flexible interest rate regime, stricter norms regarding NPAs and debt recovery, introduction to risk weights on government debt of different types and emphasis on ALM and risk management techniques by banks. Greater transparency and disclosure norms were insisted and higher responsibility and accountability was thrust on the top management of banks and their Boards.

It was during this period that the real principles of treasury management were ever thought of. Before that there was no secondary market management in Government debt or in forex market. The banks only invested and maintained the portfolios as per requirements of RBI and Government. The period after 1985, saw larger investment in government and semi-government securities for reasons of yield. In fact the share of trustee securities and other approved securities rose much faster than government debt for reasons of higher yield on the former, although SLR was lowered after 1990.

The nineties saw another feature of increasing share of investments in the total assets and falling share of loans' and advances. There was a fall in the proportion of cash credit and increase in demand loans and term loans during this period. Even when the SLR was reduced, the banks continued to invest more and more funds in Government bonds for reasons of yield.

Gross non-performing assets as a proportion of gross advance was as high as 25% in 1995 but was brought down slowly to 16% in 1999. Even so the RBI, following the Narasimhan Committee Report emphasised the need to reduce the NPAs further and improve the debt recovery performance. The banks have to observe a capital adequacy norm of 10% on a risk weighted basis. Loans and advances carry 100% risk weight, and central government securities have zero risk and the risk on other securities vary from 0 to 100%.

During the seventies and eighties, banks investments in private corporate sector were nil or negligible. During late eighties and nineties, there was some investment upto 5% of NDTL in private corporate securities either through underwriting or guarantee or through devolvement. It we take both investments and advances, the flow of bank funds going to the Government sector initially decreased from 41% during 1970-71 to 1974-75 to 29% by end of 1989-90; then it increased again to 49% by the middle of nineties but brought down to 30% by 2004. The latter increase was not due to S.L.R obligations which were lowered, but due to yield/return considerations and risk weightage. On the other hand, the share of bank funds going to private corporate sector decreased from 26% in the early seventies to around 16% by the end of seventies and has remained in the range of 15 to 17% since then. Then this share to private sector mostly in the form of loans and advances as referred to earlier and very little in investments.

Emerging Trends

The emerging trends in banks strategy of Assets Portfolio Management are as follows :

(1) The modern theory of portfolio diversification and risk reduction techniques have not so far been applied, but there is need for them.

(2) The accommodation and stock maintenance principles have been applied by banks in their Asset portfolio operations.

(3) Treasury Management in the strict sense only existed in foreign banks and not in Indian banks, until very recently.

(4) The environmental factors and RBI guidelines continued to dominate the Asset portfolio management in banks.

(5) Banks have now become more conscious than even before of the need to observe risk management techniques and reduce the non-performing assets.

(6) Banks continued to suffer from the earlier habits of conservatism, staff redundance and high costs of administration.

(7) There is a slow movement towards introduction of latest technology in banking adoption of e-banking, ATM and electronic transfer of funds, which generally help better the operations in treasury.

(8) The need for high-tech banking, cost reduction, better quality of assets and better customer service are recognised only now and it will take some time before public sector banks in India adopt them.

(9) Scientific treasury management, in theory and practice did not find a place in the present day operations of public sector banks barring SBI, but there is need for scientific approach of banks to treasury operations and trading in financial markets.

(10) Markets are still to be developed but trends toward deepening and widening of the markets are there. The volume of turnover both in government securities and in the forex market — particularly in the secondary market has shown a substantial rise in recent years indicating the scope for treasury operations of banks in money market, government debt market and forex market.

Development in Markets

The yields began to move as per the liquidity conditions and free market forces conducive to treasury operations are tending to the established. There is a greater integration of various sub-markets in the money market and gilt edged market. The spreads in yields tended to reflect the normal term risk premia and inflation expectations.

The repo market strengthened the short end of money market in which RBI DFHI and STCI generally operate to have the official policy felt. The operations of 13 primary dealers increased the volume of turnover. New instruments like short term repos, 14 day treasury bills, switches and swaps added to the depth of the market in the case of money market. In the case of government and semi-government securities, the operations of NSE brokers, FFIs, FIs and PDs have significantly widened the market. The new instruments like ZCB, FRB, Gold Bonds, Tax free Bonds, P.S. bonds etc. have added depth to the market.

Turnover in Markets

Money Market is getting increasingly inter-linked with other markets such as gilt edged market and forex market. Excess or shortfall in liquidity conditions percolates to all markets and forex inflows and outflows had their impact on interest rates and yields in other markets. The secondary market transactions in Government Securities was only rupees two or three thousand crores in 1994, when it was first allowed on NSE and SGL of RBI. The turnover in August 1999 was around Rs. 50,000 crores, of which nearly 90% ways in Central Government Securities in 1999. Turnover in Govt. Securities (outright) was about Rs. 12 lakh crores in 2004-05. Repo market has also developed very fast, with only one to two thousand crores of Rupees of turnover in 1994, when it was just initiated to around Rs. 5,000 crores in August 1999 of which more than 90% was on account of Central Government Securities. Turnover in govt. securities (Repos) was about Rs. 27 lakh crores which is 2½ times that in out right deals.

Turnover data in the forex market are also published by the RBI. These data include all spot, and forward deals alongwith forward cancellations as between foreign currencies *vis-a-vis* Indian rupees and foreign currencies *vis-a-vis* other foreign currencies. The trading can be both on account of merchant transactions and on account of inter-bank transactions. The daily transactions were in the range of U.S. 2 billion dollars in the inter-bank transactions and U.S. 700 to 800 million dollars of merchant transactions in 1999. This turnover rose to about $ 239 billion in June 2005 for interbank deals and $ 93 billions for merchant bank transactions. It will be seen that inter-bank deals are about three times higher than the merchant transactions. Besides, swaps predominate in inter-bank deals and spot deals in merchant transactions. The RBI can be both a net purchaser or seller of U.S. dollars and the volumes can vary from a few hundred million U.S dollars to a few thousand millions U.S. dollars per month in any year. These developments in markets have been conducive to treasury operations of banks to a fuller extent than at present. But very few banks take advantage of them due to fear of risk, lack of expertise and conservatism.

Needed Statutory Changes

The old Public Debt Act of 1944 regulating the issue of public debt of the Government and concerning the Government securities market was repealed. The Government Securities Bill was already approved by the Government and is passed by the Parliament in 1999. As the Act refers to the State Government debt as well, the proposed bill require the consent of all the State Governments. The new Act is more suitable to computerised dealings of banks and to hold securities in a Demat form which will increase the volumes of trading in the government securities market.

The Securities Contracts Regulation Act was also amended to give RBI, the jurisdiction over the debt markets which would help develop the debt segment of the government — Central and state securities. The Amendment Act would pave the way for a more active repos market.

The Indian Stamp Act 1899 was amended to exempt from stamp duty the transfer of securities in a Dematerialisied form, involving the transfer of beneficial ownership of debentures and securities. But there are other amendments which are yet to be completed, namely the removal of stamp duty on transfer of P.S.U bonds and debentures traded on a demat form, and on those subject to English mortgage and those convertible debentures in the secondary market and the securitised debt instruments. The secondary market in many money market instruments could not be developed due to the continuance of the stamp duty.

RBI on Risk Management

RBI stated that each bank should develop its own risk management policy as part of its treasury operations. There can be no uniform risk management system applicable to all banks. The RBI guidelines have laid down the following major norms to be adopted by each bank.

(1) The activities of the Asset Liability Management Committee and the Credit Policy Committee need to be integrated.

(2) The banks should evaluate the portfolio quality on a continuing basis rather than at the balance sheet finalisation time.

(3) Both investment and loan proposals should be subject to the same rigorous scrutiny.

(4) Risk evaluation criteria should be laid down and continuously reviewed. The total risk exposure rather than credit exposure should be looked into.

(5) Both balance sheet items and off balance sheet items, contingencies guarantees, etc should be subject to scrutiny and appraisal.

(6) Banks should manage liquidity risk by observing prudential norms and putting limits on inter-bank borrowings, swaps, etc.

(7) Banks should plan to have definite time frame for moving over to Value at Risk (VaR) and duration approaches for measurement of interest rate risk.

(8) Banks should adopt international standards for providing explicit capital cushion for the market risk and prepare contingency plans for meeting any crisis scenarios.

(9) Operational Risk particularly for operations at international level have to be provided for.

(10) Credit Risk to be controlled by stricter appraisal for which banks are asked to constitute Credit Policy Committee and Credit Risk Management Department to lay down the guidelines, enforce and monitor the compliance of Risk control parameters. The final control should be with the Board of Directors of each bank.

ALM and Treasury Function

Banks are now exposed to many types of risks due to liberalisation, privatisation and globalisation. These are exhibited in treasury operations. These risks are credit risk, market risk, interest rate risk, exchange rate risk and liquidity risk, settlement and transfer risks. Banks should reduce these risks or minimise them so as to maximise profits. The risk management system should also include proper asset liability managements. ALM function in banks is made effective from April 2000. The issues which are focussed for ALM function are :

(1) Policy Issues: information and data collection,for an analysis of all items of Balance sheet and for projection of each of the items under various scenarios including the worst scenario.

(2) Formulation of Business Strategies for maintaining liquidity and a continuing review of them.

(3) Maintenance of Trained and Skilled Manpower for ALM policy implementation, monitoring and review.

Risk Analysis and Management

(1) Gap Analysis: Interest sensitive assets and liabilities and gap between them are analysed.

(2) Duration Analysis: Average amount of time between inflows and outflows and the extent of their synchronisation are examined. The time required before the discounted value of all cash flows (principal and interest) can be recovered in respect of any asset is assessed.

(3) Value of Risk Model estimates the maximum potential loss in a position over a given holding period for a given confidence level in respect of an asset.

(4) Simulation Model: It attempts to determine bank's projected current arid future cash flows at different interest rates and market price scenarios, possible to materialise.

The success of ALM depends on the effective information system and polices and a foolproof Risk Management System. For this purpose Asset liability Managers and A.L. Committee should be put in place to minimise volatility of earnings, maintain liquidity and equity to meet all contingent changes in market conditions.

Build up of MIS

(1) *The Committee (ALCo)* should analyse all items of balance sheet and off balance sheet items, project the future inflows and outflows for which it has to build an information system and a set of policy guidelines.

(2) *Management of Risk:* It has to develop a Risk Management System to foresee the market and credit risks and prepare a contingency plan to meet such worst scenarios. It means that there should be a proper measure of risk, perpare a management system to control the risks and monitor the risks from time to time and review them on an on going process continuously.

(3) *Measuring Risk:* Guidelines for measurement of risk through volatility of earnings, maturity gaps, asset price fluctuations, duration and interest rate elasticity of its assets and liabilities.

Methods of Analysis are already referred.

The following is ALM Structure, desirable to be set up in each bank :

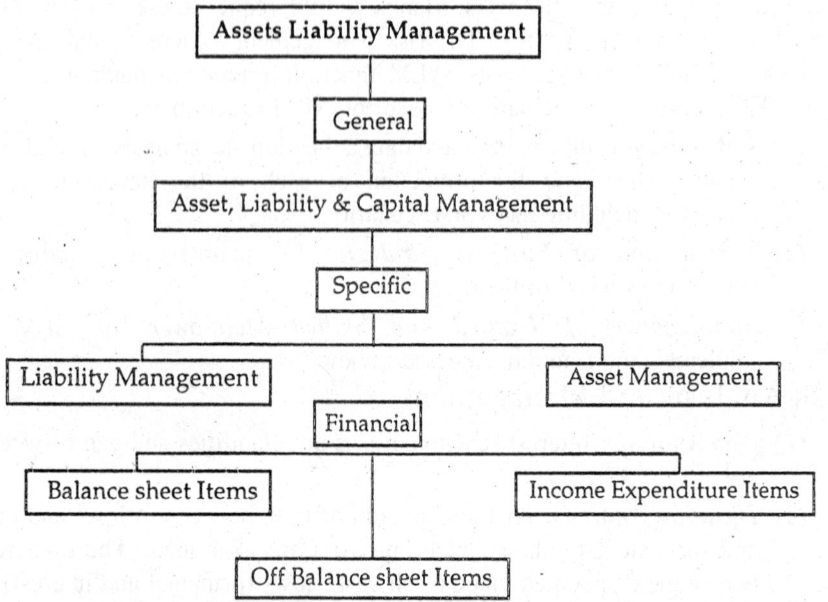

Sweep of Treasury Function

Treasury operations encompass a wide variety of services by the banks. Most of these deal with the financial markets and with other banks and financial institutions, both inside and outside the country. Treasury deals with both cash and funds management which have all-purvading interlinkages with all depts of the organisation. Cost minimisation and profit maximisation are the goals in all its operations; both physical and financial operations are connected with these objectives and hence they interact with the treasury and treasury operations impact on other activities of banks.

Treasury function involves operations in money market, Government securities market, corporate debt and P.S.U. debt or bonds, mutual funds and their schemes, as also in the forex market. With the globalised environment the access to foreign markets through GDRs/ADRs/FCN (Foreign Currency Notes) etc. is made easy. Foreign portfolio investment and foreign direct investment are now freer than before. Mutual Funds are now allowed to invest in foreign markets. The treasury operations have thus become more competitive and complex and have to be at the international standards.

The accounting and disclosure standards are now expected to be internationally (GAP) accepted and enforced by the Listing Agreement by the Stock Exchanges and by SEBI. The latest guidelines of SEBI impose a code of Corporate Governance on listed companies involving them in better investor protection, higher standards of disclosure, social and ethical obligations to the public investors and to the consumers etc.

Measure of Impact of Treasury Operations

The impact of treasury operations is difficult to measure, as it purvades a gamut of operations. The sweep of treasury operations being wide encompassing all divisions, and physical and financial operations, the impact of the treasury cannot be pinpointed.

The operations in financial markets give rise to trading profits and capital gains or losses. The corporate unit will gain through addition to non-operational income under the caption of "other income." In the case of banks, it is non-interest income. The impact of the treasury can thus be felt in the changes in other income.

The treasury operations in cash and funds management result in lowering the cost of capital and thus the overall costs of production or cost of servicing. This would ultimately lead to rise in profit margin of banks. The impact of treasury operations may be thus felt in the profit spread or profit margin and ultimately on profits.

The treasury operations can lead to better planing, budgeting and control in the operations of all departments. The financial discipline and treasury control may thus be felt in the quality of service, timeliness and in efficiency of service. The treasury function is a top level management function impinging on overall efficiency and quality of service. The impact of this treasury control on various departments should thus be reflected in the average and marginal cost of manufacture or in quality of service or after sales service or better customer service. This impact is seen in the case of banks in introduction of high-tech banking and better service and quicker transmission of funds, and better cash management.

Objectives of Treasury Operations

The overall objective of treasury operations in any company or organisation is to raise the shareholders' wealth. This is reflected in the rise in stock price of the company through rise in the earnings per share, or rise in its net worth or book value. Broadly, treasury operations should result in addition to profits or income of the company through (i) net capital gains (capital gains minus capital losses) (ii) additional non-operational income (iii) lower cost of capital leading to larger profits (iv) higher trading profits net of losses if any and (v) better efficiency in operations in cash management and in funds management leading to larger profitability.

Some of the above factors lead to larger operational profits and income while (i) (ii) and (iv) result in large "non-operational income." Since operational profits due to treasury management gets mixed up with other operational profits it is better that we concentrate on the non-operational income of the unit.

For purposes of study, let us take the case of all scheduled commercial banks whose data are available in RBI's Report on Trend and Progress of Banking in India. The "other income" of all scheduled commercial banks as a proportion of their total assets did not rise, as can be expected, as their treasury operations are not adding value to the banks' profitability. The cost of capital measure of efficiency as seen from the spread between average interest return and average interest cost (spread in net interest income) has to show improvement.

Nearly 15 out of 20 old private sector banks have reached a ratio of above 10% in respect of Capital to Risk weighted Assets (CRAR). 7 out of 9 new private sector banks and 30 out of 31 foreign banks have reached the level of above 10% of CRAR as on 2004-05. For all private sector banks (old) the gross NPA to total advances ratio was only 4.44% in 2005. This is lower compared to all the scheduled banks ratio and industry ratio of 5.2%. Similar rate for public sector banks was also higher at 5.53% in 2004-05.

Profitability and Spread

The spread between average interest income and average income cost represents the net profit and profitability of banks. The non-interest income or "other income" represents the result of Treasury operations of investment and trading in the financial markets, among others.

The table below shows the major indicators of scheduled commercial banks, in their banking and Treasury operations. Such an analysis of financial rations for each bank at micro level is necessary for assessing the impact of Treasury operations. The impact of A.L. management of treasury is seen from the liquidity position of the bank, but is measurable only through the profit margin or profitability.

Table 19.1 (on major Indicators) in percent
(All Scheduled Commercial Banks)

		2003-04	2004-05
(1)	Capital adequacy ratio	12.90	12.80
(2)	Net interest income (spread) as % of total assets	2.88	2.93
(3)	Interest income as % of Total assets	7.31	6.73
(4)	Interest expended is % of Total assets	4.44	3.81
(5)	Operating profit as % of Total assets	2.20	2.24
(6)	Net profit as % of Total assets	1.13	0.91
(7)	Gross NPA to Total assets	3.30	2.50
(8)	Net NPA to Total Assets	1.20	0.90
(9)	Gross NPA to Gross Advances	7.20	5.20
(10)	Net NPA to Net Advances	2.90	2.00
(11)	Return on Equity	19.80	13.80
(12)	Non-Interest Income as % of Total Assets (includes Trading and Forex income)	2.00	1.50

Source: Trend and progress of Banking in India RBI. Report 2004-05.

Table 19.2
Indicators of Treasury Impact

(Bank Group Wise)

	Category of Bank	As Percentage of Total Assets			
		2003-04		2004-05	
		Other Income	Interest spread	Other income	Interest spread
(1)	Scheduled Commercial banks	1.48	2.84	1.48	2.93
(2)	Public sector banks	1.39	2.92	1.38	3.04
(3)	Nationalised banks	1.86	3.06	1.30	3.02
(4)	SBI group	1.99	2.83	1.51	3.06
(5)	Old private sector banks	2.02	2.60	0.94	2.74
(6)	New private sector banks	2.10	2.03	1.74	2.17
(7)	Foreign Banks	2.85	3.59	2.51	3.33

Source: Trend and Progress of Banking in India — RBI Report 2004-05.

It will be seen from the above Tables that the impact of Treasury on banks is less significant than that of other banking operations. Broadly interest spread is better in 2004-05 than in the preceding year, but the Trading and Forex operations are less important in 2004-05 than in the preceding year. Net profitability is lower, despite on improved spread between interest income and interest expended. This was mainly due to larger provisions for NPAs and contingencies, to keep up to the guidelines of RBI for better Risk Management by banks. In sum, there is potentiality for larger and qualitatively better Treasury operations in banks, which they have to fully exploit in future.

As seen by the data on the "Other income" as percentage of total assets, the highest proportion is in the case of foreign banks followed by the new private sector banks, old private sector banks, SBI and lastly the nationalised banks in that order. As judged in the second criteria of interest rate spread between return and cost of capital, the spread is the highest in the case of foreign banks, followed by SBI group, and then the nationalised banks, old private sector banks and lastly the new private sector banks. The conclusion is obvious that in the matter of treasury operations, the foreign banks operating in India are the most active component of the market and the impact of treasury operations on them is easily seen in the data presented. In the matter of treasury operations, SBI and its associates are also important operators in the markets next only to foreign banks. These two conclusions were generally supported by other data and from the actual operations in the markets. The new private sector banks barring the ICICI bank and HDFC bank, the others are yet to make a mark in their volume of operations and their impact on the financial results of the respective banks.

The above results, are no doubt in consonance with the general impression in the markets but are to be taken with caution as we have to examine the bankwise data and study their impact at micro level to arrive at any worthwhile conclusions. As we have not examined the micro data of individual banks, the study is only indicative and serves as an example only. It is for the analysts to take indepth study of the bankwise impact of treasury operations on their profits, profitability and their contribution to the net share holders' wealth.

SHAREHOLDER WEALTH

One way the impact of Treasury operations can be felt on the company is through the change in the shareholder wealth. It will be seen that one of the factors contributing to the share price of a banking company or any other company is the efficacy of treasury operations. The information on the company's operations which should be revealed to the investors should also include the Treasury operations. In order to encourage the efficient allocation of funds by financial markets, the ability to disseminate the timely information on listed stocks and the operations of the respective companies is essential for investors to make proper investment decisions. Such information should not only be on the audited balance sheet, income expenditure accounts, but on credit ratings, physical and financial operations and treasury operations.

Both public and private sector banks are now listed on the stock exchanges as they are freed from most controls and free to access the markets for capital. Till March end 1999 eight public sector banks and 9 new private sector banks have either issued capital to the public or got listed on the stock exchanges. As at end March 2005, there are 32 scheduled commercial banks listed on the major stock exchanges for regular trading.

Listed Bank Stock

The banking stocks performed well in the stock market during the period 2003 to 2006, mainly due to encouraging fundamentals of the economy and better financial performance of the listed banks. Seven banks raised Rs. 7,444 crores from the equity market in 2004-05, as against only Rs. 1,104 crores, in 2003-04. The banking sector raised by public issues Rs. 1,478 crores in 2004-05, as against Rs. 1,352 crores in 2003-04. Larger amounts were raised through private placement — namely Rs. 10,552 crores in 2004-05, as against Rs. 6,623 crores in 2003-04.

Banking sector stocks, as represented by the Index "Bankex" on the BSE, outperformed the BSE sensex and BSE 500, and over many other sectoral indices like FMCG and PSU sectors. The following table presents the picture of the Return on Banking stocks during the past three years, 2002-03 — 2004-05.

Table (Returns)

Year	BSE Sensex	BSE 500	BSE Bankex
2003-03	–12.1	–8.0	16.2
2003-04	83.4	109.4	118.6
2004-05	16.1	21.9	28.6

Source : RBI Annual Report 2004-05.

This trend of improved returns of bank stock, continued during 2005-06 and in 2006-07, mainly due to sector specific developments. The banking sector reforms led to some improvements in Balance Sheets of banks, in addition to other factors like implementation of the Securitisation and Reconstruction of financial assets and Enforcement of security interest act, permission to foreign banks to acquire upto 75% of the weaker private sector banks and lifting of the 10% voting rights cap in private sector banks and amendment to the law to enable banking companies to issue preference shares as Tier III capital for the purposes of Capital Adequacy norms. Overall improvement of banking performance was another factor boosting the demand for bank stocks.

The table below presents in Risk Return Scenario of bank stocks listed on the stock exchange. Risk is measured by volatility, defined as coefficient of variation and Return by the rise in prices represented by the Bankex Indices on point to point basis.

Table 19.3

	Returns		Volatility	
	2003-04	2004-05	2003-04	2004-05
Bankex	+118.6	+28.6	24.0	17.1
BSE sensèx	+83.4	+16.1	23.0	11.2

Source : RBI Annual Report 2004-05.

It will be seen from the table that bank stocks had higher returns than the market returns, although their volatility is also more than the market coverage.

The relative performance of listed bank stocks are given below for illustration.

Table 19.4

	Name of the Bank	Average Daily Closing Price		P/E Ratio End March	
		2003-04	2004-05	2003-04	2004-05
	(Public Sector Banks)				
(1)	Bank of Baroda	162.1	191.1 (+ 18%)	7.4	9.5
(2)	SBI	455.9	542.5 (19%)	8.7	8.0
	(Private Sector Banks)				
(3)	ICICI Bank	212.0	309.7 (+46%)	11.1	14.4
(4)	Vysya Bank	131.7	129.3 (-2.0%)	18.3	–36.7

Note : Percentage charge over the previous year in brackets. Almost all listed public sector banks have performed better in 2004-05, but among private sector banks, out of 18 listed, some 4 banks performed worse, of which one is Vysya Bank. In all the banks which performed better, Treasury operations were in full swing or atleast reasonably well to improve shareholder wealth.

Case Study on SBI

SBI is the largest commercial bank, listed on major stock exchanges. The case study on this bank aims at identifying and highlighting its Treasury operations. Segmentwise audited Balance Sheet data for the year 2005-06 are set out below, to show to relative importance of Treasury versus Banking operations.

Table 19.5
Segment wise Revenue & Results

(Rs. Crore)

Particulars	Year ended 31-3-2006
Segments Revenue	
Banking operations	Rs. 35,266 crores (67%)
Treasury operations	Rs. 17,437 crores (33%)
Total	52,703 (100%)
Segments Results (Profit Before Tax)	
Banking operations	6,042 (149%)
Treasury operation	−1991 (−49%)
Total	4,051 (100%)
Profit unallocated to any segment	1,918
Profits Before Tax	5,499
Less: Income Tax and FBT	−2,499
Net	13,470
Extraordinary profits	936
Net Profits	4,406

Source: Audited Balance Sheet Data.

It will be seen from the above table that treasury revenue reflecting the relative importance of Treasury operations accounted for ⅓rd of total revenue. But they showed a negative profits of 49%. But presumably due to extra-ordinary profits from Investments, this loss on account of Treasury was made good. Net profits on percentage of total assets stood at 0.94 and gross profits stood at 2.39% of total assets during 2004-05 and at 1.2% in 2005-06. Operating profit to working funds was also good at 2.6% in 2004-05.

Table 19.6
Treasury Indicators of SBI (for 2004-05)

(Rs. in crores)

	Particulars	Quarter ended 31-6-2006	Year ended 30-3-2006
(1)	Capital Adequacy Ratio	11.97%	11.88%
(2)	Gross profit as % of Total income	26.75%	26.16%
(3)	Non-interest income as % of Total income	45.16%	54.94%
(4)	Interest extended as % of Total income	46.72	46.68
(5)	Interest income as % of Total income	54.84	45.06
(6)	Spread between Interest income and Interest expense	8.12	−1.62
(7)	Earnings per equity share	60.68 (Annualised)	83.73
(8)	Equity & Reserve (Networth)	27,644	27,644
(9)	Book value per share in Rs.	525	525
(10)	Return on assets (ROA)	0.64	0.89
(11)	Amount of Net non-performing assets	4,432	4,906

(12)	Gross NPA as % of total assets		—	271 (2004-05)
(13)	Net interest income margin		—	3.03 (2004-05)
(14)	Profitability (operating profit 18 working funds)		—	2.61 (2004-05)
(15)	Non-interest revenue as % working funds			1.69 (2004-05)

Source : Balance sheet of SBI and Trend and Progress of Banking RBI Report 2004-05.

SBI's Treasury operations are significant, as reflected by Non-interest income to total income. Its market price was around Rs. 800/- in june 2006. It is 1½ times the Book Value, which indicates its potential to rise in M.P. Its M.P is also having a low multiple of 13 times to its EPs (Rs. 61). This case study throws light on trading operations and market price evaluation of investment decision.

Conclusions

The impact of Treasury operations are not directly measurable, as they are an integral part of overall financing and investment operations. The magnitude of Treasury operations depends on the structure and institutional developments and the width and depth of the markets. The available risk reduction techniques and opportunities for hedge also determine the extent of Treasury operations.

In India, the needed structural changes are being developed and the Regulatory framework for proper functioning of the markets for risk reduction and for derivatives is working. The depth and market turnover are also increasing.

The first impact of Treasury operations is on the asset liquidity management and the degree of solvency and liquidity of the company. Secondly the cost of financing and sources and uses of funds are such that returns are maximised for a given level of risk or costs. Thirdly the spread between the average return and average costs is optimised and profitability of company or bank is maximised. This is dependent on the overall efficiency of banking and Treasury operations, which has to be analysed by segmental approach to their operations. Lastly the Treasury operations aim at maximisation of shareholder's wealth which is achieved by improving the efficiency and profitability through cost reduction, increase in income from other than banking services, namely investment management and Trading operations. Treasury should also help in A-2 management of the company.

❑ ❑ ❑

PART – IV

ENVIRONMENT IN TREASURY MANAGEMENT

20 TAX MANAGEMENT AND PLANNING

Introduction

Companies aim at maximisation of profit net of taxes. It is therefore necessary to plan the operations in a way that the tax liabilities are the lowest. The earnings per share (EPS) is what the shareholders look into and it is calculated by dividing the net profits after tax by the number of shares outstanding. The performance of the company is judged by its share price, which in turn depends on the EPS. Besides, dividends and retained earnings are dependent on the net profits after tax (NPAT). These flows of dividends and retained earnings are what the investors look into in a company, and these flows in the future are discounted to the present, to arrive at the Net Present Value (NPV) of these future earnings. The NPAT adds to the reserves and networth of the company which again determines the book value (Networth divided by number of outstanding equity shares). Book value is also a measure of company's performance, influencing the share price.

From the point of view of funds management, the net cash flows include net profits after taxes (NPAT) but including depreciation as depreciation is retained in the company. It is thus important for both investors and the company to maximise the NPAT including depreciation. There are various opportunities for tax planning and to reduce the incidence of taxation. Among the qualitative aspects of Management which the investors look into are the following:

(i) Tax Planning (ii) expansion and diversification (iii) consistent financial policy of dividend distribution and (iv) honesty, integrity and dependability of the management team. Tax planning helps in expansion and diversification through larger profits after tax.

Of the above qualitative factors, the incidence of taxation (tax planning and expansion) will depend on how the profits are used (for expansion and diversification or dividend distribution). A company is entitled to specified tax concessions for some investments, expansion and acquisition of plant and machinery, tax holiday for ventures into specified industries or for backward districts, export income etc., which the company should take advantage of.

Corporate Taxation

Corporate taxation has been simplified over the last few years. As the law stands now, there is only one rate of tax of 30% for all domestic companies, whether widely held or not and whether they are trading or manufacturing companies. From April 1999, there was a surcharge of 10% and education cess at 2% on corporate tax rate which takes it to about 34% in the case of India. The Asia Pacific Region had witnessed a lower average tax rate of 32.1% and the OECD countries a rate of 34.1%. There were tax cuts in France, Germany and other E.U countries and in U.K. Finland, India and Pakistan witnessed an increase in corporate tax rates. Foreign companies however pay at a higher rate of 40% plus a surcharge of 2.5% on the net income. There was however a Minimum Alternate Tax (MAT) imposed on book profits at 12% on companies which are not paying any tax at present which stands at 7.5% in 2005-06. The MAT was liberalised and surcharge to corporate tax was reduced. Income from Royalties of Patents etc. from abroad is taxed in India at 40%. Foreign companies pay at a rate of 40% domestic companies pay at 30%.

Besides, there are tax incentives for infrastructure building, industrialisation and export. The Finance Act 1995-96 provided for 100% deduction from profits and gains of an enterprise carrying on the business of development maintenance and operation of infrastructure facility for initial five assessment years and thereafter 30% of such profits and gains, is tax exempt.

There is also a concession of deduction of 30% of profits for a period of 10 years to the small-scale industrial undertakings, if such an undertaking begins to manufacture or produce articles or things during the period beginning from 1st April 1995 and ending on 31st March 2000 AD. Besides, small-scale undertakings, commencing production in an industrially backward state after 31st March, 1998 or an industrially backward district after 31st March, 1999 were entitled to these deductions, if they commenced production before 31st March, 2000 AD.

Need for Tax Planning

The company has to pay many taxes both direct and indirect taxes and there are some areas where incentives are given to the company to grow and expand by additional investments. The companies have to pay income tax, wealth tax, surcharge on income tax, capital gains tax, gift tax etc., in addition to excise, customs and sales taxes. Earnings used for provision of depreciation obsolescence etc. are given rebate. Net profits after all such provisions are taxed. The company has to carefully examine the areas where the tax liability can be reduced and tax incentives for development rebates and admissible expenses are to be taken advantage of. For example, interest paid on debt is an expense item and not taxable, while dividends are taxable. Deduction of inter-corporate dividends, under Section 80M of I.T. Act will reduce the taxable income of the company if those dividends are distributed to shareholders.

The areas of tax planning are briefly set out here. Among others, these include place of location (for backward area concessions), the capital structure decision (interest on debt is not taxable as it is an expense item), expansion into export business (export profits enjoy some tax rebates in many cases), diversification into areas with tax benefits like infrastructure, hotels, roads, bridges, electricity, shipping etc., take over of sick units or loss making units to show lower profits in total. There are a number of methods of expansion, diversification, mergers, take overs, which will help the reduction of tax liability. Entry into infrastructure industries, power generation and distribution etc. will entitle the company for tax benefits.

In corporate taxation, there are some allowed expenses and some partially disallowed expenses depending on the nature of the business. Some partially allowed expenses are advertisement expenses, entertainment expenses, business promotion travel, bonus and commissions paid to employees' perquisites and employer's contribution of P.F. and other funds, salaries and benefits to directors, depreciation and amortisation of patents and copyrights. Besides, depreciations are also permitted for tax rebate to encourage growth and investment. The erstwhile investment allowance which is now withdrawn was permitted once upto 25% of plant and machinery imported and 35% for indigenous plant. This amount is exempted over and above the depreciation allowance permitted. These rates vary from time to time and eligible methods are also subject to change. Inter-corporate dividends as referred to earlier, are exempt, if these are used to distribute to shareholders, under Section 80M of I.T. Act. Capital expenditure incentive is in the form of allowances for depreciation and obsolescence. A company can have many types of depreciation — plant leased out but owned by it (operational lease) normal depreciation by straight line method or written down method (depreciation for buildings, plant, machinery, furniture etc. is allowed) initial depreciation in the case of newly erected buildings (used for the residence of workers) and extra depreciation for plant and machinery which are used for more than one shift to reflect their use and life period.

Rebates and Provisions

Depreciation is now allowed on the basis of some limits on the total of all assets, for deduction from net income for corporate tax purpose. In order to encourage venture capital financing, income tax exemption is given on any income by way of dividend or long-term capital gains of a venture capital fund or venture capital company from investments made by way of equity shares in venture capital undertakings. The central government can also give exemption, reduction in rates or other modifications in rates of income tax or in regard to income in favour of any class or persons engaged *inter alia* in the business of prospecting for or extraction or production of mineral oils.

Export profits are also eligible for some exemptions or lower rates. Under Section 80 HHE of I.T. Act profits from export of software of computers are eligible to be deducted for calculation of tax rates. If the FTZ or export processing unit exports atleast 75% of the total sales during the previous year, then the facility of 5 year tax holiday will be applicable to it. The SEZs are now eligible for many exemptions from customs and excise duties in 2006.

This five year tax holiday is applicable for any enterprise which builds, maintains, operates infrastructure facilities in the area of highways, expressways, bridges, airports, ports etc., Under Section 80 I.A. of the I.T. Act, new industrial undertakings in hotels, shipping concerns, commencing operations before March 31, 1995 are entitled to a deduction of 30% of their income, in respect of corporate bodies and 25% in respect of non-corporate bodies.

The funds established by Trade Unions of Companies for the welfare of employees, such as superannuation, illness or death, education of dependent children etc., are having regular incomes which are now exempt from income tax from 1995-96 onwards. However, from 1996-97 all companies have to pay a Minimum Alternate Tax (MAT) at 12% of book profits calculated as under the Companies Act if the total income of the company as computed under the I.T. Act is less than 30% of book profits because of rebates, then the total income of the company is deemed to be 30% of the book profits. The tax rate was lowered to 10% in some cases and 7.5% in other cases.

NON-ROUTINE TRANSACTIONS

Tax Deduction at Source : (TDS)

The non-routine transactions are investments, trading deposits, contract services, and others etc. The companies and banks have to deduct tax at source for individuals and companies on the following basis in respect of these non-routine transactions.

TDS Rates

		Individuals	**Exemption limit (P.A.)**	**Companies**
1.	By way of interest (not interest on securities)	10%	Rs.2,500	20%
2.	By way of horse races, puzzles, etc.	40%	N.A.	40%
3.	Dividend income	20% exempt since 1997-78	Rs.2,500	
4.	Debentures / Bond income	20%	Rs.2,500	20%
5.	Long-term capital gains	exempt or 10%	—	exempt or 10%
6.	Interest income by banks	10% plus 2% surcharge	Rs.15,000	10% plus surcharge of 2%
7.	Income by Mutual funds (including venture capital funds)	Nil	Rs.10,000	Nil
8.	Services of contract, professionals, brokerage income etc.	5%	—	—

Tax Concession for Depreciation and Other Items

Depreciation on the total block of assets is allowed, from 1988. All the items of plant and machinery falling in a block repooled together for allowing depreciation at prescribed rates. Depreciation at permitted rates is allowed for tax deduction on the fixed assets of the company. The unabsorbed depreciation can be carried forward for 8 years in the same manner as business losses.

Entertainment allowances given to its employees upto certain limits are exempt from corporate tax, so also the amortised amount of preliminary expenses and amount spent on afforestation, research and RD expenditure on the matters relating to company products or technology, are allowed to be deducted from income for tax purposes. Some items are disallowed like reserves for capital redemption or reserve for contingencies, interest payable abroad or depletion allowance etc. Some others like depreciation, RD expenditure are allowed upto limits for deduction for tax computation. Depreciation of part ownership of assets in case of joint ownership is now allowed. The trade off of depreciation by loss making concerns is not allowed through sale and lease back of assets by leasing companies.

Tax Compliance and Management

Income Tax Act and the Finance Act govern the tax payable. The management has to plan to reduce tax liability by proper planning but at the same time it has to pay advance taxes as required under the Act within the time limits. The tax liability as estimated by the company can be contested by the Income Tax Officer, but the company has then to make provision for this extra amount although it may be appealed to the Appellate Tribunal.

Failure to make proper disclosure may invite/searches by Income Tax Officers and seizures of books of accounts. During such searches, if there is any undisclosed income, it was taxed at 60% under Section 132 - 133 of the I.T. Act.

The accounts of the companies have to be prepared on cash or mercantile basis uniformly. The business units have to follow the accounting standards, set out by the government in their guidelines for tax compliance.

With a view to avoid such searches or underpayments it is prudent for the management to pay the properly estimated amounts and observe proper tax compliance.

As in the case of income tax, so also in the case of the excise duties, sales tax, customs etc. They are to be paid as per the existing law under the guidelines of the authorities. The efficient management will plan tax reduction but at the same time scrupulously follow the rules of tax compliance. Introduction of MODVAT for capital goods and value added tax has helped simplification of indirect taxation. "VAT" has replaced the sales tax at the centre and by some state govts., as in 2006. (VAT is value added tax).

INCOME TAX ACT, 1961 AS AMENDED BY FINANCE ACT, 2005

The following provisions of IT Act help the corporates and individuals in their tax planning exercises. This is not exhaustive but presented for illustration only.

80C	Deduction in respect of life insurance premia, deferred annuity, contributions to provident fund, subscription to certain equity shares or debentures, etc. upto Rs. one lakh.
80CCA	Deduction in respect of deposits under National Savings Scheme or payment to a deferred annuity plan.
80CCB	Deduction in respect of investment made under Equity Linked Savings Scheme.
80CCC	Deduction in respect of contribution to certain pension funds.
80CCD	Deduction in respect of contribution to pension scheme of Central Government.
80CCE	Limit on deductions under Sections 80C, 80CCC and 80CCD.
80D	Deduction in respect of medical insurance premia.
80DD	Deduction in respect of maintenance including medical treatment of a dependent who is a person with disability.
80DDB	Deduction in respect of medical treatment, etc.
80E	Deduction in respect of repayment of loan taken for higher education.
80G	Deduction in respect of donations to certain funds, charitable institutions, etc.
80GG	Deductions in respect of rents paid.
80GGA	Deduction in respect of certain donations for scientific research or rural development.
80GGB	Deduction in respect of contributions given by companies to political parties.
80GGC	Deductions in respect of contributions given by any person to political parties.
80HH	Deduction in respect of profits and gains from newly established industrial undertakings or hotel business in backward areas.
80HHA	Deduction in respect of profits and gains from newly established small-scale industrial undertakings in certain areas.
BOHHB	Deduction in respect of profits and gains from projects outside India.
80HHBA	Deduction in respect of profits and gains from housing projects in certain cases.
80HHC	Deduction in respect of profits retained for export business.
80HHD	Deduction in respect of earnings in convertible foreign exchange.
80HHE	Deduction in respect of profits from export of computer software, etc.
80HHF	Deduction in respect of profits and gains from export or transfer of film software, etc.
80I	Deduction in respect of profits and gains from industrial undertakings after a certain date, etc.
80IA	Deductions in respect of profits and gains from industrial undertakings or enterprises engaged in infrastructure development, etc.
80IAB	Deductions in respect of profits and gains by an undertaking or enterprise engaged in development of Special Economic Zone
80IB	Deductions in respect of profits and gains from certain industrial undertakings other than infrastructure development undertakings.
80IC	Special provisions in respect of certain undertakings or enterprises in certain special category states.
80JJA	Deduction in respect of profits and gains from business of collecting and processing of bio-degradable waste.
80JJAA	Deduction in respect of employment of new workmen.
80L	Deductions in respect of interest on certain securities, dividends, etc.

80LA	Deduction in respect of certain incomes of Offshore Banking Units.
80O	Deduction in respect of royalties, etc., from certain foreign enterprise.
80P	Deduction in respect or income or co-operative societies.
80Q	Deduction in respect of profits and gains from the business of publication of books.
80QQA	Deduction in respect of professional income of authors of text books in Indian languages.
80QQB	Deduction in respect of royalty income, etc., of authors of certain books other than the text books.
80R	Deduction in respect of remuneration from certain foreign sources in the case of professors, teachers, etc.
80RR	Deduction in respect of professional income from foreign sources in certain cases.
80RR	Deduction in respect of remuneration received for services rendered outside India.
80RRB	Deduction in respect of royalty on Patents.

Such provisions as referred to above are examples of tax benefits available for companies and individuals which can make tax planning a method of reducing the tax liability. Section 80L and 88 were deleted and replaced by 80C which gives exemption upto Rs. one lakh for specific investments.

Brokerage Income and Business Profit

All firms dealings in securities will have to pay a tax on brokerage income at normal income tax rates. Their business profits or trading profits are subject to normal tax rates as also on short-term capital gains and speculative losses can be carried forward to be offset by only short-term speculative gains, later. The brokerage income is subject to a service tax of 5%.

Tax Treatment on Investments

Investments in approved categories, as in PF, LIC, ULIP, NSS, etc. are eligible for direct deduction for income tax purposes upto 20% of a total investment of Rs.60,000 P.A. Of this as an investment upto Rs.10,000 is separately set apart for approved equity linked mutual fund schemes with a tax rebate of direct deduction of 20%. Thus, under Sections 88 and 88A, of I.T. Act, a total investment of Rs.60,000 will enjoy a tax rebate upto 12,000 P.A. In 1996-97 this limit was raised to Rs.70,000 by inclusion of an additional Rs.10,000 for investment in new issues of projects for power, infrastructure development and other approved categories. All these exemptions are replaced by a new Section of 80C, giving exemption upto Rs. 1 lakh for approved investments.

Income Tax and Corporation Taxes

For income tax, individuals now enjoy a threshold exemption limit of Rs.40,000, in addition to standard deduction of Rs.15,000 for salaries incomes. The tax rates now range from 10 to 30% for individuals. As in 2006, standard deduction was removed and the exemption limit was kept at Rs. one lakh.

Corporate taxation is simplified with only one tax rate of 30% for domestic companies and 40% for foreign companies. Foreign companies pay a surcharge of

2.5% and an Education cess of 2% in all cases, of companies and individuals. A rate of 50% is charged for royalty incomes or technical fees, received from government or Indian concern in terms of an agreement entered into for this purpose. The earlier distinctions of trading and manufacturing companies and of closely held and widely held companies were dispensed with. There is however a surcharge of 15% on incomes above Rs.75,000 P.A. for companies, which was reduced to 7.5 % in 1996-97 and withdrawn in 1997-98 but was kept at 10% as in 2006-07. When incomes like lease rentals are received by a company, and it is operational lease, deduction for repairs, maintainance etc. are deductible. Depreciations made on such leased assets are also eligible for exemption, if they are not covered by sale and lease back agreements.

Capital Gains Taxation: For securities, capital gains will become long-term, if held for not less than 12 months; for holding securities for less than 12 months, there will be short-term capital gains, which is chargeable under normal income tax slabs. If it is long-term capital gains, the tax rate is only 10% for all. For investments other than securities like the house, gold, real estate etc., they have to be held for 36 months to be considered as long-term capital gains. FFIs and NRIs are given further tax benefits of paying only 10% on such long-term capital gains. The rate of capital gains taxation for domestic companies is reduced to 20%, which is the same rate as applicable to foreign companies from 1996-97. The long-term capital gains for securities or equities is granted exemption as in 2006.

For arriving at capital gains, of short-term nature the costs of acquisition, cost of improvements and cost of transfer are allowed to be deducted. For long-term capital gains, the indexed cost of acquisition (with base year 1981-82 = 100 and index for 1993-94 as 244, and for 1995-96 as 281 and so on), the indexed costs of transfer are allowed to be deducted. That means the cost of acquisition and improvements can be inflated by appropriate index numbers, given for each year by the government from 1981-82 as 100, onwards. Under some Sections such as 54 (7) if long-term capital gains are invested upto 3 to 7 years, in approved securities of Government, UTI and HDFC Bonds or NABARD Bonds, they are exempted from capital gains taxation. The semi-government bodies have issued completely tax exempt 10% and 10.5% bonds whose income is not taxable at all. New saving instruments in the form of bonds of infrastructure development were being introduced for this benefit of capital gains tax exemption.

Wealth Tax: All investments in productive assets live shares, debentures of companies PPF, NSS, Capital Investment Bonds, Natural Defence Bonds, Postal Deposits etc. are exempted from wealth tax. But other categories of assets like gold, jewellery, house and real estate etc. are subject to wealth tax, beyond an exemption limit of Rs.15 lakhs.

Gift Tax: The gift tax exemption, whether given in shares/debentures/or other forms/is exempt upto Rs.30,000. In case of marriage of dependents, a gift of Rs.one lakh is exempt from gift tax under the erstwhile tax provisions. It was abolished in 1998-99 budget.

Taxation of NRIs: Since the launching of economic reforms in July 1991 the rates of taxation on NRIs were reduced and the tax procedures for them were simplified. The investment income in the form of dividends and interest is now being taxed at a uniform rate of 20% whether they are individuals or institutions or corporate bodies. Besides, the NRIs would not lose their NRI status, even when they stay upto 181 days in India at present.

Taxation of Investment Business in India

1. Brokerage income — at normal rates of income tax as applicable individuals, H.U.F. or companies.
2. Jobbing / Trading gains — treated as business profits and taxed as applicable to business profits.
3. Badla interest income — taxable at normal income tax rates as applicable to different tax brackets.
4. Capital gains from securities — short-term gains are taxed at normal income tax rates and long-term capital gains at concessional rate of 10% or nil in some cases.

Interest on FDs, debentures etc. are taxed in the year in which they fall due, while dividend income is taxable in the year in which dividends are declared, whether received or not in that year.

Taxation of FFIs, in India

The income through interest and dividends is taxable at the rate of 20%. Income through long-term capital gains is taxed at 10% and on short-term capital gains at 30%. Transactions done outside India are not taxable in India.

Tax changes during 2004 to 2007

Tax changes affecting the corporates and banking sector are briefly set out below :

The corporate income tax rate was reduced to 30% from 35% in 2005-06 for domestic companies. The surcharge of 10% was levied on domestic companies in addition to the education cess of 2% on both individuals and companies. The surcharge on foreign companies was kept at 2.5% while retaining their corporate income tax rate at 40% while the rate of depreciation for general machinery and plant was reduced from 2.5% to 15%. The initial depreciation rate for new plant and machinery was raised from 15% to 20%. The withholding tax on technical services was reduced from 20% to 10%.

The Banking companies continue to pay service tax for the major services rendered to customers in the form of providing drafts, remittances etc. and the TDS on interest paid on deposits beyond Rs. 5,000 per annum, continued to apply. Besides, in 2005-06 Banking Cash Transaction tax was levied on any cash withdrawal beyond Rs. 25,000 in a day, except in the case of SB Accounts, at a rate of 0.1%.

A new Fringe Benefits tax was imposed on corporates or any employer for the benefits extended to employees at a rate of 30%. Such fringe benefits are defined to include entertainments, gifts, festival celebrations, food and beverages provided freely to employees, as also conveyances, tour and travel publicity, use of health clubs, maintenance of cars and aircraft for use of employees, use of Telephone and Scholarships to children of employees. The cost of all these facilities and the actual amount of contribution made by the employer for the approved super annuation funds, were all added up for arriving at the amount taxable at 30% as FBT.

In the case of co-operative banks, the exemption given under Section 80 P was withdrawn and their incomes are also taxable as in the case of commercial banks. This provision is applicable in the case of certain categories of Co-op. bank, only from 2006-07.

Minimum Alternative Tax (MAT)

The MAT rate was raised from 7.5% to 10% of the book profits with effect from April 1, 2007. The definition of assessable income is also changed. If the income tax payable on the total income as computed under the Income Tax Act in respect of any year relevant to the assessment year commencing from April 1, 2007, is less than 10% of the book profits, such book profits are deemed to be the total income and the tax payable for the relevant previous year shall be 10% of such book profits.

Capital Gains Tax

The long term capital gains tax on zero coupon bonds is kept at 10% of such gains, if the tax payer does not claim the benefit of indexation. The long term capital gains tax on securities as removed. The short term capital gains are taxable at normal rates of income tax.

Securities Transactions Tax (STT)

The STT was imposed in 2004 on the value of the delivery based transactions on equity shares and units of equity oriented funds at a rate of 0.015 percent. This was increased to 0.20 percent in the next year 2005. The budget for 2006-07, increased it further by 25% or by 0.05 percentage point to 0.25% to be shared equally by both the buyer and seller. In non-delivery based transactions in equity shares and units of Equity Oriented Funds (EOF), the STT rate will increase to 0.025% to be paid by seller. STT on transactions in derivatives and sale of units of EOF to the MF would be higher at 0.017% and 0.25% respectively.

Dividend Distribution Tax

As prevailing in 2006-07, the open ended equity schemes and close ended equity schemes are treated on par for exemption from Dividend Distribution Tax. The debt oriented funds and corporates paying dividends will be subject to Dividend Distribution Tax.

Case Study on Tax Planning (Reliance Industries Ltd.)

In 2006, Reliance has entered 32nd year of operations. It has paid up equity of Rs. 1393 crores and net worth of Rs.49,804 crores. It has been showing net profit every year, out of which reserves are built up. Depreciations and allocations to Capital Redemption Reserve, Investment Allowance Reserve, Debenture Redemption Reserve, Revenue Reserves, Amalgamation Reserves, Capital Reserves General Reserves, Taxation Reserves etc. were all built up.

Normally, tax savings come from unabsorbed investment allowance reserve, deductions for backward area investment benefits, export income, inter-corporate dividends and depreciation provisions. Reliance could take advantage of its investment in backward area (Patalganga and Hazira), it has export income and intercorporate dividend income and continuous expansion plans. What helped the company to secure zero tax treatment is a strategy of depreciation provisions and every year, there is unabsorbed depreciation and investment allowance reserves accumulated from previous years which are carried forward. Its exports constitute about 8% of India's total exports.

While depreciation provision can be carried forward, other benefits like those available under backward area investment or export income would lapse and cannot be carried forward. The Investment Allowance Reserve lapsed in 1990 but it had also the benefit of carry forward. The company took advantage of these also.

Depreciation provisions helped the company most. It showed one method of depreciation for investors under the Companies Act and another method is shown for income tax purposes (one is the straight line method and the other is the written down value method).

It has however paid taxes in the form of excise, customs, etc. for an amount of Rs.7,913 crores in 2005-06 and such taxes are paid every year. It contributes upto 8% of indirect tax revenue of the central government.

History

R.I.L. started operations in 1966 with a single synthetic future Mill in Naroda Gujarat, went into man made yarn in 1979, commissioned PFY project in 1982, P.S.F. project in 1986 and LAB project in 1988 all in Patalganga Maharashtra. In 1991-92 it started a petro chemical unit, for HDPE and PVC of Hazira, set up as a subsidiary and in a couple of years, it has merged with the parent company, namely, R.I.L. Lastly, it has taken over two group companies for polypropylane and polyethylene in March 1995. All these activities of expansion, forward and backward integration, diversification, modernisation have been planned in a systematic time schedule that the company has zero tax dues, in all the years. Besides, to help in its activities it has set up the separate units like Reliance Capital, Reliance Securities, Reliance Enterprises, Reliance Consultancy Services and so on down the line. Lastly, it has started its own mutual fund and it has eight subsidiaries

It is an extremely complicated and well thought out planning strategy that helped the Reliance from the tax net. Its assets have been growing faster year after year, than its profits and for tax returns, it has been showing no profits. Such is the mature and expert tax planning strategy that any company can present.

In the income tax return, unabsorbed depreciation and investment allowances were shown and the amounts of depreciation shown were so high that the company reported losses, for income tax purposes. For many years it had not made any provision for income tax in view of the unabsorbed past reliefs ; but has built some income tax reserves for contingencies. For 2005-06, it had provided for Current tax Rs. 900 crores and for FBT Rs. 30 crores and provision for Deferred tax Rs. 704 crores.

Once these past reliefs are absorbed the company will find other methods of showing no taxable income through amalgamation and mergers. If a company takes over the loss making company, which Reliance did in the case of RPPL and RPEL and Reliance Petroleum it can save in taxes. Reliance has a number of subsidiaries to play the tricks in this manner. More importantly, it has diversified into so many activities that the losses in some can be offset by the profits of the others for income tax purposes. Thus, depreciation benefits will continue to protect the company from tax clutches. If the company can show assets base growing faster than profits, the tax liability can be overcome.

Reliance was brought under the tax net through MAT. In 1998-99, for example it had gross profits before tax, interest and depreciation at Rs. 3,317 crores, but provided only for a nominal tax of Rs. 30 crores in the Balance sheet as at end March, 1999 and paid a tax on dividend of Rs. 41 crores, as per the existing tax provisions. Since then it has been providing for direct taxes also in the Balance sheet and making payments as per the Tax laws, but still observing all Tax planning techniques available. Thus, RIL is an ideal example of a law abiding listed Company still observing the Tax planning methods possible for a corporate.

Conclusions

This chapter highlights the importance of tax planning for Treasury Management. Any corporate unit, big or small, has potential to gain from proper tax planning and achieve the objectives of good. Treasury management, namely through Financing and Investment decisions. Tax planning can help in reducing the costs of capital, increase the PAT and enhance the shareholder's wealth.

❑ ❑ ❑

21 GOVERNMENT POLICIES AND INDUSTRIAL REGULATION

The Government policies are a single important environmental factor which influences the treasury operations in a bank or a corporate unit.

The state of the financial market depends to a great extent on the state of the economy, which in turn is a function of a number of economic and non-economic variables. The most important of these variables are *inter alia* the monsoon in the case of India and the government policies affecting industries. The monsoon although is important for the Indian economy due to its predominant influence on the performance of the economy with a contribution of one-third of the national income and with two-thirds of the population depending on agriculture either directly or indirectly, it is one of the fundamental factors affecting the markets referred to earlier. But equally important is the direction of the government policies in regard to the economy and industry. The operations of the Treasury manager either in the new issues market or the secondary market depend on the flows of money or savings into the market on the one hand and the flows of information on the other. The information may be on the economy, industry or the company, bulk of which emanate through the PTI tickers, newspapers, journals, etc. on the policy aspects of the government — central and state. All financial markets are influenced by government policies to a great extent.

The operations of treasury are the result of a vast number of buy and sell orders from their own demand for and supply of funds which depend on the information flow on a daily, hourly and minute by minute basis. Government policies being the most important single factor influencing the economy the markets reflect and absorb them first and prices of securities are the result of these forces.

In choosing an instrument to buy or sell a study of its features or terms is necessary. Before the choice of an alternative, the treasurer has to first select the industry and then study companies within the industry by a careful comparison of the companies within the industry with regard to their fundamentals. This is true for investment in both the new issues market and secondary market, in respect of investment management by treasury operating in the capital market. The RBI and Government Policies similarly influence operations in gilts and money market.

International factors influence all the financial markets and the forex market in particular. Now that FFIs and FIIs are allowed to operate even in government debt market, the influence of foreign flows either side influence gilts and money market. These foreign flows also depend on the government policies.

Government Regulation — Legal Basis

There are various government policies which influence the markets, the more important of them are set out in the table at the end of this chapter as having direct effect on the market (Chart I). The financial markets in which the treasury manager operates are the money market and capital market, Government bonds and forex market. In addition to these policies, the public sector policy influences the infrastructural industries, their growth, prices and distribution which account for a weight of about 28% of the total industrial output of the country and most of which are in the public sector. These industries provide the inputs to other manufacturing and mining industries which would thus influence the industrial growth in the country. The growth of infrastructural industry would thus severely affect the overall growth of the industry and hence the importance of public sector outlay and policy in this regard. Since in 1991-92, there have been many changes in this policy to improve their working efficiently and to make them autonomous and market-oriented so that they increase their productivity and output, reduce costs and increase profits. There has been privatisation of some PSUs which are profit-making and the PSU shares and PSU bonds are available for trading and investment, in the money market and stock market.

Industrial Policy

In India, the industrial policy has a legal basis in the Industries (Development and Regulation) Act, 1951. The objectives of policy enunciated when India became independent are to promote the rapid agricultural and industrial development of our country, expansion of opportunities for gainful employment, progressive reduction of social and economic disparities, removal of poverty and attainment of self-reliance. Originally, it was directed to the attainment of a socialistic pattern of society through economic growth with an egalitarian pattern of distribution. The 1956 resolution gave primacy to capital goods industries and to the role of state in development of industries. This gave rise to growth of heavy capital goods, basic industries, etc. as also rapid expansion of public sector in the economy.

The subsequent industrial policy changes in 1973, 1977, 1980 and 1991 have revolved around the development of priority industries, small-scale and cottage industries and rural industries. In 1980, in particular the policy emphasised the need for competition, foreign investment, technological upgradation and modernisation as also to exports. Since 1985, a number of policy changes were made to liberalise the economy, promote competition, productivity and reduce costs and improve quality. The accent was on opening up of the economy and the domestic markets to competitive forces abroad, liberalise imports and promote exports and help the Indian industry to stand on its own in the face of international competition. Some of the price and distribution controls, as well as licensing requirements were liberalised since 1985, with the starting of Seventh Five Year Plan.

The effect of these measures was that India could now boast of a wide base of infrastructural industries, a net work of all capital goods and basic industries and whole range of raw materials, intermediates and finished goods are now available in India. New growth centres, industrial estates, export processing zones, etc. have been in operation. All these made India one of the top ranking industrial nations and the annual average rate of growth of industry in India was around 8% in the five years 1995-2000 and around 6% during 2001 to 2005.

Some of the policy measures initiated since 1985, particularly during the Seventh Plan 1985-90 have helped India to grow industrially and to broad-base its industrial structure. The liberalised licensing policy, broad banding of licensed capacities, dispensation with licensing requirements and import control requirements in many cases and other trade controls have all helped the growth of industry. Besides, greater autonomy was given to public sector units and a memorandum of understanding was entered into with them as referred to earlier and with the process of privatisation, the financial markets have grown faster than before.

The year 1991-92 saw far reaching changes in the economic and financial policies. These reforms encompass the industrial policy, foreign exchange and trade policy, fiscal policy, MRTP and PSU policy, etc. They aimed at deregulating the industrial sector and liberalising foreign investments and technology imports. The reforms in major areas are set out below :

Industrial Licensing

As per the Industrial policy announced in 1991. Industrial licensing was abolished in July 1991 for all industries except a list of 18 industries specified for compulsory licensing. Barring the eight industry groups like arms, atomic energy, coal, mineral oils, mining, minerals, railways, etc. which are reserved for public sector, all the rest are thrown open to private sector. Even electricity, steel, etc., which are infrastructural industries have been kept open to private sector.

Industries reserved for the small-scale sector, continue to be reserved. The existing system of registration schemes, DGTD registration, exempted industries registration etc. are all abolished. Entrepreneurs have only to file an information memorandum on new projects and substantial expansion. The convertibility clause imposed by financial institutions on borrowing companies has been withdrawn except when interest and repayment instalments are in arrears.

Policies for PSUs

Though some reservation for public sector is being retained, a gradual opening of the areas to private sector and privatisation of some PSUs is being followed. The sick PSUs like the private sector units are referred to BIFR for necessary action. The government has aimed at professionalising the PSU management and improve their accountability and profitability by giving them greater autonomy. Many PSUs are thrown open to private sector participation and their shares are sold to mutual funds and FIs and to the public. A memorandum of understanding was entered into with many PSUs by the government to make them accountable and to improve efficiency and profitability. BIFR was later replaced by competition commission and sick PSU were either merged or allowed to private parties.

Foreign Investment

A special empowered board comprising the top government secretaries (Foreign Investment Promotion Board) would negotiate for attracting foreign investment into India through large multinationals. This Board is now in the industry ministry. Besides, a Foreign Investment Promotion Council is set up to do mainly promotional work in this field. The government has assured automatic direct investment approval upto 51% of the total equity in Indian companies by foreigners in selected industry groups. Automatic clearance for some cases are granted by the RBI itself while others are to be sent to the Ministry of Finance also. Besides, automatic clearance for foreign investment in specified industries and for capital goods imports if the foreign exchange is available through collaborators is also granted. Besides, the government made it clear that import of foreign technology is freely allowed in specified industries if the outgo is covered by export earnings. Besides, no permission is required for employment of foreign technicians or foreign testing of indigenously developed technologies. A list of industries with 34 categories in it is provided automatic approval of foreign technology agreements by the government. Foreign borrowing by Indian Companies through GDR, FCCB, Euro Bonds or notes also require government and RBI approval and subject to some limits on amounts, maturity and rates. After 1999, single window clearance was provided for many categories of FDI. A Foreign Investment Implementation Authority was set to further facilitate foreign inflows.

There was a sharp rise in foreign direct investment in more recent years. The data on direct and portfolio investments in recent years are set out in the following table. The fall in portfolio investment in 1998-99 was due to net outflows taken away by FIIs and less amount raised through GDRs by Indian corporates.

Table 21.1 : FII Investments in India

(in $ Million)

Years	Direct Inv.	Portfolio Inv.	Total Inv.
1995-96	2,133	2,214	4,347
1998-99	2,462	–61	2,401
2001-02	6,130	2,021	8,151
2004-05	5,653	9,313	14,966

Source : RBI Bulletins.

MRTP Control

The MRTP Act was amended to delete the provisions relating to the threshold limits of assets for MRTP companies. All restrictions on their expansion, acquisition and mergers etc. have gone. They are also freed for any need for government approval for establishment of new undertakings, expansion, mergers, etc. The MRTP commission will initiate investigations *suo motto* or on complaints received from individual consumers only in regard to restrictive and unfair trade practices. Thus, the concept of MRTP companies and dominant undertakings has gone and government controls on their activities have disappeared. But emphasis is now placed on controlling and regulating their restrictive and unfair trade practices, and anti-consumer policies and practices. Following the agreements with WTO, all restrictive trade practices were dropped and a competition law was passed.

Nature of Control

The nature of control on industrial enterprise extends from the conception of the project to the point of winding up of the enterprise. Some of these controls like a letter of intent, MRTP restrictions depending upon the size of the assets, etc. were dispensed with more recently. The DGTD registration and other bureaucratic controls were also dropped. The Capital Issues Control Act was repealed and issues of capitals to public are freed from prior permission with regard to terms and pricing of issues. But the other controls still continue. The CIC guidelines were replaced by the SEBI guidelines and control through industrial licensing is replaced by a system of reporting and submission of statements of information.

From the genesis of the project upto the process of implementation of the idea, the project has to be vetted by the merchant banking activity. This involves the project preparation, liaison with the government agencies, financial institutions, Registrar of Companies, stock exchange, co-managers, brokers, underwriters, registrars to the issue, bankers, etc. All these are part of the new issues activity and marketing of new issues. Inter-corporate funds market, commercial bills, bills discounting and other operations of similar nature depend on the performance of the companies. The finance manager is involved in many of these activities.

The nature of the control by the government has continued to be wide-ranging but more recently some discretionary controls of bureaucracy like granting of industrial licences, import licences in some cases and pricing of shares and permission to raise funds from the public etc. are dispensed with. Even so, the control mechanism exists in some form or other, on corporates and more so on banks which the treasury managers have to be familiar.

Major Policies

Other policies which affect the stock and capital markets either directly or indirectly are the following : Of these, banks are in particular directly affected by the monetary and credit policy.

1. Fiscal or budgetary policy.
2. Monetary and credit policy.
3. Trade policy.
4. FERA policy, (now FEMA policy)

(1) Fiscal Policy: Fiscal policy influences the government securities market mainly and other markets to a lesser degree. Fiscal policy refers to the government income and expenditure, tax and non-tax revenue, resource raising methods, borrowing and spending pattern of the government, pattern of financing of its expenditure and investment outlays, the budget deficit and projected creation of currency etc. The fiscal policy is reflected in the government's annual budget presented once in a year which also contains changes in tax rates and other non-tax measures. All these influence the demand for goods and services, the disposable incomes of the public and profitability and performance of the corporate sector. These in turn influence the industries and the expectations regarding corporate performance and the demand and supply for shares and securities in the market. Government budget is an indication of the government outlays, fiscal deficit excise and direct taxes on the corporate sector, import and export trade policy, etc. all of which have a bearing on the performance of corporate sector and savings and investment in the economy and money supply and credit cost and availability. Government debt policy and its management which influences all financial markets are reflected in the fiscal policy.

(2) Monetary and Credit Policy: Monetary policy refers to the cost and availability of money and credit, expansion and contraction of money supply and the interest rates on various types of money or credit. Money Market, in particular, and all other financial markets in general, are influenced by cost and availability of funds. Monetary and Credit Policy of the RBI tries to influence the cost and availability of funds with the banks and the financial system. The budget deficit and government outlays influence the money supply in the economy. The RBI pursues the monetary policy which is consistent with the requirements and performance of the economy. The requirements of money for expansion and monetisation in the economy and for the government for its outlays and to meet its budgetary gap and of the industry and public in general, are to be met by the RBI through its monetary policy. The interest rates and cost of credit are also determined by the monetary policy. The credit policy is an adjunct of the monetary policy dealing with the control on the supply of credit; creation of credit and interest rates on various types of lending are all part of the credit policy which is also formulated and implemented by the RBI. These influence the markets through flow of money into the markets, cost of financing, cost and availability of credit to companies affecting their profitability etc. The larger the credit creation and larger the money supply, the larger is the demand for securities and better is the market position. The RBI Policies stipulate credit disposition, liquidity requirements through CRR and SLR, priority lending, valuation of investments, capital adequacy and income recognition norms for banks to follow.

(3) Trade Policy: Trade policy refers to the licensing of imports and exports, control on the quantum of foreign trade, the duties on various types of exports and imports etc. These in turn influence the cost and availability of capital goods, intermediates and raw materials which are necessary for industrial growth and expansion of output both for domestic use and exports. The easy and quick availability of imports and the cost of imports particularly of raw materials and intermediates for domestic industries and for exports are important to be known in advance for an assessment of the performance of the company. These are announced by the government in its trade policy before the beginning of the financial year in April. The constraints on the foreign exchange availability and balance of payments position may necessitate the control on the imports or the shortage of domestic supplies may affect exports. The foreign trade of the country has an important bearing on the industrial performance and corporate profitability. The stock market and share prices are therefore dependent to a large extent on the trade policy, duties imposed and ease or difficulty with which imports can be secured or exports can be made and the relative costs of imports and exports. Thus, trade policy as announced in April every year and any changes made during the year have a bearing on the financial markets and prices of financial instruments and in particular on the Forex market.

(4) FERA Policy: The Foreign Exchange Regulation Act provides for control on foreign investment in India and Indian investment abroad, foreign technical inflows and other outflows of funds, employment of foreign nationals in India and of Indian nationals abroad. The controls are tightened or eased depending on the balance of payments position of the country. Since 1992, many of these restrictions have been relaxed and rupee has been made partly convertible upto 60% of export earnings. Earlier rupee has been devalued by about 20% in July 1991. Foreign investment in Indian equity was permitted easily upto 51% of the total paid up capital of a company at present as against 40% before. In the case of some industries this foreign investment can go upto 76% and even 100% as for example in the case of sick units, export oriented units, etc. The foreign multinationals and NRIs, overseas corporate bodies have been now permitted to invest more freely in India and foreign technology is also more liberally welcome in specified priority sector industries. Foreign equity for import of capital goods and in projects with export orientation which can earn enough export earnings to pay for dividends and royalty abroad are freely allowed. The bureaucratic controls and red tapism have also been reduced. The NRIs are also given special tax incentives to invest in India. The FERA was replaced by FEMA in 1999 with emphasis on development rather than controls.

Trade policy together with foreign exchange policy influence all the financial markets and forex market in particular. The Rupee was made fully convertible on Trade Account in March 1993 and fully convertible on Current Account in March 1994, whereby the Forex Market has become a free market to a large extent. The permission granted to FFIs and Foreign security firms to operate in Indian capital market has opened up floodgates for free inflow and outflows of funds to a larger extent than before. The investments of FIIs registered with SEBI from November 1992 when they were first allowed to operate in India were already referred to. There was also net inflow every month and their contribution to portfolio investment in the capital market was significant. Convertible rupee with larger flows of funds across borders has made the forex market a highly volatile market leading to larger risks and better returns but require a high degree of expertise for the treasury manager.

NRI's Facilities for Investment

The facilities available for non-resident Indians and overseas corporate bodies (OCBs) are the following :

(A) Direct investment is investment in new issues of shares and debentures of new or existing companies. Direct investment on repatriation basis is allowed upto 100% in hospitals, advanced diagnostic centres, shipping, export oriented deep sea fishing and oil exploration. The NRI equity should cover the foreign exchange requirement for import of capital goods but the terms are further liberalised. Investment on non-repatriation basis is permitted without limits in new issues of public limited companies and investment in non-convertible debentures and sick industrial undertakings is permitted upto even 100% of the total issue. In the Annexure III industries of the Industrial Policy Resolution, investment upto 51% is allowed on a repatriation basis.

(B) Portfolio management scheme refers to the purchase/sale of shares/ debentures/UTI units etc. through recognised stock exchange and their brokers. Total purchase by non-resident Indian or OCB both on repatriation and non-repatriation basis should not exceed 24% of the paid up equity capital of a company and 24% of the total paid up value of each series of convertible debentures of the Indian company. Any single NRI should not exceed 1% of the total equity, preference shares or convertible debentures of any listed company if it is on a repatriation basis, but additional investment to reach upto 24% of the total can be made on non-repatriation basis. The RBI's special permission is not necessary for the portfolio investment. The NRI has to nominate a specific branch of a bank for credits and debits and authorise an Indian resident or a broker or a financial consultant as his agent for such deals with a properly executed power of attorney. Investments on non-repatriation basis are to be done through NRE (RA) accounts while those on repatriation basis NRE (B) accounts. The minimum period of holding of one year was also dispensed with; the NRIs can give interest free repatriable loans upto $ 2.5 lakh with a maturity of 7 years. No RBI permission is required for interest free non-repatriable loans to Indians. Transfer of funds from one NRE account to another is freely permitted. NRE participation in venture capital funds is permitted as like any foreign investment.

NRI deposits are now kept in the following forms and their total balances in all forms stood at $ 34,376 million at end of February, 2006.

Table 21.2 : NRI Deposits

($ US million)

Item	At end March outstanding		
	2003	2004	2005
FCNR (B)	10,199	10,961	11,452
NRE (RA)	14,923	20,559	21,291
NR (NR)D	3,407	1,746	232
Total	28,529	32,266	32,975

Source: RBI Bulletins.

1991-92 Reforms in the Economy

Since July 1991, a number of far-reaching reforms in the economy were initiated. These reforms are exchange rate adjustments, fiscal reforms and structural reforms. The Rupee was devalued to the extent of about 18% to 20% on July 1 and July 3, 1991, followed by the abolition of cash compensatory support to exports and introduction of Exim Scrips which were transferable and tradeable for providing the export incentives. This exchange rate adjustment was followed later by freeing of the rupee in the exchange market to the extent of 60% of the export proceeds, while the rest of 40% had to be sold to the banks at the official rate. With this liberalisation, the policy of Exim Scrips was found unnecessary and dropped. In March 1993, rupee convertibility on trade account and in March 1994 on current account were adopted, which were referred to earlier.

Fiscal reforms include curtailment of government expenditure, reducing the fiscal deficit to 4% of GDP from the earlier level of 8.5% of GDP. A number of subsidies were withdrawn or lowered and unproductive expenditure curtailed. Many foreign loans and IMF assistance were secured to tide over the balance of payments constraint. But after 1992, the fiscal deficit began to grow again and budgetary policy later did not reflect the policy statements made earlier.

Structural reforms were also initiated in the form of freeing the industry from the shackles of controls, encouragements to the private sector and to competitive market forces. In agriculture, prices of both inputs and outputs were raised to align to the market forces and reduce the artificial props. Both in trade and industry, bureaucratic controls are reduced and freer entry and exit policies are pursued.

A number of other liberalisation measures in FERA were also made to benefit the industry and trade. FEMA namely Foreign Exchange Management Act was passed in 1999 for removing the Control Regime and replace it by facilitation of all foreign flows. Permission to keep foreign currency accounts abroad, larger foreign currency allocations for business travel abroad and freer conversion of foreign exchange and a number of other measures were announced to benefit the trade and industry. Trade policy was liberalised to keep many imports in OGL and removal of import licensing system in respect of many goods, rationalisation of import duties and freer imports of capital goods through foreign equity investment or foreign collaboration agreements, etc.

Financial reforms were also announced introducing free lending rates by banks beyond a limit and freeing of deposit rates of banks, removal of ceiling on debenture rates, introduction of new short-term instruments in the money markets and a host of other liberalisation measures were introduced in the financial system. The bank rate was raised by stages from 10% to 12% which was reduced in stages to stand at 8% at the end Feb. 2000 and to 6% in April 2003 and a number of other banking reforms were initiated since 1991, which were all relevant to treasury manager. During 1998-99, the Central Government pumped in additional of Rs. 400 crores for the capital of three nationalised banks and as at end March, 1999, the overall capital contribution of government to nationalised banks stood at Rs. 19,803 crores. Government have written down a sum of Rs. 2,066 crores during 1998-99 from the existing capital base of 4 nationalised banks as against their accumulated losses. Public sector banks are allowed to write down the accumulated losses to the extent of Rs. 6,037 crores so that they can borrow from the public as Tier II Capital. The Government made it clear that the centre would pump no more funds into the banking system and that they have to stand on their own and have recourse to the capital market or foreign sources for their capitalisation or for Tier II capital requirements in future. Banks are given autonomy and have to operate at international standards in future. In 2006, the Government was in favour of banks capitalisation through issue of preference shares to the public.

Other Reforms

As at the beginning of new millennium year 2000, the concept of universal banking was accepted by the RBI, following the recommendations of S.H. Khan Committee in May 1998 and Narasimham Committee in 1991-92. Banks and D.F.Is should move gradually to a new uniform system of universal banking and there will be only two categories of Financial Institutions in future, namely Banks and Non-Bank Finance Companies. Banks can now provide a diversified set of services at the international standards and tune themselves to serve as universal banks. The regulatory system should provide mechanism for ensuring financial stability through their conforming to international standards of transparency, disclosures, prudential and supervisory norms.

The recommendations of the First and Second Narasimham Committee 1991 and 1992 were being implemented in stages. Financial stability is the goal, which means that smooth and orderly functioning of the institutions comprising the financial system is to be ensured. There should be internal checks and balances within each bank, coupled with market discipline and stricter surveilance by the RBI.

Policy Announcements by RBI

(1) Capital Adequacy Rate : Banks should achieve a minimum CRAR of 9% by March end 2000, and 10% thereafter.

(2) Risk Weights to be Given : Risk weight of 2.5% for market risk in respect of government/approved securities and of 20% for other approved and government guaranteed securities. Loans and Advances are to have 100% risk weight whether government guaranteed or not. The Foreign Exchange open position has to carry a risk weight of 100%. These were effected from April, 1999.

(3) Provisioning Norms: For standard assets, a general provision of 0.25% was allowed for the year ended March 2000. A doubtful asset is one which is under substandard category for more than 18 months and banks have to provide 50% on these assets by end March 2001 and another 50% by end March 2002. By end 2003 all investments were to be marked to the market values.

(4) NPAs : Banks have to reduce the NPAs and Asset classification, and provisioning norms have to be applied to all government guaranteed advances also.

Legal Basis for Government Policies
Chart — I

Policy	Enabling Act	Nature of Influence
1. Industrial licensing policy. policy.	1. Industries (Development and Regulation) Act, 1951 Mostly dispensed with	1. Governs the setting up of industrial enterprises and expansion, etc., now used for statistical reporting.
2. Capital Issues Control.	2. Capital Issues Control Act 1947 Repealed in May 1992.	2. Regulates the pricing and issue of shares to the public.
3. Import and Export Trade Policy.	3. Trade Control Act, 1947 Liberalised to a large extent and simplified..	3. Licencing of imports and exports and their regulation in regard to price and quantum imposition of duties and tariffs.

4. Foreign Investment policy.	4. Foreign Exchange Regulation Act, 1973. Highly diluted to move to current account convertibility of the rupee now replaced by Foreign Exchange Management Act in 1999.	4. Regulation of foreign investment and technology in India and investment abroad by Indians.
5. Monopoly control on industry and trade.	5. MRTP Act, 1969 partially scrapped.	5. Control on monopoly and restrictive trade practices in industry only exists now.
6. Sick industry rehabilitation policy.	6. Sick Industrial Companies Act, 1985.	6. Board for Industrial and Financial Reconstruction given powers to restructure and revitalise the sick units, both in private and public sector wound up early in 21st century.
7. Labour Policy	7. Industrial Disputes Act.	7. Arbitration and adjudication of industrial and labour disputes through Labour Tribunals.
8. Price/ Distribution controls on industrial products.	8. Essential Commodities Act and Maintenance of Supplies of Essential Commodities Act.	8. Regulation of industries with regard to their prices and distribution, stocking, etc.
9. SEBI Policy or Capital market	9. SEBI Act, 1992	9. Regulation of Stock & Capital Markets and the players in them.
10. RBI Policy and Banking Regulation Policy on Money and Forex Markets.	10. RBI Act and Banking Regulation Act.	10. Control on banking, Money Market, Govt. Debt, Forex Market etc.

❑ ❑ ❑

22 BANKRUPTCY MANAGEMENT

Introduction

Treasury Management encompasses bankruptcy management also, which can be called crisis management in a company. Failure of liquidity and default in payables may arise from many causes, which the Treasury Manager should be able to deal with. Non Performing Assets (NPAs) of banks are closely associated with sickness in industrial units, to which banks have advanced money. Both the managements and financial institutions which are creditors of those units are involved in bearing the responsibility for this. Financial management and treasury operations in such potentially sick and actually sick units are vitally important for regaining their health and viability through what is called Crisis Management. Banks and Financial institutions are responsible to appraise the projects strictly and monitor and review their progress on continuous basis and give early warning signals to them.

Sickness in industries has become a rampant phenomenon and its occurrence has assumed increasing dimensions during the eighties and nineties. Many factors, both external and internal play a role in making the unit sick, but the lapses on the part of the management are a major factor to reckon with. The symptoms of sickness, if visible and identified at early stages can be attended to so as to make it a viable unit. This is called nursing the sick unit. If sickness goes beyond a point and the unit becomes non-viable then the banker to the unit has to consider the following possibilities :

(1) Rescheduling the repayment of existing loans and postponement or writing off the interest component of the debt burden.

(2) Granting a working capital term loan at concessional interest rate to allow the company to continue operations and make it break-even again; this term loan is to meet the deficit in working capital advance granted to company.

(3) Stipulation of suitable changes in production, sales, cutbacks in bills, receivables so as to realise some amounts and economise expenditure.

(4) Ask the promoters to bring in their own fresh funds.

The financial institution lending to the company or the banker arranges for pumping in some funds, from their own sources or the sources of promoters, which helps the sick units to revive or through writing off of government dues on account of sales tax, excise etc. Sometimes the bankers or FIs would keep their own director on the Board to help the management revive the unit, through proper changes in policy. Industrial Investment Bank no longer finances potentially viable sick units as the erstwhile IRBI.

Financial Crisis and Bankruptcy

To start with, what is financial crisis ? It relates to the short falls in receipts in relation to committed expenditure. The inflows of funds continuously fall short of outflows. Current liabilities are increasing, and some bad and doubtful debts have cropped up. Receivables fall short of the expected amounts. The current ratio has deteriorated from the standard of 2 : 1 (ratio of current assets to current liabilities). When the norm of banks, namely, the ratio of 1.33 :1 has been crossed, banks find it difficult to extend further credits. Inventories may be piling up, sales are falling down or profit margins are declining due to rise in costs, fall in demand and market recession. It is also possible that due to poor productivity the quality of the cutputs declines and costs rise which will make their products unsaleable as compared to its competitors.

Thus, financial crisis exhibits in various forms, namely :

(1) Shortfalls in cash and liquidity and thus payments are delayed.

(2) Receivables are not materialising and payables are increasing faster leading to larger outflows than inflows.

(3) Current ratio and quick ratio show a deterioration indicating liquidity crunch.

(4) The borrowings from banks are already upto the hilt and further advances become difficult from banks.

(5) FIs also find it difficult to make any term loans at this stage.

(6) The company's directors and promoters could not find enough resources to tide over the financial crisis or willingness and ability for revival may be absent.

(7) The raising of deposits from public becomes difficult, if the financial position gives already red signals. The credit ratings will go down.

(8) After a few months, the income and expenditure statement will show losses and these losses are credited to the balance sheet as assets and the reserves and equity capital (networth) will be eroded.

(9) The long-term solvency reflected in the prudent debt equity ratio will disappear and the standard of norm D/E ratio of 2 : 1 will deteriorate with increasing debt burden and further losses will be incurred.

(10) When the financial performance is poor all the available sources of finances will dry up one after the other and resort has to be made to draw on the net worth of the company.

(11) When 50% of the net worth of the company has dried up, then the unit becomes potentially sick unit and when 100% of networth is wiped out, it will become completely a sick unit, which may or may not be viable. There will be no takers at this point and the company has to be declared as bankrupt and winding up proceedings have to be initiated.

Causes of Financial Crisis

There are usually many factors which cause temporary or continued financial crisis leading to sickness of the company. These factors are classified into internal and external. The details of them are set out below for illustrative purposes.

I. External Causes

(a) Infrastructural bottlenecks, like chronic power shortage, transport bottlenecks and shortage of raw materials, noticed by units as in A.P. and Tamil Nadu.

(b) Natural causes like political and social riots, war, communal disturbances, floods, labour unrest and strikes.

(c) Market recession, changes in tastes and fall in demand for product and technological absolecence, in the case of many units as in jute and cotton textile industries.

(d) Changes in government policy, higher levies or taxes, distribution and price controls as in the case of many sugar units.

II. Internal Causes

(a) Poor planning of technical and financial flexibility.

(b) Low productivity of labour, strikes/lockouts etc.

(c) Cost over-runs and poor budgeting and performance in operations.

(d) Weakness in materials management, high costs due to improper purchase policy, poor quality of inputs and shortages of supplies.

(e) Production problems — poor quality of goods, wrong product mix, inadequate maintenance, obsolescence, high wage, poor capacity utilisation, diseconomies of scale.

(f) Diversion of funds into capital account or in investment in subsidiaries or in other companies.

Banker's Role in Emerging Crisis

So far as the company's banker is concerned they will notice symptoms of financial crisis or emerging crisis through the operations of working capital account:

(1) Inability to maintain margins and delay or non-submission of stocks/receivable statements and other control statements to the bank.

(2) Continuous irregularity in cash credit account and excess drawings over limits granted.

(3) Dishonour of bills or return of bills drawn etc.

(4) Delay in payments to creditors and delay or non-payment of interest instalments to the bank.

(5) Opening of another account with other banks to deposit fresh collections so that the old account is kept frozen for the time being.

(6) Decrease in working capital limit due to increase in debtors, decrease in creditors and accumulation of stocks unsold, etc.

These symptoms in relation to bank accounts are a reflection of the basic operational defects of the company such as :

(1) Underutilisation of capital, strikes and lockouts.

(2) Slow movement of stock for sales and reduced order books and high rate of rejections.

(3) High fluctuations in profits or decline in profit margins and of incurring losses.

(4) Statutory obligations like P.F. contributions are not met or delayed or in default.

(5) Quick turnover of key personnel and /or of professionals.

(6) Diversion of funds, delay in project implementation and cash over-runs.

(7) Poor current ratio, and deteriorating position of receivables.

(8) Payables delayed or defaulted and guarantees invoked.
The responsibility of banker is to locate incipient sickness and give warning signals to the company and even provide corporate counselling and advice as to the measures to be taken.

(9) Poor marketing management and inefficient administration — over centralisation, weak organisational setup, lack of professionalism and lack of internal controls and audit, poor efficiency of departmental heads, lack of profits monitoring etc.
Poor sales strategy, inadequate demand, poor after sales services defective pricing policy, high credit sales and low realisations, dependence on single defective marketing network and distribution channels, improper stocking, irregular deliveries etc.

(10) Poor financial management — defective planning or no planning, faulty costing and pricing, laxity in financial controls, frauds, overtrading and speculation, inadequate monitoring, too much unnecessary expenditure, inadequate working capital, large proportion of credit sales and lack of effective collection machinery etc.

Finance manager being the kingpin of operations, he or his team has to be very effective and efficient. If he is not efficient and competent, the first axe will fall on the liquidity of company. Even if he is efficient his counterparts in production materials and marketing managements may let him down by their defects or lapses, such as through increasing purchase costs, poor quality control, inefficient sales strategy, high credit sales and poor receivables etc. But if the finance controller is very efficient he can overcome some of these difficulties by proper advice and strategy.

Managing Financial Crisis

The management of any financial crisis whether leading to bankruptcy or not is a great art and needs a high level of expertise. Identification of early symptoms like shortfalls of cash, increasing inventories, shrinking order books etc. is a first step for the management to act quickly in different directions.

(1) Better quality control, better production strategy or change in product mix, if that is possible in the short run.

(2) Change in marketing strategy, adoption of discount sales, cash discount, larger cash sales, aggressive marketing etc.

(3) Finance Manager has to readjust the financial structure to changing conditions, increase inflows through short-term credits from banks, FIs, public deposits, shift from high cost debt to low cost financing, long-term credits to short-term credits. The strategy is to delay payments while quickening the cash inflows, arrange credit lines and reduce or delay payables.

Depending upon the maladies and causes of financial crisis, the management team has to act quickly and efficiently to meet the situation, before it goes out of controls and the bank account becomes irregular. Sometimes, the banker can be taken into confidence when the reorganisation and financial restructuring is taking place. The banks and financial institutions can also help by postponing some instalments of payment of interest and principal. But basically the management team has to be committed to revive the unit and overcome the crisis by taking the remedial measures promptly. These measures should be both short-term and long-term; in the short run inflows have to be accelerated while postponing the outflows and give the company a breathing time. If necessary, the promoters should bring in fresh funds.

Early Warning Signals

I. Outward Signals

(1) The company started defaulting in some instalments of P.F, and other statutory dues.

(2) Delay in payment of principal, and interest to the bank and FIs or margins to banks are falling short.

(3) Inflows of cash are falling short of the outflows continuously.

(4) Bank limits exhausted and fresh limits are asked or another bank is approached.

II. Inward Signals

(1) High rate of rejections and poor quality of goods.

(2) Order book declining and underutilisation of capacity.

(3) Increasing stocks and poor receivables position, increasing credit sales etc.

(4) Quick ratio started becoming adverse with increasing current liabilities as against available bank limits and cash and bank balances.

(5) Cash payments exceed receipts in a chronic fashion.

The finance manager has to see these early symptoms and before the situation goes out of his control, start remedial measures. He will ask for change in bank limits, increase in cash sales, aggressive marketing, resort to public deposits or new issue or rights issue or change in financial strategy and resort to lowest cost of financing. He will start crash management of cash in working capital.

The financial crisis if temporary and not due to poor top management then restructuring of current assets and current liabilities and increased cash sales, strict timely realisation of credit sales and of bills and book debts and resort to lower cost of financing like loans and advances from promoters, directors, shareholders and public deposits can help the process of recovery. These measures have to be supported by changes in marketing and production plans in a crash programme.

If the management's commitment is there, that is half the battle. Thus, the fund requirements for each level of operations are assessed, the arrears of interest and debt repayments are funded and sometimes interest component is waived. Internal cash accounts period-wise are estimated and then the gap between requirements and internal generation of surplus will be met by a fresh term loan with a deferment of repayments including interest for a period 5 to 7 years.

Fig. 22.1

The package of nursing may include :

(1) Concessional interest for the amount sanctioned and waiving of the penalties imposed earlier and funding the interest component and rescheduling the repayments. The arrears of debt and interest will be kept in a separate funded account and converted into working capital term loan.

(2) Past cash losses led to irregularity in cash credit account of banks, which banks would take care, as shown above but there may also be non-payment of taxes to government, statutory dues such as PF, workers dues, credit dues to creditors etc. In the process regularising these, some write offs from state governments concessional tax treatment (sales, excise etc.) or sharing of the expenses between banks and FIs involved with the company.

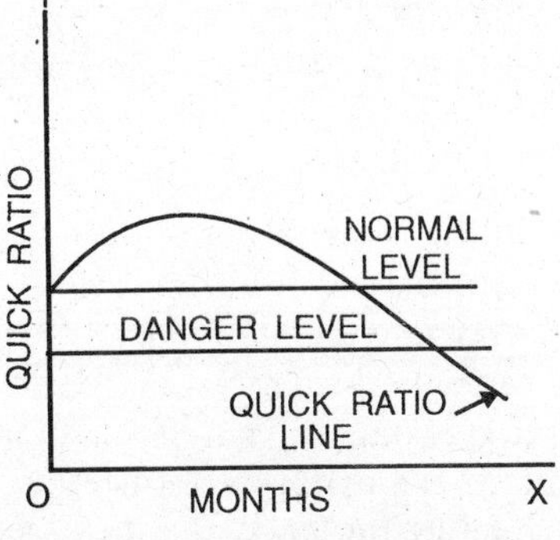

Fig. 22.2

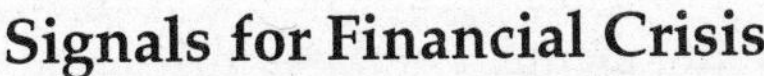

Signals for Financial Crisis

Early action will help overcome the crisis and possible bankruptcy.

Signal No. 1 : Payables are increasing faster, than receivables on a monthly basis.

Solution : Improve the receivable position, increase cash sales and bank borrowings. (Figure 22.1)

Signal No. 2 : Borrowing falls, quick ratio is deteriorating, eligible bank borrowing is declining.

Solution : Resort to public borrowings, improve current assets and liquid assets, cash sales and promoters' funds to be brought in. (Figure 22.2)

Banks' Lending : Current ratio of 1 : 1.33 is generally tolerated by banks and below that, they ask for larger margins, reduce the bank finance and even refuse to lend.

General Guideline : Improve the efficiency of production, increase capacity utilisation, increase sales and cash sales in particular, lower costs and improve profit margins if possible with the cooperation of the trade unions and workers.

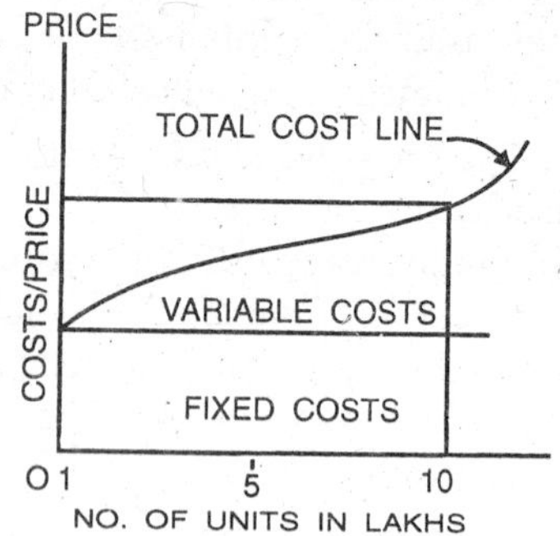

Fig. 22.3

Signal No. 3 : Falling profit margins. Increases cash losses, rising costs and declining profit margins.

Solution : Lower the costs and raise prices relatively to cover both fixed costs and variable costs or increase sales with even lower margins when total profits will increase.

After 10 lakh units price remains constant while variable costs increase leading to rise in total costs — that will lead to increasing iosses, a symptom of inefficiency. (Figure 22.3)

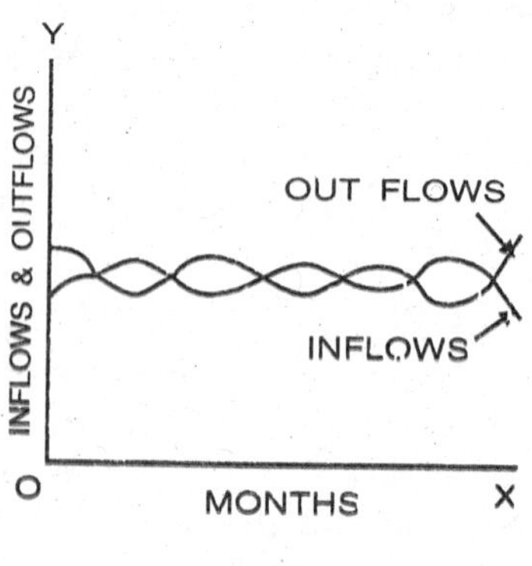

Fig. 22.4

Signal No. 4 : Liquidity Crunch : Cash outflows outpace cash inflows, leading to liquidity crunch; bank borrowings and private credits will dry up.

Solution : Rearrange the cash and credit sales, give premium and discount to cash sales, arrange private credits and short-term inflows. (Figure 22.4)

Priority Claims of Some Categories

In the event of winding up, the claims of the various parties are met in the order approved under the Companies Act and in the rules made thereunder by the government. The secured creditors, like debenture holders and even before that banks and financial institutions whose loans have a floating charge or fixed charge on company's assets will get priority in repayments. Then the unsecured creditors, depositors, suppliers etc. will get the amount due to them to the extent of available funds. Lastly, if there are leftover funds, the preference shareholders and the equity shareholders, including promoters and directors in that order will get funds on a prorata basis. The above distribution and the scheme of arrangements for repayments is looked after bý the official liquidator, appointed under the Company's Act.

Even before the public financial institutions can get their dues or part thereof, all the dues to the government, statutory dues like P.F., employees dues, etc.

have a prior claim and have to be first met. It is only then that creditors of various categories and finally the owners of different classes can get any share in the left over proceeds.

It is generally the creditors who can initiate such winding up proceedings. If the debts are more than the credits and if all the networth is wiped out, the company has no means of paying the creditors who will then initiate proceedings and request the ROC to act as per the provisions of the Company's Act for voluntary liquidation or official liquidation.

Settlement with Creditors : Creditor relations: As the creditors are having powers to ask for liquidation, if they are secured creditors, the company generally tries to compromise with them in a court of law or outside the court. Such compromise or settlement can be arranged by the company before they go to the court provided the creditors are willing to have a compromise and secure atleast 50 paise or more per rupee of their dues. If the compromise of this nature is not possible and the matter goes to the court, the official liquidator has the powers to call the creditors for a meeting and arrange for a settlement.

The settlement scheme in that case, has to be approved by the court as the matter is pending with them. The approved scheme of settlement drawn up by the liquidator has to be submitted to the court and as per their directions, the settlement has to be implemented.

B.I.F.R and Sick Company

If the company has some net worth, but not fully wiped out, employees and bankers may like to revive the company. In such case it may be referred to the B.I.F.R. The reference may be made by the government, the company, or its creditors. But the case can be taken up by B.I.F.R. *Suo motto* also :

Then the company's future fate will lie with B.I.F.R.

Voluntary Liquidation : If the company wants to go in for voluntary winding up, it may arrange for merger, take over or a compromise with the creditors. It may, in some cases decide to go for voluntary winding up, if it has no other chances of survival or merger. In some cases the company declares itself insolvent or bankrupt and the creditors will be left with no other chance except to go to the court for any possibility of getting some money from the leftover funds of the company.

In the case of voluntary liquidation, it has to be approved by the ROC/CLB and there is no chance of revival of the company. Not only there will be no takers for acquisition, mergers or bail out deals, but the management itself declares its unwillingness and inability to pump in more funds and to make it viable. The management, the unions and other interested parties would have given up hopes for any revival if the company goes for winding up.

Legal Provisions for Winding Up

The Company's Act 1956 provides for the regulation of companies from birth to death. Starting with their regulations, the Registrar of Companies (ROC) controls all the activities of companies who have to report to ROC regularly in the form of half yearly Reports and Annual Balance Sheets etc.

Besides, under Section 234 of the Act the ROC can order inspection of the books of accounts of the companies, call for information, accounts and resolutions. If any irregularities or violations of the provisions of the Act are found, the Central government can order an investigation into the affairs of the company under Section 235. The subsequent Sections 236 to 241 deal with inspection, and reporting of the inspecting officer etc. Under Section 242 the company can be prosecuted by the government for any violations under the Act. It is also possible that under some complaints from the clients, creditors, etc. ROC can conduct investigations, under Sections 247, 248 and 249.

The Central government has powers for asking the company for voluntary winding up under Section 250 (A), or application for winding up under Section 397 or 398 can be made under Section 243. CLB can use these powers of the government and ask for voluntary winding up.

When a deposit has fallen due for repayment and remains unpaid the creditors can seek remedy in a civil court or can file an application for winding up of the company to the court, after serving a notice of written demand requiring them to repay the deposit under notice. Sections 433, 434 and 439 of the Company's Act deal with this notice period and the petition to the court for winding up under Section 433. A creditor or debentureholder of the company can send this notice, under Section 434 of the Act, asking the company why it has not paid its principal amount and /or interest on the amount due and if no satisfactory reply comes, the creditor can file the winding up petition under Section 433 of the Act. Creditors of the company can drag the company to the court, particularly if they are secured creditors. It is also provided in the Act, that on a written and documented complaint, the ROC can institute proceedings in a court of law, with the permission of the government.

Winding up and Liquidation

Under the law, there are three modes of winding up : (i) members voluntary winding up (ii) creditors voluntary winding up (iii) under court order due to insolvency proceedings.

Besides the above, the BIFR can also direct the winding up of the company, if their attempts at revival or rehabilitation or merger fail to materialise.

If the financial crisis reached a stage that net worth of the company is wiped out, the company will have the above methods of winding up. Any arrangement between the company's members and creditors has to be sanctioned by a special resolution of ¾th in number of members. Even if the company is not insolvent, this method of winding up can be adopted by ¾th majority. Then the company has to give notice in *Official Gazette* and regional Newspapers within 14 days of the passing of the Resolution.

Secondly, the creditors can force winding up by the court appointing the liquidator. This is called the creditors voluntary winding up. The company can call a creditors' meeting after the general meeting of the members of the company and registrar of company has to be informed within 10 days. Under Section 495, a meeting of the creditors is to be called if the company's assets are not adequate to meet all dues of creditors.

The appointment of liquidator by the company has to be informed to ROC within 10 days. In case of court order of winding up, the court will appoint an official liquidator. The liquidator will have the powers of the Board which will be dissolved on the appointment of liquidator.

So long as the liquidator is functioning to realise the assets, he stops all the activities of the company except those necessary for winding up every year, he calls for the general meeting to report the status of winding up, until all the assets realisable are realised and a scheme of prorata payment for creditors is arranged. A final meeting and dissolution of the company will be arranged to give an account of the realisation and payments and closure of the accounts of the company.

The proceeds of the realised assets are distributed as per the Act. The liquidator has to deduct his pay, costs of collection and incidentals relating to liquidation.

(1) Then Income Tax Commissioner will assess any tax dues and after payment of their claims, if any, the clearance of the commissioner is obtained which is necessary for further payments.

(2) Statutory dues to the government, for excise sales tax, P.F. for employees etc. are the next item to be paid in the order of priority.

(3) Dues to employees for the period worked, their gratuity, P.F., salaries, D.A. etc. are to be cleared.

(4) Secured creditors whose claims are admitted will get in full or prorata depending upon the available funds.

(5) Unsecured creditors where claims are admitted will get in full or prorata depending upon the available funds, after meeting the prior claims of others, referred to earlier. Power to compromise, agree to a scheme of payment etc. lies with the liquidator and if he is in doubt, he can secure court rulings in this regard or on any other matter.

If still, any funds are left over they are distributed to the members on a prorata basis and the dissolution of the company is announced by the liquidator and approved by the court. The ROC will record the same and the name of the company will be deleted from the list.

Public Interest in Winding up of Companies

Companies Act has provided enough safeguards to ensure public interest in the event of a company going for liquidation. Public interest is involved in many ways, apart from those of creditors, debtors and members who are owners of the company. The owners who cannot sustain the company's working both in terms of financial and human resources would prefer the closure of the company. The creditors are interested in the closure, if they can get atleast some amounts due to them from the company. Debtors are for the closure as it might help them delay and compound for the dues to the company. But the closure which is asked by all the parties may not always be in the interests of the public, for reasons given below :

(i) The company's employees and workers will be unemployed and increase the ranks of unemployed.

(ii) The company's consumers may be denied the products which they were used to for the reasons of their habit or the nature of the product of the company.

(iii) Competitors will gain an advantage which may be to the disadvantage of consumers due to increasing cartelisation or due to higher prices that they have to pay now or due to poor quality of the goods.

(*iv*) Although the management and promoters are for closure of the company, the public members who are the investors, but are a minority will suffer and have to abide by the majority holding of the promoters.

(*v*) If the company's product is in the essential commodity group and consumer goods, the public interests will again suffer.

Generally, public interest is supposed to be taken care of by the central government, through the C.L.B. and Registrar of companies and by the State governments. Even, voluntary winding up is not possible without a court order or without the prior sanction of the C.L.B. Earlier the state and central governments used to take over the sick companies or nationalise them which are about to be closed, if it is in the public interest. Now the governments have reversed the policy due to privatisation. This job of reviving is entrusted to Board of Industrial and Financial Reconstruction which will order the winding up process if no scheme of revival is possible. Although the central and state governments are not taking over any sick company now but they are encouraging the NRIs and cash rich companies to take over the sick companies through merger and amalgamation. The public interest being dominant, the B.I.F.R., C.L.B. and governments are expected to safeguard the interests of the public.

B.I.F.R. was set up in 1987 for determining the preventive, ameliorative, remedial measures to be taken in respect of sick companies. It can initiate measures *suo motto* or on a reference from any of the interested parties, to bring any sick or potentially sick company under its fold of investigation.

Case of Genelac Ltd. with B.I.F.R.

A recent example of tax benefits from mergers is that of Sick Genelac Limited, which has been under the charge of B.I.F.R. for revitalisation or rehabilitation. The B.I.F.R. has approved a scheme of amalgamation of Genelac Ltd. with the Shaw Wallace & Co. as prepared by the IDBI. Under this scheme approved, the Shaw Wallace & Co. (SWC) will invest Rs.22.91 crores from its internal accruals and in turn, it is entitled to a tax benefit of Rs.9.77 crores.

The entire loss of the Genelac will be wiped out and all outstanding dues to the financial institutions and banks, through a one time negotiated settlement, so that the company will have no debt burden.

Similarly, a settlement is arrived at with the shareholders of Genelac Ltd. whereby they will be given one 15% preference share of face value of Rs.10 for every 10 shares, held by them. These preference shares will be redeemable after 10 years.

In this case two things are clear. One is that the B.I.F.R. is the final authority in such revival packages. As against the normal 14% for preference shares, it has granted 15% to these shareholders. Secondly, the burden of losses are borne partly by the government through loss of tax dues (to the extent of Rs.9.77 crores), partly by the financial institutions and banks for agreeing to a one time settlement and shareholders for getting something like 15% p.a.

Case Study of a Company in Financial Crisis (Example : Hindustan Shipyard Ltd.)

Objectives: (*i*) to examine how a company, rated as sick can be revived.

(*ii*) to see how revival of a company with its networth completely wiped out can be effected.

Background Facts : Hindustan Shipyard Ltd. is a P.S.U. which is based at Visakhapatnam. It is one of the oldest ship building companies, employing more than 10,000 workers with an equity capital of Rs.76.31 crores.

Hindustan Shipyard Ltd. was hit by the recession of eighties in shipping industry and in 1990-91 it was rated as almost a sick company. Later, it was about to be given up as a sick company to be closed. Even in 1992 it had a negative net worth of Rs.654 crores. Its entire equity capital was eroded by accumulated losses.

How Revival Started

Firstly, Management prospective has changed and secondly, the shipping industry has revived from the recession. Because of the new financial package adopted by the Management, during the two years of 1993-94 and 1994-95, it has emerged as a surplus company, after wiping out the accumulated losses.

The package of revival is three pronged.

(1) Asset Revaluation.

(2) Capital Restructuring.

(3) Adoption of cost cutting methods.

Asset Revaluation: It has real estate and fixed assets which were acquired many years ago and the present market prices are nearly 10 times or more. The company got them revalued at current market prices and wiped out all accumulated losses.

Capital Restructuring: Through changes in capital structure, the debt equity ratio is being brought down from the earlier level of 8 : 1 to a planned level of 2 : 1. In view of the surpluses, the fresh cash inflow from the government was not necessary. For additional cash resources, a leading shipping company based in Denmark, Kreanor A.S. has taken a sizeable equity stake in joint venture with Hindustan Shipping Ltd. for bringing in $ 10 billion.

Cost Pruning: Exercises in cost reduction are carried out for about two years and profit margins are improved.

All the above exercises, spread over three years, have made the company good for private participation and the government may privatise this company, as the company has turned the corner and there are takers for it, both in Indian private sector and foreign sector.

If the revitalisation can be done in public sector, it will be more possible in the private sector, if there is a will on the part of management.

Conclusions

This chapter has highlighted the emerging symptoms of bankruptcy and it is for the Treasury Manager to stall such a process through identification of early signals. Most of the causes of bankruptcy are emerging from liquidity problems, which are in the domain of the Treasury management. By efficient handling of financing and investment functions of the Company, the Treasury Manager can ward off all impending bankruptcy symptoms.

❑ ❑ ❑

23 RBI POLICIES AND INDUSTRY

One of the most important environmental factors influencing the treasury operations is the RBI policies, next only to government policies. RBI as the source of currency and controller of banking and credit has been referred to in earlier chapters. Its monetary and credit policy influences treasury operations in money market. Its public debt policy and management influences the gilt-edged market and its operations. Its foreign exchange policy and control on foreign operations under FERA would influence the forex market and operations in it. RBI's policies and regulations encompass the whole of the financial system, banks, non-bank financial institutions and money changers, authorised dealers, dealers in money market, government securities market and all related institutions and areas.

As the name itself indicates, treasury involves the government and RBI as sources of operations, issuers and controllers, of the treasury markets. Treasury managers whether in banks, financial institutions or companies are influenced and controlled by the Reserve Bank and their policies.

In this chapter, discussion is confined to one aspect not referred to above, namely, the regulators of banking and credit in respect of industrially sick units.

RBI and Industrial Sickness

The RBI has been laying emphasis on the prevention of sickness through early warning signals and as next best, early revival of the potentially sick units. By proper amendments to Sick Industrial Companies Act, an early identification of sickness in industrial unit was aimed at. These amendments include revised definitions of sick units and potentially sick units as banks are involved in financing them. Treasury Management has the basic objective of protecting liquidity of the company and thus forestall possible sickness.

New Definitions are as Follows

Sick Industrial Company means an industrial company (being registered for not less than 5 years) which has at the end of any financial year accumulated losses equal to or exceeding its entire net worth. A potentially sick industrial unit is one which has accumulated losses as at the end of any financial year eroding 50% or more of its peak net worth during the preceding four financial years.

As provided by the RBI data, regarding sick industrial units, the number of sick units and the bank credit, standing against them are showing increases during the recent years. The total bank credit locked up in industrial sickness or Gross NPAs has increased from Rs. 11,533 crores at end March 1992 to 15,682 crores at end March 1998 and Rs. 64,439 crores at end March 2004 and Rs. 59,516 crores as end March 2005. Amount written off during 2004-05 was Rs. 1,519 crores.

As regards the non-SSI units, namely, medium and large units, their number has increased by 69% during the years of 1991-98 and the amount involved rose by 132% during the same period. These trends are a hurdle for the industrial growth of the country and poor reflection of the financial management. The major cause of sickness was identified as managerial deficiency in many studies made by the RBI and ICICI. RBI has given guidelines to banks on asset classification as NPA sub-standard, and Doubtful assets, Loss assets, and stipulated level of capital adequacy for each of them. The data on sick units has not been published separately for small, medium and large units by the RBI, but shifted emphasis to NPAs with banks, during the early years of the 21st century.

As per the RBI data, those which are potentially viable are helped by the banks through appropriate nursing programme. This means that bulk of the units which are potentially viable are helped by banks. The others belong to the managements who are stubborn, not interested in revival or are not in a position to comply with the requirements of banks.

SSI-Sickness

Credit extended by scheduled commercial banks to 1,38,811 sick units of SSI stood at Rs. 5,285 crores at end March 2004. Of these only 2,385 units were found to be viable, with an outstanding bank credit of Rs. 421 crores, which accounts for only 8% of the bank credit extended to sick SSIs. Banks have placed 783 units, with an outstanding credit of Rs. 385 crores, under Nursing Programmes.

After 1999, RBI ceased to emphasis on the health codes of sick and potentially sick units, but has delegated powers to the banks for debt recovery from all units. During July to October 2004, it has directed banks to operate one time settlement or compromise schemes to recover debts due, to the extent possible. Lok Adalats and Debt Recovery Tribunals were set up by the government to help the banks to recover from the units which have defaulted their loan repayments to the banks. Debt Recovery Appellate Tribunal was also set up for appeals against the verdicts of the DRTs. The Securitisation and Reconstruction of financial assets and enforcement of Security Interest Act 2002 (SARFAESI) was passed to streamline the recovery of debts due to banks, expeditiously and it was amended in 2004.

During 2004-05, a total of 3,62,576 cases were referred to for one time settlement, or Lok Adalats, or DRTs and for enforcement under SARFAESI of these cases, 368 cases were taken over by ARCD and an amount of Rs. 14,506 crores was recovered. All the above cases, including those taken over by ARCs involve an amount of Rs. 29,674 crores of which an amount of Rs. 20,578 crores was recovered (69% of the total due)

The RBI has since been insisting on the banks to reduce the NPAs and to raise the capital to achieve the capital adequacy norms.

Working group on SSIs (A.S. Ganguly)

The working group on flow of credit to SSI sector under the chairmanship of Dr. A.S. Ganguly had submitted its report in April 2004. It has made as many as 31 recommendations, of which some are being implemented by the RBI. These include the adaption of cluster based approach for financing small and medium enterprises, sponsoring of specific projects, publicising the successful working models of NGOs, exploring new instruments for promoting rural industry and special package for SSIs in the north-east region, etc.

As recommended by the working group, the structure of interest rates on deposits placed by foreign banks with SIDBI, in lieu of shortfall in priority sector lending operations was modulated by increasing the tenor of deposits from one to three years. SIDBI continued its efforts to encourage lending to SSIs and prevent possible sickness among SSIs.

The working group made many other recommendations some of which pertain to other agencies like Ministry of Finance, Government of India, SIDBI, Credit Guarantee Fund Trust for small industries, Credit Information Bureau of India (CIBIL) and the IBA. The respective agencies are examining them and some are being implemented.

NPAs in Scheduled Commercial Banks

Gross non-performing assets as percentage of total assets was brought down from 4.6% in 2001-02 to 2.5% in 2004-05, due to deliberate efforts of banks and RBI. Gross NPAs of all SCBs as percentage of Gross Advances has also fallen from 10.4% in 2001-02 to 5.2% in 2004-05.

Sector-wise, the NPAs with respect to PSBs, was the highest as end March 2005 and in respect of Non Priority Sector at 50%. The same with respect to private sector banks for non-priority sector was higher at 74.65%. In respect of SSI sector, the NPAs for all public sector banks was only 16.4% and for all private sector banks, it was 10.96%. The same picture emerges in respect of other priority sector Advances, evidencing the fact that the NPAs are more in the case of non-priority sector for all classes of banks. In the case of advances to weaker sections of all PSBs, they were at Rs. 51,445 crores out of total non food credit of Rs. 931, 466 crores (accounting for 5.5% of total Non-food credit). Out of the advances to weaker sections, only 11.2% are NPAs as in 2004-05. It can be concluded that in terms of absolute figures or percentages the NPAs for all priority sectors and weaker sections, are less than those for Industry and Non-priority sectors.

All loan assets are classified into the following categories, depending upon their quality.

All scheduled commercial banks at end March

(in %ages)

Loan Assets	2002	2003	2004	2005
Standard assets	89.6	91.2	92.8	94.9
Sub standard assets	3.1	2.6	2.3	1.2
Doubtful assets	6.1	5.1	4.0	3.3
Loss assets	1.2	1.2	0.8	0.6
of which Total NPAs	10.4	8.8	7.2	5.1

Source : RBI – Report on Trend and progress of Banking 2004-05
Loss Asset, have come down while standard assets have increased, due to better credit appraisal and efforts to bring down NPAs, made by banks.

In House Group in RBI

During the Nineties, the emphasis was on preventing industrial sickness, which shifted to prevention and reduction of NPAs of banks in the early 21st century.

To prevent the rising sickness, the RBI constituted an In House group to examine the causes and remedies of industrial sickness. This group emphasised the need for upgradation of appraisal skills in banks, stricter credit monitoring and observance of working capital norms, coordination and exchange of credit rating information among banks and financial institutions and building up a data base on the industry. The Reserve Bank has initiated steps for implementation of the above recommendations and moved in the direction of better coordination with Board for Industrial and Financial Reconstruction (BIFR) by sharing the information of banks and RBI.

Goswami Committee : The Committee on Industrial Sickness and Corporate Restructuring under the Chairmanship of Dr. Omkar Goswami in its report submitted in July 1993 recommended a package of measures, aimed at ameliorating the problems of industrial sickness and creating an economically rational, market-oriented competitive industrial structure.

The policy measures recommended by the committee include *inter alia* :

(i) Shift in the responsibility of industrial and corporate reorganisation from secured creditors and the state to defaulting debtor firms.

(ii) Fast Track facilitator role for B.I.F.R.

(iii) More frequent use of the winding up provisions of Section 20(4) of Sick Industrial Companies Act (SICA) and

(iv) Amendments to SICA to allow for alternation in the form, content and scope of the company. The Committee has highlighted the importance of close monitoring by the banks and FIs, and accelerating the face of financial reforms and to enable the restructuring of industrial sector.

The committee has, among others underlined the need for early detection and prevention of sickness, rather than providing concessional packages. There is need for adoption of such schemes of revival and restructuring of units which will reduce the losses to financial institutions and at the same time help the company to secure a good return on equity. This would tantamount to boosting the efficiency and productivity of the workers as also improving the managerial efficiency in running the unit. So far the resort to winding up was very limited, but attempts to mergers and acquisitions bail out takeovers etc. are encouraged by healthy and efficient units.

Viability and Nursing Programme

If a sick unit, as defined above is to be nursed back to health, the RBI has laid down some guidelines. First, it is to be ascertained whether it would be viable or not on a commercial basis. Secondly, the management confidence and their commitment to the unit are to be assessed.

RBIs guidelines for determining the commercial viability are as follows :

A unit is regarded viable, if it would be in a position, after implementing a rehabilitation package spread over a period not exceeding 7 years from the commencement of the package to continue to service its repayment obligations as agreed upon including those forming part of the package, without the help of concessions after the aforesaid period. The repayment period for restructured debts should not exceed 10 years from the date of commencement of package.

For the purpose of assessing the viability proper feasibility study has to be undertaken by the bank or F.I. The study should cover the past operations and the weaknesses determine the viable level of operations to create internal surplus; the cost of production and profitability estimates for 7 to 10 years have also to be worked out.

The points covered under any project appraisal have to be formally repeated again. Most important of all aspects is the managerial aspect, which has to be examined from the point of view of (i) their willingness to submit to the financial discipline of the package (ii) their ability to bring in fresh funds and fresh expertise in management (10 to 20% of the additional funds as required).

RBIs Health Code

The RBI has laid down the broad criteria for monitoring the individual accounts of companies, as adjudged by the quality of the account (either cash credit or loan account).

Accordingly these accounts of borrowing companies, firms, etc. are classified as follows :

Health Code 1 : Classified as follows: Satisfactory : Conduct of operations, margins kept, regularity of repayments and safety of the advance are all satisfactory.

Health Code 2 : Irregular: Account is sometimes overdrawn, but safety of advances is not doubted. Instalments in respect of term loans are overdue for less than 6 months or instalments under deferred guarantee or import bills under L.C. are overdue for less than 3 months (10 to 15% of bills overdue).

Health Code 3 : Sick — Viable — under nursing — units in which nursing and revival programmes are taken up.

Health Code 4 : Sick — Non-viable — sticky advances Irregularities persist for more than six months — apparent stagnation of business — strikes/ lockouts slow movements of goods, poor order book position, current account deficits persist and cash flows are inadequate, diversion of funds, current liabilities more than current assets etc.

Health Code 5 : Advances recalled — Repayment doubtful and nursing not considered worthwhile.

Health Code 6 : Recovery proceedings under public Debt Recovery Act initiated; suit filed on these accounts and cases are in the court.

Health Code 7 : Decreed Debts : Court decree has been obtained for recovery of advances but execution delayed for less than 1 year to 5 years and more.

Health Code 8 : Debts classified by the bank as bad and doubtful against which 100% provision has to be made in the bank books as per the RBI guidelines.

The above procedure was in operation since 1985 and bank branches are expected to classify the advance accounts of Rs.1 lakh and above. The provision for these accounts and the method of dealing with them has been laid down by the RBI. Health Code No.1 to 3 are generally safe for the bank. But from 4 to 8 the bank branch has to initiate action in a Court of Law for recovery of funds. Debt Recovery Tribunals were set up by Government in Kolkata, Delhi, Bangalore, Jaipur and Ahmedabad and an Appellate Tribunal at Mumbai for the purpose of quick recovery of bank loans; more powers are given recently for DRTs. Depending on the recoverable position, it has to be classified under the proper code and for the NPA, a provision has to be made for making good the short fall in the books of account of the branch and the bank. An account is classified as NPA if interest or instalment of principal is in arrear for any two quarters and not for two consecutive quarters in a year as it used to be before.

The constituents and companies who are borrowing from the banks have from time to time to be warned of the state of their accounts. The management and in particular finance manager will have to be given a chance to reorganise the unit, take corrective action and improve efficiency and productivity so as to bring theft financial position into a healthy state. Treasury Manager has also a responsibility in this regard.

Some examples are given below from the past on the companies in financial problems.

Case Studies — Temporary Financial Crisis Hind Ciba

Hind Ciba has witnessed some set back to its operations during 1994-95. Its sales, rose only by 6% and gross profits destined by 20%. This deterioration was accelerated during April to Sept. 1995 half year with sales rising by only 3%. EPS for the half year has also shown a fall. Its account with the banks became irregular and it became potentially sick.

Being a well established old blue chip company, it could face this problem, due to labour strike and lockout in its factory at Corlim near Panaji; Santa Monica plant has been under lockout since January 1994. The striking workers passed a resolution withdrawing the strike after 21 months of closure. The permanent employees and those whom the company has not chargesheeted are taken back. But the losses to the company on account of such closure was Rs.50 crores in total and Rs.20 crores during 1995. The lockout was lifted on October 31,1995. Here is a case of financial problems due to internal labour problems. At end 1996, it was finally decided to merge to Ciba with Sandoz on mutually agreed terms.

Case of Lan Esada

This company started computer software work in 1990, but bulk of the income during the early years was due to trading and not in manufacture. Then it has diversified into steel, hardware etc. They have moved out of software business to get into hardware in collaborations with Tulip India. Tulip held 80% and the rest is given to Mr. Shyam Bhatia, the Promoter of Lan Esada. This is a case of voluntary merger due to company's poor show in the original plan of software production. The company has shifted from software to trading and then to steel and hardware.

In the above two cases, the moral is clear. The issue is how did the management meet these challenges ? One is labour problem and the other, the failure in the products mix. In the first case, the management has the advantage of strong financial position and met the threat of labour by lockout. After 21 months, the labour realised its mistake and resumed duties although the company lost Rs.50 crores in the process in a period of two years.

In the second case the company has no other go except to diversify and the management has to concede to the terms of Tulip India and take a minority stake, in it for manufacture of hardware, completely changing the product mix.

The conclusion is that management has to respond quickly and in time before the company becomes bankrupt and winding up proceedings are initiated. In both the above cases, the management who are running the show got into difficulties but did succeed to salvage their problematic state into a viable state.

U.C.P.L.

In Nov., 1995, B.I.F.R. has directed United Clutch Products Ltd. to be wound up, following the failure of the rehabilitation scheme prepared for the revival of this sick company. The rehabilitation scheme was sanctioned on December 1993 but the existing promoter has no will and means to pursue the rehabilitation programme. Accordingly, the B.I.F.R. has concluded that the company needs a management change, but there was none willing to come forward to take over the management; there was no other choice except to order for its winding up.

Apollo Tyres : Apollo Tyres has launched Black Cat Scooter Tyres, but did not catch the market imagination. It did not make any profits on this division for nearly two years and their projections of break-even and profitability have gone haywire.

In December 1995, they have changed the plans to produce new moulds and totally modify the product to lead to a completely new tread pattern.

Many instances can be given of the financial problems leading to changes in plans and corrective measures taken by companies. U.B group Company (Bangalore based) dropped the Bulate Rubber Project scheduled to be set up in A.P., due to financial problems. U.B. Elastomers has planed the setting up of the new project on bulate rubber in Parvada mainly for which it acquired land in 1991. Here is a case of a change in plans in the beginning itself.

Vikrant Tyres : A case of a company in losses is Vikrant tyres (Mysore based) with losses running upto Rs. 12.36 crores In April-September 1994. The loss was brought down to Rs. 5.39 crores during April-September 1995 due to improved production, higher productivity. Fall in rubber prices and better marketing strategy have helped the company to reduce the losses. The change in strategies of production and marketing has helped the financial position of the company. It will thus be seen that the willingness and ability or expertise of management will decide whether the company can be revived or not.

Calico : BIER has ordered the winding up of (CALICO) as there are no takers for this sick company which is non-viable. It has losses of around Rs.480 crores and tax liabilities to government of Rs. 75 crores. Arvind Mills which has come forward to take over and the Gujarat government which wanted to help 6000 workers who will be unemployed could not come with any concrete proposals to the B.I.F.R. In December 1995 the order of winding up was passed by B.I.F.R.

ITC Classic : This was set up by ITC but within a short period of 5 years or so, it became non-viable and sold of to ICICI securities. It was a case of industry acquisition by ICICI securities as both were in the same line of activity.

The above are brief examples from the real corporate world on the potentially sick and sick units and what measures were taken. The objective is to highlight the role of mismanagement and lack of proper financial planning in making a company sick potentially viable or non-viable. The role of the Treasury Manager is to,make good the above deficiencies in the company.

24 BANKING RELATIONSHIPS

Need for Finance

From the inception of the company or firm the need for funds both for inputs and outputs was already emphasised. The sources of funds for companies vary from the purpose and the period for which funds are required. To start with, long-term finance is required for project finance and for setting up of the factory, plant and machinery etc. The sources of such long-term finance for the project, expansion and diversification are set out below :

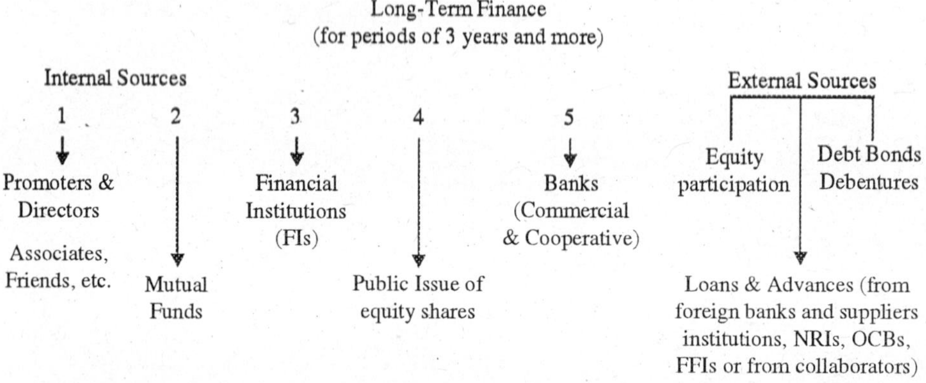

Fig. 24.1

For a new company, there will be no internal accruals, or surpluses. They have to depend on the funds raised from promoters, banks, FIs and mutual funds in a private mutually agreed basis and on new issues to the public. As per the SEBI guidelines, all new issues to public should be atleast 25%; promoters and directors should have a minimum of 25% of the total issue, if the total is less than Rs. 100 crores and 20%, if the total issue is more than Rs. 100 crores and this quota is subject to a lock-in period of 5 years. The rest of the amount of about 50% of the project finance can be raised from other sources listed above, and there should be a minimum offer of 25% to the public to get the shares listed on any stock exchange.

Bank Finance

The most important source is the bankers, for the simple reason that banks provide both term loans and working capital loans and that their relations continue to subsist in some form or other until the company is wound up. So the selection of banker is very crucial for a company. Proper introduction and a knowledge of banking law and practice is necessary for this purpose. The banker has generally relations with the company on a daily basis for operating current accounts, overdrafts, loan accounts and even for term loans. The banker-company relationship is therefore a long-term sustainable relationship of a personal and confidential nature. Both the banker and the company have to carefully weigh the consequences of their relations and the need for sustaining their relations, the management of the company, their credit rating, honesty and integrity and their dependability. Similarly, the company should take the bank into confidence as the bank will continue to be a friend, philosopher and guide and will not let down the company in the normal course. It is this mutual trust and confidence that is the basis of selection of a bank by the company and the acceptance of the company by the banker as its customer. Sometimes if the operations are large, there can bo more than one banker, or a consortium of banks.

Other Sources of Finance

If the company is an existing company and they want funds for expansion and diversification or for working capital their sources can be set out as follows :

Main Sources for Existing Company

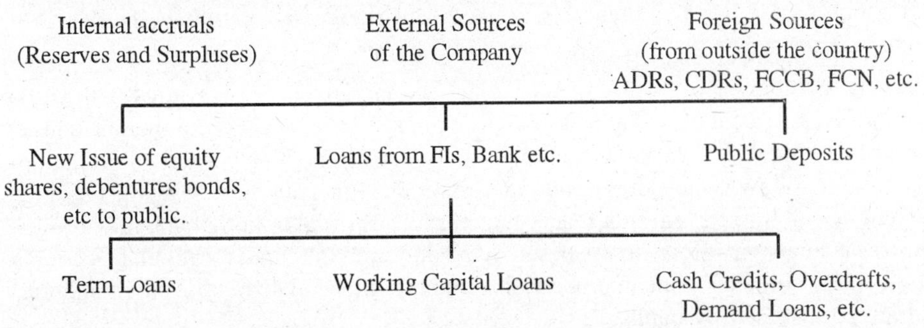

Fig. 24.2

The short-term sources of funds for a running company are slightly different from those referred to above and these are setout below :

Short-Term Sources

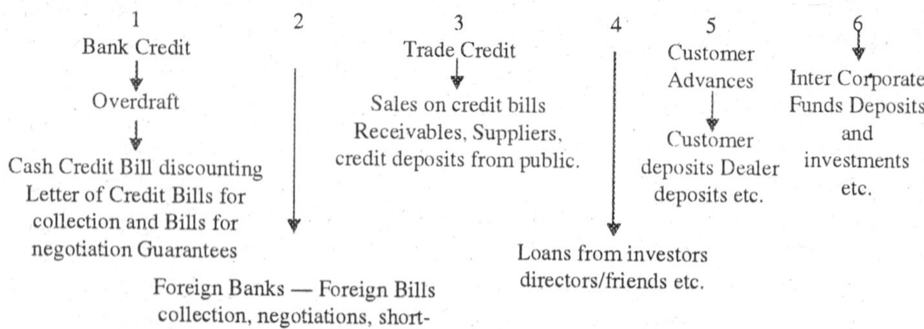

Fig. 24.3

Banks and Short-Term Funds

As referred to earlier all companies require bank finance for working capital purposes and for meeting the gap between the receipts and payments. Production is carried on a continuous basis but sales and other income are realized in discreet and discontinuous fashion depending on the extent of credit sales, terms of sales and the volume and velocity of flow of goods. Normally, the banker to the company provides working capital on the basis of their assessment of operations of company, their inflows and outflows and the forecasted needs of credit, as arranged and planned in the beginning of the year and reassessed from quarter to quarter. Bankers' services to the company and latter's dependence on the banker are continuous. Banker-customer relations and their inter-dependence are too well known.

Other Services of Banks

The company has to use the banks' services in a variety of ways and not necessarily for working capital purposes or for term loans. Basically, the services that banks provide to companies is finance. But there are a number of other non-funded services.

The companies can only open current accounts, overdraft accounts with banks and not savings accounts. The banks can provide need based finance either as loans or advances, secured by the hypothecation or mortgage of goods in process of production or stored in godowns etc. They can grant term loans for fixed periods against security of fixed assets. In the event of arrears of interest or principal or both, bank may provide working capital term loan to fund such overdue amounts under irregular accounts, provided the company appears to be viable and the financial difficulties are temporary and are so assessed by banks.

The Companies secure various other services from the banks which maybe set out as follows :

(i) Monthly statements of their accounts.

(ii) Collection of bills and Negotiation of bills etc.

(iii) In case of export/import trade, collection negotiation, guarantee confirmation of credit, credit rating and foreign exchange information of foreign countries, etc.

(iv) Cheques of outstation for collection or purchase and discount of cheques/bills etc.

(v) Remittances from one center to another through MT/TT/Pay Orders/Bankers Cheques etc.

(vi) Remittances against tender of cash.

(vii) Availability of credit cards for savings in cash.

(viii) Issue of duplicate drafts/ cheques/Pay Orders and revalidation of them.

Charges for Services

For current account holders, the bank charges at the rate of Rs.40/- or above per ledger page. These charges have now increased and vary from bank to bank on a cost plus basis. For accounts maintained on computers a page with 40 entries or part thereof will constitute one ledger page for such levy, if the average credit balance is above a level say Rs.10 of Rs. 15 lakhs all ledger pages are maintained free and the charges vary depending on the average credit balances maintained with the bank by the party.

The bank provides financial guarantees, performance guarantees, etc., for which they charge separately depending on the transactions whether they are in land or foreign. The bank also does processing of applications for advances/ cash credits/loans/etc., for which there is an application processing fee depending on the amount. A minimum fee of Rs.10,000 is generally charged as processing fee and it may increase with the amount involved or vary from bank to bank.

Handling of bills/cheques, whether honoured or dishonoured attract bank charges. Safe custody of valuables, documents and money for which the charges vary from Rs.300 or above per annum. collection of inland and deposits receipts/outstation cheques etc. and carrying out the standing instructions of payment of bills, taxes etc. are also attended to at charges varying with periodicity and amounts involved in such instructions.

Inland guarantees, issue of duplicate pass books, dishonoured cheques, lost deposit receipts etc. are also attended to by banks at appropriate charges. The schedule of charges is now left to the discretion of each bank, subject to the minimum floors for each of the transactions as fixed by Indian Banks Association (IBA). The commissions, fees, charges etc. are all fixed for each bank separately within the ambit of IBA circulars and RBI guidelines if any. Even the RBI and IBA are now asking banks to charge on the basis of their own costs.

Banks' services are very wide ranging and not just acceptance of deposits and making loans and advances against such deposits. These services vary from inland trade to foreign trade and a wide variety of non-fund financial services. Companies are open to use these services, particularly relating to collection, guarantee, remittances, discounting, safe custody, standing instructions, and so on.

Choice of Bankers

Companies select a banker for their efficient service in the first place, their branch net work for remittance and collection work and modern technology in the form of computerisation, adopted by the bank. The banker has to be properly introduced or must have had relations earlier. The company generally operates through one branch of the bank and that branch should be nearby or knowing to the party and has all operations of domestic as well as foreign nature in the sense that they should also deal in foreign exchange, financing of foreign trade etc. Banker's flexibility, their readiness to help, easy access and understanding are the other criteria for selection of a banker.

The choice of a banker is generally a matter of personal contact, past dealings and convenience. A number of factors other than pure efficient service count in such matters. The customer-banker relationship being of a fiduciary nature, the mutual trust and dependability of one on the other is very important. The company's requirements of credit, non-credit services and foreign exchange services, if the company has dealings abroad are to be catered to by the bank chosen. Normally all the public sector banks have these facilities, atleast in some selected branches. Some companies choose even private sector banks if they offer a wider range of services and better service. Some export-oriented units prefer foreign banks and the PSUs and semi-government enterprises prefer SBI and associate banks for their past relations with the government.

Credit Card Business

Six nationalised banks, SBI and its associate banks and five foreign banks were engaged in Credit Card Business at present. Besides, ten public sector Banks and more than ten private sector banks have entered into this business by having tie up arrangements with other banks or foreign banks.

New Technology in Banking

A Committee on Technological Issues of Banking setup by RBI reported in December 1994. This Committee suggested far-reaching changes relating to payments cheque clearances, securities settlement and training in High-technology to banking personnel.

Consequent on the agreement between IBA and employees' unions in October 1993, 4000 branches of public sector banks have become eligible for computerisation. IBA has also suggested setting up of a shared payment network system of Automated Teller Machines (ATMs) to improve customer service.

Mainframe computers were installed in many banks, and mini computers at some centres (Zonal /Regional Offices). Electronic clearing services are being provided and tele-communications in seven big cities have been brought under BANKNET, for giving and receiving messages. This was extended to smaller cities also later on. The offices of RBI and Government of India (Banking Division) have been connected to this dedicated communication network. Banks as well as FIs have already entered the world of Information Technology and Computer Networking.

Management vs. Bankers and Lenders

Bankers and Management relations depend on the efficiency of the latter with which they manage the affairs of the company. Banks can provide clean advances sometimes, if the party is good and credit rating is high. Otherwise the same facility is given as overdraft or a demand loan against a collateral or mortgage. Banks are now discouraging cash credit accounts but are encouraging demand loans and term loans.

At the next stage, if the company has inventory, banks keep a margin of 20 to 50% and lend against inventory and receivables; working capital limit is fixed on the basis of sales, cash inflows and outflows of the company based on the estimated receivables and payables (net current assets). The gap in the amount and time between sales realisation and the expenditure for sales is met by working capital from the bank. The management has to submit their funds position month-wise for each quarter.

Efficient managements forecast properly their requirements of funds on a realistic basis, without over valuation or under valuation. After keeping a minimum cash with itself, the company credits the bank account from realisations of credit sales, book debts, bill receivables etc., when the bank's loan account or cash credit account is reduced. The company may again draw on the bank account for its expenditure and the circle starts again in banker-company relationship.

Good management also ensures that there is no diversion of funds from working capital to long-term assets or for trading and speculation or investment in subsidiaries. Besides, management should be prudent, conservative and honest in that they do not allow any diversion of funds but that the end use of bank credit is for the purposes meant for and for productive use. This will enable them to repay the loans in time and promptly.

Current strain and financial stress will arise due to internal and external factors and management has to take corrective action in time and keep the bankers informed so that their support will be forthcoming in time to tide over the temporary financial strain.

Communications and Negotiations

The current strain referred to above is controllable, if corrective action is taken promptly and immediately. The quality of output is to be improved. The inventory has to be reduced by quicker sales and bad receivables have to be properly managed to realise the best out of them, improve the sales and after sales service to increase the cash inflows. It requires a reshuffling of current assets and current liabilities and improve the quality of assets. If there is a time lag, the banker can help the management in the transitional phase provided there is a mutual understanding and good will between the management and banker.

The management is rated for their honesty, integrity and commitment to the unit. They should be running the bank account in a regular and committed manner. They would take measures for rectification of the lapses or weaknesses and keep the bank informed from time to time. Communication should be timely and proper, true and factual without exaggeration and over-valuation. The bankers and creditors are to be kept in good humour and well-informed, by the company whereby they will willingly help the company in times of stress or financial crisis, referred to above.

Similarly, the management should have the competency and expertise for communication skills and they should be in a position to negotiate with bankers and creditors, commute any part for future payment or seek time for settlement of dues and their success in this regard will depend upon their past record, their skills at negotiation and their commitment to improve the unit.

Honesty and Integrity of Management

For all the dealings of the management with the creditors and bankers the voice that convinces them is the sincerity, honesty and integrity of management. This requires special skills at communication, negotiation and power to convince the other party. In such negotiations the financial data, projected inflows and outflows and measures taken for rectification of the weaknesses etc. are to be put forward by the finance manager. The finance function being the kingpin of all the operations, the realistic projections and presentation of factual data along with measures to improve the quality of assets such as receivables book debts etc., should be the basis for re-negotiations with bankers for fresh limits or temporary accommodation. For all these functions, the finance manager or treasury manager is the mouthpiece or the frontliner for the top management.

In all these efforts, the finance manager is responsible to convey the right picture of the company and build an image of honesty and integrity in projections; and realism in estimates for fund requirements. If the bankers and creditors are convinced of the genuineness of these estimates and bonafides of the measures taken for rectification and management's commitment they would readily come forward to help the company to tide over such temporary financial strain or crisis. Ultimately, it boils down to the function of quality improvement in receivables, book debts, inventories etc. on the one hand and increase the realisations from these sources and at the same time postpone the outflows due to creditors and payables, etc.

Consistency in Bank Relations

Bank relations are very crucial for the financial health of the company. If and when any help is needed, the company should be able to count on the bank. The banker-customer relationship is therefore very important and such relations should be fostered carefully by satisfying all the requirements of banks in terms of reporting, keeping the required margins and keeping them informed of the state of finances of the company. In this task, the finance manager plays a key role.

Consistency in reporting, observing the guidelines and conditions for bank loans/finances and to build up a good image in the eyes of the bank is necessary. The finance manager has to be very versatile in his accounts, sound in his practices and more importantly good in relations with bankers, creditors and other counterparts in similar organisations.

The treasurer should be alert and well prepared with contingent plans, if the original projections fail. Restructuring of short-term assets and liabilities and if necessary long-term capital restructuring, resort to inter-corporate funds, public deposits, etc. should be well planned as the next order of support to the company and as alternatives, many such avenues should be kept ready and planned in advance to be implemented at short notice. By such prudent planning and preparedness short-term crisis can be tided over and financial health of the company can be preserved.

Electronic Banking (High-Tech Services)

The latest technology in banking is slow to come, as mass banking and high-tech banking are at opposite poles. The need of the new millennium is that banks should converge high-tech banking with mass banking. In India, bank employees and customers are slow to adopt to any changes and as such the extent of computerisation adopted by banks is poor, even today after a decade since the recommendation by the RBI for introduction of computerisation was made. In 1984, the first report on computerisation by Rangarajan Committee made recommendation for stage-wise implementation of electronic banking. It was followed by a Second Report in 1989.

The main highlights of these two committees are as follows: The first committee recommended:

Automatic ledger posting machines, introduction of unix machines in banks, use of MICR technology for cheque processing, introduction of credit cards, clearing of intercity cheques by RBI in four metro centres, setting up of a BANK NET by RBI and putting up of SWIFT gateway at Mumbai.

The second committee (1989) recommended for a perspective plan for computerisation of banks at selected branches, on line banking at branch level, electronic fund transfer, installation of ATMs and other self service machines by banks, training in banks' manpower in computerisation, etc.

Some banks are not in a position to keep pace with the degree of computerisation needed for customer service firstly, due to their low profitability, poor deposit mobilisation and conservatism.

Banks being used to spoon feeding both from RBI and IBA, they do not take any initiative in any of these lines for historical reasons. Only the foreign banks are exception in that they act in their own interest in the few branches, they have in India. As theirs is a select banking rather than mass banking, they have achieved a high degree of computerisation. As at end of 1999 many branches are fully computerised and have installed advanced ledger posting machines (ALPMs). The 24 Hour Banking, Electronic banking and Electronic transmission of funds have been in operation in respect of many foreign and private sector banks.

The Indian Financial Network (INFINET) is a wide area satellite based net work, using VSAT technology, setup jointly by the RBI and IDRBT and has facilitated the connectivity with in the financial sector.

Present Position of Bank Automation

Many banks have computerised their Head Office work, their accounts and returns etc. But only a few branches have teller machines, and automatic ledger posting machines. Some private sector banks have already adopted them. Even ordinary equipments such as money changers, note counters, exchange counters etc., which are so essential for branch work are not widely used. ATMs are not still adopted by many branches of banks, and there is no possibility of 24 hour banking with many Indian banks, at the present juncture.

BANKNET envisages the connecting of every branch of bank to BANKNET. Each bank has to be connected to other banks by electronic network in each centre and each centre with other centres, so as to secure quick clearance of cheques, money transfers on spot and signature verification electronically etc. are absolutely necessary for quick and efficient service by banks. Some banks like GTB, UTI Bank and ICICI Bank have adopted e-banking for corporate customers.

The practices of banking, for introduction of opening an account, cheque payments, signature verification, money transfer etc. are different from bank to bank and even from branch to branch within the same bank. If that is the state of affairs, Indian banks with a vast network of branches will find it extremely difficult to introduce high tech services like on the spot payment of cheque immediate/spot transfer of funds anywhere in the country, use of credit card, by all customers, machine operated accounts, audit etc. Services to customers through electronic network are yet a far cry for Indian banks, as also automatic credit for local cheques, not to speak of outstation cheques, which take 15 to 20 days.

For quick transmission of RBI messages within the offices of RBI - RBINET has been designed and connected all RBI Offices to BANKNET. (Electronic network for banks). Electronic Clearing System (ECS) was already adopted by some FIs, mutual funds, and banks are providing this service.

Presently the total number of live users of the Society for World wide Inter bank Financial Telecommunications (SWIFT) network stands at around 60. Several banks have connected their upcountry branches to their computer based terminals at Mumbai. Financial messages can be transmitted through a code number by Head Office to branches and *vice versa* in this SWIFT system. Many corporates are using electronic clearing services of banks for customer services.

Banking in Prospect

With banking being increasingly privatised, companies have better choice in selecting banks with specialised electronic network services and corporate service branches. Some 95 banks have industrial finance branches; 181 have SSI branches, 15 have capital market service branches 5 have corporate finance branches and many specialised branches are now operating even among Indian banks. At the same time, banks are now free to charge higher rates based cost-profit considerations, but some nationalised banks still follow the guidelines set by the IBA for all charges, fees, commissions, etc. Companies will thus face a new banking scenario where banking is a cost based service and services will be better in banks operating through electronic network connections The banks will also be choosy in entertaining corporate clients as banks are now conscious of risk weighted assets and non-performing assets in their portfolios. Profit being the main consideration with the banks in the private sector as also in public sector, efficient and financially sound companies will have better access to banking services and for this, finance and funds managers have a heavy responsibility. The alternative avenues of accessing funds and the free entry into the capital market for corporates both in India and abroad, accompanied by a high degree of financial deregulation in bank operations have opened up new challenges to the corporate finance managers.

RBI'S Directive on Debit Cards

In November 1999, the RBI has put additional restrictions on the issue of debit cards by banks. The RBI has barred banks from tying up with non-bank entities and to use such cards to withdraw cash/make deposits from points of sale. It has also imposed existing reserve requirements on card balances. These deposits and withdrawals of cash tantamounts to the acceptance or creation of deposits through the route of debit/Smart Cards. Banks have to get their Board's approval for issue of these cards and have to advise the RBI about the details of the operations, the terms and conditions of the Debit/Smart Card scheme, as submitted to their Boards and the latter's approval.

Electronic Card

The Master Card issued by City bank is being converted into electronic cards through an electronic tape, it records all transactions done through it and can be used only in places and branches where electronic scan and identification is possible. The plastic money leaders, Master card has launched an electronic card, which is claimed to be the first of its kind in India. The waiting time of customers is reduced by this. The card can be accepted at points of sale with electronic authorisation terminal. The electronic programme offers Indian consumers the flexibility, designed to work at all points of sale with this facility and gives added convenience of a new payment product and financial facility for easy transactions.

Debt Recovery : Amendments to DRT Act

Debt recovery by banks would now be quicker. The Amendments to DRT Act proposed provide for more teeth to the Act. Provisions are now made for summary attachment of property of defaulters at the time of filing a complaint, as against the time of judgement, speedier loan recovery process, provisions for counter claim by the borrowers, easy transferability of cases from one DRT to another, besides empowering the processing officer to execute the decree of the official receiver based on a certificate from the Tribunal. Besides, provision is made for summary attachment of property of the defaulter. The attachment would begin at the time of complaint made and not at the time of judgement. This would mean that the borrower would not have time for bleeding of the assets of the company.

As a result of these Amendments to the Debit Recovery Tribunal Act, greater security is provided to the lenders, and an institutional mechanism is extended to reduce the NPAS of the banks and FIs. The provision for certificates ensures that the processing officer would be able to proceed immediately and there would be no delays at the DRT level. It is also important that provision is made for the borrower to prefer counterclaim on the lender which removes the impression that the DRT Act is one sided and favours only the lenders. Now the Act is more balanced and gives more powers for attachment and recovery and delays at the DRT levels would not affect the recovery as at present. If DRT takes time for giving judgement and meanwhile the company goes sick by erosion of assets over the consecutive three years it is referred to BIFR, when it becomes impossible to recover anything from the company.

Internet and Tele Banking Services

Many banks have started Internet banking in India. Vijaya Bank, and Indus Ind Bank, ICICI Bank and many other private banks have totally computerised branches which offer tele banking services. Linked to credit cards the banks are planning to have web sites where cross payments in a business deal can take place. The e-commerce initiatives would facilitate cash management services for corporate clients, where all their accounts in-different branches are consolidated and their cash position is known instantly. The banks can operate a payment highway, where all payments and receipts are credited and clients can operate these accounts.

The City bank has launched a e-commerce service, called Suvidha, with prominent on line service providers, Fabmart, Rediff-on-the net, Satyam on line, COM and LG. Soft. Suvidha customers now have the added advantage of paying for their purchases on the internet directly from their bank account through the debit facility.

Indus Ind Bank has plans to widen its network of automated teller machines. The bank has 21 onsite ATMs now. Till recently it has concentrated on wholesale banking operations with a customer base of only 30,000 and a limited product line. It has launched its first retail products only in the year 1999-2000 with autoloans, housing loans and loans against shares and property. The e-commerce facilities are expected to be made available on the web, for better cash management and for the whole amount of cross payments to be effected in business deals.

GTB has 65 branches all over the country and has started late in 1999 the internet banking services including customer access to their depository accounts and world class products to its customers. It was taken over by OBC in 2004.

ICICI Bank was the first to offer internet banking in India. It has more than 10,000 regular internet accounts, of which more than 50% are those of NRIs. They are provided account opening facilities on the web sites. The ICICI group has also launched an internet payment gateway Christened I payments to handle cash transactions of its client over the net.

UTI Bank has tied up with Comsat-Max to create a communication network for its customers. The network had fifty VST terminals at strategic locations which would help in ATM servicing Internet Management Information System through Lotus Notes and ISRS for the banking industry. UTI Bank has 39 branches, all filled with ATMs and 12 off site ATMs.

Revolution in Banking

With banking industry, integrating, I.T. and harnessing all the internet facilities and electronic banking is in for a regulation in the services. The private banking sector has been the pioneer in using the internet and underlying technologies in vat only banking but in all aspects of finance and commerce. The other service providers and e-commerce companies like business, Tourism, Transport, Traffic etc, tic up with banking to increase their revenue base and their turnover. The private sector banks were the first to cash in the opportunities.

Following the merger deal of HDFC and Times Bank, the Stock Market began to focus attention of private sector banks which are entering into Internet banking services. The consolidation and financial strengthening on the one hand as seen from the mergers in offing (as in the case of OBC and UTI Bank) and their entry into I.T. and Hi-Tech Banking have enhanced their investor values. The funds remittance facilities launched by Time Bank called India link in association with World Exchange Centre of Bahrain for remitting money from Bahrain to India in just 48 hours through a special software was an added attraction for the banking on the Internet.

The table on next page provides data on some internet providing banks.

Table 24.1

Some Financials of Private Sector Banks

in *2004-05*

(in ratios/percentages) **(in rupees)**

Private Sector Bank	Net Profit as % of T.A	Average M.P. of share in Rs.	EPS	P/E ratio	Non-interest income as % of WF
HDFC Bank	1.29	437	17.3	25.3	1.44
ICICI Bank	1.20	310	21.5	14.4	2.52
IndusInd Bank	1.35	49	6.9	7.1	1.79
UTI Bank	0.89	160	8.0	19.8	1.50
Centurian Bank	0.54	11.5	0.185	62.2	1.81

T.A means Total Assets, M.P is market price

EPS = Earnings per Share P/E multiple = MP/EPS

W.F. = Working Funds.

Source: RBI—Report on Trend and Progress of Banking 2004-05.

The above banks are new private sector banks with internet facilities and quoted and listed on the BSE and NSE.

It will be seen from the above table that EPS is relatively higher only for ICCI Bank and HDFC Bank, whose market prices are also high. Net profits as percentage of Total Assets are also high. For the IndusInd Bank, however, its net profits as percentage of T.A. are relatively higher than other banks in the table but its EPs and Market price are relatively lower, which is mainly explained by relatively higher NPAs (as percentage of advances) and declining capital adequacy ratio in recent years.

The item of Non-interest income is presented in the table to reflect of the Treasury operations in banks. This item represents the income from Treasury trading, fees, charges, etc. This again is high in the case of ICICI Bank which also justifies its high market price. Although not shown in the table, the foreign banks have relatively higher non-interest income reflecting their larger treasury operations and nonfunded income. The market price is the result of various factors, sometimes not reflecting the true intrinsic worth of the share.

At the start of the new millennium, the rally of the markets has been contributed largely by Info-tech, Bio-tech, Multi-media, entertainment and finance sector stocks. In India, not all finance sector stocks are in the forefront, largely due to the high NPA of public sector banks and FIs. But some private sector banks are in demand due to internet facilities, e-cornmerce and electronic funds flows.

Of the private sector banks, referred to above HDFC Bank and ICICI Bank have largely kept out of the corporate lending but concentrated more on investments, personal and housing loans, Their NPAs are at a lower level. But in the case of UTI Bank, and Indus Ind Bank, high-level of NPAs are a matter of concern. The Earning per share of ICICI Bank is the highest and so is its Book value per share. Indus Ind bank has the lowest EPS, as also of the Centurion Bank. The UTI bank and Indus Ind Bank are on similar lines with the respect of EPS and NPA, as also of equity and net-worth (not shown in the Table).

E-BANKING : PAYMENT GATEWAY

Payment Gateway

A Payment Gateway is third party network that acquires the transactions from an e-commerce portal and processes it through the banking or credit card system. It serves as a link between the banking net work and the Internet, as the public will have no access into the banking net work.

Payment Gateway acts as an intermediary for effecting transactions between the merchant and the bank's payment processing system. It translates the internet messages into other message formats (like Visa Net) that are used for the authorisation and settlement of merchant transaction.

All payment gateways are based on Secure Electronic Transaction (SET) Technology for ensuring the security and privacy of finance transactions on the internet. It was supported by Master card, Visa, Micro soft, Net scape and others.

Payment Service

A payment service is internet banking provided by a bank on a portal site of a merchant. Payment service is vendor and bank specific. Payment gateway is different in that it provides linking several banks together and is a general service to all banks. It takes a transaction, then certifies it and routes it after securing it with encryption. It also manages the translation and de-cryption.

What is SET

SET is an encryption technology that helps protect the transfer of payment information over the internet. If uses advanced security technology which allows card holders to make secure payments to merchants on the internet.

E-Commerce and Payment Gateway

In India payment services are provided by ICICI Bank, HDFC Bank and Satyam. Consumers interact with the e-Commerce site only. They do not come in direct contact with the payment gateway. When they submit the Credit Card number, this information is forwarded to the Payment Gateway which completes the transaction. The e-Commerce sites are required to have an agreement with bank and the payment gateway provider to access these services. The e-commerce sites do not come to know about the Credit Card authentification and information on customers. This ensures risk free payment mechanism and obviates any misuse of the information.

Payment gateway enables banks to allow real-time transactions from one account to another and from one bank to another. It helps merchants doing on-line business to focus on their products and customers rather than on the payment mechanism. The payment gateway enables secure, fast and standardised e-commerce and e-business. It improves trade turnover and bank transactions are facilitated.

CELL PHONE BANKING AND INTERNET BANKING

The latest craze in banking using electronic media is internet banking. By visiting the web site of each bank, one can enter his key pass word and know the account balance and even pass his own credit and debit entries. Such internet banking facility is opened up by some banks. This means that you can do your banking through your Personal Computer, sitting at home; banks may soon allow zero balance savings accounts through internet facility only, that will obviate the need for bank clerks to pass entries and maintenance of books of account. Each account holder maintains his own account in the web site of the Bank by opening up his pass book page. Banks have been asking for a minimum balance in saving accounts to cover cost of accounting – fixed costs of rent, electricity, furniture, paper, clerical time, etc.

While customers can now make only balance enquiries download statements and open fixed deposits' over the net, they will soon be able to carry out all these transactions over the net and visiting a bank branch would then become needless. Similarly, the increasing use of ATMs, and then installation of offsite areas by banks has done away with personal visits to bank branches.

The credit card base in India is expected to grow from the present level of 3.5 million to 11 million by 2007. The plastic money is expected to account for 15% of all transactions in India by a decade next from just 1% at present. That means that the use of cash will come down further. The Debit Cards will out do Credit cards in numbers, but credit cards are expected to account for a lion share of business transactions in the current millennium. In the years to come, Mobile Phone will drive banking transactions. These mobile phones will be equipped with Smart Cards that are embedded with banking and other information. Instead of going to the Bank ATM, all you do is to punch up your bank account through your cell phone. ATM then loads the card up with whatever sum you wish to add to it and the Smart Card automatically deducts the amount of cash purchases. It is also possible to make enquiries on balance in the account and transfer of funds from one account to another through your mobile phone. This mobile phone banking facility is yet to come but the mechanics of linking the banking with the cell phone is being worked out.

Already the linking of banking with the internet is completed. The banks can be interconnected branch-wise and bank-wise, through the internet facility which was done already by some banks like OBC. The increase in the installation of teller Machines for all branches is the first step for the electronic banking facility. The use of e-mail for banking will open up the gates for internet banking. The next step is the smart banking by the use of cell phone, where banking will be on the wheels and mobile. These facilities will increase the volumes of turnover of credits and debits in banks and increase in transactions electronically.

WEB-BASED BANKING SOLUTIONS

City Bank has launched in Jan. 2000 two new web based corporate banking Solutions in India namely speed collect 2000 and Citi commerce. These two products, provide their corporate customers with essential link in the present day e-Commerce environment on line information, financial settlement and reconciliation. Speed collect 2000 is an extension of the city bank's cash management product, which can now be accessed by customer through a regular internet browser. Citi commerce is a seller centric e-commerce solution, which links corporates with their dealer net work.

ICICI Bank is another private bank which is a leader in providing internet banking facilities to its customers. It is the first bank to provide credit card to its customers through a tie up with visa which enables the customer to see the transaction details and make payments over the internet. It provides the web site commerce and links it with bank payments through the credit card. It is the final link in the bank's chain of personal products that were launched over the last three years. It is a coherant strategy of leveraging technology and existing customer base to increase its market share in e-Commerce.

The e-Commerce has come to stay and increase in volumes and Gateway providers help the linkage of banking to the merchant business and trade. The internet banking will revolutionise banking in India. Cell Phones help this growth by linking the Satellite Communications with internet banking. These new financial products will grow in the years to come.

Mobile Banking

Internet and well-based banking has some limitations, like a P.C. and a Net connection. As against this, wireless cell phones are more accessible to all and sundry, reaching a total of 80 million and growing at a rate of 3 million, a month. Initially, banks use this mobile phone numbers to transmit account information through alerts by **SMS**, WAP, and SIM Toolkit. The customer sends an SMS by Typing the predefined code name for accessing his specific account information along with a password to the number published by the Bank. The reply is received from the bank's system as SMS.

The bank can send alerts through SMS on the account balance, insufficient funds, credits and debits, etc. Once the customer opts for this service, banks' system sends automatic alerts to the Customers' handsets, anywhere in the world. The customer can react and pass orders of what is to be done from anywhere in the world through his cell phone. Such banking is very useful to the customer, particularly for the corporate clients of banks. Advances in encryption and other technologies can ensure high security for any financial transaction with the Bank.

❑ ❑ ❑

25 MANAGING INVESTOR RELATIONS

Investor is the backbone of the Joint Stock Companies. He is the owner or creditor and takes the risks involved in the enterprise. In that sense the promoters of the company are themselves the owners and investors. The investing class is a general term and encompasses in the legal sense all the following categories :

(i) Promoter/Director and their associates.

(ii) Collaborators if they are involved either with equity stake or with loans/advances to the company.

(iii) Banks and financial institutions who are having equity through underwriting commitments or firm allotments of the stock of the company.

(iv) Mutual funds and corporate bodies, who invest in their own capacities for the benefit of their constituents, who are themselves savers and investors.

(v) NRIs, FFI, Pension Funds, GIC and LIC, UTI, etc.

(vi) The individuals or HUF who invest in their capacity as savers.

Of the above categories, the major groups are (i) Institutions (ii) Individuals. The former hold nearly 40 - 60 % and the rest by individuals. Sometimes the category of individuals hold much less, if the promoters and financial institutions hold a larger proportion from their own resources. In good companies like Tisco, ACC, Reliance, the holdings of individuals, running into 5 to 20 lakhs in number would account for about 30 - 40 % of the total holdings. In recent times only 25% need to be given to the public for purposes of listing and their holdings may be lower, after listing. Now the SEBI is insisting on continued observance of all listing requirements by listed companies.

Importance of Investor Community

As referred to earlier, they have a large stake in the company and the activities of financial nature of the company are related to the investors, as shown below.

Corporate Financial Management

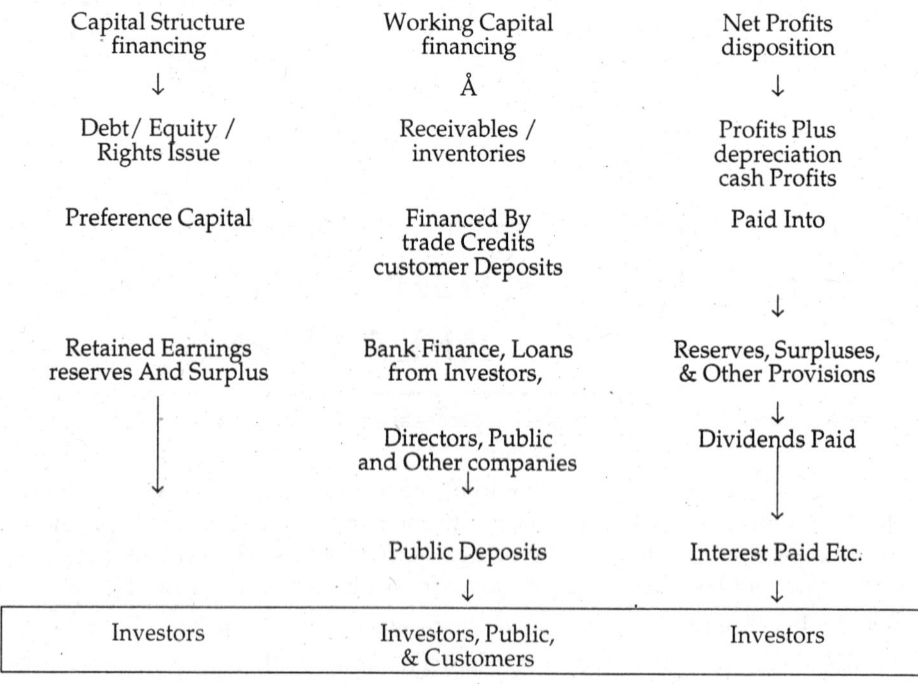

Fig. 25.1

In the above chart, investors help finance the equity and debt in the capital structure. As equityholders, they are owners of the companies, entitled to all privileges of voting, rights, bonus dividend, etc. They are the owners of the net worth of the company comprising of equity plus reserves and surpluses. There are also preference shareholders who are the owners as well as creditors. Besides in many companies, they provide funds through deposits, for working capital, supply raw materials, inputs etc., and sometimes the directors/promoters provide loans to the company. Even when banks and financial institutions provide funds for working capital, the companies which need funds more than those sanctioned amounts by banks, have to resort to the public in the form of loans and deposits for short-term periods of one to three years. More recently reliance on capital market (investing public) is found to be a cheaper source of finance, than banks.

Investors as a class thus provide financial backbone to the company and have to be kept satisfied and happy in their relations with the company. Many employees, are investors; even promoters, directors and their associates and collaborators are investors. Investors as a class are interested in rising share prices, which in turn depends on the intrinsic worth of the company, their profits, dividends, right and bonus issues. All these depend on the efficient financial management of the company and management perspectives of the promoters. In a sense the investors are, as a class, the owners of the funds and hence finance and treasury managers have to keep their interests in mind.

In respect of the above regular entitlements to investing shareholders, the investing class may have complaints of many types, against companies.

(i) As regards non-receipt or delayed receipts of dividends, rights, bonus, etc.

(ii) Non-receipt or delay in despatch of letters of allotment, for new issues.

(iii) Delay in listing and manipulation of prices before listing.

(iv) Delay in transfer of shares into own name. The normal limit is one month for listed companies to effect share transfers and two months under the Companies Act.

(v) Delay in receipt or non-receipt of debenture interest or repayment of principal to debentureholders.

(vi) Delay in payment of interest or non-payment of principal in respect of fixed deposits.

(vii) Issue of duplicate certificates in cases of lost certificates and delay in rectification of bad deliveries.

(viii) Issue of odd lots and problems of their sale. The above complaints are to be minimised by prompt action by companies and their Registrars and Transfer Agents of the Company.

Investors as Analysts

Investor community are not necessarily passive and sleeping members. Some of them take active interest in the company's affairs and analyse their performance, based on the available data from time to time. For this, they need the information flow regularly and periodically, through press reports on Board meetings and their decisions, press interviews of the top executives of the company, half yearly and quarterly results published by the company, AGM and EGM and their proceedings, their expansion and diversification plans, if any, etc. The speech of the Chairman at the AGM/EGM contain a future perspective of the company. The report of the directors contain the factual position of the company and an explanation of the factors leading to such position. Some developments like change in market conditions, labour problems, raw material scarcity, natural calamities or government policy changes, which all effect the company's performance will be contained in these reports. Besides the financial statements, namely, profit and loss account, balance sheet statement, profit allocation statements and notes accompanying them contain data which investors use for their own analysis and interpretation. Most important of all these data are the accompanying schedules, and auditors' notes on the accounting practices and procedures.

The investors, both potential and actual, analyse these data and project the future earnings flow to estimate the share price on the basis of company's past and likely future performance. The equity analysts and research groups specialise in different methods of research on corporate performance. These methods are financial data analysis, collection and collation of the information from press reports and plant visits and, if necessary, interviewing the company executives, their suppliers, distributors, and consumers. This type of market and equity research is the basis of investors' decision on their purchases and sales of corporate shares and securities. The share price of the company is the broad index of the corporate financial performance.

Financial managers and public relations officers of the companies provide the basic picture of the company to the investors. The financial position, for which the finance manager is responsible, will be the basic framework, which the investors look into. The public relations officers, investors service cells and share transfer agents also provide many services to investors. They provide immediate contact with the investors and as such they are expected to keep the investors, satisfied with the services. But basically the operations of finance or treasury managers alongwith the top management determine the shareholder's wealth and the share price in the market.

Companies which are progressive bring out the progress of the company, an outline of their operations, expansion plans, etc., in brochures for distribution to investors. Some companies have video cassettes and information literature ready for investors at request. Such progressive companies who have these investor relations departments or service cells are Reliance, Raymond Industries, L & T, Essar Group etc.

SEBI and Investor Relation

The SEBI is now inviting all Companies for better investor relations and is collecting the data from companies about the number of total investor complaints of which how many are satisfactorily disposed of. The time limits within which transfers are effected, the time taken for redressal of grievances of investors etc. are also looked into by the SEBI. During new issue process, the merchant banker and registrars are held accountable and they have to report about the investor complaints to the SEBI. The corporate code of conduct and the rules of corporate governance the transparency and disclosure norms are enforced by the SEBI through the listing Agreement of the Stock Exchanges.

Only in January 1995, the SEBI got penal powers on companies for their lapses in respect of new issues and investor relations. SEBI is also publishing from time to time investor guidance series like Dos and Donots, Rules and Guidelines and other information needed for investors. Major stock exchanges like Mumbai, Delhi and Kolkata are also publishing information on companies, their performance data and information on the record dates, book closure dates, dates of Board meetings and the purpose of meetings etc. There is also computer software data in a consolidated form on all listed companies with some computer software companies. Mumbai Stock Exchange is publishing Directory of information on companies giving the history, objectives, pattern of shareholding, price data, volume data, financial ratios, data on the income and expenditure and Balance Sheet data over a period of 5 to 10 years. The investors analysing these data as equity research are increasing in number in the recent past. The Mutual funds, financial companies and investment trusts etc. are also having full fledged equity research wings for analysis and recommendations for purchase and sale of equity shares. Portfolio managers are also involved in hightech equity research, sometimes involving the plant visit and spot enquiries and research through personal contacts and questionnaire methods. These research methods include both fundamental analysis and technical analysis and the basis of both are the available data with companies and stock exchanges.

Intermediaries

The image of the company is in many cases spoiled by the foul play of intermediaries, their lapses and malpractices. Thus, price rigging may be done by brokers, and sub-brokers, independent of the company, or by poor services by Registrars and Transfer Agents. The reputation of RIL & Tisco was spoiled by their Transfer Agents and so is the case with many other companies. It is therefore necessary for companies to choose efficient registrars competent to deal effectively with investor complaints and with necessary infrastructure to service a large investor base.

The companies have to choose carefully transfer agents, and other intermediaries for their dealings with the public, for say new issues or for secondary market. All well established companies have started their own subsidiaries to service their investors so that complaints are reduced. They choose reputed brokers and merchant bankers noted for the quality of services. The enlightened companies have started investor service cells in important centres where a large number of their investors are located, as they have to depend on them for their future expansion plans.

Companies' Service to Investors

The companies organise investor conferences at various centres, where the investors are located, post them with informative news letters or brochures on the progress of the company's operations, their expansion plans and diversification at the time of rights or public issues. They keep their investors satisfied with regular dividends and bonus. Not only they organise their annual general meetings, where investors get the annual reports and balance sheets through statutory obligation, but through EGM and also investor conferences from time to time, particularly when they have plans to approach them for rights, debentures, new issues, public deposits, etc.

The companies have to keep the investor relations good for their own interest and mutual trust. This is done by periodic reports, news letters, investor conferences, EGM & AGM, etc. This can obviate any influence of rumours, by interested parties on the investors. They can give correct and unbiased information to investors so that investors can make a correct assessment of the company, instead of depending on the biased reports of financial journalists or rumours spread through "Market Khabar" etc. The healthy relations between company and investors can be built on the sound financial and accounting practices efficient financial management resulting in increasing profits and keeping the correct data and information before the investors and transparency in their operations. The treasury operations and finance function play an important role in the gamut of investor services. The malpractices of insider trading, rigging up of prices and other frauds can be eliminated by such healthy traditions and good investor relations, which is an important part of the code of corporate governance observed by the listed companies.

Programme of Investor Relations

Each company should thus have its programme of investor relations, a service cell, efficient transfer agency and effective public relations office. Such programmes can be drawn up on an annual basis and information can be passed on through public relations office. The service cell will look into the grievances of investors, complaints against various departments of the company and the intermediaries like merchant bankers, collecting bankers and registrars.

The company can also plan monthly or quarterly press conferences or make press releases available to investors either through the press or directly. These can be supplemented by sponsored visits of investors to the company and proper and timely response to investor queries, complaints and correspondence. In the new Companies Amendment Act, there is a provision for companies to keep a fund for investor services and education, which can be used for financing the investors in the above objectives.

Grievances of Stock Exchanges for Investors

Complaints against members were in the nature of non-payment of sale proceeds, non-settlement of accounts etc. Of the total complaints against members, about 85% were settled during the year, itself. There are more complaints with stock exchanges against listed companies.

The complaints against companies are in the nature of non-receipt of allotment letters, refund orders, non-receipt of dividends, interest etc. delay in transfer of shares and in splitting and consolidation. The clearance of these complaints is also attended to by the Investor Service Cell by writing to the companies, follow-up telexes, etc. and finally by warning to delist the companies, concerned. But the clearance of these complaints is slow due to the non-compliance or slow compliance by the companies to the references made by the cell. The powers of the stock exchange are limited to warnings and delisting of shares and as such compliance by the companies was poor. SEBI has now powers to penalise companies for offenses of such nature, particularly when companies violate any provisions of the listing agreement, entered into with stock exchanges.

Customers' Protection Fund

The Customers' Protection Fund is constituted by some exchanges to safeguard the interests of the investor clients from defaults of the stock brokers. The fund is financed by way of a levy on the turnover of members collected at the rate of Re.1 per Rs.10 lakhs of turnover and at the rate of 2% of the listing fees, earmarked by the exchanges, or at any other rates, as decided by the governing Board of the Exchanges.

Investors' Responsibility

Investors in stock and capital markets need a word of caution. Firstly, these investments are more risky, returns are uncertain and share values are subject to wide fluctuations. Secondly, such investments require an art and expertise to pick up the right stocks, failing which the investors would burn their fingers. Thirdly, the players in the market, namely, brokers and issuers of securities, namely, companies, are not rated high for their honesty with the result that investor complaints against stockbrokers and companies have been increasing over the years. It would, therefore, be necessary for investors to prepare themselves well before entering into the capital market.

Preparing to Invest

Investors desiring to invest in stocks require a lot of preparation. The weak-hearted and risk-averter should first make an entry into the capital market by buying only debentures, with a buy back arrangement particularly convertible debentures of good companies, or subscribe to new issues of promising and well-established companies and aim at fixed returns. After sufficient study and preparation, the investor should act like rag-pickers in the market, picking up good scrips on a selective basis. The main selected companies from promising and growing industries should be picked up after collection of all relevant information and data on the companies and a scientific analysis of their fundamentals. The undervalued scrips should be purchased at the right time with the help of fundamental analysis and technical analysis.

Balance Sheet Study

Investors entering the stock market should also get into the habit of detailed and careful study of the balance sheets of companies in which they wish to invest. Similarly, they should examine carefully the detailed prospectus before subscribing to the new issues of companies. The habit of relying on rumours, or advice of brokers or friends should be replaced by the habit of self-study of balance sheets and prospectuses of companies. The factors which should be looked into and ratios that should be analysed are based on financial data of the company. The Finance Manager or Treasury Manager has a good role to keep the investors of the company happy.

Protection in the New Issues Market

The main source of information on which investors depend in the new issues market is the prospectus, which should contain correct statements of fact. Any false statements, fraud, etc. are punishable under the Companies Act. Under Section 56 of the Companies Act, the Directors are subject to civil liability for any misstatements of facts or untrue statements.

Under Sections 63 and 68 of the Companies Act, the Directors are also liable criminally for any fraud or false statements in the prospectus. Companies' liability for misstatements arises from untrue statements and statements which are material for investors and particulars on which investors depend to make investments. The directors or promoters of the company are thus subject to both criminal and civil liability under the Act for any misstatements in the prospectus. Although Directors take the final responsibility, it is the expertise of Finance Manager or Treasury Managers who has to help the company in all such cases.

Protection for Fixed Deposits

Section 58A of the Companies Act deals with the subject of Fixed Deposits. There are some rules which apply to non-banking companies, private and public limited companies, who wish to raise deposits from the public.

No deposits can be invited from investors or the public unless the companies follow the rules and guidelines made by the Department of Company Affairs in consultation with the RBI. Interest rates, maturity period of deposits, and the amount permissible to be raised by the companies are all given in the form of guidelines by the Department of Company Affairs. The companies have to follow these guidelines while accepting deposits from the public. Renewal and repayment are also regulated by the Companies Act and the rules framed by the Department of Company Affairs. When a company fails to repay the deposit, the depositor can complain to the Company Law Board (CLB) in the specified form duly filled in, together with the fees for the application for non-payment of interest or non-repayment of deposit. The order of the CLB is final and binding on the company and the company has to comply with it. Any non-compliance with the order of the CLB or violation of the provisions of the company law would invite penalty of imprisonment and fine. This provision however, does not apply to sick companies, referred to B.I.F.R.

Legislative Protection of Investors

The Companies Act and the Listing Agreement of the Stock Exchanges provide certain safeguards to investors. The normal complaints against companies and the protection available are listed below :

	Complaints	Legislative Provision	Relief Prevent
1.	Delay in refund of excess application money or allotment letters.	Section 73 of the Companies Act as amended by Amendment Act of 1988.	Payment of interest for the delayed period beyond 30 days from the closure of subscription list at the rate of 15%.
2.	Delay in transfer of shares.	Section III of the Companies Act. This Problem does not arise for shares in Demat form.	A time limit of two months provided in the Act for effecting transfer. As per the Listing Agreement, the time limit is only one month from the lodgment of shares.
3.	Refusal to transfer shares.	Section 22(A) of SC(R) Act. This section lists the reasons for which transfer of shares can be refused.	Transfer can be refused only for specific and valid reasons given in the Act and not otherwise.
4.	Problem of odd lots.	Listing Agreement provides for issue of certificates in marketable lots and avoidance of odds lots. This problem does not arise for demat form of holdings.	Need for consolidation of odd lots and ensuring the issue of shares only in marketable lots through conversion of debentures or rights issue, provision of an odd lot trading session and listing out brokers willing to trade in odd lots.
5.	Take-over bids.	New clauses of 40(A) and 40(B) of Listing Agreement SEBI Regulations and takeover code of SEBI.	Purchases or acquisition of shares beyond 5% to be notified to the stock exchange. Acquisition beyond 10% take over code puts an obligation on the transferor and transferee and intermediary to notify the Stock Exchange and the public and offer to the other shareholders of the company to buy at their price or the highest market price during the preceding six months.

6.	Insider trading, rigging and other malpractices.	SEBI (Insider Trading) Regulations 1992.	The investors have to guard themselves regarding the price and their investment.
7.	Delay and non-payment of interest fixed deposits by companies.	Section 58(A) of the Companies Act.	Complain to the Company Law Board.
8.	Delay and non-payment of dues or non-delivery of shares, etc. by brokers.	Rules, Bye-laws, etc. of the Stock Exchange.	Complain to the Grievance Cell of the concerned Stock Exchange and to the SEBI.
9.	Delay in Defective Deliveries.	Stock Exchange Guidelines to the company to accept the attestation of Registered Stock Broker.	As the signature differences are the main cause of the defective delivery these can be rectified by the attestation of the Registered member broker and delivery can be quickened.

Note: The SEBI has also been receiving investor complaints and besides taking up the matters with companies, merchant bankers, etc., they are publicising such complaints in the newspapers for the public to know and isolate the concerned companies and their Registrars. The Department of company affairs is also receiving complaints against companies and the matter is also pursued by the SEBI which has now powers to penalise the companies for investor complaints.

CRISIL Ratings and Investor Protection

Investors should also be familiar with the ratings given by the Credit Rating and Information Services of India Ltd. (CRISIL) or any other credit rating agency, for protecting their interests. The CRISIL ratings are given only for debt instruments of companies, namely, Commercial Papers (CP), debentures, bonds and fixed deposits. Since early 1992, the ratings of Investment Information and Credit Rating Agency (ICRA) are also used by companies. These are given on a voluntary basis and may be publicised or not, depending upon the company's own perception of the impact of these on the investors. Another agency rating company is the CARE (Credit Analysis and Research Ltd). The ratings used by the companies are published by the "CRISIL Rating Scan." The companies use them only when the ratings are favourable to them and when they are making any public offer for deposits or debentures, etc. The investors should examine these symbols with regard to their benefits and their implication. Since a rating given can be revised upwards or downwards, the investors should keep a watch on any such revisions. Unfortunately, the CRISIL itself would not publicise them for the benefit of the investors as it is a private and autonomous organisation and is under no obligation to do so. The SEBI guidelines now insist that all companies should get these ratings and publicise them compulsorily, if they are borrowing from the public through issue of debentures. Many companies accepting fixed deposits are also using these ratings. Under the new companies Act 1993, credit rating for acceptance of deposits is compulsory.

The implications of the ratings used are as follows:

For Debentures, simple A and B are used; for preference shares, "PF" is prefixed. For fixed deposits and short-term instruments "F" and "P" are prefixed.

Debenture Ratings	Implication
Triple A - (AAA)	- Highest Safety
Double A - (AA)	- High Safety
Single A - (A)	- Adequate Safety
Triple B - (BBB)	- Moderate Safety
Double B - (BB)	- Inadequate Safety
B, C & D	- High risk and default-prone
Fixed Deposits Ratings,	
F Triple A - (FAAA)	- Highest Safety
F Double A - (FAA)	- High Safety
F Single A - (FA)	- Adequate Safety

FB, FC and FD are inadequate, high-risk and default -prone instruments.

Crisis Situation and Investor Hostility

Companies in financial trouble or with problems of labour, electricity etc. will be in Crisis situations. When in any year or half year, the results are disappointing, the investor hostility will crop up. Similarly, if company is involved in rigging up of prices or insider trading or other malpractices for which in fact the company may not be directly involved, the investor hostility with biased reporting will again emerge. There may be other reasons, why investor hostility, indifference and antogonisum will arise. The best way to tackle such situation is for the company's public relations officer to give corrected picture of these developments, admit of any mistakes and inform the corrective measures taken and try to win back the confidence of the investors. Yellow journalism and rumours can be nipped in the bud, by such correct press statements, given by the company in time and inform the same to the stock exchanges where its shares are listed and to the SEBI so as to keep its record clean and overcome the hostility situations in time and keep healthy and good relations with investors. In sum, investor is more important or equally important as the consumer and investor confidence and loyalty will help the financial management and expansion and growth of company. Investor rating of the company is important, if the company wants to raise fresh funds through equity, debentures or deposits. It is thus, investor rating which has to be influenced by the Finance Manager or Treasury Manager through

(1) Sound Financial Principles of Capital Structure.

(2) Efficient financial operations leading to rising profitability, net profits and cash inflows.

(3) Prudent financial management for ensuring long-term solvency (leverage) and short-term liquidity (Current ratio).

(4) Plan for building up increasing reserves, net worth and expansion plans with a view to rising the market price of share in which the investor is ultimately interested.

The wealth of the investor can be increased by growing share prices and rising market capitalisation, for which the efficient Treasury Management is a pre-condition.

❑ ❑ ❑

26 MIS FOR TREASURY OPERATIONS

Introduction

Treasury Manager has to operate in the financial markets and the factors influencing these markets are of paramount importance to him. If he has to operate efficiently and plan for these operations, he has to be well-informed of all the current developments in economic and financial field. For this, he will have to develop a management information system (M.I.S.) of all events of importance to his work. Such information can be stored in files or in computers and updated from time to time as changes take place on a daily basis, as reported in the press, journals, etc.

The M.I.S. in which the Treasury Manager is interested consists of information and developments, which can be classified under the following heads.

1. ***Current Economic Developments:*** Events happening in the economy, sectors, industries and the government policies influencing them.
2. ***Current Monetary and Credit Policies:*** Policies of the Reserve Bank of India, which influence cash, currency, M1 to M4 and credit system of the economy — cost and availability of cash and credit; Liquidity trends affecting money market and monetary and banking trends are evidenced from these policy changes, in which the treasury operations are critically involved.
3. ***Fiscal and Budgetary Policies,*** which determine tax system, budgetary expenditure and deficits, public debt and the financial markets particularly in debt instruments and the gilt-edged market, and factors influencing them as Treasury Manager operates in these markets.
4. ***Foreign Trade and Foreign Exchange Policies,*** which influence the exports and imports cost of financing them, and the foreign exchange

reserves of the country, foreign inflows and investments in the financial markets, in India. The changes in these policies affect the operations of the treasury manager in the Forex Markets in particular and all markets in general. The spot and forward rates, interest rates in foreign markets, forward premiums etc. and factors influencing them, including all the derivative markets in them are relevant to the treasurer.

5. ***Trends in Financial Markets:*** Current developments in the money market, stock and gilt-edged markets and in each of the segments of these markets vitally influence the financing decisions and investment operations both in short-term and long-term in which Treasury Manager is involved.

   Trends in gilt-edged market and forex markets are relevant to him directly if he is operating in them and indirectly, even if he is not operating in them, as all the markets are interlinked in the present liberalised economic and financial environment and open-economy.

6. ***International Developments:*** With the opening of the economy and globalisation in process and with the present system of current account convertibility of the rupee, international events influence the forex market, the government debt market, particularly because of a good component of external debt of the government of India and the business sectors in India and through them all the other sectors and financial markets generally in the context of the above inter-relationships, international trade and growth and foreign currency trends etc., influence the economy and financial markets.

All these developments can be incorporated in the MIS and made available on the website of his P.C.

Current Economic Developments

In the backdrop the quinquennial average rate of growth of the economy at around 5% during Nineties, the economy was projected to grow at 8% in the next five years. This compares well with 7.8% in 1994 - 95 and 7.6% on 1995-96 which itself reflected the economic recovery seen in the earlier years. The rate of growth was around 6.5% in the second half of Nineties and early in 21st century.

This rate of growth of the economy is supported by strong upswing in savings and investment. As per the C.S.O. estimates, gross domestic savings at current prices constituted around 28% of the G.D.P. now at current prices as against relative stagnation of 21% during the preceding three years. Gross capital formation stood at around 30% of G.D.P. and this rise is explained by large inflows of funds for investment. The savings of household sector and private sector have contributed to this uptrend. Actual growth rate of manufacturing production was about 9% in the Tenth plan period 2002-07.

The CMIE estimates show that there is a slackening in growth of the infrastructural industries and particularly in power sector during later half of Nineties. Although services sector may grow at around 8-9%, the growth of agricultural sector in the Nineties was good due to good monsoons in many parts of the country. But the average growth rate of agriculture in the second half of Nineties was only 2-3%, and was lower in some years during 2001 to 2007.

In any assessment of the real economy, both the stock position and flow position should be considered. It is in this context that food production should be viewed against the background of existing stock and industrial production against the backdrop of the earlier growth rates and the stocks position. Taking the overall position of the economy including the services sector, and the various components of it, a view has to be taken of the likely trend of the fundamentals of the real economy, by the treasury manager.

As part of the economic fundamentals, the corporate treasury manager has to study the industry prospects and the present state in the background of the past growth. Although the general picture of all related industries should be known to him, he has to specially study of the industry to which his corporate unit belongs. Thus, the treasury in a bank should know thoroughly of the banking industry and treasurer in leasing industry should be thorough of the leasing industry and its fundamentals, in addition to all other knowledge.

In the study of the industries, the industry analysis which is generally recommended is the same as is recommended in the fundamental analysis in investment management. He should be familiar with the product lines, raw-materials and input capacity installed and utilised, industry features demand nature such as income elasticity, price elasticity of the products market etc., government policy and its attitude to the industry, labour relations, personnel management (HRD) etc. in the industry. The past, present and prospects for the future should be reviewed from time to time with special reference to his competitors in the industry.

In the present scenario, the sectors to be watched for growth prospects are banks, finance, cement, hotels, auto, textiles, petrochemicals, drugs, healthcare, informatics, computer software, telecommunications, and infrastructure industries in particular. These will change from time to time. The industries have also stages of growth, decadence and stagnation or recession, etc. All these require a close watch and study by the treasury manager, when he is operating in the financial markets.

Aim of Financial Reforms

Financial reforms aimed at improving the health of the banks and financial institutions. The budgetary support is stopped to all public sector banks so that they can depend more on the market and their performance judged by the market forces. Competitive efficiency is increased and intermediation costs are brought down and direct access to savings of the public is provided. These are part of the structural reforms undertaken since July 1991, aimed at improving efficiency in the banking industry.

The administered tiers of interest rates on both bank deposits and advances were brought down. Interest rates are now freed from controls. Capital adequacy norms were brought into force within a time frame and banks and FIs were given direct access to capital market to strengthen their capital base and improve operational efficiency and profitability. Prudential norms for income recognition, classification of assets on the risk weighted basis and provisioning for bad debts and NPAs (Non Performing Assets) were provided for. Special Debt recovery tribunals were setup to recover bank dues faster than before. Branch licensing policy was dispensed with and closure of non-viable branches including foreign branches was allowed.

Trade Union support in banking sector paved the way for quicker computerisation of operations and better customer service. For grievance redressal of bank customers area-wise, particularly with respect to advances, special ombudsmen were appointed. The guidelines for improving customer service in banks and for reduction of NPAs, and provisioning for bad debts, were provided by the RBI. Computerisation and faster clearing and quicker services were aimed at. At the same time, these services are charged on a cost plus basis so that their profitability will improve in the immediate future.

Current Monetary and Credit Policy

The Monetary indicators, namely, currency with the public (c), Money supply with the public (M_1) and aggregate Monetary Resources (M_3) have shown a faster growth rate than warranted by real economic growth during the decade of Nineties.

During this period, the average rate of growth of currency was 17%, M1 of 19% and M3 of 18% per annum. These have to be compared with the average rate of growth of GDP of around 4-5%, and of industrial production of about 8%. These factors have led to an average rate of inflation measured WPI or CPI of more than 8%. So during 1995-96 the rate of growth of money supply was brought down to around 15%, which led to liquidity crunch in the system. The RBI wanted to control inflation through a straight curb on credit and accordingly inflation rate was brought down to around 6% in 1996, and to 5%, early in the 21st century.

The currency expansion is at a faster rate, particularly due to budgetary deficit surpassing the estimates in 1996-97. With the deposit growth decelerating to around 5 to 10%, there was a wide gap in the resources of the banking system in some years. There were spells of liquidity crunch in the financial system during 2001 to 2007, due to slow down in the growth of M_1 and M_3.

The impact of these developments is seen in gyrations in call money rates which skyrocketed to as high as 130% in Sept.-Nov. 1995. The liquidity crunch in the banking system persisted after Nov. 1995 despite the lowering of the CRR from 15% to 14%, in two stages. The CRR was brought down further from 14% to 12% by stages in 1996, and further to 10% in stages, in October 1996 and January 1997, to improve the overall liquidity position of banks. The CRR was lowered further to 5% by October 2004. The SLR was also lowered to 25% in October 1997 from the earlier rate of 34.75% in September 1994. The call rates and interest rates in general continued to persist at higher levels than initially anticipated. The ICD rates went up to 25% (inter corporate deposit rates) and the rates on certificates of deposits shot up to 18% - 20% and other rates have also gone up sharply. Some of the treasury managers who have thrown caution to the winds have burnt their fingers by lending at higher rates, leading to some defaults in repayments particularly in I.C.D. market. In a volatile market, the treasury manager will become avaricious and greedy and jump in to the fray to make quick profits which may land him into troubles. This happened during 1995-96. During 1996-97, treasury markets have become sober and more stable. With the policy of deregulation of interest rates, the RBI has removed ceiling rates on credit limits beyond Rs.2 lakhs granted by banks. The deposit rate ceilings and lending rate floors etc. were removed in 1996-97.

The prime lending rate of banks with banking sector was changed in tune with the monetary policy. Along with the deregulation of interest rates, the lending norms of banks as also the discriminatory limits, margins etc. were also left to the respective banks to be decided. Advances against shares and debentures have been relaxed; although there are no bank wise limits for bank advances against shares, the individual limit of Rs.10 lakhs is still maintained. A number of relaxations have been made in the directives relating to banks. In addition to underwriting and investments in shares and debentures, and they are also allowed to trade in the stock market. Restrictions in granting bridge loans were maintained but ceilings on term loans were relaxed, as at end of December, 1996, but those controls were removed in 1998 and 1999.

Bank credit to NBFCs was tightened particularly to leasing and hire purchase companies, as they seem to compete with banks, in mobilisation of public deposits and banks are now allowed to undertake all these activities themselves,either directly or through their subsidiaries. Bank credit limits to the NBFCs were restricted to one to three times their NOF.

Measures were also initiated to reduce volatility in the maintenance of cash balances by banks in the form of fixing a minimum level of 85% of CRR requirement to be maintained on the first 13 days (barring holidays) and banks can fall short of this requirement of 85% on the 14th day, provided they adjust the average of daily balances to the required 100% level — over the fortnight.

A loan system of delivery of bank credit was introduced in April 1995, instead of the prevailing cash credit system to improve the credit discipline on large borrowers. As per the credit policy prevailing early in 1996, existing cash credit limit, of borrowers with MPBF (maximum permissible bank finance) of Rs.20 crores and above have already been bifurcated the accounts into loan component and cash credit component. The cash credit component is brought down from 100 % earlier to 50% in 1996-97 and loan component is raised accordingly. The issue of commercial paper is in lieu of part finance under MPBF and limited to 75% of the cash credit component. These restrictions on C.P., Bills discounting etc. were mostly removed. Cash credit system was replaced by loans by banks.

The present level of S.L.R. is 25% of aggregate NDTL and CRR at 5% at end March 2006. RBI refinance facility is available to banks upto 1% of the average outstanding deposit on a basis with 0.5% against treasury bills and 0.5% against government securities. All types of refinance except export credit refinance were withdrawn in 1996. Liquidity support for Ledger Adjustment facility was given to banks. The objectives of Monetary policy during the recent period were to moderate the growth of money supply to contain the inflationary pressures, to keep its growth of M3 at around 15% to 18% and to attempt at moderation the growth of net RBI credit to government, and to improve the deposit resource mobilisation of banks; interest rate control was removed and banks are given freedom to fix their rates.

The Average growth rate of M_3 during the second half of Nineties was around 17% and in the period 2001 to 2006, it was at about 15%. The Average GDP growth during the same period was about 6.5% and the average rise of WPI (Inflation) was around 5%, during 2001-06.

As part of the changed policies eight private sector banks were licenced to operate by the RBI and some more are to be approved in the months ahead. The B.R. Act was amended to allow an individual shareholder in a private bank to have ceiling of voting rights upto 10% of the paid up capital and to have a non-executive chairman, to be approved by the RBI and some more reforms are to be implemented in the months ahead. The RBI has also started licensing small local banks under a scheme, approved by the government in the budget. These measures are intended to allow private banks to offer effective competition to public sector banks. Such banks can raise capital contribution from financial institutions upto 20% and NRIs upto 40%.

To improve the supervisory system on the banks, Board for financial supervision within the RBI (BFS) was setup in 1993 and RBI Regulations relating to BFS were framed under Section 58 of the RBI Act, and become effective from July 1994. The RBI has also set up a separate department within the bank to give operational support to BFS, under the caption of Department of Supervision (DOS) since December 1993.

Fiscal and Budgetary Policies

Many fiscal reforms were initiated since 1992 to bring about more financial discipline in the government sector, reduce the budget deficit and subsidies and budgetary support to PSUs and financial institutions. Financially, the gross fiscal deficit which is the excess of total expenditure including loans, net of recovery over revenue receipts and non-debt capital receipts like grants was brought down from 8.33% of GDR in 1990 -91 to 5.89% in 1992-93, and although it went up again to 6.87% in 1993-94, the centre had an average Gross Fiscal deficit of 5.5% during 1993-94 to 2003-04. The conventional deficit which is the difference of all receipts and expenditures on both capital and revenue accounts, as also the monetised deficit of the centre, which is the increase in the net RBI credit to the government, comprising of increase in RBI holdings of 91 day TBs net of cash balances of government with the RBI and increase in RBI holdings of dated government securities, have been decreasing over the last few years, due to an agreement of the government with the RBI to reduce the government's reliance on the RBI to a ceiling of Rs.9000 crores in 1994-95 and taper this limit slowly by 1998 and to eliminate the reliance of the government on Adhoc Treasury bills from 1997-98. These adhocs are replaced by ways and means Advances to the centre so as to reduce RBI credit to the government.

The government has in consultation with the RBI increased the interest rates offered on their debt to the public from low levels 8 to 9% in 1985 to 13.5% to 14.0% in 1996. In the subsequent years 1997 to 2000, interest rates were brought down to 11-12% and further to 7-7.5% by 2006. Besides, the government's reliance on the RBI and banks is reduced and that on the market is increased. The interest burden is rising due to (a) increase in interest rates to market related rates on larger components of government debt and (b) the raising of the short-term debt as a proportion of the total debt in recent years. Total external debt in recent years has stood at U.S. $ 105 billion which is not high relative to Indian' GDP (20%) but the debt servicing ratio at 16% was also low. On the similar lines, the internal debt burden also moved up in the recent past. In recent years interest payments alone would account for about 38% of the revenue receipts of the centre. Both the central and state domestic liabilities are about 90% of GDP in 2004, which is relatively high.

Tax System

Direct taxation was simplified and exemption limits were raised but at the same time the incentives for savings and investment were reduced and simplified. Rationalisation of the corporate tax structure was aimed at, with uniform rates of taxation for all domestic companies at a maximum of 35% since 1997-98 with a 10% surcharge after a level. Rates of taxation were lowered but at the same time, the implementation was made stricter and incentives were given for disclosing incomes and imposed also severe penalty and high tax rates for non-compliances. A new Minimum Alternate Tax MAT was imposed at 12% of book profits, in 1996-97.

Indirect tax system was also rationalised and simplified and the rates of taxation were brought down drastically in stages from 100-150% to 50-65% by 1999-2000 and further to 10 to 15% by 2006-07. The import duties were simplified and reduced and the peak customs duty was lowered to 50% by 2000 and to 10% by 2006. Many export duties were abolished, or reduced. The availability of MODVAT to manufactured outputs provides tax credits for inputs used in the final products and the real burden of taxation is brought down. In general the structure of excise and customs duties was simplified and the impact was brought down to a large extent. What was more important is that a number of small duties on innumerable items were removed and the irritating system of administration was sought to be eliminated by this rationalisation. Many quantitative restrictions were removed, subsidies were reduced and rates were rationalised. These reforms in the tax system were effected in accordance with the recommendations of Chelliah Committee Report on tax system in its reforms in India.

Public Debt Management

The issue of government securities and of treasury bills was made to be on the basis of market determined rates, through the adoption of auction method of issue. This system of auctions and zero coupon securities and other innovations have been initiated during 1992-94. During recent years, there was a deterioration in the financial position of the centre due to larger subsidies interest burden and other non-plan expenditure. There was substantially lower reliance on adhocs and RBI support to government debt only for 1994 and 95. But during 1995-96, and in next three years the net market borrowing was placed higher as compared to 1994-95. The government has issued treasury bills and to retire them, they have funded them into medium and long term debt. The government debt was offered in various instalments to the market with fixed coupons or on the basis of auctions, but the market absorption was only 50-60% of the total offer; in the latter half of Nineties and the rest was absorbed by the RBI under the reforms, new instruments of issue and new methods of raising funds were adopted. Mostly auction system was resorted to for the market to decide the interest rates during 2001 to 2006.

The poor public response to government debt was due to slow growth of bank deposits leading to lower demand of banks for the government debt for S.L.R. purposes. Besides, there was acute scarcity of funds in the market, during the greater part of 1995 and 1996 due to increase in demand for funds from the manufacturing sector and also due to diversion of funds from banking to non-banking channels. Large amounts of money were immobilised in stock market investments which was in a continued bearish phase for more than three years from 1996. Funds were also diverted to gold, black channels and into informal sectors. Because of the poor response to divestment of P.S.U. shares the government borrowing needs have increased further and hence greater reliance on RBI, took place in 1996-97. In 1997 there was surplus funds with banks and devolvement on RBI came down and interest rates were brought down, during 1998-2000. After 2000, interest rates policy was made flexible and the rates fell as well on gilted securities, Money market and other markets. Bank rate was lowered from 11% in Jan. 1998 to 8% in July 2000 and further to 6% by April 2003.

Reforms in Exchange Rate Mechanism

The system of managed exchange rate for the rupee on the basis of a stable rate linked to dollar was given up in March 1922. Under the liberalised exchange rate management system which was in operation from March 1, 1992 to February 1, 1993, a dual exchange rate system was in operation, which had seen the coexistence with one official exchange rate and the other market determined rate. As per the arrangements, 40% of the export proceeds were to be surrendered to ADs at the official rate and the other 60% at the market related rates. The dual system could not be sustained for long, as the remittances on capital account (namely, N.R. Deposit Accounts) were allowed full conversion at market rates.

The dual exchange rate system was given up in March 1993, in accordance with the recommendations of the Rangarajan Committee Report on Balance of payments submitted in 1992. This Committee's Report contained wide-ranging recommendations regarding management of the exchange rate system and exchange reserves, including gold, launching of gold bonds, long term external borrowings only for periods above 25 years, etc. The short-term debt was permitted only for trade related purposes. The committee recommended long range planning for realistic exchange rates — a level of reserves of not less than the import value of three months, development of NRI bonds, market for medium term debt and a National Investment Law for codification of the existing policy and practices relating to foreign investment, dividend and employment of foreign nationals etc.

Foreign Trade and Foreign Exchange Policy

The Treasury Management is influenced by various foreign factors, referred to in earlier chapters. They may be set out under the following heads :

1. Imports – cost and availability of imports.
2. Exports – sales abroad and prospects of sales.
3. Foreign collaboration and Technology imports.
4. Borrowing facilities of short, medium and long-term duration.

As regards first two imports and exports the Exim policy as amended from time to time contains all the features of policy. The trade policy aimed at supporting a broad based export strategy minimising the export incentives, progressive dismantling of all quantitative restrictions. Modifications are made every year to make necessary adjustments in the long-term policy. Reference was made earlier to import and export duty reductions and rationalisation of all duties. Trade reforms, which are part of the structural reforms programmes, started in July 1991 were continued year after year with necessary modifications. The modifications made to Exim policy upto May 1995 continued the philosophy of trade, and greater access of imports to agricultural sector and needed capital goods and inclusion of a number of consumer goods on O.G.L. and S.I.L. were effected. Negative list of imports was reduced. Exporters were given the facility of importing zero duty capital goods upto a value of Rs. 20 crores, with an export obligation and deemed export category was expanded. A new trade instrument was introduced for exporters for enjoying the back to back letter of credit access to goods from indigenous suppliers. Since March 1994 when the full current account convertibility of rupee was initiated, the rupee was maintained at a stable level by the RBI giving a reference rate, followed by the FEDAI's own indicative rates, to the ADs. The ADs are however free to vary the rates, subject to their own demand and supply position of currencies. The RBI's buying rate was maintained at around Rs.31.37 during 1993-94 and 1994-95. The rupee was under pressure since March 1995, but recovered to the normal level of Rs.31.37 – 31.40 for the major period upto September 1995.

During April to September 1995, the foreign exchange situation deteriorated due to increased imports, debt servicing abroad and deteriorating fundamentals of the economy, due to inflation and continued high fiscal deficits. Starting from a level of Rs. 31.40 in September 1995, the rupee fell to around Rs. 35.64 by end October 1995 and after remaining around that level for about three months slumped again to Rs. 36.80 on February 2, 1996 and further down to Rs. 38 at one stage in February 1996, mainly due to hedge and speculative transactions by importers and exporters. The payments in A.C.U. were stopped since January 1996 due to turmoil in the forex market. Besides with full convertibility of Rupee on Current Account the need for Acu or SDR was eliminated. The RBI has announced a series of measures to support the rupee, in addition to its pumping out dollars to the market. Foreign exchange reserves fell from a peak of $ 20.8 billion dollars in March 1995 to around $ 17 billion by February 1996, due to the RBI operations in the market and some outflow due to slackening in FFI's operations and slow down in the net inflow of funds. The volatility of forex market was heightened during this period (1995-96), due to steep depreciation of the rupee. The rupee rate established at round Rs. 36.5 per dollar later in February 1996. In 1997 the exchange rate remained more or less stable at around Rs. 35.85 per dollar. The forex market witnessed crisis situations again in Dec. 1997, when the rupee fell from Rs. 36 to 39.5 per dollar and again in July 1998 when the rupee fell to Rs. 42 per dollar and the rate stood at Rs. 44.6 at end March 2000 and Rs. 46 by mid July 2006. The Rupee has seen both appreciation and depreciation during 1999 to 2006, due to many domestic and external factors and exchange rate stood at Rs. 46.495 at end June 2006.

RBI Measures in Forex Market

The turmoil in the forex market since September 1995 led to a depreciation of the rupee by about 20% in seven months as against dollar. The RBI operations in forex market involved large-scale sale of dollars, resulting in depletion of foreign exchange resources during this period and foreign inflows had slowed down with the result that the supply of dollars in the market fell while the demand continued to grow for imports and debt service payments. Although exports were rising at a rate of 26%, in dollar terms, imports are rising faster by about 32%, with the result that current account deficit widened during 1995-96 to 1999-2000. Later, Current A/c was in surplus for three years from 2001-02 to 2003-04 during recent years due to growth of invisibles.

The RBI has directed the banks not to make any forward deals and cancel them later which may be speculative in nature and not for genuine transactions. The other measures of RBI included raising of interest rates on NRE deposits and non-repatreable NRNR deposits, imposition of surcharge of 15% on interest for import credit, fixing up of floor on interest rates for the post-shipment credit for exporters, removal of reserve requirements for NRE and NRNR deposits etc. Banks were advised to discourage advance payments abroad and asked the exporters to bring back the export earnings at the earliest so that outflows are reduced and inflows are increased. Bank's open position, in foreign currencies which used to be Rs. 15 crores on any day was made flexible and changeable, and later RBI removed many of these restrictions. RBI intervened in the forex market by supply of dollars, when there is pressures and purchased dollars also when there is excess supply. There were large inflows during 1998 and 1999 with the result that the level of forex reserves with RBI stood at around $ 34 billion at end of March 2000, and $ 163 billion at end June 2006.

Financial Markets

Among the financial markets, the short-term market of call money ruled generally tight during 1995-96 as compared to relative stability earlier due to liquidity crunch, slow down in deposit growth of banks and diversion of funds from banks to non-bank finance companies and private corporate sector. Call money rates ruled as high as 25% to 130% in 1995-96 as against the rates of 5% to 27% during the preceding years. During 1996-97, the rates came down however due to easy money conditions and lowering of CRR to 12% consistent with the general liquidity crunch. Interest rates continued to rule high during 1995-96. The rates on CDs were as high as 15-18% and on CPs 16% to 20%. The banks found it difficult to satisfy the requirements of credit from their own resources, due to slow deposit growth and fast rising demand on non-food bank credit. This led to growth of participation certificates of banks in the markets.

All the short-term markets experienced tight conditions during 1995 and 1996 as against very comfortable conditions during the preceding three years of 1991 to 1994. The emergence of tightness during 1995 and 1996 was in particular due to : (1) reducing the monetary growth by the RBI (2) tight monetary and credit policy to curb inflationary pressures and (3) out go of funds from the domestic markets to foreign markets due to the continued depreciation of the rupee and the need to support it and finally (4) moderation in capital inflows into money and capital markets in India, due to their depressed conditions.

During the subsequent period 1997 to 1999, money market conditions ruled generally comfortable due to lowering of CRR and SLR easy credit policy of RBI and excess liquidity. The interest rates fell from 14% to 12% in the giltedged market and the call rates were also lower.

Reflecting these trends, the bids received in T.B. Auctions and of sales of government securities rose. The devolvement of RBI went down correspondingly and the government which was forced to postpone the proposed disinvestment of P.S.U. shares and sale of P.S.U. bonds in 1995 and 1996, raised their borrowings significantly in 1998 and 1999. During 2000 to 2006, CRR was further lowered to 5% and the yields on gilted securities fell to 7.5%. The call rates were stable at around 5-6%.

Capital Market Reforms

The Treasury Manager operates also in Stock and Capital Market. Capital Market Reforms started with the setting up of Securities and Exchange Board of India (SEBI) in April 1988, to regulate and oversee the capital market. Later, by the passing of SEBI Act 1992, it has got legal status and powers to regulate all the players in the Capital market, in India.

The setting up of over the counter exchange of India (OTCEI) in 1989, for computerised trading in shares of small companies and venturesome enterprises and of National Stock Exchange (N.S.E.) for trading in both equity and bond markets of bigger size companies in 1993 were the other landmarks in the Reforms process.

The issue of P.S.U. bonds and disinvestment of P.S.U. shares were the other developments, started in 1985 even before the present reforms. All government and semi-government bodies including banks were allowed direct access to the capital market and not to depend on the budgetary allocations.

The entry into capital market was free and pricing of shares was also left uncontrolled since May 1992. After the introduction of computerised trading in the OTCEI and then the N.S.E. The B.S.E. has also started the electronic trading under the caption of BOLT (B.S.E. ON LINE TRADING). Electronic trading with terminals all over the country increased trading volume.

Options and futures trading in stocks and shares was permitted since 2000-01 and attached trading floors are allowed to operate in places where there are no recognised stock exchanges, in principle, through electronic trading.

The other reforms included the entry of FFIs and Foreign security firms, opening of mutual fund business to private and foreign firms, registration and licensing of all intermediaries in the market, including stock brokers, sub-brokers etc. SEBI has powers to control merchant banks, mutual funds stock brokers etc. and even listed companies, in respect of their operations in the capital market.

Insider trading, take overs, frauds, bought out deals etc. are also being controlled by the SEBI for which regulations were set out. During 1992-94, there were boom conditions in the primary market, which slowed down in 1994-95 and later. During the year 1994-95 the amount raised by Non-government public limited companies of by corporate sector through equity bonds and debentures etc. stood at a high Rs.26,456 crores as against Rs.19,502 crores in 1993-94 but during 1995-96, the capital mobilisations showed a fall in the terms of amounts to Rs. 16,000 crores which reflect the sluggish and bearish conditions in the markets, during 1995 and 1996. Afterwards these new capital issues continued to fall to reach Rs.3,721 crores by 2003-04 but rose to Rs. 13,079 crores in 2004-05, and further to Rs. 21,154 crores.

In the secondary market, as also in the forex market, there were undue gyrations and turmoil due to depressed conditions. In the stock markets the cessation of financial and fiscal reforms, liquidity crunch and slow down in the investments by FFIs have also led to continued bearishness in the market during 1995 to 1999. Later the markets became bullish spurred by IT Software, Tele Communications stocks. The rupee depreciated in the forex market by about 20% *vis-a-vis* dollar during September 1995 to February 1996. The fall of rupee is due to large interest payments and growing import needs in the background of lower export growth than of import growth, slow down in invisible receipts and of capital account receipts for short term and medium from investments in India. The fundamentals in the economy and of the balance of payments position were all reported to be sound. The fiscal deficit reached 6.5% of GDP in 1998-99 and 4.34% in 2005-06 while balance of payments (current account) deficit reached 2% of GDP by 1995-96 and 1% of GDP in 2004-05. The problems of the economy were not solved by the reforms due to continued unemployment, inflation and poverty. The process of reforms slowed down since 1995, and this resulted in an effort at heart searching so that the shortfalls and weaknesses of the reforms could be rectified. The election year 1996 also saw some changes in policy, slow down in reforms and economic activity due to weak government at the centre. The installation of a strong Government in October 1999 and recovery in the stock markets in the economy and a slow down in inflation led to the economic recovery and bullishness in 1999 and 2000.

It will thus be seen that almost all financial markets were is a state of euphoria and sansex reached 6000 mark in Feb. 2000. There were again boon conditions from 2003 to 2006, taking the Sensex to a high of 12,000 by May-June 2006. This was attributed to the effect of reforms in the relocation of resources and introduction of efficiency in market forces. Generally, financial markets will undergo various phases of turmoil, disturbances and varying growth rates and cycles.

Forex Market and Forward Premium

The turmoil in the forex market was noticed many times from 1994 to 2000. In view of the persistent pressure on the rupee from the dollar, the forward premium for one month rose sharply to an annualised rate of 10 paise in the beginning of October 1995 from hardly 1 or 2 paise early in September 1995. The forward premia rose sharply thereafter with one month forward rising to 30 paise per $ and three month forward to 21 paise per $ by the middle of February 1996. The one month forward was at an average rate of 35 percent per annum in March 1996 but declined due to return of stable conditions to 6 per cent per annum in March 1997 before rising again to 21% per annum in Jan. 1998 and stood at 5.3% per annum is Sept. 1999. During the latest period of 2005 June, the premium came down to 1 to 2% for one month to six months.

The data show how the premium changed with the perceived risks, expectations of interest rate and currency rate changes, etc. Various forces operate to influence forward premium.

Premia are the indicators of expected changes in interest rates and currency rates in the respective centres. In the case of India, however, the demand and supply factors play a very important part rather than the economic forces, namely, interest rates and currency rate expectations with the continued depreciation of the rupee since September 1995, the premium on the dollar began to rise despite the fact that the dollar was itself weekend *vis-a-vis* the DM and yen, during same periods of the year since than. The turmoil and fears of depreciation in the forex market have kept the traders on their tenterhooks and there was a scramble to hold on to the dollar. All importers began to buy forward contracts or hedge for their forthcoming payments in foreign currencies. All the debt service payments and current account outflows are hedged by swaps, forward contracts etc., with the result that the forward premium shot up and hedge and speculative deals began to increase in number. Forward rate agreements and swaps etc were encouraged and derivatives are being developed in the forex market. These conditions in the later half of Nineties were reversed during 2003 to 2006, when markets were stable and forward premia came down to less than 1% per annum.

International Developments

World economic indicators show that during the latest period 2004-2006, the world output grew at a higher rate of 4 to 5%. Developing countries recorded a still higher growth rate of 6 to 7% and Developing Asia at 7-8%. Inflation in developed countries was only 1.5 to 2.0%, while that of developing countries was higher at 4.5% to 6%. Fiscal imbalances continued for both developed and developing countries alike. Current account balances were growing for advanced countries in terms of deficits; while the surpluses for developing asia were relatively stable. So far as foreign trade trends are concerned, the imports are uniformly higher than exports for developing asian countries, while the reverse is true in the case of developed countries.

World trade trends show that in volume terms exports are growing faster at 6.8% than that of imports at 6.3% in 2006. Similar trends were noticed in the earlier years. Asian countries and Indian in particular are recording larger growth rates. But still, the practices of D.C.s are acting as hassles for the growth of exports of agricultural products and market access for the products.

The establishment of W.T.O. in January 1995 was expected to accelerate world trade, in particular of agricultural products, textiles and services, etc. The prospects of trade and commercial borrowing from world capital markets of London, New York, Tokyo and Frankfurt were good for India with its country rating of BB+. There was continued flow of funds from abroad through FFIs and the Indian Capital Market is expected to grow at a higher rate than before.

The foreign debt of many countries, including India is growing leading to debt servicing burden and larger reliance on commercial borrowing where the rates of interest are higher. The larger export growth and better economic performance would therefore be the only solution to the problems of India *vis-a-vis*, other developed countries. The high growth rate of foreign debt and export sluggishness have made India a country with lower credit rating than that of the investment grade.

In addition to the general economic trends of output, prices and trade, a number of other economic and financial factors, like tax rates, customs law, practices and procedures, interest rates and market conditions in foreign money and capital markets as also in forex market influence the treasury operations in any unit. International markets and foreign currency and foreign exchange are in particular affected by many social and political factors, expectations, rumours and also extra-economic forces, which the treasury manager has to keep a watch.

Leaving aside general trends of output, trade and aid, and developments, affecting all sectors of the economy, the unit in which the treasury manager is operating is also affected by any developments, national and international in addition to those in his own industry, service or activity. Thus, the treasury in leasing industry is affected by general trends in the world on the leasing industry and the law and practices abroad relating to leasing.

Multinational companies, international corporations and international banks are more acutely affected by any and all the factors, both economic and financial as also social and political developments. The law, practices and procedures in the countries in which they operate, or export to or import from have special relevance to the treasury manager, who should know not only the developments but their implications to his operations, for which he should have the expertise of analysis and interpretations of all factors, national and international. He has to build a proper M.I.S. and lead a competent research group to support the front office investment and finance operations.

Corporate Borrowing Abroad

To augment resources for investment, the government has allowed banks, FIs and non-bank finance companies among others to raise funds abroad in the form of equity to promote lending for genuine transactions and not for speculation or diversion into stock market or real estate. For corporates, there is no restriction on the number of euro issues they can make in a year. Infrastructure and related companies are allowed access to foreign funds upto 35% of the project cost. For capital restructuring corporates can raise GDR funds upto 25%. Corporates and institutions are allowed to raise ECBs upto $ 3 million, to pay Telecom Licence fees, exporters and 100% EOUs can raise ECBs upto $15 million. Instead of average maturity of 7 years allowed before, ECBs with a minimum of 3-5 year maturity are permitted and the industries which get easier access to foreign funds are oil exploration, gas, telecom and infrastructure projects. Relaxations were made for foreign investment in India and in Indian banks and corporates borrowing abroad, particularly for I.T. companies, for JVs and acquisitions abroad. The RBI is authorised to give automatic clearance for ECBs upto a limit. Many restrictions were liberalised in the second generation reforms since 1999.

Conclusions

This chapter has set out the more important constituents of the MIS for the Treasury Management. Economic and financial developments, policy changes in the fields in which the Treasury Manager is interested, namely, Monetary and Credit Policy, Fiscal Policy, Tax Policy, Public Debt Policy, Foreign Trade and Forex policy and related areas are briefly set out in this chapter.

The financing and investment operations of the Treasury Management involve trading in the money and capital market, giltedged market and forex market. The developments in these markets are to be dovetailed and codified in the MIS for the Treasury Managements. These areas are briefly discussed and set out in a succinct manner in this chapter. It is for the Treasury Manager that he builds up an MIS in an appropriate manner for his efficient operations in the Treasury.

❑ ❑ ❑

BIBLIOGRAPHY

1. RBI, Functions and Working of RBI.
2. RBI, History of the RBI.
3. RBI, Publications and Annual and Monthly Bulletins and Reports.
4. V.A. Avadhani, *Theory and Practice of Central Banking in India,* Somaiya Publishers, 1978.
5. V.A. Avadhani, *Studies in Indian Financial System,* Jaico Publishers, 1979.
6. V.A. Avadhani, *International Finance,* Himalaya Publishing House, 1986.
7. James C. Van Horne, *Financial Management and Policy,* Prentice Hall of India.
8. I.M. Pandey, *Financial Management,* Vikas Publications.
9. Kulkarni, P.V., *Financial Management,* Himalaya Publishing House.
10. L.M. Bhole, *Financial Institutions and Markets,* Tata MacGraw Hill.
11. B. Ramachandra Rao, *Balance Sheet Analysis,* Progressive Corporation.
12. Vinayakam and Sinha, *Management Accounting,* Himalaya Publishing House.
13. TAXMANN's Publications, *Companies and Other Corporate Laws.*
14. Harbans Lal Varma, *Management of Working Capital,* Deep & Deep Publications.
15. R.R. Bari, *Selected Readings in Cash Management.*
16. V.A. Avadhani, *Investment Management,* Himalaya Publishing House.
17. Richard Ensor & Peter Muller, Eds. The Essentials of Treasury Management Euro Money Publications.
18. Derek Ross, Jan Clark & Seragul Taiyab Eds. International Treasury Management.